THE [partially covered] NCE

THE MARROW OF HUMAN EXPERIENCE

Essays on Folklore

By
WILLIAM A. WILSON

Edited by
JILL TERRY RUDY

with the assistance of
DIANE CALL

UTAH STATE UNIVERSITY PRESS
Logan, UT

Utah State University Press
Logan, Utah 84322–7800
www.usu.edu/usupress/

Manufactured in the United States of America
Printed on acid-free paper

Library of Congress Cataloging-in-Publication Data

Wilson, William Albert.
The marrow of human experience : essays on folklore / by William A. Wilson ; edited by Jill Terry Rudy with
the assistance of Diane Call.
p. cm.
Includes index.
ISBN-13: 978-0-87421-653-0 (pbk.)
ISBN-10: 0-87421-653-2 (pbk. : alk. paper)
1. Folklore and nationalism. 2. National characteristcs. 3. Folklore--Finland.
4. Mormons--Folklore. I. Rudy,
Jill Terry, 1963- II. Call, Diane. III. Title.
GR41.5.W55 2006
398.2094897--dc22
2006021243

Contents

Acknowledgments

The editor would like to acknowledge the Brigham Young University English Department for the semesters of research assistance that Diane Call provided this project and for the encouragement of endearing colleagues. Many thanks to Diane herself for her organizational skill and her persistence. I also thank the contributors for their introductions and enthusiastic responses to my requests to write them. I hope again someday to work on a project that is so warmly received by its participants. Additionally, I appreciate the many colleagues who would have been willing to write introductions if room had allowed.

The readers for Utah State University Press, including Barre Toelken, made helpful suggestions that improved the final version, and John Alley provided the perfect organizing scheme for the essays and great patience in guiding me through my initial publishing foray. I have read manuscripts and proofs of this book at dance rehearsals, baseball games, and late into the night and thank Bill, Katelyn, Matthew, and Spencer Rudy for not minding. My gratitude to Bert Wilson is eternal, and for everyone who knows him, the work in this book displays our debts, always, to Hannele.

INTRODUCTION

I often misplace certain William A. "Bert" Wilson articles and then find them in unexpected locations. When researching Mormon folklore, I may need "On Being Human" and finally find the article in a folder marked "Definitions of Folklore" or "Folklore and the Humanities." The article might be tucked in the folder I use for the Introduction to Folklore course or even in the folder for my advanced writing class. The process gets repeated for the "Deeper Necessity" article, the "Herder" article, and others. For this very personal reason, I have wanted a book compiling Bert Wilson's essays. I want a good variety of his writings in one easily accessible and transportable collection.

More seriously, and less selfishly, I requested to work on this essay collection with Bert so others could receive and study the work of an excellent teacher and champion of folklore studies and the humanities. The essays won't convey exactly what it was like to be in his classroom, what it was like to experience the variety of personal experiences, lectures, slide shows, guest speakers, films, and other multimedia displays he used to present folklore in all its varieties to his students. But these writings will introduce new and ongoing students of folklore to useful definitions and functions of folklore study. They may guide readers who know little of this field, as well as seasoned folklorists, to recognize and remember the imperatives of traditional expression—the powerful needs to create, to know, and to commune within the realms of change, continuity, and a common humanity. These essays in folklore will immerse their readers in Bert's passion for folklore as a way to negotiate recurring human needs, to recognize the values and concerns of particular groups, and to understand what it means to be human.

MAKING THIS COLLECTION

When studying folklore, it seems important to indicate that the creation and sharing of knowledge takes place through face-to-face contacts as well as by reading and writing. I studied folklore with Bert as a master's student at Brigham Young University and heard him give several of the invited lectures on Mormon narrative traditions now included here. As a folklore doctoral student at Indiana University, I discovered that he had a wider influence than Mormon folklore when my professors expressed their appreciation for his work on Finnish nationalism and folklore in the academy. Knowing of the regard for Bert and his contributions to the field, I more fully understood the scope and impact of his work. When we began to make this essay collection, I invited his scholarly peers and former students, whom he always treats as peers, to contribute introductory notes to the essays so readers could more easily see this impact. By gathering in one collection Bert's words from four decades of work, we can better understand his vision of folklore studies that builds bridges across academic disciplines and unites such seemingly diverse areas of specialty as romantic nationalism and Mormon folklore.

It is fitting that Michael Owen Jones wrote in his introductory note to "On Being Human" that "All of us are influenced by the writing of others." The format of this book is based on Jones's essay collection, *Exploring Folk Art: Twenty Years of Thought on Craft, Work, and Aesthetics.* In his collection Jones included introductory headnotes explaining the personal and disciplinary context of his writings, and I enjoyed reading the notes as much as reading his articles. Contributors have been enthusiastic and thoughtful in providing their introductory responses to the essays and commenting on their relationship with Bert and his ideas. Some contributors refer to Bert informally by his first name, while others use his last name; either name is a sign of esteem and respect. As mentioned in most of the introductions and especially in the biographical sketch by his daughter Denise Jamsa, Bert Wilson is recognized as a community builder; therefore, it is particularly appropriate in his essay collection to include the voices of others interacting with his life and work. Many other colleagues and former students could have provided commentary on Bert's influence, but the mirror I have held is influenced by my relationships with Bert and these contributors at this particular time.

Selecting essays to include has been a delight; deciding which essays to eliminate from the collection has been difficult. I made initial selections, invited the writers to contribute introductory notes, and grouped the essays somewhat thematically by folklore and the academy, folklore and religion, and folklore and Finnish nationalism. The initial order of sections and essays was improved by the careful reading of John Alley, our USU Press editor. On more than one occasion with Bert, I have compared the process of essay selection to compiling a "greatest hits" collection, suggesting that creating another volume later could be an option. Bert has preferred instead to winnow some previously published articles and include some unpublished papers in order to consider this as his standard. He consistently has chosen to add more recent works, preferring to present how his ideas have developed and matured rather than simply using the collection as a documentary of past thought. For example, later in the manuscript process he announced that he wanted to replace "Fact amid the Legends" with the more recent "The Folk Speak," explaining that the two pieces expressed similar ideas but he liked the later iteration better. In the midst of making final changes to this manuscript, he also traveled to Finland to present another paper on the *Kalevala.* Perhaps knowing of the looming deadline from the publisher, he did not even ask about including the new paper in this collection, but the paper will be revised and published. For these reasons, not all of Bert's work could possibly be included, and interested readers should attend to the bibliography and consider this collection as some of the highlights of an ongoing academic career.

RECOGNIZING THE IMPORTANCE OF FOLKLORE THROUGH USEFULNESS AND ARTFULNESS

Although there is a tendency to shield students from committee work and institutional administration, it is important to know that professors do more than lecture in a classroom and sit in an office reading and writing. The first essays in this collection acknowledge Bert's many roles as a teacher, scholar, archivist, and cultural critic while also providing a helpful introduction to folklore studies and a clear definition of folklore. Through essays in this section, Bert demonstrates the usefulness of folklore in the ways that stories, sayings, artifacts, and customs afford creative and artful responses to the human condition. In his memorable essay "The Deeper Necessity," Bert upholds the human need for order and beauty as a necessity that cannot be restricted only to certain gifted individuals or elite groups. He claims that the impulse to create, or to be artful, is an essential component of being human. Moving beyond restricting definitions of *folk literature* to *literature* or from *folk art* to *art*, he notes that folklore crosses disciplinary boundaries showing a deeply human need to be creative. In advocating that folklore study be infused in the humanities curriculum and attended to by policymakers, he teaches that our traditions are a useful and artful display of our humanity.

Bert combines and transcends academic categories by building bridges or dismantling walls between the arts, humanities, and history. In essays on folklore in the academy, on tradition and cultural policy, and on contemporary views of the past, he shows that folklore is an imperative form of expression that must be considered to fully understand human creativity and endurance. As Beverly Stoeltje notes in her introduction to "Building Bridges: Folklore in the Academy," Bert's work links folklore study with action and connects ideas with their implementation in society. He explains in several essays that these connections are inherent in folklore itself and that the study of folklore, therefore, should be integrative. For example, in writing about folklore and history, he asserts that folklore shows what people value from the past by documenting the stories, sayings, and attitudes that they share in the present. The historical record, he explains, will be minimized without adding in the facts expressed through lore.

Access to traditional expressions is enhanced by thoughtful archival work, and in "Documenting Folklore" Bert explains why and how students should become contributors to folklore archives. In this essay he also defines folklore as the things people make, say, and do and introduces the three main categories of folklore studies: material, verbal, and customary lore. While the categories help clarify, especially for new students, the myriad forms of traditional expression that folklorists claim in their studies, the example of birthday party traditions shows how folklore performances combine and transcend categories in contexts that are understood and enjoyed by participants. We may not label the birthday cake "material lore," the birthday song "verbal lore," or the giving of presents "customary lore," but many cultural groups would have a hard time recognizing a birthday without these traditions. Placing labels on traditions may help us appreciate them in new ways. Through Bert's writings, he teaches that we are all the folk who use traditional expressions because we are human beings working through similar needs and situations in culturally specific groups of people.

UNDERSTANDING OTHERS THROUGH FOLKLORE

Although much of Bert's career is centered on his study of Mormon folklore, his scholarship on the role of folklore in constructing national identity is also a significant contribution. Bert's work shows that folklore study is not only a warm, fuzzy collection of one's own deeply cherished traditions but also a politically and intellectually charged act of interpreting and shaping reality. Essays in this section connect with Bert's work on folklore, cultural policy, and the humanities to show that scholarship is a form of action that cannot be isolated to classrooms, academic disciplines, or universities. Exemplified by his study of nationalism, Bert's position as a sympathetic outsider to Finnish culture has given him challenges and opportunities that have affected his personal and professional life. By acknowledging that intellectuals can use traditional expressions to fabricate a national past and influence the present, Bert's work provides a timely reminder that ideas must be thoughtfully pursued because there are consequences when individuals and groups are led to act on their knowledge, values, and beliefs.

This section includes Bert's writing on folklore and Herder, romantic nationalism, and Finnish American identity construction. These essays show that folklore study may lead to self-understanding and to awareness of the humanity of others, but they acknowledge that folklore study also can be constructed to fulfill the wishes of scholars. Phillip McArthur, in introducing "Folklore, Nationalism, and the Challenge of the Future," points out that Bert is well aware of the dual nature of folklore as it is performed and as it is studied. Folklore can be used to denigrate other groups and create boundaries to keep a group isolated, while folklore can also be used to celebrate a group and make connections between individuals and other groups. Folklore study can be used for nationalistic propaganda to promote a group beyond all other groups and to argue for political and territorial privileges, while it can also be used to critique misuses of authority and to make legitimate claims for cultural and political autonomy. In all this, Bert sees human impulses at work and at play; he advocates an understanding of traditional expression that includes self-awareness, appreciating diversity, and honoring a common humanity.

STUDYING CLOSELY ONE GROUP— RELIGIOUS INDIVIDUALS

While understanding what it means to be human is a consistent theme in Bert's writings, he admits that his own research has sought the universal through the particular. In this respect, his methodological practices match the preferences of folklore as an academic field. Students who learn through concrete examples before leaping to abstractions will appreciate that folklorists collect particular expressions as a way to work toward generalizations about individuals and groups. As suggested by Jackie Thursby's introduction to "The Concept of the West," Bert frequently will use his own, and his family's, experiences to introduce a particular kind of traditional expression. He then will add examples from archival collections and evoke his audience's experiences to lead to generalizations. Especially notable in "On Being Human," he often concludes that people use folklore to release tensions, to negotiate boundaries, and to draw meaning from uncertain circumstances.

Some of the headnotes and the biographical sketch describe Bert's involvement as a practicing member of the Church of Jesus Christ of Latter-day Saints, also known as the LDS church or as the Mormons, for accepting the Book of Mormon as scripture. As a folklorist, Bert does not study primarily the theology and doctrines of the church but rather the stories, customs, and humor that members of the group share. In his introduction to "The Study of Mormon Folklore," David Hufford acknowledges that Bert's participation in the religious group he studies has caused some concern among academics who prefer the appearance of objectivity in scholarship. However, many of his peers acknowledge the value of his insider status both for members of the academy and for members of the religion. Steve Siporin explains in his introduction to "Freeways, Parking Lots, and Ice Cream Stands" that Bert's work on Mormon folklore demonstrates that religious belief and practices do not disappear in the face of claims that such expressions are outdated or unnecessary in modern life.

After some discussion over what would be included in this section, Bert convinced me that his initial article on Three Nephite legends in Indiana, although significant as his first publication on Mormon lore, was not as helpful for students as the more analytic discussion in "Freeways." This collection of essays, therefore, shows a scholar changing his approach to his subject after years of study. He first changed from the textual approach of collecting legends and comparing them with a motif index to a more performative approach of analyzing a collection for function and meaning. Over the years, Bert increasingly calls for study of the less sensational expressions of religiosity and for the scholar to account for his or her biases in presenting the values of other people. As "Freeways" was being published, Bert was turning attention away from the supernatural legends to call in "An Uncertain Mirror for Truth" for stories that represent the more common acts of service and faith performed by members of the LDS church. This change is articulated most clearly in the essays in this section where Bert shifts focus from *folk religion* to *religious folklore* and asks that folklorists study the daily acts of service and other practices of religious individuals.

Whether one is a religious individual or not, he or she can find in Bert's extensive study of Mormon lore another use for folklore. Bert's work shows how studying the traditions of particular individuals in specific groups can encourage deeper insights into human behavior. This collection concludes with "The Family Novel," a piece that echoes the sentiments of "A Deeper Necessity" by advocating the necessity of artful expression in family relationships and the power of personal stories in living well amid the struggles of life. The essay makes a bold claim, consistent with other ideas developed through this body of work, that scholars should consider their own traditions and experiences as they seek to understand the expressions and motivations of others. Intensely personal and honest, the essay highlights the significance of intertextuality and community in understanding and appreciating family stories. The essay leads fittingly into a biographical sketch written by one of Bert's daughters, who concludes the sketch by quoting the final lines of "A Family Novel." A constant teacher, Bert turns his audiences to their own experiences of folklore and their own opportunities to thoughtfully value the traditional expressions of others and themselves.

The majority of essays included here were originally presented as lectures; they often begin with Bert directly addressing his audience and inviting them to consider his topic of discussion. Many have been published and republished in venues that are acknowledged in each essay or in the bibliography at the conclusion of the book. While a primary purpose of this collection is to emphasize the value of studying folklore, another reason is to show the development and breadth of a scholar's work. Scholarship is a human activity, and the introductory notes and biographical sketch, as well as the essays, are meant to introduce readers to the man who presents these ideas as well as to the ideas themselves. New students of folklore should focus their reading on Bert's words because of his clear ideas, writing style, and voice. The introductory notes will be particularly useful for more experienced students who want to learn how a scholar's work draws from and influences others. Promoting folklore as a scholarly field has been a major undertaking in Bert's life that has seeped into mine as well. We will be most pleased if readers of this collection come to see their worlds differently because they recognize and understand the function, complexities, and beauty of folklore performances in their own and other's lives. Through his essays on folklore, Bert Wilson reaches the core of human expression and honors the capacity to adapt traditions to prevail over life's challenges.

—*Jill Terry Rudy*

The Importance of Folklore

THE DEEPER NECESSITY

Folklore and the Humanities

In his address at Los Angeles, Bert Wilson offers a grand message of hope. The style is plain and direct, the spirit soars. If folklorists would take as their goal the discovery of our common humanity, topical interests would coalesce, academic disciplines would unify, invidious distinctions among people would fade away. Within a universal humanity, cultural differences would seem trivial, the past and the present would mesh. Folklorists would assume a leading role in an advanced cultural program.

His call for unity clarified and perfected old tendencies in folkloristic thought. He locates two essential aspects of human action: the godlike capacity of the individual consciousness to bring splendid order out of chaos, and the social desire among people to communicate with consequence. That duality lies buried in every mature formulation. If we speak of folklore in terms of tradition, we acknowledge the process by which individuals reshape the shared past to create a shared future. In speaking of identity, we recognize that individuals are inviolably themselves, alone in psychic continuity, yet linked to the others with whom they identify. If we speak of performance, we concentrate on the instants when individuals forge connections with others through artful enactment.

We are born alone, we die alone: we are, each one of us, individuals. We are born, we live, we die among others: we are, all of us, members of society. That universal duality, the unity in being of the personal and social, is, at its peak, made sensate in creative acts. Those acts are called, depending upon one's presuppositions about social class, folklore or art. Call them folklore, call them art, but this is what they are: momentary fulfillments of what it is to be human.

In the days when the discipline of folklore was consolidating professionally—in the early sixties, in Dick Dorson's days—what seemed most important

---

This paper was an address given at the University of California at Los Angeles, May 31, 1986, in celebration of the twenty-fifth anniversary of the university's Folklore and Mythology Program. It was printed in the *Journal of American Folklore* 101 (1988): 156–67. Reprinted by permission of the American Folklore Society.

was defining folklore as something distinct. Folksong was not pop song. Folk art was not fine art. Folk history was unlike the history the professors taught. In confirming folklore as different, as complementary and compensatory, folklorists established their discipline and put it, as Bert Wilson argues, into a position of servitude—humble and marginal, capable of no more than contributing minor episodes to the big story by which the powers of the status quo preserve their authority. But when two decades had passed, and the discipline had developed, unity seemed more important than difference. Then Bert Wilson proclaimed that there was no folk literature, no fine literature, but only literature, and at exactly the same time, I wrote a long book to demonstrate that all logic of difference breaks down: the distinction between folk art and fine art is not phenomenal or qualitative, but a mere matter of academic perspective.

That was the mood of the late eighties, when Dorson was gone and the students of the sixties had hit their stride. But however laudably democratic and empirically accurate it was, it bore within it a danger. Distinctions between folklore and literature, or folk art and fine art, were founded on more than intellectual confusion. They were based on clear prejudices of class and gender and race, prejudices that have hardened more than they have diminished in time. If, in the study of literature, it makes no difference whether we study Shakespeare's plays or the narratives of Mormon missionaries, then academics will choose Shakespeare—because, as Harold Bloom unintentionally reveals in *The Western Canon,* Shakespeare raises the psychological issues that interest academics—and folklore will become less than marginal. It will be neglected, utterly. What we used to call folklore, or folk art, contained alternative virtues, the virtues of the local, communal, and sacred that shaped in opposition, in resistance to the onrush of power—virtues that, though of slight concern in the academy, must be confronted in any quest toward the universally human. The route to unity runs through difference.

The problem of diversity in unity spills through the fullness of Bert Wilson's complaint about the limitations of folkloristic practice. If we search the past for sameness, then the universally human will come clear, but the real differences between historical eras will blur into a history that is no more than a prelude to the present. We will, perhaps, distance rural life into a vanished past and turn to focus only on the urban, industrial, capitalistic creativity of the contemporary United States, even though at this time, in our time, there are more peasants in India (who work on the farm by day and sing ancient songs at night) than there are people of all classes in the United States and Europe combined. Fixed on sameness, we will surrender the options that lie in the past. The critical capacity of history will become closed to us, lost in an evolutionary trajectory that leads inevitably to ourselves. If we dismiss as romantic nationalism the energies that brought us to security, we will fail in compassion for those who, in this post-colonial world, still struggle for cultural survival against the violent forces of neocolonial expansion.

Bert Wilson was brave to put his manifesto before us. He is a great scholar, and, better than that, he is a good teacher, a good friend, a truly fine man. And he was right when he wrote. We should be hard at work in the field, out there among the people where all of the answers abide. We should recover the courage of comparative research, crossing the divides of class and gender and race, of social and political and religious affiliation. We should seek the universally human.

And that—our common humanity—is a matter, I believe, of both the fundamental sameness upon which our right to study is founded, and the differences among people that require our study to be patient and respectful. For all people are alike in their humanity, in their individuality and their modes of social belonging—that is, in their uniqueness of personality and experience, their difference. We differ in conditions, in predicament, and what makes us most human is the will that enables endurance, that grants us the ability to turn chaos into order, and the ability to turn order into chaos.

—*Henry Glassie*

I SERVE ON THE BOARD OF DIRECTORS OF THE UTAH ARTS COUNCIL. FOR several years we have been working to make the arts (and I include arts in the humanities) a required part of the Utah secondary school curriculum. With the rising waters of the Great Salt Lake eating up larger and larger portions of Utah tax dollars for flood control, money available for the public schools—and thus for arts programs—has been pirated away. The argument has been that in these difficult times, only the most essential courses should remain in the curriculum while interesting but nonbasic courses should be eliminated. Considerable debate has been generated in the state legislature, in educational circles, and in newspaper columns over what these essential courses should be. A few months ago our governor gave his answer. Arts and humanities curricula might have to be cut back, said the governor, in order to maintain excellence in fundamentals such as reading, writing, math, science, and computer science (Browning 1986, 1).

Anyone who might find comfort in the governor's reference to reading and writing should understand that the reading referred to is, I fear, the basic skill necessary to pass a driver's license examination or read instructional manuals, and the writing is that required to apply for a job or fill out an application for a loan. However important these skills are, the reading and writing we value—that dealing artistically with significant human issues—fall under arts and humanities and must give way to courses designed to make our students computer literate.

Legislators less moderate than the governor have gone even further. For example, a resolution was recently put forth in the Utah Senate proposing that all classes in Utah's secondary schools be designated basic or nonbasic and that in the future the students themselves be required to bear the costs of the nonbasic courses. The resolution failed on a close vote, but it will be back again. If it should become school policy, arts and humanities classes will be available only to those students wealthy enough to pay for them. Economically disadvantaged students will be denied opportunities to develop their artistic talents and thus to discover, with others, their common humanity.

As I became involved in the effort to save arts and humanities classes in the public school curriculum, I became more keenly aware than I have ever been not only that such courses ought to form the core of any respectable public and university curriculum, but also that folklore should be a central component of this curriculum. Those are rather brave words, considering the fact that many of our colleagues in arts and humanities colleges and departments consider folklore, if they consider it at all, to be ancillary to the more traditional and respected dance, music, painting, theater, and literature courses. Brave words or not, they are true; and we folklorists ought to be doing a better job of defending the legitimacy of our discipline and arguing for its primacy in the humanities curriculum. Let's look at that issue more closely.

In a recent issue of *National Forum*, University of California president David P. Gardner gave one of the best definitions of the humanities I have seen:

> The humanities are animated by the urge to understand human beings in all their complexity and contradictions. . . . They connect us to our past, linking us to what other human beings have thought and felt and believed and suffered in the process of finding their own humanity.
>
> But the humanities not only connect us to our cultural heritage; they also hold out the potential of connecting everything in our experience. . . . They offer us the experience of wholeness because they touch us at the deepest levels of mind and personality. They are inclusive disciplines, helping us to create larger and more comprehensive meaning out of the fragmentariness of every-day life. In the broadest sense, they are devoted to the task, as one scholar puts it, of "discovering what it means to be human." (1986, 9)

Surely no other discipline is more concerned with linking us to the cultural heritage from the past than is folklore; no other discipline is more concerned with revealing the interrelationships of different cultural expressions than is folklore; and no other discipline is more concerned, or no other discipline should be more concerned, with discovering what it means to be human. It is this attempt to discover the basis of our common humanity, the imperatives of our human existence, that puts folklore study at the very center of humanistic study.

In 1840 Elias Lönnrot, compiler of the Finnish national epic, the *Kalevala*, wrote:

> If someone were to ask when music and song came into being, we would not go far astray if we were to answer that their origin was not much later than the origin of the entire human species. For the very first people had the same reasons as we have for music and song. ([1840] 1982, ii)

In a somewhat similar vein, Edward Ives wrote recently:

> Music is a universal in human culture: so far we have never found people without it. That in itself is a remarkable thing, and I can in no way satisfactorily account for it. I can understand why all peoples have to gather food, construct some sort of shelter, or develop systems of kinship or political and social organization. But why they have to make music is beyond me. Yet make it they do, always. (1985: 74)

Ives's wording is especially interesting. He does not wonder why people make music—he wonders instead why they "have" to make music. The answer, of course, is that making music is one of those imperatives of human existence, one of the things humans have always done, as Lönnrot pointed out, in order to meet similar needs—in order, that is, to be human. What is true of music is equally true of those other "einfache Formen," or fundamental expressive forms that folklorists study across time and space, in all of their cultural manifestations. The point that many of the "back to basics" people seem never to grasp is that the so-called "nonpractical" arts and humanities courses they would remove from the curriculum are the courses fundamentally important in our development as human beings, the courses that deal with our basic human imperatives.

A few years ago art historian Kenneth Ames put together an exhibit of American folk art at the Winterthur Museum and called the catalog accompanying the exhibit *Beyond Necessity* (1977). This title at first intrigued me, suggesting that art comes into being when people who create utilitarian objects move beyond practical need—beyond necessity—and make the objects beautiful for their own sakes. Thus a woman who spends days stitching an intricate log cabin design into a quilt moves beyond the practical necessity of creating a covering that will keep her warm and creates instead an object that gives her aesthetic pleasure. I have liked this phrase very much and have used it again and again in my folklore classes to explain the development of folk art. But I have recently come to understand that the phrase may be more facile than accurate.

Art, music, literature, and dance come into being not when we move beyond necessity but when we move to a deeper necessity, to the deeper human need to create order, beauty, and meaning out of chaos. It is this human need to combine words, sounds, colors, shapes, and movements into aesthetically satisfying patterns that separates us most clearly from the rest of the animal kingdom and makes us most like God. And it is this need, or the satisfaction of it, that answers Ives's question and explains why all people at all times have had to make music, or paint, or tell stories, or dance. If we ignore this fact, if we neglect the deeper human necessity lying behind the arts and humanities as we determine what is *basic* to a good education, we will do so at the peril of our society. And if in our preparation of arts and humanities curricula we ignore the contributions folklore study can make to the understanding of fundamental expressive forms, we will do so at the expense of proper humanistic education.

The great contribution of folklore study, of course, is that it crosses most disciplinary lines, tying all expressive forms together, and especially that it examines the artistic and creative efforts of all human beings, not just the elite or the professionally trained. It thus provides us information we can get in few other ways and brings us about as close as possible to achieving that goal set by David Gardner—understanding what it means to be human.

Considering this fact, one would expect university arts and humanities programs to welcome folklorists with open arms. We all know how far that is from the truth. It is easy enough to criticize our colleagues for being unreceptive to folklore and for failing to grasp the contributions folklore can make to our understanding of expressive behavior. Certainly, some of them deserve such criticism; but in many instances the fault lies not so much with them as with ourselves, with approaches we sometimes take to our subject that do little to persuade non-folklorists of its significance. Though there may be many such approaches, I shall focus here on only three: the tendency to treat folklore as handmaiden to other disciplines and thus to undermine its own intrinsic worth, the tendency to be preoccupied with the past at the expense of the present, and the tendency to pay more attention to individual folk groups than to the broader humanity they share.

As I speak about the first of these approaches—the use of folklore in service of other disciplines—I shall focus primarily on folklore and literature, but what I say can be applied to other art forms as well.

I recently read the introduction to Steven Swann Jones's 1984 publication, *Folklore and Literature in the United States: An Annotated Bibliography of Studies of Folklore in American Literature*, and looked through a considerable part of the extensive bibliography. Jones states that one of the purposes of his work is to break down "the assumed differences between folklore and literature," and, by showing how much they share in common, to demonstrate that "they are equally impressive forms of human art" (1984, xxiv). I am fully in accord with Jones's aspiration. But I find little in the bibliography to suggest that scholars have spent much time discovering what folklore and literature share in common. A great number of the studies simply catalogue the folklore in the works of a particular author or show how this lore contributes to the success of a literary work in which it is used. However worthy these goals might be, one frequently leaves such studies with the feeling that the folklore itself is far less significant than the uses to which it is put by individual poets and writers of fiction.

The problem is particularly critical in folklore textbooks, in those works that introduce students and colleagues to our field. In *The Dynamics of Folklore* (1979), for example, which I consider the best of these books, Barre Toelken comes close to literary exegesis in his chapter on connotation and in some of his interpretations of folklore meaning. But in only two subsections of the book does he explicitly get at the relation of folklore to literature. In the first he points out that in folk artistic works, community taste, as opposed to an individual aesthetic, determines the outcome of artistic creation. And in the second he, once again, shows what folklore contributes to the artistic success of the literary works in which it appears (1979, 199–223, 181–94, 334–43).

What we must have, if we want to win for our subject greater academic credibility, is not more studies of folklore *in* literature, but rather careful analyses of folklore *as* literature. Otherwise, we will continue to be viewed by our literary colleagues as the folks who do the hack work for their more sophisticated and important literary analyses.

Another unfortunate result of focusing on folklore in music, art, or literature instead of on the musical, artistic, or literary merit of the folklore itself is that such a focus contributes to an evolutionary view of folklore still prevalent among our colleagues in other disciplines, and occasionally among ourselves, and, in the process, diminishes the humanistic value of the lore. Many faculty members in arts and humanities colleges and departments view folklore in a condescending way—as unsophisticated, aesthetically inferior material from which the more sophisticated fine arts may have developed or to which writers, composers, painters, and others may occasionally turn for the themes, motifs, and images that they, supposedly, will give fuller artistic elaboration. But they seldom see this material as significant artistic expression having originated from the same human imperatives as the works they study. If they treat folklore at all in their classes, they usually do so historically—that is, they tend to treat it as primitive, subliterary artistic or musical material from which the "higher" art forms eventually evolved. And they view folklore always as subservient to these higher forms. Anyone who doubts this need only walk into almost any arts or humanities department across the country and ask what contribution a folklore course might make to the curriculum. When I suggest to my colleagues that folklore ought to be taught in their departments on an equal footing with other courses—that a course in American folklore, for example, ought to be just as important as a course in American literature—they look at me as though I have taken leave of my senses. We can bemoan this fact all we wish, but until we ourselves begin more seriously to treat folklore *as* music, *as* art, or *as* literature, we are not likely to make much headway with these people and will probably never win a solid place for our discipline in arts and humanities curricula.

Serious literary studies have long been made, of course, of folksongs and folktales; and in recent years scholars have charted new paths to a better understanding of rhetorical strategies in folklore and of the art of folklore performance. But much remains to be done. What we need now are willing workers in the vineyard.

From what I have been saying, it should be fairly obvious that in the studies I envision I would draw no sharp lines of demarcation between folk artistic expressions and artistic expressions in general. Though some may consider me a heretic, I have come to the conclusion that there is no such thing as folk literature—there is simply literature, which I would define as the artistic expression in words of significant human experience. Sometimes that expression is made through the written words of individual authors, sometimes through spoken words in face-to-face encounters among people usually sharing the same social identity. These different modes of transmission and the different audiences to whom the folklore is addressed will, of course, require somewhat different methods of analysis. But that should not obscure the fact that behind each expression lies the human urge, that deeper necessity, to communicate significant experience and emotion and to influence the surrounding social world through the artistic, and therefore powerful, use of language. And neither of these expressions is any less literature, or art, than the other.

As I wrote these words, my thoughts moved back across the years to a young Finnish scholar-patriot, Carl Aksel Gottlund. On October 9, 1815, on a hunting trip near his home in central Finland, Gottlund asked some of the local men accompanying him to sing—they were in a boat rowing across a lake. He described what followed in this way:

> I asked them to sing for me to pass the time. Then from the bow of the boat, Torvelainen began to raise his voice against the wind, so that the boat shook. He sang the old forest songs which were formerly sung as men left to hunt bear. The beautiful words and his clear voice, not in a childish but heroic tone, so affected my young mind that I began to cry. . . . Now for the first time I comprehended the beauty and gracefulness of the Finnish language and discerned in my heart an emotion that words cannot explain. (Heikinheimo 1933, 124)

Forty-five years later, in 1860, the Russian scholar P. N. Rybnikov, crossing Lake Onega in northern Russia—not far, actually, from Gottlund's home country—was forced to take shelter from a storm on a small island. There he heard a *byliny* singer and, much like Gottlund, was moved to tears by the beauty of the performance (Oinas 1964). Surely there was no question in the minds of Gottlund and Rybnikov that what they were hearing was literature, powerfully and artistically performed.

I have not had an experience quite so dramatic as these, but I have on numerous occasions been as moved by witnessing skillful folklore performances as I have by reading the works of *belles lettres* that I teach in my literature courses. A former Mormon missionary, I have for the past fifteen years been collecting, studying, writing about, and especially *enjoying* the folklore of Mormon missionaries. The value of working with a fairly limited corpus of material like this missionary lore—at the moment I have on hand about five thousand narratives—is that one can know it well, just as one can know well the works of a single author. Reading through this material and *remembering* and *envisioning* the contexts in which it has been performed has for me been closely akin to reading again and again a favorite novel. The lore makes me laugh, makes me angry, and, yes, sometimes moves me to tears. More important, it has the same impact on the missionary narrators and audiences to whose lives it directly relates and from whose experiences it develops.

In his Nobel Prize acceptance speech, William Faulkner argued that it is the privilege of the creative writer

> to help man endure by lifting his heart, by reminding him of the courage and honor and hope and pride and compassion and pity and sacrifice which have been the glory of his past. The poet's voice need not merely be the record of man, it can be one of the props, the pillars to help him endure and prevail. ([1950] 1960, 1249)

That is equally true on the Shakespearean stage, in one's private encounter with *Moby Dick*, on a rain-swept island in Lake Onega, or among a group of Mormon missionaries coming to terms, through the fictive world they have created in their lore, with pressures that might otherwise be their undoing. To treat these folk performances as anything less than literature would be to demean our field and to detract from its central position in humanistic pursuits.

A second hindrance to the humanistic credibility of folklore is a persisting romantic, or antiquarian, view that recognizes the artistic and humanistic worth of folklore but values the creations of the past much more than those of the present. I don't want to generalize more than I should and must be cautious about what I say, but I believe this view, though it can be found everywhere, is frequently most evident among those whose task is to present folklore to the general public.

During the four years I served on the National Endowment for the Arts Folk Arts Panel, I worried a great deal about some of the ends we were achieving. I remained on the panel, and served one year as its chairman, because the panel, more than any organization in America, struggled to win public recognition of the artistic merit of folklore and because it brought acclaim and feelings of self-worth to countless Americans whose considerable artistic and creative efforts would otherwise have gone unnoticed.

The problem was, or so it seemed to me, that the artistic achievements of numerous Americans still went unrecognized—not because they lacked merit but because they did not fall into the established, and frequently old-timey, categories of American folk art, or under what Jennie Chinn calls "more conservative textbook definitions" (1986). Thus, a woman who saved scrap pieces of fabric and stitched them together into a quilt would have had an easier time winning funding than would an automobile assembly line worker who saved scrap pieces of automobile frames and welded them together into a metal sculpture—at least she would have had the panel not grown so weary of quilting applications.

To be fair, this predilection for the past and the concern for objects generally perceived by the public to be "folk" were not necessarily emphases of the Folk Arts Panel but rather of the people making grant applications, including a number of folk arts coordinators. After all, the panel cannot fund grant applications to highlight contemporary folk art if no such applications are submitted. Grant writers, on the other hand, may have shaped their grant proposals according to what they perceived the NEA would fund. So we have a Catch-22 situation. Whatever the case, instead of applications to support surveying and presenting the salvage art so popular on many western ranches, we would receive applications for funds to present the "safer"—that is, more generally recognized as folk art—saddle-making and rawhide and horsehair braiding. We were frequently asked to support Native American legends but seldom the "war stories" construction workers tell at lunch breaks; Easter egg decoration but not the decoration of recreational vans; wheelwrighting but not lowrider construction. Though there were notable exceptions (and, fortunately, the number is growing), too many applications clearly grew out of romantic, antiquarian notions of folklore and focused primarily on ethnic, rural, and, especially, older art forms. There is certainly nothing wrong with rural, ethnic, or immigrant folklore presentations; indeed, they should and will continue to demand our attention. But in these presentations, the focus should be on contemporary art forms, not just on those surviving from the past or from the old world—many of these will die out no matter how much grant money is poured into attempts to keep them alive.

Reading through these grant applications, I frequently had the desire to send to the writers the words of Elias Lönnrot, one of the most famous of all romantic folklorists. In 1840, in the preface to his *Kanteletar*, a collection of Finnish lyrical folk poems, he wrote:

> When customs and life have changed, then one should not be surprised to see earlier singing changed [to fit] the present, for songs depict the times in which they originate. Nothing is quite so laughable as a person who does not value the present [and] looks askance at everything that does not fit the patterns of former times. Every age has its own character, life, and essence, nor can the former time be brought back, no matter how we drag it by the coattails. . . . I say this because of those people who sorrow over the falling of an old tree and do not understand that from a sprout a new tree can rise up if it is not trampled under foot. ([1840] 1982, xxxiii)

In folk arts grant applications I discovered a lot of people sorrowing over fallen trees, tearfully pleading for money lest a wonderful folk tradition disappear forever. I had no quarrel with keeping art forms alive so long as it seemed at all possible to do so. But I was distressed by the naïveté of people who believed that if the old forms disappeared nothing would ever take their place, no new trees would replace the fallen oaks of the past.

Some may think I am beating a dead horse and will probably argue that folklorists long ago gave up survivalist, antiquarian views of the field and understand perfectly well that folklore is more a key to the present than to the past, and that, as Lönnrot said, it grows out of and reflects the vicissitudes of contemporary living. That may be the theory, but—after reading hundreds of grant applications, reviewing nominations for state folk arts awards and National Heritage awards, and visiting and evaluating numerous folk festivals—I can assure you that it is often *not* the practice. In many instances the agrarian world of yesteryear still occupies center stage.

The difficulty with this past-oriented view is, once again, that it detracts from the humanistic value of folklore. If, as I have argued, painting, sculpting, singing, dancing, and narrating are human imperatives, things we *must* do in order to be human, then it makes little difference what era they come from or precisely what forms they take. What is important is the enduring human spirit coming to terms, through art, with the world that exists at the moment. To ignore the present—to value the people still doing the old things over those doing the new—would be to deny the humanity of our contemporaries.

We must not, of course, ignore the past. Most of us understand that we cannot know where we are until we understand where we have come from, but that does not mean we must forever struggle to keep alive artistic expressions no longer functional. We must be willing to let old forms go, no matter how beautiful, and search out and present (and probably defend) to the public those artistic expressions that have taken their place. We must learn to see in the Hmong story cloth a new form just as viable as the earlier Hmong needlework and fully capable of meeting the needs of Hmong struggling to survive in a new world. And, yes, as Michael Owen Jones has argued, we must even be prepared to recognize in the ways people arrange garbage cans along a street curb the enduring human urge for order and design (1987a, 88–94).

A third impediment to the development of folklore as a humanistic discipline is what I consider an overweening reliance on the concept of folk group, too much emphasis on the particular occupational, regional, ethnic, and religious clusters of people who keep the lore alive. I disagree with the notion that individuals who plan careers in academic or public sector folklore can best prepare for their work by studying the lore of different groups. I find nothing wrong with such study so long as it is comparative and seeks to find common inspiration for apparently different group expressions. I oppose this study if the focus is primarily on the unique characters of the groups studied.

In the introduction to a book on Finnish proverbs, Matti Kuusi wrote: "What kind of people actually are we? What is the Finnish national character?" He continued: "There really is something that separates us from Italians, Americans, Russians, even from the Swedes." He then explained that he would use Finnish proverbs to identify the unique Finnish national character and to cast it in sharp relief (1953, v).

In America, especially since midcentury, when Richard M. Dorson began studying the different social groups living in the Upper Peninsula of Michigan and argued that we had to quit talking about *the* folk and focus instead on different *folks*, that is, on different folk groups ([1952] 1972, 6–7), the emphasis in American folklore study has been not so much on the national character but rather on the character of the different groups that make up our pluralistic society. However, the attempt to discover the uniqueness of the group is closely parallel to the romantic-nationalistic attempt, with all of its inherent dangers, to discover the uniqueness of a particular nation. The brochure advertising the NEA Folk Arts Program states:

> The folk and traditional arts have grown through time within the many groups that make up any nation—groups that share the same ethnic heritage, language, occupation, religious or geographic area. The homegrown traditional artistic activities of such groups are sometimes called folk arts, and they serve both to identify and to symbolize the group that originated them. (*Folk Arts 85/86* 1985)

Notice the wording. The lore symbolizes not recurring human features, not those things that link members of the species together, but individual—that is, unique—group characteristics.

Both Kuusi's statement and the statement of the Folk Arts Panel brochure fall squarely in the center of mainline folklore study. In spite of that, I still believe there are better approaches to the study and presentation of our subject matter. Instead of focusing on what makes us different from each other, why not stress that which unites us? I recently returned from a conference in London aimed at discovering the impact on Finnish identity of the numerous celebrations held in 1985 and 1986 in honor of the 150th anniversary of the publication of the *Kalevala.* It seemed to me that the conference missed the main point. The great value of the *Kalevala* is that it illuminates not just the Finnish spirit but also the human spirit. Like all good literature, it confronts again and again those enduring human problems with which human beings have always struggled. The great value of folklore is that it does the same thing—that is why folklore is, or should be, primarily a humanistic discipline. When we focus our attention predominantly on what it means to be a Finn or on what it means to be a member of a particular American ethnic, occupational, religious, or regional group, we limit our vision and miss that which is most important in what we study.

I am convinced that we generate and transmit folklore not because we belong to a particular nation or to a particular group—not because we are westerners, loggers, Catholics, or Finns—but because we are human beings dealing with recurring human problems in traditional human ways. The Mormon missionary who initiates a new arrival in the field by having him save worthless bus-ticket stubs, with the idea that they can later be turned in for a rebate, is not much different from a boy scout who sends a tenderfoot on a snipe hunt or a logger who tests the temper of a greenhorn by cramming his lunch bucket full of grasshoppers. To be sure, folklore usually is expressed in and is given color by the groups to which we belong; it can serve, therefore, as a means of understanding and increasing our sympathy for these groups. But the source of the lore, we should always remember, lies not in our differences, but in our common humanity, in our common human struggle to endure.

Some may wonder how one who has spent much of his career studying a particular folk group—the Mormons—can make the statements I have just made. True, I have studied Mormons and have tried through that study to better understand myself and the culture that has produced me. But my principal interest has really not been Mormons, but people, not a particular ethnographic fact, but the universal truth manifest in that fact. And I am vain enough to believe others should follow the same course. My real view of Mormon folklore study, one that has echoed throughout this article, is expressed in my conclusion to an essay on missionary folklore:

> What missionaries share with others is not so much common stories or common practices but rather common reasons for performing them—common means of achieving these ends. From studying the folklore of missionaries, or railroaders, or college professors, we will, to be sure, discover what it means to be a missionary, a railroader, or a college professor. But if we learn to look, we will discover also what it means to be human. (Wilson 1981, 21–22)

I return now to the point with which I began: the humanities should lie at the heart of both public sector and university education, and folklore should lie at the center of the humanities. About 180 years ago the poet William Wordsworth stood on Westminster Bridge, watched the morning sun break over London, and was moved by "all that mighty heart" of the still slumbering city ([1807] 1948, 223). It is all that mighty human heart that is the object of our study as humanists and as folklorists. If in the pursuit of particular theoretical approaches and specialized research interests we ever forget that, then we will have bartered our birthright for a mess of pottage and will have lost the vision that should have brought us into folklore in the first place. We must never fail to recognize and honor all the artistic murmurings of that heart; we must see it as equally important and equally inspiring in all ages, past and present; and we must hear its beating in all places, among all cultures.

In the Nobel Prize acceptance speech I mentioned earlier, William Faulkner said, "I believe that man will not merely endure; he will prevail. He is immortal, not because he alone among creatures has an inexhaustible voice, but because he has a soul, a spirit capable of compassion and sacrifice and endurance" ([1950]

1966, 1249). It is my firm belief that folklore will give us the best picture we can get of our fellow beings struggling to endure. And it is my even stronger conviction that we have a duty to use the knowledge we have gained from folklore study, and the skills we have developed, to help each other prevail.

Building Bridges

Folklore in the Academy

In an effort to address the perennial questions of where a person with a PhD in folklore could find an academic position and how to succeed in the profession, I proposed that the Folklore Institute at Indiana University host a symposium in 1995 entitled, "Folklore in the Academy: The Relevance of Folklore to Language and Literature Departments." It was my intention to feature Bert Wilson as the role model because he had been an inspiration to me since I encountered him at my first meeting of the American Folklore Society in Austin, Texas, where we had a memorable discussion about his work on folklore and nationalism in Finland. Indeed, in May of 1995 when we held the symposium, Bert did inspire folklore students, and the many other colleagues present, to pursue their folklore scholarship within the larger context of the humanities. He presented his scholarly life history, a tale of "Building Bridges: Folklore in the Academy," with instructions for the next generation of folklorists who would like to succeed in academe.

More than a story of personal achievement, however, Bert's career narrative shared in this article embodies the principles of success for folklorists: the integration of scholarship and activism, of ideas and the work involved in implementing them. Both his scholarly work and his leadership have been built on the bridge that links folklore and society together. Utilizing this concept in academe, he pursued an interdisciplinary approach to his graduate education; in addition to his master's degree in English from Brigham Young University (BYU), at Indiana University he earned an MA in anthropology, an MA in Finno-Ugrian studies, and a PhD in Folklore, before winning a Fulbright Research Scholarship to Finland. With his faculty position at BYU in the English department, Bert effectively applied the principles he had learned in graduate school by establishing folklore courses in the curriculum and creating relationships with his colleagues. In fact, he deserves much of the credit for creating the foundation of folklore throughout

---

This paper was read at a conference on Folklore in the Academy at Indiana University, May 20, 1995. It was printed in *Journal of Folklore Research* 33 (1996): 7–20. Reprinted by permission of the Folklore Institute, Indiana University.

the state of Utah. This article describes Bert's painstaking process of promoting folklore studies, which involved not only conversations and guest lectures at the university campus but presentations to public schools and organizations all over the state. He continued with his campaign to contextualize folklore in the social life of Utah citizens when he shifted to the English department at Utah State University in Logan. He expanded his folklore responsibilities there to include direction of the annual summer Fife Folklore Conference. Having been invited by Bert to speak at the conference, I found the event to be a lively example of building bridges between the academy and the public.

Especially important during the 1970s and early 1980s, Bert gave influential national service on the NEA Folk Arts Panel in Washington, D.C. He also continued his attendance at the annual meetings of several scholarly disciplines, where he not only remained current in scholarly developments but encouraged and directed younger scholars who, like myself, enjoyed his sense of humor as well as his broad intellectual reach. With these achievements came recognition and visibility and the offer to chair the English department at BYU. Lending his scholarly leadership in the capacity of chair, he encouraged interdisciplinary work in the English department, including cultural studies and feminism as well as folklore. He remained at BYU until retirement, directing the Charles Redd Center for Western Studies in addition to his many other responsibilities.

Paralleling his successful efforts to establish folklore in the academy and consistent with his intellectual vision of the field, his scholarship on nationalism and folklore in Finland remains central today. "Building Bridges" describes the training in Finnish language, literature, arts, history, and political life that Bert undertook to write the book *Folklore and Nationalism in Modern Finland*. In the book, Bert outlines with clarity the complex project by which folklore, identity, scholarship, and politics interacted in the phenomenon of Finnish nationalism, yielding the epic narrative we know today as the *Kalevala*. Not only does his scholarship on the subject outline the particulars of the process in Finland, contextualized in its historical moment, but it also provides the guidelines for those of us who continue to study the subject in its many guises around the globe as well as in the U.S. His work provides the blueprint for a very popular course I teach on "Nationalism and Symbolic Forms" in which folklore figures prominently. In his major scholarly work on a topic as relevant today as in 1976 when it was published, Bert has explicated the intricate relationship between folklore and society and made evident the role of folklore in political movements.

In the conclusion of "Building Bridges," Bert identifies Elias Lönnrot, compiler of the *Kalevala*, as an inspiration for him in the pressing work of collecting and sharing folklore as widely as possible. By linking folklore to the larger scholarly enterprise, to the humanities especially, and linking folklore to society, Bert Wilson has built bridges to establish and sustain the relevance of folklore in an interdisciplinary setting. His "Building Bridges" paper makes available the story of his success to any scholar with hopes of implementing his integrative ideas in an academic setting.

—*Beverly Stoeltje*

Folklorists normally study and interpret stories of others. I intend to alter that role and play storyteller myself. The story I tell will be my own. I pick up the narrative almost at its end.

Last year I turned sixty-two, which means that retirement looms closer each day. As I look at friends and colleagues in the American Folklore Society, I realize that large numbers of them are about my age, give or take a few years. That means that very soon folklorists holding major positions in universities across the land will be leaving those positions. At one time I thought our departure would be a good thing, opening up job opportunities for a younger generation of folklorists eagerly seeking university employment. Now I'm not so sure. Too many folklore slots, I fear, will be pulled back into other departments and offered to candidates in other specialties. If that happens, and it already has in some instances, much of the fault will lie with us. We will not be replaced by other folklorists because we have not built necessary bridges between ourselves and our colleagues and have not adequately demonstrated that what we have to offer is crucially important both to English departments and to the humanities in general.

To build these bridges, we must take an interdisciplinary approach to our subject matter; and, abandoning isolationist tendencies, we must be willing to rub shoulders with colleagues from a variety of disciplines and work with them in the nitty-gritty task of building programs that will benefit both them and us. These efforts should begin with the training of students in our major folklore institutions and should continue as these students later take positions somewhere in the academic community.

I entered the PhD program at Indiana University in 1962, committed to earning my degree in folklore but interested also in a host of related disciplines. I understood well that if I hoped to find a job some years hence, I would have to know more than just folklore and would need to connect folklore to other disciplines. I had already earned an MA in English and could have used that degree to satisfy one of my PhD minor requirements. I elected instead to pick up minors in both anthropology and Finno-Ugrian studies. I also took courses in language and linguistics. After passing qualifying examinations, I won a Fulbright Research Scholarship to Finland to conduct the study that led ultimately to my book *Folklore and Nationalism in Modern Finland* (1976a). In Finland, I attempted to contextualize my research by reading everything I could about Finnish art, literature, theater, music, education, and cultural and political history. The cross-disciplinary approach I developed through this research and through my earlier course work at IU has proved invaluable over the years, opening doors that might otherwise have remained closed as I developed my university career. In 1967 I left IU behind and settled comfortably into an English department at Brigham Young University—but, because of my training, I could have settled just as comfortably into history, anthropology, or humanities departments.

Now let me jump ahead for a moment to the present world and speak as a recent English department chair. Folklore students currently in training for academic positions, as well as the faculty members training them, sometimes live in an encapsulated world where folklore is the be-all and end-all of their existence. They seem not to realize that very few new PhDs will find positions that approximate those in the folklore departments they have just left. If these new graduates are lucky, they may find one other folklorist in the departments they join. More often they will be lone folklorists in departments that expect them to do more than just teach folklore.

If I were interviewing a candidate for a position in my department, I would look that individual in the eye and say something like this: "I enjoyed your presentation to the faculty. Your folklore credentials are excellent and testify that you could do a good job in teaching our folklore courses. Now tell me what else you can do. Could you teach composition? What literary periods are you most comfortable in? Have you had any training in rhetoric?" And especially I would ask: "What current literary theories do you find most compatible with your own teaching and research interests?" Successful candidates will most likely be those whose cross-disciplinary training has prepared them to answer questions like these.

Actually, answering those questions should be easier now than it was when I was hired. The received literary canon and formalist critical theory that held sway when I began my career have given way to postmodern theories that can bring folklorists squarely into the center of contemporary literary study: deconstructionist approaches that peel away layers of meaning to get back to the context that generated a text; reader-response theory that views a text as the collaborative creation of both teller and audience; new historicism that attempts to situate texts in their historical/cultural settings before hazarding interpretation; intertextual studies that see individual texts stitched together into much larger cultural fabrics; research efforts that focus on discourse, or interpretive, communities; multicultural emphases; the linking of aesthetic and cultural functions. These and other contemporary literary approaches should set bells ringing for most folklore students. If folklore candidates for English department positions will resist the urge to insult potential employers by telling them, "Oh, we folklorists have been doing those things for years" and will focus instead on shared approaches in a common interpretive venture, they should be able to demonstrate that they can indeed do much more than "just teach folklore" and should thereby increase their chances of being hired. The key is careful planning.

First, they should find out what is really going on in academic departments throughout the country and, early in their training, begin tailoring their programs to fit possible hiring needs. In this effort, they should be assisted by the faculty. In my judgment, it is unconscionable for faculty members to remain aloof from career planning and to pass students through their classes like objects on a conveyor belt, giving no thought to their futures.

Second, students entering the market should prepare carefully for specific job interviews. If I were applying for a position in a particular English department today, I would learn everything I could about that department and then I would make a presentation that would show how my folklore training could tie into and support central departmental concerns. To do that, I would get a catalogue and look at the department's course offerings. I would get a list of the faculty and spend some time in the library discovering what they had published. And, if possible, I would look at the titles of theses and dissertations completed in the department in recent years, since these would give good insight into the department's present research emphases. Candidates for positions in our department sometimes show up believing we are an old-style traditional department and gear their presentations accordingly, only to miss the mark pretty badly. A quick look at recent departmental thesis titles would have given them a better sense of what we are about. To be sure, some of these titles reflect fairly traditional lines: "Illusion and Reality in Willa Cather's *One of Ours*"; "Failed Marriages in Jane Austin." But many other titles would reveal a picture of the brave new world into which our department has moved: "Words That Sustain Life: The Life Story of Louie Jean Bahr"; "Trickster Discourse as a Model of Postcolonial Hybridity"; "Gender Roles in Popular Culture: A Sociolinguistic Analysis of Gender in 'Star Trek'"; "Postcolonialism and the Emergence of African Feminism: An Islamic Arab Perspective"; "Electronic Mail and the Composition Classroom: An Ethnographic Study"; "Redefining the Slave Narrative Genre: From Traditional Autobiography to Contemporary Fiction"; "Off Roaders: The Cohesion of Western Folk Groups"; and "Daughters of China: Telling Stories of Separation, Suffering, and Hope."

Most of the theses in the second group were informed by theories familiar to folklorists. In fact, during the last year I served either as director or co-director of one-fifth of the theses completed in our department—a task that nearly killed me but that demonstrates our department's recognition of the centrality of folklore, including anthropologically oriented folklore, to our discipline. Clearly, in preparing for careers in departments like ours, folklore students would do well to heed the words of Annette Kolodny in a recent essay in *American Literature*:

> If we are ever to have what Andrew Wiget calls "a new literary history that is both just and useful," then American literary specialists must move beyond the training that prepares us to analyze only texts written in English or to recognize only European (or "Western") antecedents. And we must become the intellectual colleagues of those, from a variety of disciplines, who can teach us to read across cultural boundaries. . . . American literary scholars must begin to create their own new frontiers, openly declaring their agenda as radically comparativist, demandingly interdisciplinary, and exuberantly multilingual. (1992, 15)

I mentioned above our department's recognition of the importance of folklore to the discipline of English. I don't want to overstate the case. Folklore still has its detractors, but the bulk of our faculty now supports our folklore program. Such was not always the case. Nor did our present circumstances come about by accident. They have resulted from years of hard work.

In a discussion of the state of our profession that developed on an e-mail list last November, Lee Haring referred to the intense "force of marginalization" lone folklorists experience in many departments; he suggested that folklorists have done little to remedy this situation because they prefer "to get on with what they do rather than build up their position[s]" (1994). Haring is correct: unless we change our priorities, unless we devote ourselves full tilt to building up our positions, we may in the near future have no remaining places where we can get on with what we do.

When I arrived on the Brigham Young University campus in 1967, eager to put my folklore training to work, I quickly experienced the isolation Haring talks about. For several years I did not even teach folklore—I taught mainly composition and lower division literature courses. Dismayed over prospects for the future, I realized that if things were going to change, I would have to change them.

My first step was to make myself part of the departmental team. I taught every class I was asked to teach, served on every committee I was asked to work on, accepted every extracurricular assignment that came my way. As a result, colleagues began to view me as a real person after all, willing to work for larger departmental interests. At the same time, I began practicing what my wife calls "hallology"—that is, I strolled the halls of the English department talking about folklore with any department member who would listen. But I did not just talk about my work. I asked these colleagues about their work as well and, when possible, tried to tie our interests together. Before long, invitations to give classroom guest lectures began coming my way. Then, as people across campus learned about me, other invitations came along. I never turned any of them down. I talked several times in a library lecture series; I gave a talk sponsored by the honors program. I even made a presentation to the American Association of University Professors.

As a result of these and other efforts, the department gained confidence in me and eventually added two undergraduate folklore courses and one graduate class to its curriculum—additions that had seemed beyond hope when I first arrived on campus. As soon as I had prepared syllabi for these classes, I took them to the chair of the anthropology department. He liked what he saw and cross-listed the classes in his department, thus assuring a continued cross-disciplinary approach. As students in these classes began submitting folklore collections, we developed them into the BYU Folklore Archive, which further strengthened the folklore presence on campus.

But I did not confine my activities to campus. As soon as word spread that there was "this folklorist" at BYU and that he could talk about some pretty interesting stuff, speaking invitations began arriving from the community. I accepted them all. I talked at junior colleges and in the public schools, at local libraries and historical societies, at genealogical organizations and at church gatherings. I talked to the Catalyst Club, a group made up of spouses of chemistry professors, and I talked to the Sons of the Utah Pioneers. I even talked to the Forest Service and to miners about forest and mining lore, subjects I knew almost nothing about. Both the State Historical Society and the Utah Endowment for the Humanities sponsored lecture series in local history and signed me up. Like an itinerant preacher, I dragged my tired bones across our large state, never knowing whether I would end up speaking to an audience of three or three hundred, but always willing to talk about folklore with whoever showed up. Always my aim was to increase the visibility and credibility of folklore in the state and thereby to make it difficult for the university to ignore this growing awareness.

Early in this process I became president of the Folklore Society of Utah, an organization that had struggled along weakly for years. I got together with the director of the Utah Historical Society, Charles Peterson, and worked out an agreement whereby the Folklore Society could hold its yearly business meeting at the annual meeting of the Historical Society if the folklorists would sponsor one of the sessions in the program. This provided us an opportunity to take the message of folklore to a still broader audience, and it gave students from folklore classes at BYU and from the University of Utah an opportunity to present papers in a "scholarly" setting.

These activities persuaded editors of the *Utah Historical Quarterly* that we were pretty good folks and, as a result, opened the pages of the journal to folklore publication. In 1976 I edited a special issue of the journal on Mormon folklore, drawing on papers submitted by students in a graduate seminar I had just led on the subject—two of those papers later received best article awards for that year (Wilson 1976d). In subsequent years, Margaret Brady edited a special issue on ethnic folklore in the state (1984), and Thomas Carter edited another on material culture (1988). What's more, the pages of the journal have remained open to individual articles on folklore.

In 1978 Charles Peterson, who had left the State Historical Society and accepted a position in history at Utah State University, persuaded me to join the faculty there and to continue the work begun earlier by prominent folklorist Austin Fife. During my USU years, I continued the same pattern of activity I had begun at BYU. In addition, I accepted a five-year appointment as editor of *Western Folklore*; served four years on the NEA Folk Arts Panel, serving the fourth year as panel chair; and served eight years on the board of directors of the Utah Arts Council, this last position making me automatically the chair of the Utah Folk Arts Panel. These positions, though time consuming, again added to my leveraging power and helped make possible the expansion of the folklore curriculum at USU (this time with courses cross-listed in the history department), the establishment of the Fife Folklore Archive, and, especially, the development of the annual Fife Folklore Conference into a nationally recognized summer program.

In 1984 I returned to BYU as chair of the English department, a position I held until 1991. Many of my colleagues supported this appointment because they had come to believe that a folklorist actually had something to offer the department. As chair, I worked hard to hire new faculty trained in contemporary literary theory and especially to establish a strong emphasis on cultural studies. I also worked hard to support the legitimate research efforts of department members in all areas of our discipline, not just in those related directly to folklore. And I continued to practice hallology, discussing with the faculty their research and teaching projects and, where appropriate, suggesting related reading in folklore. Some of them responded by incorporating folklore approaches into their teaching and by encouraging so many students to take folklore classes that we have not been able to handle them all. Most important, they also made folklore a major field of emphasis in a recent departmental curriculum revision.

Though I am no longer chair, this cooperation has continued. For example, four of us—a poet, a rhetorician, a feminist critic, and I—recently developed and team-taught an exciting new course in cultural studies. Such a class would have been unthinkable not too many years ago. In the class, we viewed the quilting film *Hearts and Hands*, read literary works with references to quilting, and then made a quilt in the class. Students individually made blocks from a particular fabric or with a design representing something important to them. A few of the more experienced students next stitched these different blocks together. Then we set up quilting frames in the classroom and spent one long class period tying the quilt. Each student submitted a narrative explaining his or her block. Later, at a gathering at one professor's house, we recorded the stories. With each block and accompanying story representing a different life, the experience opened the door for us to talk about everything from narrating to cultural diversity. On one of the walls of the stairwell leading to our departmental offices hang portraits of all the English and American winners of the Nobel Prize for Literature, symbolizing the traditions we have come from and still cherish. On the facing wall now hangs our quilt, symbolizing the culturally diverse and rich world we are moving toward, a world in which folklorists have much to contribute.

I have also continued my efforts to build bridges to other disciplines. I have spoken several times in an anthropology symposium; I have met with historians to discuss ways we might cooperate on local history projects; I have spoken twice to the theater department on the folklore backgrounds of plays currently being produced; I have given several university-wide honors lectures; and I have published several general-interest articles in the university alumni magazine and have by this means taken the message of folklore to some 150,000 alumni and university supporters. Finally, as the new director of the Charles Redd Center for Western Studies, I have broadened the scope of the research we support to include not just history but all the arts, humanities, and social sciences. For the first time in its history, funds are now flowing from the center in support of folklore research.

I am aware that some may be appalled by the story I have just told, considering me a braggart of the worst order or, worse yet, someone who has abandoned the pure scholarly life for politics and administrative advancement. I can assure you that, given a choice, I would much rather have devoted myself fully to scholarship and teaching and left to someone else the task of building up the discipline, of securing folklore positions. But who might that someone have been? Whatever some might think of my efforts, I take comfort from the knowledge that at BYU we now have a limited but solid folklore program, that we have developed a folklore research archive, that many of our undergraduate and graduate students now see how folklore relates to their particular disciplinary interests, that we have trained and sent out graduate students who have done well in folklore doctoral programs, and, above all, that we have enriched the lives of numerous students who see the world differently as a result of having taken a folklore class.

In all the efforts described above, I have had one principal goal—not to lionize myself but rather to develop my credibility to the point that my voice, speaking on behalf of all those voices we folklorists represent, cannot be ignored. I have always been inspired by the life and work of the Finnish scholar-patriot, Elias Lönnrot, who, while serving as a district doctor in remote northern Finland, battling cholera epidemics, and struggling with his own ill health, managed to trek mile after mile on foot through the Finnish hinterlands to collect the epic poems from which he eventually composed the *Kalevala.* As he brought the epic to completion, he wrote to a friend: "A lot of work these poems have been, but I'm not sorry, if they are at last suitable" (Lönnrot 1990, 1: 91). A lot of work it is to earn a graduate degree, to train ourselves broadly in our own and related disciplines, to establish programs in the universities that hire us, and to sacrifice ourselves for the advancement of the discipline. But if in the process we find the means to give voice to the carriers and performers of the traditions we study and value, then our work will also prove suitable, and we will have no reason to be sorry.

Arts and Cultural Policy

Early in his career, Bert Wilson questioned the value of public folklore, which in America is mostly situated in the nonprofit arts sector. He then, and still today, worried about the political purposes to which folklore could be put. When I interviewed Bert in May 2003, I learned that it did not take long for him to accept the idea that helping people appreciate their own heritage through public programs like festivals and exhibits is a valuable endeavor (Thatcher 2003, tape 1, page 4 of transcript). Soon after this realization, which he says started when he participated in the 1976 Smithsonian Folklife Festival, he began actively to support public sector folklore by serving on panels and boards, participating in fieldwork, and consulting on presentation projects. After twenty years of such participation, he gave presentations and put down on paper some of his thoughts about government's role in the arts.

In "Arts and the Family," Bert discusses the creativity that is inborn in the human animal and makes a case for recognition of all kinds of artistic endeavor, whether it be performed by professionals on a concert stage, or performed in the living room by people who earn their livelihoods outside the arts. This notion of creativity as a human imperative is one embraced by most folklorists, but Bert brings it home, literally, by using his own experience with his family and their stories as examples. While he does not advocate directly for public funding of the arts, he suggests that if the public is to accept and appreciate all the arts, a beginning must be made by teaching children to recognize the creativity that flows within their own families. He suggests that schoolteachers should encourage children to recognize their families' traditions, along with teaching them about the world's great artists like Beethoven, Matisse, and Melville.

"Arts and the Family" was published in *Ovations* (Fall 1996): 2, and is reprinted by permission of the Utah Arts Council. "Misquotes and Misfires: William Wilson Responds to Christopher Caldwell and George Will" was published in the *American Folklore Society News* 28 (February 1999): 24–25, and is reprinted by permission of the American Folklore Society. "The Role of Religion in Cultural Policy in Utah" was published in *Cultural Policy in the West: Symposium Proceedings*, 103–10 (Aspen, Colorado: Aspen Institute, Western State Arts Federation, 2000), and is reprinted by permission of the Western State Arts Federation.

This seemingly innocuous piece of writing stirred up a bit of a storm, however, when it was republished by the National Endowment for the Arts. The endowment, especially in the culture wars of the 1980s and 1990s, had become a lightning rod for some people with particular political agendas, and thus Wilson's words became fodder for the political press. He then wrote "Misquotes and Misfires" as a response to two conservative writers who had twisted his words and his intent. This piece is more informal and displays not only Wilson's considerable skills at forming an argument, but also his wit. Wilson's response to these politically motivated misrepresentations of public policy is more important than it might appear. Wilson was in a position to speak plainly about the value of arts in the public sector, and about the value of folk arts as one part of the arts. It is unfortunate that "Misquotes and Misfires" did not appear in every newspaper that carried the George Will column that inspired the piece in the first place.

The essay "The Role of Religion in Cultural Policy in Utah" is another important work on folklore and cultural policy because it speaks openly about issues and practices that are often guarded and controversial. With the thoughtful balance and articulate expression that are hallmarks of Bert Wilson's writing and speaking, the essay describes the Mormon/non-Mormon divide in Utah's arts. Wilson even-handedly discusses the biases of Mormon leaders and non-Mormon arts advocates and describes events from his own experience in which he had to walk the policy tightrope or advocate for consistent application of the rules in decision making. He communicates the truth of the matter that mixing religion, politics, and arts is a balancing act of no small proportion.

One of the reasons Bert's essays on folklore and cultural policy are so valuable is that few public folklorists have taken the time to write about the work they do. Notable exceptions are Robert Baron and Nicholas Spitzer, who edited *Public Folklore* (Smithsonian Institution Press, 1992), and others who have written or compiled reports such as Ormond H. Loomis, who edited *Cultural Conservation: The Protection of Cultural Heritage in the United States* (Library of Congress, 1983). Most writing on public folklore has been for the folklore field and primarily focused on best practices or on the academic-public divide. Little discussion has dealt with the basic question of whether, or how, government should be involved in the folk arts. Wilson's writings have reached broader arts policy audiences with messages about the value of folk arts in the schools, in arts institutions, and elsewhere in personal and public life.

—*Elaine Thatcher*

ARTS AND THE FAMILY

I grew up in a family of railroaders. My father and an uncle were section foremen, my brother a road master, one uncle a fireman, another an engineer, still another a train master. Holiday dinners at my grandparents' home were day-long storytelling events. As my grandmother prepared a dinner, which was always an artistic feast, the cousins gathered in the back room and terrified each other with ghost stories. Later, as we gathered around the dinner table, my uncles, all excellent raconteurs, would regale us with heroic stories of how they had almost single-handedly saved the Union Pacific Railroad from disaster, each narrator trying to top the others in recounting dramatic exploits. Later, when the dishes had been washed and put away and the talk had finally died down, we children would curl up in corners of the room and listen to our parents join in song. My grandfather's and Uncle Albert's clear tenor voices would lead the way, and then other uncles and aunts would join in, harmonizing wonderfully. On the drive home, my head full of story and song, I would feel a closeness to my family that could not have been engendered in other ways.

Through all the years of my public education, no teacher ever suggested to me that what I had experienced in my family on those occasions was of any artistic worth. Art was something we read about in books, not a crucial part of our own lives.

The recent *American Canvas* forum in Salt Lake City, sponsored by the NEA, pondered the question of how the arts can strengthen families. Family bonds are tightened, of course, when family members attend and participate in artistic events together. Anyone who doubts this need only visit Cedar City's Shakespearean Festival and observe the families who year after year make that occasion a family pilgrimage.

But if we really hope to strengthen families through the arts, we must move away from the notion that art can only be found on the museum wall, at the concert hall, or on the performing stage. We must understand that art includes the expressive behaviors of ordinary people, like my railroader relatives, as they respond creatively to the circumstances of everyday life. If we will look, we will find art all around us—in the things we make with our words (songs, stories, rhymes, proverbs), with our hands (quilts, knitting, rawhide braiding, piecrust designs, dinner-table arrangements, garden layouts), and with our actions (birthday and holiday celebrations, worship practices, playtime activities, work practices). As Franz Boas noted long ago, "All human activities may assume forms that give them esthetic values" ([1927] 1955, 8).

Art, then, is not something that exists "out there" in a world alien to many families but is rather an essential part of the lives of most families. The problem is that they just don't know it. If we want to help families through the arts, we must help them recognize, nourish, and value the art they already possess. As they begin to recognize the artistic merit of their own creative efforts, they may discover also the creative power of those art worlds that once seemed so foreign.

It is important, of course, for teachers to acquaint their students with Mozart and Beethoven, with Matisse and van Gogh, with Shakespeare and Melville. But it may be even more important to acquaint them with their parents and grandparents, their aunts and uncles—to send them home with new eyes, prepared now to recognize the artistic merit of what they had been led to believe was simply the routine flow of everyday life. The family pride that can develop from such endeavors is well worth the effort.

Teachers can enhance that pride even more by encouraging students to bring some of those relatives to the schoolroom to share their talents with the entire class—to sing for them, tell stories, show how to embroider an intricate pattern. The children of one immigrant couple always encouraged their parents to remain upstairs when guests visited because the children were embarrassed by their parents' old-world ways. Then these parents and their ways were discovered by a scholar who recognized the great worth of their customs and traditions. Suddenly the children saw their parents in an entirely new light—and the family was strengthened because an educator valued the art of ordinary people.

Similarly, I encourage students in my English and folklore classes to record the stories that have circulated in their families. Just last month one of these students completed a first-rate master's thesis on the stories told by her grandfather. She had always considered him rather cool and stand-offish. But as she for the first time listened closely to his stories and was captured by their artistic power, she discovered what an excellent narrator he was. More important, the grandfather to whom she had never been close now occupies an important place in her heart. And, perhaps equally important, members of her family, who initially questioned the value of such a research project, have now asked for copies of the thesis.

I am fortunate to have had a mother who read to my sister and me each night at bedtime and introduced us to the exciting world of books. I am equally fortunate to have had a mother who told us wonderful stories—stories that illuminate her girlhood in a homesteading community in Idaho; vigorous stories full of passion, humor, joy, and tragedy; stories that have shaped my life and persist in my mind as powerful and as artistically moving as the works of literature that line my library shelf. Once we realize that all people, from all walks of life, have the capacity to create and enjoy beauty, and once we begin seeking much of that beauty in our own homes, we will have taken great strides toward strengthening families through the arts.

MISQUOTES AND MISFIRES: WILLIAM WILSON RESPONDS TO CHRISTOPHER CALDWELL AND GEORGE WILL

Well, I've made the big time. In today's paper (*Deseret News*, April 5, 1998), I was quoted by the conservative George F. Will in his syndicated column. The summer before last I participated in a forum in Salt Lake sponsored by the National Endowment for the Arts. In a project called *American Canvas*, the NEA held regional forums around the country, focusing on different themes at each forum. The Salt Lake meetings focused on the arts as a means of improving family life and education. After the conference I wrote up the things I had said under the title "Arts and the Family," and the Utah Arts Council published them in *Ovations* (1996, 2). I sent the article to NEA as part of the follow-up report I was to make after participating in the Salt Lake forum. Gary O. Larson synthesized all the reports from the various forums in *American Canvas: An Arts Legacy for Our Communities*, published last year by NEA, and cited several passages from my article.

In February of this year, Christopher Caldwell wrote an article called "Arts for Politics's Sake," published in the conservative *Commentary* and attacking the goals outlined in *American Canvas*. Deploring the breakdown of the distinction between "high" and "low" culture, "in favor of the latter," he decries NEA's more inclusive approach to the arts. "This," he says, "is certainly what the Clinton administration had in mind in recently naming William Ivey, a folklorist and the head of the Country Music Foundation, to succeed the outgoing Jane Alexander as head of the NEA" (1998, 56). To underscore his point that folklorists can be trusted only to dumb down our culture, Caldwell quotes from a passage Olson had quoted from me:

> We must move away from the notion that art can only be found on the museum wall, at the concert hall, or on the performing stage. We must understand that art includes the expressive behaviors of ordinary people . . . things that we make with our words (songs, stories, rhymes, proverbs), with our hands (quilts, knitting, rawhide braiding, pie-crust designs, dinner-table arrangements, garden layouts), and with our actions (birthday and holiday celebrations, worship practices, playtime activities, work practices). (ibid., 56)

Caldwell conveniently omits, with the use of ellipsis, the important phrase in which I had argued that we should look at the expressive behaviors of ordinary people "as they respond creatively to the circumstances of everyday life." From Caldwell's perspective there can be no creativity among ordinary people. During the rest of the article, he scorns using art for such social causes as improving children's school performance, preventing crime, and contributing to the quality of life. All these efforts, he claims, are part of President Clinton's program of "mainstreaming the agenda of the Left, wrapping it in the uplifting mantle of populism, and co-opting as many sources of real or potential opposition as possible." He concludes that for the NEA these efforts mark "a pitiful coda to the career of a now hopelessly corrupt institution" (ibid., 56, 57).

Picking up where Caldwell leaves off, George Will argues that both the National Endowment for the Arts and the National Endowment for the Humanities have taken a populist road to survival. Once again he quotes me, this time with the same omission as in Caldwell but without benefit of elliptical marks. He also drops any reference to me as the author of the passage and instead makes the NEA the author of my words, as though I were some sort of synecdoche for the entire organization. As does Caldwell, Will deplores the "embarrassing embrace of cultural democracy" in which all can participate and gives as evidence of our downward drift the appointment of folklorist William Ferris as head of NEH and folklorist William Ivey as head of NEA. Immediately following the quotation from me he writes:

> Everything from singing in your morning shower to setting your dinner table is eligible for NEA support, which makes it easy to spread support, like honey on bread, across 435 congressional districts. The chairman of the NEA, William Ivey, is a folklorist. (1998, AA6)

Will, of course, gives no support for his argument. He merely refers to the expressions of ordinary people in mocking tones and assumes that all right-thinking people will see that such expressions can have no artistic merit. He argues that both NEA and NEH will exclude nothing from their purview and will devote their efforts to studying and supporting "mundane things [simply] because they are ubiquitous" (ibid.). No one I know would make the ridiculous claim that everything created by ordinary people is of equal artistic merit—that would be as foolish as saying that all novels, symphonies, and ballets are equally good. During the four years I spent on the NEA Folk Arts Panel, one year as chair, we did pay heed to the social implications of the grants we awarded, but at center stage was always our concern with artistic quality. One need look no further than Steve Siporin's *American Folk Masters: The National Heritage Awards* (1992) for ample demonstration of the NEA's concern with aesthetic excellence.

Will continues in the same vein throughout his article. He ridicules the notion that by studying food one can learn a lot about regions. And he derisively holds up for public scorn the following statement by Ferris:

> Today the lives of ordinary American people have assumed a place beside volumes of European classics in the humanities. . . . We must recognize those voices which seldom touch the printed page. A sharecropper in Alabama and a steelworker in Indiana have a voice in the humanities. Their view of truth and wisdom complements traditional learning in a new and exciting way. (ibid.)

Will completely misses the point that the new approaches suggested by Ferris "complement" rather than "replace" traditional learning. As one who has spent much of his life promoting what Caldwell and Will would probably accept as art, I am put off by their pseudo distinctions between high and low culture and by their assuming an either/or approach to the arts: either we can have William Shakespeare or we can have Ray Hicks, but we can't have both. Nonsense! That's like saying you can enjoy a vegetarian meal or you can enjoy fried chicken, but you can't enjoy both. In our pluralistic, multicultural country, the greater variety of food we can put on the plate, the richer will be our lives—to say nothing of our honoring the long-ignored artistic traditions of many of our citizens. Neither Caldwell nor Will seems capable of recognizing artistic excellence in any but the established artistic canons (what a simple-minded approach that is: if it's in the canon, it must be good). They fail to realize that the artistic impulse resides not just in a privileged few but is inherent in the species, one of the few forces that separates us from the rest of the animal kingdom. Realizing that ordinary men and women everywhere have moved beyond necessity to create beauty in their lives ought to be cause for rejoicing, not denigration.

Aside from the fact that both Caldwell and Will jerk people's words out of context and distort them to drive home their own ideological agendas, the most disturbing thing about them is their cynicism, their inability to comprehend that some people might really prefer to act in other than self-serving ways. As they question the motives of others, they are, I fear, simply listening to the beatings of their own jaded hearts. They can't comprehend that some people might want to take a more inclusive approach to the arts because these people genuinely believe that the canonical approaches of the past have overlooked art of great significance and ignored artists of great accomplishment. As a result, Caldwell and Will have to explain a broader approach to the arts as nothing more than a populist attempt to win the financial support of Congress and to serve mean ends. I will never apologize for my own democratic approach. I am proud to belong to a profession that values the equal worth of all people and respects and honors their artistic efforts. I only regret that we have done such a poor job of getting our message across that we have left columnists like Caldwell and Will free to speak glibly and irresponsibly, and with impunity, about art worlds of which they are largely ignorant.

THE ROLE OF RELIGION IN CULTURAL POLICY IN UTAH

I have been asked to address the interplay between art and religion in making cultural policy. Because the connection between art and religion is far too broad a subject to treat in one paper, I will focus on that interplay as it occurs in my state—Utah—and address the topic from the perspective of someone who has spent much of his life in arts reviewing and programming and is also a practicing member of the Church of Jesus Christ of Latter-day Saints—the LDS, or Mormon, church.

While artistic and religious impulses seem to be fundamental forces in the lives of most people, it is obvious that these forces are sometimes mutually supportive and sometimes end up at cross-purposes (or at least the people who put them into action end up at cross-purposes). This has been my experience in Utah. I want to focus on three specific issues: the LDS church's support of the arts, the tension between the LDS church and LDS artists, and the tension between the LDS church and non-LDS artists in the state of Utah.

In Utah, it is difficult to separate church and nonchurch into two artistic camps—there is too much exchange back and forth. Many people think that all Mormons live in Utah, but in fact, 80 percent of them live outside the state, and more than half live outside the United States. It is true, nonetheless, that Utah is a Mormon state; approximately 65 percent of the state is Mormon. For Salt Lake City, that figure drops to 45 percent, which means that the great majority of residents in rural areas are LDS. These demographics have important implications for the arts. Since most members of the Utah legislature are Mormon (and almost all Republican), LDS values will guide them as they make decisions regarding arts funding. This is so not because the LDS church forces these values upon them but simply because they have absorbed a Mormon point of view in the process of growing up.

I would like to offer a brief example of how the lines between Mormon and non-Mormon cross. The church-owned *Deseret News* recently published an article about Salt Lake City's magnificent symphony hall, the home of the Utah Symphony Orchestra (Reichel 1999, Focus Section). For the first forty years of its sixty-year existence, the Utah Symphony had no home. In its first few years, the symphony played in whatever venue was available, in whatever high school auditorium could be rented for the night. In 1947, maestro Maurice Abravanel became the symphony's music director. He was not a Mormon, but he had a good relationship with the Mormon church and worked out an agreement in which the symphony could present its programs in the Mormon Tabernacle without paying any rent. This relationship lasted for thirty-two years, with the symphony using the tabernacle and the church providing support by waiving rental fees.

During the 1970s, when folks were planning the nation's bicentennial and looking for a bicentennial project in Utah, it was decided that the symphony needed its own hall. The U.S. Congress had initially promised to appropriate funds for such projects throughout the United States but then backed off and did not come up with the money. About this same time, leaders of the Mormon church issued this statement: "We are pleased that plans are being considered to construct a concert hall. . . . Our city and state have long needed such a facility. Its construction and use will coincide with the policy of the church followed from earliest days of our history of encouraging and supporting projects which improve the cultural and artistic life of our community" (Reichel 1999). The Utah legislature (our good Republican legislators) appropriated $6.5 million for the construction of the hall, and the symphony had to come up only with matching funds and private donations. Because the symphony had trouble raising this money, the Salt Lake County Commission ordered a bond election; the bond passed, additional money was appropriated, and the symphony got its hall. This would not have happened without the support of the Church of Jesus Christ of Latter-day Saints.

Examples abound of the church encouraging and supporting the arts, from the time Mormons arrived in Salt Lake Valley in 1847 to the present. Brigham

Young shrugged off the prevailing asceticism of his day, teaching that God had given music, dancing, and theater for the pleasure of His children. Young frowned on the reading of novels, especially by young women, because he believed these fictional works might corrupt their morals. But from the outset church support for music, dance, theater, and the visual arts has been strong.

Most of that art, I must concede, has been didactic. Church leaders have seldom supported "art for art's sake." Rather, they have viewed artistic creation as a means of promoting spirituality and building faith in the church. Joseph F. Smith, president of the LDS church at the beginning of the twentieth century, told church members: "I wish to say to the Latter-day Saints that I hope they will distinguish themselves by avoiding the necessity of being classed with people who prefer the vulgar to the chaste, the obscene to the pure, the evil to the good, and the sensual to the intellectual" (Smith 1938, ch. 35). What is to be regarded obscene remains always open to interpretation, but Smith's view has become the policy Mormon artists have been expected to follow.

In spite of this stricture, during the Mormons' first century in Utah good results were achieved in all artistic fields except one, literature, where the results were pretty dismal. To counter the "corrupting" influence Brigham Young had attributed to novels, the church in 1888 began a home literature movement. The result was a series of sentimental, nonrealistic, didactic works that are still being produced and read in the church today. Not for almost a century later, when in 1977 church president Spencer W. Kimball made the following statement, was new terrain opened for literary exploration. Said Kimball:

> For years I have been waiting for someone to do justice in recording in song and story and painting and sculpture the story of the Restoration, the reestablishment of the kingdom of God on earth, the struggles and frustrations; the apostasies and inner revolutions and counter-revolutions of those first decades; of the exodus, of the counter-reactions; of the transitions; of the persecution days; of the miracle man, Joseph Smith. (1977, 5)

For many Mormon writers, Kimball's statement meant that they could now focus not just on the smiling aspects of Mormon life, but also on the conflicts, struggles, and frustrations. From that time to the present, there has been a flowering of Mormon short stories, novels, and personal essays written by faithful church members. In the 1930s and 1940s, an earlier generation of Mormon writers called "The Lost Generation" had produced quite good literature; but the authors, though coming out of the Mormon pioneer tradition, for the most part rejected the church and moved away from it (see Geary 1977). Those writing since 1977 have in the main stayed within the church and have argued for what they have called "faithful realism," a realistic view of the problems encountered in this world but a view motivated by faith (see England 1996).

There have been counter views, however, expressed mainly by Boyd K. Packer, one of the most influential members of the church hierarchy in the last twenty-five years. In 1976, a year before Kimball made his statement, Packer delivered a major address that has been widely republished. In "The Arts and the Spirit of the Lord," he criticized Mormon writers for aping the style and techniques of non-Mormon artists and for not using their work to build faith and promote Mormon values (Packer 1977).

Despite President Kimball's statement advocating fuller artistic expression, the opposing view tends to have prevailed at the church's Brigham Young University, where I taught for many years. This view has not fully thwarted the creation and expression of Mormon literary arts, but it has at times had a chilling effect. As the English department chair at BYU, I frequently had to answer letters from angry mothers upset over their children's reading assignments in their English classes, assignments they were convinced did not meet uplifting church standards. During those years we had a fine creative writing program—we still have a pretty good one—but we lost two of our best creative writers, both of them nationally recognized award-winners. One of them was forced out; the other left of his own accord, feeling stifled by the prevailing atmosphere. The theater department has some excellent playwrights, but they too have sometimes been confronted with the choice of rewriting parts of their work or of not seeing it produced.

Although I am not particularly sympathetic to the view that Mormon literature must always reflect church positions, I should say in defense of those who hold this view that the church has the right to establish whatever policy it wants for its people. What's more, during my last years at BYU, I learned that the issue is more complex than I have presented it here, as I ran head on myself into the conflict between individual and institutional freedom. After stepping down as chair of the English department, I directed the Charles Redd Center for Western Studies. At that time, the center began moving away from promoting primarily historical interpretations of the West and began publishing serious creative works as well. We were considering publishing a fine collection of poetry by a friend of mine. Two of the poems were sexually explicit—not in a prurient way, but I knew they would present problems. I went to my friend and said, "Henry, I can't publish these two poems. If I were the publisher myself and if the decision to publish would draw negative attention only to me, there would be no problem. But the university is the publisher, and I can't afford to jeopardize the Redd Center by offending the powers-that-be." Of course, I could have been heroic and said, "I'm going to publish these poems no matter what anyone thinks." But that could have spelled the end of the center. I couldn't bring myself to undermine what former directors had worked so hard to establish. And so, though I certainly did not relish the role, I was forced to become a censor myself, balancing precariously between the tensions of faith-promotion and faithful realism.

I served for eight years on the Utah Arts Council. The demographic makeup of the council was quite different from that of the rest of the state. Membership varied, of course, as some members retired and new appointees took their place. However, at any one time the council would be comprised of participating Mormons, lapsed (or nonpracticing) Mormons, and non-Mormons. One thing was clear: council decisions were not governed by the church position on the arts. The council wanted to make sure that Mormon voices were not the only voices heard in the state, that minority religious and ethnic groups would have their time in the sun, and that the values and interests of the 35 percent of Utah residents who were not Mormon would be protected and promoted. The council was successful in achieving this laudable goal, especially in folk arts and in community outreach programs; but the problem with this focus was that, in making sure minority groups and programs were not smothered and overwhelmed by the Mormon majority, Mormon artistic programs were often ignored or denied funding.

For example, the council wished to provide supporting funds for literary magazines at all of the universities in the state—with the exception of BYU's magazine, even though it had won national awards for artistic excellence. Because I was English department chair at BYU at the time, I could not participate in the discussion of BYU's grant proposal. I was permitted to stay in the room, but I couldn't speak or vote on the matter. I had to listen as council members argued that the church had lots of money and that BYU really did not need the funds. I knew exactly how much university money was available and that it was not sufficient to publish the kind of magazine we wanted. In the end, the council voted not to grant BYU's proposal and then began discussing similar proposals from the other universities. I was free to speak now. I said, "Well, I had planned to vote for these magazines and I would very much like to, but in turning down BYU's proposal, the council has established criteria that will make it impossible to fund these other proposals. If we are to be consistent, we must adhere to the criteria you have just set." The council backed off; it funded both the magazines at the other universities and BYU's magazine as well.

In another instance the 1999 Madeleine Festival, focusing primarily on an excellent series of musical programs and sponsored by Salt Lake City's Cathedral of the Madeleine, received partial funding from the Utah Arts Council. The 1999 Mormon Arts Festival—also a very good program featuring first-rate artists—received financial support from the Mormon Arts Foundation and the BYU College of Fine Arts, but none from the Utah Arts Council. I suspect, though I do not know, that Mormon Arts Festival directors did not even ask for Utah Arts Council money because they assumed they would not get any. Again the problem has been lack of consistency. The Utah Arts Council can give money to religious groups, so it has been argued, not to promote any particular religion, but to support artistic components of religious programming. That approach has worked fine for Catholics, Baptists, and Lutherans, but not very well for Mormons. Whenever the issue of funding Mormon arts programming has arisen, the sometimes hostile sentiment against promoting the dominant religion has often come to the fore, and the funding has not been forthcoming.

Several decades ago, a group of the Mormon faithful wrote and produced a musical called *Saturday's Warrior*—a sentimental production that was disliked by professionals in theater and music groups both in the church and out but was almost universally acclaimed by Mormon popular audiences. The musical is still very popular and is still produced. Some years following the debut of *Saturday's Warrior*, a group in Salt Lake City put together a very salacious parody called *Saturday's Voyeur* and asked the Utah Arts Council for funding.

I still remember that discussion very well. The council had always been very careful not to offend different ethnic and religious minority groups in the state. Now, however, when we were dealing with a work directed against the majority religion, some threw that caution to the wind and argued that we should make our decision on this particular grant proposal on the artistic merits of the production only, a criterion that seldom came fully into play in making other awards. Just as publishing my friend's poetry might have brought about the demise of the Charles Redd Center, so too funding *Saturday's Voyeur* in a state 65 percent Mormon could have spelled disaster for the Utah Arts Council.

This issue also brought up the thorny question the National Endowment for the Arts has had to struggle with in recent years: How much should those who pay the taxes supporting the arts have to say about arts programming? Further, in a state in which nearly three-quarters of the citizens belong to a particular religion and pay the bulk of the taxes, is it all right to filter very little tax money through the state arts council to support art in harmony with the values and beliefs these taxpayers cherish?

As we have seen, religion can inspire and nourish artistic production, can suppress artistic expression, and can turn people from different religious persuasions against each other. So long as both religion and art continue to play significant roles in the lives of our citizens, questions like those raised above will continue to plague those who must develop and carry out public cultural policy.

"Something There Is That Doesn't Love a Wall"

When Bert Wilson in 1991 delivered this talk, "'Something There Is That Doesn't Love a Wall,'" the Folklore Society of Utah was holding its annual meeting in conjunction with that of the Utah State Historical Society, an arrangement that had then continued for twenty years. Bert had been the driving force behind this supportive agreement. At that time, the Folklore Society had a tiny membership and few resources, but the quality and interest of the folklore session made it annually one of the most popular and best attended at the meeting. The hospitality of historical society director Charles Peterson and of his successor, Melvin T. Smith, proved absolutely essential in providing the Folklore Society an arena for meeting, which in turn allowed it to survive, grow, and eventually prosper, so much so that we now have an independent annual meeting featuring as many as twenty-four papers by undergraduates and graduate students, several of which are published by the society.

Fostering cooperation in mutually beneficial enterprises is a hallmark of Bert Wilson's work, within the universities he has served, in the public arena, and in his own intellectual life. That drive for cooperation and understanding is exemplified by "'Something There Is That Doesn't Love a Wall,'" a title he borrows appropriately from the opening line of Robert Frost's poem "Mending Wall," with its frequently misquoted and even more frequently misunderstood line spoken by the next-door farmer, "Good fences make good neighbors." In fact, the poem's point is to question the building and maintenance of walls, whether between pine trees and apple orchards or between human beings.

Bert has devoted his career to tearing down walls where they exist and encouraging others to think past the walls that we create in our career, our institutions, and our thinking. At Brigham Young and Utah State universities—at both of which he increased course offerings in folklore, expanded the folklore archives, and encouraged the hiring of other folklorists—he has sought cooperative arrangements

---

This paper was a dinner address delivered at the combined meetings of the Folklore Society of Utah and the Utah State Historical Society at Park City, Utah, July 12, 1991.

with colleagues in English, history, and social sciences; with librarians and archivists; and with such institutions as the Charles Redd Center for Western Studies at BYU, the Mountain West Center for Regional Studies at USU, and the Festival of the American West in Logan. In his teaching, his deeply interdisciplinary interests allowed him to intertwine perspectives drawn from a variety of folkloristic approaches along with those of written and oral history, the new historicism of literary theory, performance and contextual approaches from folkloristics (the theory and practice of folklore study), and behavioral and functionalist approaches from the social sciences.

The same can be said of his scholarship, nearly one hundred articles and several hundred public presentations on many topics, particularly Mormon and Utah folklore. His ability to place folklore within the context of the humanities, to demonstrate that folklore contributes to the quality of being human for all people, has helped scholars and the general public alike to appreciate the human potential for shared, cooperative, and supportive interaction. Rather than seeing folklore as something possessed, invented, perpetuated, or even lost by a group of "the folk," by those markedly different from the observer, Bert has shown us the universality of tradition, performance, and communication in all our lives.

As a builder of institutions and programs he has been exemplary. Not only has he helped to lower the barriers between folklore and history, he has also shown the ways folklorists and historians can achieve a common cause and a common goal while learning from each other. As a Mormon working in an academic discipline whose national and international membership is, on the whole, profoundly ignorant of Mormonism, he has collected, analyzed, and explained not the archaic lore of difference but the contemporary lore of similarity. His long service as the first folklorist appointed to the board of the Utah Arts Council helped immeasurably to increase the understanding and importance of folk arts among the arts community, and paved the way for later board members Barre Toelken and Meg Brady. His understanding and support of folklore in the public sector—the Folk Arts Program of the Utah Arts Council and of the National Endowment for the Arts, the Fife Folklore Conference at Utah State University, the Western Folklife Center in Elko, Nevada, and fieldwork in Nevada for the American Folklife Center of the Library of Congress—has helped break down long-standing barriers between public-sector and academic folklorists.

This article exemplifies his multidisciplinary and humanistic approach. It encompasses the history of folklore studies and various theories concerning "the folk." It emphasizes the innate artistry and performative instincts of humans, an approach linked to contemporary developments in folklore theory. It demonstrates from an anthropological and sociological perspective that folklore occurs in social situations and that it is a vital component in the formation and maintenance of human groups. It shows the vitality and importance of folk history and the way it reflects values, hopes, and fears that written, verifiable history may not. And, near the end, it emphasizes the importance for every group of people and every community of a "common body of shared beliefs," what Bert calls a "value center." This value center, often expressed through folklore (stories, songs, jokes, customs, rituals, and other kinds of expressive culture), is at the heart of how we regard ourselves and how we regard others. Rather than creating walls between human groups or between academic disciplines, Bert argues, we need to seek out and to find the commonalities that link us.

—David Stanley

THE REALIZATION THAT WE CELEBRATE THIS YEAR TWENTY YEARS OF COOPeration between the Folklore Society of Utah and the Utah State Historical Society has pulled my thoughts toward the subject I would like to address in this paper.

On March 6, 1971, Austin Fife, realizing that the Folklore Society of Utah had sputtered along for years, recommended that it disband, that it turn its records over to the State Historical Society, and that it encourage the historical society "to recognize folklore as an integral part of its activities." On March 21, I countered by proposing that the folklore society seek closer cooperation with the historical society, that it meet jointly with the historical society at their annual meeting, but that it continue to maintain its independence and to pursue those activities peculiar to folklorists alone. We put the issue to a vote of our meager membership; by an 87 percent majority we voted to remain independent (Wilson 1971).

Officers of the folklore society then met with officers of the historical society on May 15, found them receptive to our initiatives, and planned a special folklore session for the historical society's annual meeting to be held at Brigham Young University on September 18. In that session, Jan Brunvand spoke on Mormon jokelore, Thomas Cheney on the J. Golden Kimball legacy, and John B. Harris and I on Mormon missionary lore. Thus began a pattern that has continued until today with the folklore society's participating each year in the historical society's annual meetings—to the mutual benefit of both.

At the annual meeting the following year, I gave a talk, "Folklore and History: Fact amid the Legends," which was well received, was published in the *Utah Historical Quarterly*, and even received the Rosenblatt Award for the best general interest article of the year. That also was a beginning, as the *Quarterly* opened its pages to folklore articles and, in addition to individual essays, published over the years three special issues devoted entirely to folklore—one to Mormon lore (Wilson 1976d), one to ethnic lore (Brady 1984), and one to material culture (Carter 1988).

Elsewhere in the state, partly as a result of these initial advances, the marriage between folklore and history continued to grow stronger. Folklore courses at Utah State University have been cross-listed in the history department; the annual Fife Conference at USU has always welcomed historians; the Jensen Living History Farm brings together folklore and history; the Folk Arts Program of the Utah Arts Council has always endeavored to set its work in historical context; the Western Folklife Center, based originally in Salt Lake City, later in Elko, Nevada, has attempted to increase our understanding of western history, especially through its work with cowboy poetry; and the state historical society, in its preservation efforts, has paid attention to folk architecture. A year from now, when I return from a leave of absence, I will assume the directorship of the Charles Redd Center at BYU, a step I hope will make the marriage of folklore and history still stronger.

In Utah, then, historians and folklorists have cooperated to a degree unknown in almost any other state. One hopes that the next twenty years will produce equally rich results. But before that can happen we must learn to understand each other still better. In spite of general good will on both sides, I sometimes fear we talk *past* each other instead of *to* each other.

Both historians and folklorists are interested in stories people tell about the past, but while historians are primarily interested in the events illuminated by these stories, folklorists are often more interested in the stories themselves—as artistic performances worthy of study in their own right; or folklorists are interested in the tellers of the stories and in the ways they use narratives to project personal values or to place themselves center stage in a world that has not often acknowledged their worth. Once these differences are understood, however, cooperation and mutual endeavors are still possible.

A much more serious problem occurs when folklorists and historians use the same words but attach different meanings to them, or when one camp views a term positively and the other pejoratively. I would plead, therefore, that the historians among you pay closer heed to definitions of terms folklorists have coined, including the word "folklore" itself, even if you eventually choose to use them in different ways; and I would urge folklorists to seek ways of making our language more palatable to historians and thus to cause them to view our work with less skepticism.

As I write these words, lines from Robert Frost's "Mending Wall" keep haunting me. "Something there is," said Frost, "that doesn't love a wall." "Before I built a wall," he continued, "I'd ask to know what I was walling in or walling out" (1969, 33–34). That's what definitions are, of course—walls that can separate us from each other and hinder our cooperation. Still, if we are to do business with each other, we must have some mutual understanding of what we are about. I would like to consider two terms that have sometimes given us trouble—first "folk" and then "folk history." As a folklorist, I must, of course, speak from a folklorist's point of view, but by explaining that point of view to the rest of you, I hope to eliminate some of those walls that occasionally divide us.

The way some historians use the first of these terms, "folk," will frequently set the teeth of folklorists on edge. Who are these people, "the folk," who occupy our attention? Properly to answer that question, we must look briefly at the antecedents of contemporary folklore study. Serious folklore study began in Europe in the nineteenth century—on the continent under the inspiration of romantic nationalism and in England under the impulse of the idea of progress and of evolutionary anthropology. The romantic nationalists considered the folklore which eager collectors were bringing to public attention to be relics, or survivals, from an earlier Golden Age; the evolutionists, on the other hand, considered this same lore to be survivals not from a glorious past, but from savage or barbaric ages of cultural development which all people had passed through or would have to pass through on their unilinear path to civilization.

Though divided on questions of folklore's ultimate origins, advocates of both these schools shared a number of views in common. Both believed that folklore had survived in and could be found only among the rural peasant classes or, as some put it, among the "ruder orders" who had remained relatively untouched by education and by the more sophisticated and cosmopolitan life in the cities. Both saw folklore as a tool for reconstructing the past—for the romantic nationalists a glorious past which they hoped to restore and for the evolutionists a savage and barbaric past which they believed most of the race had happily, and forever, left behind. Neither school would have given credence to the notion that folklore might help us understand the dynamics of the present or of the recent past, and both schools, therefore, would have found quite ridiculous any attempt to use folklore to better understand our contemporary world.

Almost all serious folklorists have long ago abandoned these nineteenth-century concepts. Though twentieth-century folklorists have made many theoretical advances beyond the monistic views of the previous century, three in particular are germane to our discussion. First, we now understand that folklore has come into being not just in the distant past but in all ages. Just as people in earlier eras generated and transmitted folklore in response to the circumstances of their lives, so too people in the present create and pass along folklore as they react to the strains, stresses, joys, and sorrows of their lives. Folklore expressions, therefore, are not static survivals, like potsherds, but dynamic responses to dynamic and current social situations. Even if these expressions have originated in the distant past, they will have been reshaped to meet the demands of contemporary life. In other words, folklore may have been born in the past but it lives in the present. Second, we now understand that folklore belongs not just to peasants and to rural people nor to the unsophisticated and unlettered but to all people. All of us, really, are the "folk." We generate, transmit, and enjoy folklore because these acts are imperatives of our human existence—that is, we tell stories, sing songs, recite proverbs, and participate in rituals because these are the ways we have as human beings of dealing with basic and recurring human problems, the social situations I mentioned above. Third, we now understand that while folklore is indeed universal, occurring throughout time and among all peoples, it is also culture specific—that is, those universal folklore forms available to us are given shape and meaning by the attitudes and values of the social groups to which we belong. Folklore study, therefore, helps us identify the universal in the particular. It teaches us what it means to be human while at the same time showing us what it means to be a member of a particular locality, a particular ethnic or immigrant group, a particular occupation, a particular religion, a particular family. Since historians are interested in these same cultural groupings, folklorists and historians have good cause to cooperate.

The problem is that some historians—and notice, please, that I said *some*, not *all*—got stuck back in the nineteenth century in their understanding of folklore and never made the transition to the twentieth. They still consider the people who keep folklore alive as simple, unlettered country folk; and they view this lore as curious customs and usages, survivals from an earlier era. Consider, for example, the following two passages from Jon Butler's *Awash in a Sea of Faith: Christianizing the American People*, published in 1990 by Harvard University Press:

> Significant evidence suggests that the folklorization of magic occurred as much in America as in England. As in England, colonial magic and occultism did not so much disappear everywhere as they disappeared among certain social classes and became confined to poorer, more marginal segments of early American Society. (83)

> The legal activity against witchcraft demonstrated the broad range of early American religious expression. The persistence of belief in witches after witch trials had ended reflected the folklorization of magic in the twilight of early modern Western society on both sides of the Atlantic. Although upper social classes largely abandoned occultism, other colonists continued to believe in witchcraft, astrology, and the ability of wise men and wise women to find lost objects and cure disease. In this regard, folklorization prevented the complete suppression of occultism and magic. Opponents lacked the means to eliminate it completely, and magistrates and ministers tolerated its minimal expression, in part because such views seemed quaint and in part because they were held by the folk. (96–97)

No nineteenth-century English evolutionary anthropologist could have said it better. According to this nineteenth-century point of view, through a process Butler calls "folklorization," as the majority of the population progressed out of the darkness of the past, elements of an earlier folk mentality supposedly persisted among uneducated, marginal, and lower class individuals.

These same ideas can be found in Ronald W. Walker's "The Persisting Idea of American Treasure Hunting" (1984), which places Joseph Smith's treasure seeking in the context of practices current in Smith's time. In this otherwise excellent piece, Walker, like Butler, still clings to the notion of the marginalized, unlettered folk versus the rest of us—as is evident in phrases like, "an immemorial but now forgotten world view" (430–31), "an old but fading way of life" (431), "myths" (431), "part of a significant but now largely forgotten belief system" (435), "old lore" (435), "surviving folklore" (443), "an old cultural system that rapidly was passing into obsolescence" (450), and "the old way that eventually faltered before the onslaught of modern science and the triumph of a new world view" (452).

And these ideas become centrally important in D. Michael Quinn's *Early Mormonism and the Magic World View* (1987). Since I have discussed Quinn's work elsewhere (Wilson 1987b), I will not repeat myself here, except to point out that, like Walker and Butler, Quinn locates folk practices, especially magic and the occult, "in rural areas and among people with limited education" (21) and reduces the practitioners of traditional knowledge to "rural folk" (14), "the common people" (20), people among whom there existed an "indifference to the priorities of the educated elite" (11). Further, he finds in the folk mentality "a magic world view" that has persisted relatively unchanged from days of the ancient Egyptians, little influenced by circumstances of geography, culture, and history—a worldview which can be put behind us only through increased education and through accepting the more rational, scientific thought of the contemporary world.

The problem with the approach taken by these scholars is not their argument that as certain segments of a social group, for whatever reason, abandon once widely held beliefs and practices, other members of the same group will continue to adhere to them and will keep them at least temporarily alive. Of course this occurs. The problem is calling those people among whom the generally abandoned practices persist "the folk"—otherwise why the term "folklorization"—and thus assuming that the rest of the supposedly more enlightened population are not folk and consequently will have no folklore.

A related problem with the approach is that, since the model of these scholars does not allow for the persistence of earlier practices in a more educated world, they have not looked for them—as their badly outdated references to folklore publications will quickly make clear. It is difficult for me to understand, for example, that anyone can argue that treasure seeking is a thing of the past, a survival of an earlier intellectual climate, when tales of lost Indian or Spanish gold mines or of hidden outlaw wealth comprise one of the most vibrant themes in American, and particularly in Western American, folklore. When I taught at Utah State University, a fellow came into the archive who had heard stories of outlaws having once buried their ill-gotten gain somewhere on Samaria Mountain near Malad, Idaho. Having failed to uncover the wealth through conventional digging, he was now trying to raise money to find the treasure by bulldozing away the entire mountain. Such treasure legends are everywhere, as is made clear by the 1977 publication of Byrd Granger's *A Motif Index for Lost Mines and Treasures Applied to Redactions of Arizona Legends and to Lost Mine and Treasure Legends Exterior to Arizona.*

Folklorist Alan Dundes sees such legends as part of the ongoing American dream of "unlimited good." "It may be significant," he suggests "that most accounts end with the treasure still not recovered. This suggests that Americans think that America remains a land of opportunity, that boundless wealth is still readily available to anyone with the energy and initiative to go dig for it" (1971, 97). One can certainly quarrel with Dundes's interpretation but not with his awareness that the legends reveal much more than an earlier "folk" way of thinking.

It is also difficult for me to understand that scholars can consider the use of the divining rod, either to find treasure or water, as a practice that has faded with the advance of rationalistic thought. A quick walk through the BYU Folklore Archives should provide one with evidence that the practice is still alive and well in Utah. In their very important *Water Witching U.S.A.*, published in 1959, Harvard professors Evon Z. Vogt and Ray Hyman, taking a functional rather than a survivalist approach, argue that use of the diving rod has continued to flourish, even in a more sophisticated environment, because it gives its users a sense of control in an unsure world—that is, it persuades them that even in our arid West, where a high degree of uncertainty exists concerning the availability of precious water, means are still available through which one might hope to find this precious liquid (191).

This is precisely the point—that folklore arises in response to felt need—which Wayland Hand has made in explaining the persistence of magical folklore in a world that one would expect to be hostile to magic: "Folk beliefs and superstitions," says Hand, "arise naturally out of situations of hazard and doom. . . . Physical hazard is bad enough; far worse, however, are pursuits fraught with psychological hazard such as the stage, stock market operations, gambling, and sports" (1983, 53). In other words, in certain desperate and trying circumstances, in both rural and urban life, and among the educated and uneducated, many of us turn to cultural means outside ourselves to save the day. The point I would stress is that these are not "folk" ways of dealing with life's vicissitudes; they are human ways, common to the species, not just to a segment of the race. We call them folklore because they find their cultural expression within the different folk groups I have mentioned above.

For example, while the twentieth-century Mormon world is not the nineteenth-century world of Joseph Smith and his contemporaries, much remains constant. So long as present-day Mormons continue to believe, as did their predecessors, that through intercessory prayers and rituals they can manipulate supernatural powers to their advantage, they will continue to do so. Hence, though supernatural experiences are not the sum of their religious values, many Mormons today still divine the future, experience dreams and visions, invoke angels and spirits, exorcise devils, seek information from the spirits of the dead, heal the sick through ceremonial means, and use talismans to ward off evil.

I am not suggesting that all remains as it once was. Clearly, in response to changed cultural circumstances, some forms of folklore diminish or disappear altogether. But, and this is the crucial point, others develop to take their place—because folklore is fundamental to the human condition, arising, as I have noted, in response to recurring human situations. Another, and more serious, problem with the evolutionary approach to folklore, therefore, is that it denies this fact and argues for the eventual disappearance of folklore altogether. For, if the folk are to be seen as marginal and unlettered individuals, bound together by their nonscientific and nonrational worldview, and if folklore is to be seen as the expressive manifestations of this worldview, then it follows that once the folk become educated, they will cease to be "folk," and folklore will cease to be. If we accept this point of view, then we "wall out" from serious consideration not just magical and supernatural practices but also the folklore that exists all around us and is part of all our lives. And we hinder, in the process, the cooperation that should exist between folklorists and historians as they seek to understand the social groups that make up our society.

Students often bring these older notions of the folk to introductory folklore classes. When they learn that they must actually collect folklore as part of the course requirements, some panic, thinking they must head off to some hinterland to uncover quaint and curious stories and practices. Others grow ecstatic when they are able to discover potential informants so old they are just about to totter into the grave. When I suggest that they forget such enterprises and begin by interviewing their roommates or people at their work places or in their families, they often look at me in amazement, never having considered that they or their acquaintances might know any folklore. They have been conditioned to think of folklore as something belonging to people other than themselves—to those strange, or exotic, or quaint "folk." By midsemester, however, they wonder not where they will find folklore but rather how, for their research papers, they will cut out a narrow enough focus from the world of traditional material that surrounds them.

One student, convinced she could never locate any folklore, came to talk with me. "Where do you work?" I asked. "In my father's office." "What does your father do?" "He's a doctor." "All right, then, put together a collection of doctors' folklore." And she did. By semester's end, she had gathered a rich body of medical lore collected from her father and his medical colleagues (Barton 1974).

Though doctors and nurses must work closely together, they do not always admire each other and frequently tell stories that reflect and warrant their opinions. Thus from doctors we often get stories like the following (nurses, of course, will have their own stories about doctors):

> This doctor was in the hospital, and a nurse came by to get a urine specimen from him. She left the specimen bottle with him and told him that she would be back in a few minutes to collect it. Well, this doctor had just had some visitors, and they had brought him a jug of apple cider, so the doctor decided to play a trick on the nurse. He filled up the bottle with cider. The nurse returned a few minutes later, and he asked her how she thought the specimen looked. The nurse looked at it and it seemed OK to her. But the doctor took it and held it up to the light. "Looks a little cloudy to me," he said.

> "Let's run it through again"—accompanied by a hearty drinking-it-down gesture. (Barton 1974, no. 25, 26)

> One morning, the silence in the hospital was broken by a patient, running down the hall, pursued by a nurse who was wielding a large pair of scissors, followed by an intern, who was calling out, "No, no nurse. I said slip off his spectacles!" (Barton 1974, no. 23, 24)

Doctors also tell stories about dumb patients, who do not know where to put suppositories; they tell war stories about heroic operations; they engage in rituals initiating new medical students into the field; they develop strategies for telling some patients they are going to die; and they use a jargon that goes far beyond standard medical terminology. A careful study of the full range of doctors' lore will give us an understanding of their strains and stresses, joys and sorrows, values and attitudes that we are not likely to get in other ways—just as, for example, a study of the full range of the lore of the Mormon missionaries, from faith-promoting stories to trickster escapades, will help us better understand their world (see Wilson 1981). What a pity it would be to miss collecting and studying this lore because its possessors somehow seem to be people more like ourselves than marginal, or rural, or old, or unlettered "folk."

If folklorists are occasionally troubled by the definition some historians ascribe to the term "folk," historians are on occasion equally troubled by the use some folklorists make of the term "folk history." And thus definitions once again "wall us in" or "wall us out" from the cooperation that ought to exist between us.

I have always been dissatisfied by the term "oral history" because it seems to include under one heading what strike me as two kinds of history, each of which yields a different sort of data about the past. So when I wrote an essay for the recent book *The Mormon Presence in Canada* (1990), I tried to distinguish between these different forms of oral history. I wrote:

> Folklorists had been collecting and studying oral history for at least a hundred years before Allan Nevins set up the oral history program at Columbia University in the 1930s and thus set the course many historians in subsequent years were to follow with increasing enthusiasm. If what these scholars study is oral history, what, then, have folklorists been studying all these years? Well, another kind of oral history. To avoid confusion, I would suggest the terms "personal history" and "folk history"—both of them oral. Personal history is comprised of accounts of historical events collected from people who observed or participated in the events they describe. Folk history, on the other hand, is simply history that circulates within a community by word of mouth—that is, accounts of historical events collected from people who learned the stories

> from others and who did not themselves observe or participate in the events they describe. (1990, 155)

These comments passed muster with most reviewers, but one historian took angry exception to my comments. Taking me to task for muddying the waters of historical research by inventing a new term, "folk history," where other, already existing, terms would serve better, the reviewer said, "Folk history in the way he [Wilson] uses that term is rather more appropriately called folklore or myth. It is not history" (reader's report to Utah State University Press on Wilson's manuscript, 1989).

Well, I really can't take credit for inventing the term. It appears at least as early as 1957 in the important "A Theory for American Folklore," written by Richard M. Dorson, folklorist and distinguished professor of history at Indiana University (210). The same mail that brought the reviewer's comments brought an advertisement for a book entitled *Eats: A Folk History of Texas Foods* (Sewell 1989), and a collection of essays on oral narratives that arrived from Finland about the same time contained a piece by a prominent Finnish folklorist called "What the People of Sivakka Tell about Themselves: A Research Experiment in Folk History" (Knuuttila 1989). So the term has been around awhile.

The reviewer's suggestion that I avoid confusing readers by simply calling what I have termed "folk history" folklore would be akin to suggesting that we could avoid confusing the musical world if we would only call pianos nothing more than musical instruments. Of course, folk history is folklore; but it is part of the whole, not the whole—and it was the part I was trying to define.

I could devote many pages to the reviewer's use of the word "myth," but that will have to wait another day. I will say simply that his or her suggestion that I seek instruction on how to use folklore for historical analysis by turning my attention to books like Henry Nash Smith's *The Virgin Land: The American West as Symbol and Myth* (1950) reveals the conceptual chasm that can separate the work of folklorists and historians and frustrate what ought to be common efforts. I have read *The Virgin Land*; I have even assigned it to students; it's a great book; the only problem is that it contains almost no folklore. As Richard Dorson, a contemporary and friend of Smith, has noted, "Smith made extensive use of unconventional sources, such as dime novels, but he did not dip beneath subliterature into the wells of oral tradition" (Dorson 1964, 225). And again:

> The folklorist goes to folk sources, to word-of-mouth utterances, to people in their homes or business places or leisure spots. The cultural historian goes to the library, to the writings of intellectuals. Even when Henry Nash Smith plows through hundreds of dime novels to extract popular conceptions of Western heroes, he is reading the productions of professional writers, of intellectuals. The people who write for the folk are not the folk. (Dorson 1969, 231)

As I reworked my essay in response to the reviewer's comments, I tried to clarify my definition by changing it to read: "Folk history is . . . simply a view of the past that circulates within a community by word of mouth." Otherwise, I stood by my use of the term "folk history," and the press stood by me.

Later, as my own anger cooled for having so patronizingly been taken to school again, I pondered over why the reviewer had responded to my rather innocuous definition as though hit on the toe with a large hammer. The reviewer was probably a decent enough person who loved his or her spouse and treated the family dog well. Why the anger? So I read the review again and discovered another of those walls that keep us apart when we should be working together. And the fault was as much mine as that of the reviewer—in this instance, I had not paid close enough attention to the way at least some historians use their language.

The reviewer stated:

> The basic facts of history are verifiable through documents created in the past or through the memory of people who participated in those events. Far from avoiding confusion, the use of the term "history" in connection with folklore or myth *creates* confusion by leaving the impression that the facts alluded to in the narrative are verifiable when they are not. What is verifiable is that the ideas conveyed in the folklore or myth are believed by the informant. (reader's report)

Therein lies the crux of the problem—verifiability. Working from my own comfortable propositions and having in the past written primarily for people who accept those propositions, it never occurred to me that anyone would take my references to folk history as references to verifiable past events. I was speaking, I thought, of nothing more than what people believe the past to have been, not necessarily to what it really was—though I would not want to leave the impression that the details of folk history can never be verified; sometimes they can. I certainly agree with the reviewer that what is verifiable in folk history is that people believe the stories they tell about the past. That I had made such an argument seemed self-evident. Obviously, I was wrong—and in my error "walled out" someone who may actually share more common interests with me than differences.

I do not intend to quit using the term "folk history"—even if I did, others would continue to use it. But in the future, I will more carefully define my terms. For this evening, let me, in the words of a former president, "make myself perfectly clear." Real history, at least from the point of view of the reviewer, is a story of the past whose details are believed by the person who puts them together because these details can be supported—that is, verified—by documentary evidence. The ideological commitments and the worldview of this person will, of course, influence how he or she interprets the details. Personal history is the story of a past event told by someone who has witnessed or participated in that event. Personal history must be used with great caution, given the fallibility of memory, but at least it has the validity of the eyewitness account.

Folk history, on the other hand, is third-person history, a story of the past whose details may or may not be verifiable, but which are usually believed by the person who passes them along to others because this person has confidence in the individual from whom he or she heard them. Because folk history is kept alive not by print but by the spoken word, it follows that there can be no official version. Each teller, influenced by his or her own interests and psychological makeup, as well as the circumstances of the storytelling occasion, will tell a story at least slightly differently from the way anyone else tells it. From the many recountings within a social group of a folk historical narrative, one can, nonetheless, abstract a consensus view. More on that later.

In space remaining I would like to explain why some of my fellow folklorists and I consider stories that cannot always be verified and that are not fixed in form are worthy of study and would like to plead that we not let language barriers keep us from a fuller understanding of our culture.

Anyone who would like an exercise in verifying accounts of past events should drive a few miles north of Preston, Idaho, and visit the monuments located near the highway commemorating the Battle of Bear River. I say monuments (plural), because, standing a few feet from each other are two placards recounting the battle. The first, erected by the Daughters of Utah Pioneers in 1953, states:

> Attacks by the Indians on the peaceful inhabitants in this vicinity led to the final battle here January 29, 1863. The conflict occurred in deep snow and bitter cold. Scores of wounded and frozen soldiers were taken from the battle field to the Latter-day Saint community of Franklin. Here pioneer women, trained through trials and necessity of frontier living, accepted the responsibility of caring for the wounded until they could be removed to Camp Douglas, Utah. Two Indian women and three children, found alive after the encounter, were given homes in Franklin.

The other placard, erected recently to give an account closer to the Indian point of view and entitled "Bear River Massacre," states:

> Very few Indians survived an attack here when P. E. Connor's California Volunteers trapped and destroyed a band of Northwestern Shoshoni. Friction between local Indians and white travelers along this route led Connor to set out on a cold winter campaign. More than 400 Shoshoni occupied a winter camp that offered ideal protection in Battle Creek Canyon. But they suffered a military disaster unmatched in Western history when Connor's force struck at daybreak, January 29, 1863.

How might historians and folklorists try to reconcile these accounts? I hesitate to speak for historians, but I assume they would be fully aware of and interested in the way different ideologies inspire different interpretations of the Battle of Bear River, that they would realize the full story of what transpired before and during the battle can probably never be recovered, that they would nevertheless attempt to come as close as possible to that story, and that they would do so through the use of verifiable, documentary evidence.

Folklorists would also be interested in what really occurred at the battle, but their principal interest would be in oral narratives underpinning these two accounts, narratives circulating among the people that would reveal what members of the opposing camps believe precipitated the battle and took place there. Why this interest? Because people govern their lives not on the basis of what actually happened in the past but rather on what they believe happened—that is, on folk history—and because these beliefs will have important consequences in the lives of those who subscribe to them, as well as on the lives of those who must deal with those who subscribe to them.

For example, I recently collected stories from a man whose grandfather had worked at the Winter Quarters Mine near Scofield, Utah, shortly before the disastrous explosion that killed some two hundred miners in 1900. Because the grandfather was active in attempts to organize a union, the company evicted him and his family from their home in Winter Quarters and deposited him, his furniture, and his family in Scofield in midwinter. After explaining this, my informant added: "They [the family] never did join the LDS church because of this eviction—the mine at that time was owned by the church. Being dumped there in the wintertime, they had some bitter feelings. In fact, my uncles had quite bitter feelings all the time because of this" (Herlevi 1986). Though the church, according to my historian friends, did not own the mine, the family believed it did and remained antagonistic to the church because of these beliefs. In other words, their behavior was determined not by actual, verifiable history but by folk history, by an explanation of the past kept alive in family stories.

Whether or not the LDS church owned the mine is a fact that can be verified. The following story told by the same informant cannot:

> My grandfather, when that mine explosion happened, he'd been working up there in Winter Quarters; and his dog used to always walk with him up to the mine and wait and then come home with him when he got out of the mine. That morning the dog wouldn't go with him, and my grandfather said he had a funny feeling about going to work. He said, "If that dog doesn't want to go, I'm not going to go"—because that dog every day would go up there and just wait for him. And so he didn't go to work that day, and that's when the mine explosion happened.... Otherwise, he'd probably been in the mine and gotten killed. (Herlevi 1986)

There simply is no way to verify this account—it lives only in family stories. As a result, some scholars might accept it as a bit of interesting local color but then dismiss it as inconsequential for serious analysis. But the family believes the story just as steadfastly as it believes the LDS church owned the Winter Quarters Mine. The one story justifies family hostility to the Mormon church; the other persuades family members that a kindly providence once smiled on them and kept their grandfather from being killed—a fact that might also persuade them that he was a decent person in spite of his unpopular activities as a union organizer.

Sometimes folk history can take a much more vicious turn. In his *Dynamics of Folklore* (1979), Barre Toelken recounts a story in which a young white boy is attacked in a drive-in restroom by members of a minority group and is then castrated. Toelken traces the story, or one like it, to a number of U.S. cities and centuries back in time. In some instances, members of the minority group are Indians, in others Mexicans, in others blacks, and in one occurrence they are even hippies. Though something akin to this event may have happened at one place at one time in history, Toelken's comparative study clearly demonstrates that we are dealing with a migratory legend that could not really have occurred in all the places where it has been reported.

Yet many of the people in these places believe this nonverifiable story, believe that Indian, or Mexican, or black thugs actually committed this dastardly act against a fine young white youth. Toelken argues that the story keeps "cropping up in cultures where minority groups of one sort or another have posed a threat to the security of the majority group," providing "a succinct and usable traditional experience for any majority group that wants to rationalize and vivify its symbolic fears of the minority group" (176–78). I would add that it not only symbolizes majority fears, it also provides, or can provide, members of the majority the evidence they seek to justify repressive measures against the minority. In a society still charged with racial tensions, if we dismiss stories like this because they cannot be verified, we do so at our own peril.

Toelken's account should remind some of us of events that took place in Utah during late 1969 and early 1970, during the months preceding the April General Conference of the LDS church. At that time, blacks had not yet been granted priesthood privileges and the church had come under sharp attack for its racial policies. At the same time, apocryphal prophecies about racial wars and bloodshed to precede the last days spread widely through the area. As a result, many Mormons became convinced that black-white conflict was imminent and would reach its peak during the April conference. Stories that justified this belief spread like wildfire throughout the intermountain region. The following account is typical:

> Did you hear about the kids who were on their way to California and got jumped by some blacks as they stopped for something to eat? I think it was in Nevada somewhere. Anyway, they were going

> to eat. They stopped and were jumped by some blacks who happened to see their BYU sticker on their car. They messed up the car and drove it off the road and then beat up the guys and did who knows what to the girls. It's weird that they would do that just because they saw a BYU sticker, don't you think? (Ryan 1970)

Other stories claimed that cars with Utah license plates were not safe out of state, that carloads of blacks were on the way to Salt Lake, that the Black Panthers were sneaking into the city with guns, that all the hotels around the temple were filled with blacks, that the Lake Shore Ward Sacrament Meeting had been interrupted by blacks, that the SDS and the Panthers planned to blow up Mountain Dell Reservoir, that black children were to sell candy bars laced with broken glass, that two bombs had been discovered on Temple Square, and that blacks would storm Temple Square during conference.

Conference came and went—peacefully. The stories proved groundless, or at least nonverifiable. But in the days before the conference they had a powerful influence on many who believed them. Some formed neighborhood defense groups; others stored guns and ammunition; and some who had planned to travel from elsewhere to attend the conference remained home. And in all these instances it was not actual history, verifiable accounts of what had really happened, but *folk history*, what the people believed had happened, that governed their lives (Bowman 1972; see also Wilson 1973a, 57–58).

One final point here. The reviewer of my article did admit that studying folklore is important in comprehending the mentality of a group. I would insist that it is folk history which will give us some of our best insights into that mentality. For example, a young Mormon missionary in Canada had a frightening experience which he and his companion at least believed to have been an encounter with evil spirits. He recorded the experience in his journal and related it to a few close friends. Three years later, now a member of my university folklore class, he decided to do a class project on the folklore of his mission field and began collecting stories from recently returned missionaries. Much to his surprise he collected versions of his own experience from informants who did not know that he was the missionary in the story. He was amazed to discover that the further the story had moved from his original telling of it, the more he and his missionary companion, who had done nothing wrong, had been converted into rule-breaking missionaries who, because of their misconduct, had become subject to the power of evil (Vernon 1968, nos. 15–27, 15–21). One can quibble about whether or not the missionary's frightening experience was really an engagement with an evil spirit, but the experience itself, whatever it was, was real enough. In just three years, that personal experience had, through the process of oral transmission, been transformed into the folk history of the group, serving now as a cautionary tale to warn other missionaries not to step out of line lest they too be subjected to the buffeting of Satan.

What we must remember is that changes like those in this missionary account do not occur randomly but are dictated by cultural determinants. Every group of people, every community, will have what I have called a *value center*, a common body of shared beliefs—what my reviewer called a "group mentality." It is this value center which determines what is retained and what is changed in narratives as they are passed from person to person; it produces that consensus view I mentioned earlier. Whether a story is a migratory tale, like the account related by Toelken, or a personal experience that becomes the shared possession of a group, like this missionary story, it will be shaped as it is passed along, usually unconsciously, to conform to the group's value center, to express group members' interests and attitudes and to meet their needs. For example, considering the discomfort the earlier practice of polygamy brings to a fair number of contemporary Mormon women, what needs might be met, or attitudes expressed, or behavior governed through the telling of the following stories:

> This man had one wife, and he was going to take a second one. The first wife went with the couple to the temple to see them married. They lived a day or two from the temple. On the way there the man slept with his first wife in the wagon, and his little fiancée slept on the ground under the wagon. But on the way back from the temple, the wives reversed positions. The second wife slept with the husband in the wagon and the first wife slept under them. (Campbell 1970a, no. 3, 3)

> I heard once about three wives who were helping their husband push a new piano up the hill. They stopped to rest for a moment at the top of the hill and the husband said, "You know, this piano will belong to Martha." "What about us?" the other two said. "No," said the husband, "it's for Martha alone." So the two wives jumped up, pushed the piano down the hill, and watched it bust into a thousand pieces. (Hansen 1971, no. 26, 30)

Readers can draw their own conclusions. Whatever they might be, it should be reasonably clear that the stories people believe and tell about events in the past—that is, their folk history—can and should provide valuable data in our attempts to delineate the behavioral patterns and the mentality or ethos of the social groups to which they belong.

Just as it would be a pity to avoid studying the lore of certain groups because their members do not happen to be unlettered agrarians, so too would it be a shame to neglect a community's own view of its past because the stories which embody that view may not always be verifiable. By no means am I suggesting that we abandon attempts to authenticate accounts of past events. On the contrary, I am suggesting instead that in our attempts to understand ourselves and our culture, we should view the pursuit of both verifiable history and folk history as mutually supporting endeavors.

I end with the plea with which I began. As we move into the next twenty years of cooperation between Utah's folklore and historical societies, I urge historians seeking additional ways to augment their understanding of the past to pay serious attention to contemporary folklore study and to discover what folklorists really have been about. Of the nine references to the *Journal of American Folklore* in Michael Quinn's *Early Mormonism and the Magic World View*, the most current is from 1932. Had Quinn paid attention to cutting-edge, current folklore study, he might have avoided any number of pitfalls. At the same time, I would urge folklorists to pay more careful heed to the conceptual frames from which historians work and to make their own work more understandable within those frames. And I urge all of us to be less defensive, more willing to listen, less territorial. I recently delivered BYU's annual faculty lecture. By examining the stories my mother had told about the frontier community in which she spent her youth, I tried partly to recapture the life of that community but primarily to view my mother's stories as projections of her personal worldview and as statements of her own self worth. Afterwards, some friends wondered whether my interpretation had been historical, literary, or folkloric. I answered with a question: "Did you learn anything?" "Yes," I was usually told. "Then what difference does it make? Why worry so much about disciplinary boundaries? Something there is that doesn't love a wall."

The Folk Speak

Everyday Life in Pioneer Oral Narratives

One of my first introductions to folklore studies was attending the Fife Folklore Conference at Utah State University (USU) as an impressionable undergraduate student. I had been told by one of my professors at Brigham Young University (BYU) that I needed to introduce myself to Bert Wilson, who at that time was director of the folklore program at USU. I made the introduction, and during lunch, Bert sat down with me and talked about folklore and the fact that he was going to move to Provo to become chair of the English department at BYU. I became excited to know that he would be coming to BYU and that I would be able to work with him. Little did I know that I would eventually carry that excitement to graduate school at Indiana University to do a doctorate in folklore from Bert's alma mater. That particular lunch encounter is so indicative of the kind of man Bert is. He is a scholar of international repute who had time to sit with an excited neophyte and influence him in more ways than he'll ever know, the strongest influence being his kindness and humanity. During our twenty-plus-year relationship, it has been an honor to try to live up to the human values that he taught me, not only as a student in his courses, but as a human being in everyday life.

In February 2003 there was an exhibit at the Lee Library at BYU honoring William A. Wilson and his contributions to the field of folkloristics and Scandinavian studies. Thirty years before the exhibit, Bert published an article called "Folklore and History: Fact amid the Legends" in the *Utah Historical Quarterly* (1973a). In this article, Bert tells a story of trying to interest the special collections curator at BYU into accepting "the burgeoning collections of folklore," but that ultimately, special collections was only interested in "authentic historical documents." Wilson used this story to talk about how folklore could be useful to historians in putting

---

This paper was read at a conference on Everyday Life in Pioneer Utah. It was printed in *Nearly Everything Imaginable: The Everyday Life of Utah's Mormon Pioneers*, 485–503, eds. Ronald W. Walker and Doris R. Dant (Provo, Utah: Brigham Young University Press, 1999). Reprinted by permission of BYU Studies, Brigham Young University.

a human face on history and providing a more complete interpretation of events in the past.

In that article, Wilson attempts to speak to the validity and even necessity of using folkloric materials as part of historiography, arguing that up to that point in time the "only historians to make extensive use of oral traditions to reconstruct the past have been students of Black African history, forced to these traditions by the paucity of written documents." Many scholars at this time were making similar arguments about the under-represented voices in historiography: Michel Foucault, *The Archaeology of Knowledge* and the *Discourse of Language* (1972); Hayden White, *Metahistory: The Historical Imagination in Nineteenth-Century Europe* (1973) and *The Content of the Form: Narrative Discourse and Historical Representation* (1987); and later cultural critics like Fredric Jameson, *The Political Unconscious: Narrative as a Socially Symbolic Act* (1996); and the New Historicists, *The New Historicism,* ed. H. Aram Veeser (1989). What all these scholars have in common is the idea that historiography is a political enterprise representing voices of elite, ruling classes. Wilson alludes to this point in the article; the voices of seemingly insignificant protagonists in the American historical narrative, "of trapper and homesteader to that of the factory worker and sophisticated suburbanite," are missing and forgotten.

Folklore, Wilson argues in "Fact amid the Legends," is what can provide a glimpse into the attitudes, values, and beliefs of a community at a particular moment in history. He gives several examples from Mormon culture and history to illustrate this point. These include J. Golden Kimball stories, Mormon Nephite narratives, Mormon polygamy, folk heroes of the American West like Butch Cassidy, and Mormon missionary narratives. Those attitudes, values, and beliefs expressed by folklore may reveal communities at their best and worst, but they complete an official "factual" history of the community by describing what people of the community "believe to be fact." These ideas on folklore and historiography were later expanded by Wilson into two separate articles, "Something There Is That Doesn't Love a Wall" and the following article, "The Folk Speak: Everyday Life in Pioneer Oral Narratives."

Wilson begins this article by stating that "A common misperception holds that the study of folklore is useful primarily for illuminating the past," but that really this point is only one way folklore can be used in historiography, as was also shown in "Fact amid the Legends." Folklore can be useful also to "give us a picture not so much of what 'really happened'" in the past, "but rather of what those of us living in the present believe happened." Grounding his ideas in Mormon pioneer narratives, Wilson uses the stories to illustrate the process of "communal re-creation" and that "the stories come in time to reflect the attitudes, values, and beliefs of the people keeping them alive and lose at least some of their credibility as accurate accounts of the past. That is, the narratives will tell us much more about those who relate them than they will about the events they recount."

It is a tribute to Bert Wilson, in addition to many of his contemporaries, that he was grappling with salient issues that would eventually change the face of folkloristics and even other related disciplines, including history. To know the influence of folkloristics in the humanistic disciplines, one need only look at the changing study objects and research questions in cultural studies, history, cultural anthropology, sociolinguistics, and sociology. This example of working across academic fields, then, shows the kind of man and scholar Bert Wilson is: a facilitator and consensus-builder rather than a fence-builder against other disciplines. It is also poetic irony and, unquestionably, a tribute to Bert's persistence that the exhibit in the Lee Library that honored him in 2003 also celebrated the renaming of the BYU Folklore Archives as the William A. Wilson Folklore Archives and acknowledged the merging of the archives into the L. Tom Perry Special Collections at BYU four years earlier.

—*George H. Schoemaker*

AS WE LOOK AT THE EVERYDAY LIFE OF COMMON PEOPLE IN PIONEER UTAH through the lens of folklore, we should make sure that we understand what kinds of images will be reflected by that lens. A common misperception holds that the study of folklore is useful primarily for illuminating the past. Just the opposite is true. To be sure, folklore is born in the past and relates events that occurred at earlier times, but it lives in the present. It will give us a picture not so much of what "really happened" in pioneer Utah, but rather of what those of us living in the present believe happened.

The reason for this circumstance is simple. Folk narratives are kept alive and are passed from person to person by the spoken word, by people who hear stories, like them, and then tell them to other people. As they participate in this process, narrators of the stories change them—not consciously, in most instances, nor in any attempt to deceive, but in response to the cultural imperatives of the moment. Like most of us who tell stories about events important to us, these narrators will selectively remember details from the past, will highlight and sometimes embellish those that appeal to them, and will leave others in shadow. Through this process—a process folklorists call "communal re-creation"—the stories come in time to reflect the attitudes, values, and beliefs of the people keeping them alive and lose at least some of their credibility as accurate accounts of the past. That is, the narratives will tell us much more about those who relate them than they will about the events they recount. What Elliott Oring has said about the truth value of folksongs can be applied equally well to the stories we tell about nineteenth-century Utah:

> If a song is to continue, a generation must find something in it worth continuing while altering aspects which are no longer consonant with its own values and beliefs. . . . A song cannot be adequately conceptualized as the reflection of some ancient past [or in our case, the pioneer past]. At any point in its history, the song is the distillation of generations of cumulative modification. If it

> can be said to reflect any group at all, perhaps it can only reflect the group in which it is currently sung—that group which has (for conscious or unconscious reasons) maintained and transformed elements from the past in the creation of a meaningful, contemporary expression. (1986, 10)

Applied to the stories contemporary Mormons tell about the practice of polygamy, for example, Oring's dictum would suggest that these Mormons would remember and relate narratives about plural marriage in terms meaningful to them in the present. And that, indeed, is the case. In those families that hold positive views of polygamy, narratives of harmony and cooperation between the families of plural wives circulate. In families that hold a less sanguine view of the practice, stories of heartbreak and discord, like the following, predominate:

> A kind and mild man received instructions to get another wife. The first wife, knowing that this was a principle of the gospel, willingly accepted the situation and helped prepare for the wedding. She prepared the nuptial chamber and the wedding dinner. [Her husband] . . . and his new wife went upstairs, and [she] . . . was left to do the dishes. Then something happened. As she was doing the dishes and thinking things over, she got madder and madder. She went outside, picked up a hatchet, rushed upstairs, and chopped down the door. The new wife was so terrified she left and never returned. (Campbell 1970a)

Historians are sometimes dismayed by what they perceive as folklorists' lack of interest in the truth about the past. Truth is an illusive creature, seldom fully capturable, but folklorists are as much interested in it as are any other scholars. They simply seek different kinds of truth—truths of the human heart and mind. Folklorists understand that it is not what really happened in the past that captures the attention of most people and moves them to action, but what they "believe" happened. And they know that one of the best ways to get at what people believe is to examine the stories they tell about former times. If, for instance, one wants to know what polygamy was really like, one will be much better off relying on standard historical sources. But if one wants to know what contemporary Mormons believe polygamy was like, how this belief could influence the manner in which the historical record is interpreted, or, perhaps more important, how this belief reflects and shapes present attitudes and influences current behavior, then one would do well to turn to folk narratives like the one above.

So it is with stories of the pioneer era in general. Many people, most perhaps, do not learn of life in nineteenth-century Utah by reading historical treatises. They learn what life was like "back then" by listening to stories—stories told in their homes, at family reunions, in Sunday School classes, in seminary classes, and occasionally across the pulpit. While these stories may have originated in actual historical happenings and may at times square with historical reality, they will have developed, through the processes of communal re-creation described above, into accounts that reveal how the common people of contemporary Utah view the everyday lives of Utah's common people of yesteryear. More important, the stories will have become something other than mere reflectors of beliefs about the past. As usually occurs in the process of myth formation (and I use the word in its positive sense), the narratives have become projections onto the past of what we value in the present, historical constructions, as it were, after which we hope to conduct our own lives.

In saying this, I should make clear that, while folklore is communal in nature and reveals concerns common to a group, it would be a mistake to assume that a folk community is some sort of monolithic body whose members all think and act alike. No two members of any group will ever see the world through quite the same lenses. Still, the stories collected and submitted to the BYU Folklore Archives over the past four decades—the stories upon which this paper is based—present a fairly uniform view of the past held by those who have told the stories.

It should come as no surprise that this view is heroic. Most people seeking in their lore historical warrant for present-day action will see the past in heroic terms. Mormons are no different. The dominant theme in their pioneer narratives is struggle—struggle against nearly insurmountable forces of nature and humankind, carried on by valiant men, women, and children who do not yield to opposition. They may suffer severe deprivation and even death, but they do not falter or waver in the faith, and they remain ever true to their vision of the kingdom of God restored. They and their stories thus serve as exemplars of the way we should confront the challenges of our lives in our contemporary world.

Though the stories cover a broad range of subjects, they tend to cluster around three major themes: struggles on the trek West, struggles with Native Americans, and struggles to survive in a new land.

THE TREK WEST

Although accounts of the migration to Utah lie generally outside the focus of this paper, the telling and retelling of these stories was very much a part of the life of nineteenth-century Utah, as settlers in a new world sought courage to face present hardships by remembering the price paid to get to their new homes. One storyteller, for example, noted that his grandmother had told him trek stories when he was young "to impress on his mind the suffering of his ancestors to get across the plains and enable him to be born and raised in a Mormon environment" (Wixom 1975).

Some of the most poignant trek stories tell of the travails of children on the trail:

> Grandma would tell the stories about walking the long, long way across the plains and some of the hard and frightening experiences of being at Winter Quarters and burying loved ones on the plains. She'd also tell of evening, as they were stopped for the night. Wagons and handcarts in a circle. Parents trying to keep warm by dancing the Virginia Reel and little children playing tag or Ring-around-the-Rosie or, if they needed to be quiet and rest, to just try to catch the sunbeams in their aprons. (Bryant 1972a)

Unfortunately, the stories reveal few sunbeams in the children's lives. Many tell of the youngsters' tragic deaths:

> My great-grandmother . . . was a member of one of the numerous pioneer companies that came across the plains to Utah. One night, when the company was within the region of Wyoming, my great-grandmother slept next to a little girl. The weather was especially bad and the temperatures that night went far below zero. When they awoke the next morning, they found that the little girl had frozen to death and my great-grandmother's long hair was frozen to the stiff body. The only way they could get them separated was to cut my great-grandmother's hair. The pair of scissors they used has been passed on from generation to generation since that time and are now in the possession of my aunt. (Strong 1965a)

Other stories tell of children mourning parents' deaths:

> My great-great-grandmother . . . decided to go to Salt Lake with the hand carts. But she died along the way and was buried on the plains. Her little girl cried and cried. The rest of the company got ready to go after the burial, and started off. When they camped for the evening, they noticed that the little girl was not with them. They sent back some scouts to see if they could find her. They retraced the entire day's journey and found the little girl crying on the grave of her mother. . . . They took her with them back to camp and eventually to Salt Lake. (Tometich 1967)

Still other stories tell of both parents and children attempting to show love and affection for each other in ways made more difficult by life on the trail. When a little girl lost her "precious doll that she had taken care of since her family had been forced to leave Nauvoo," she was heartbroken. Her mother, "sad to see her daughter so sad, . . . made a new doll with a face made out of an apple core and a dress made of an old rag" (Steed 1984). Another girl, wishing to give her mother a birthday gift but having no means to do so, "would pick the flowers that she thought were prettiest along the way and dry them somehow. When they finally reached the valley, she had a lot of flowers. She pressed them in a glass frame and gave them to her mother for a birthday present" (Smith 1982).

The stories about the suffering of adults focus on their hunger, their chills, their weariness, and their deaths. The following story is representative of tales that are legion:

> As one of the early wagon trains was nearing Utah, . . . their provisions were already nearly exhausted, and the people themselves were near exhaustion. During the storm, three members of the party died. After the storm had passed, their relatives and loved ones made arrangements to bury them. The ground, however, was frozen so hard that the poor pioneers were unable to dig the necessary graves. The people were faced with the problem of not knowing what to do but of having to do something fast. They had only a few blankets, but from those few they took three. They wrapped the bodies in these blankets. They hung the bodies from trees with ropes. They were high enough so that the wolves could not get to them. Thus, the wagon train continued on its journey toward the promised land, leaving their loved ones and friends taken care of as well as possible. (McCauley 1968)

Some of these pioneers, once arrived in their promised land, carried marks of the journey throughout their lives. "Grandma could never understand," said one narrator,

> why anyone would want to cultivate a cactus plant. She and her husband had both walked across the plains as children, and as they made their journey west there seemed to be so many thorny weeds and rocks. Grandpa said, "My feet were torn and bleeding and many times I could hardly walk." His widowed mother . . . had brought the fatherless family through to Payson, Utah. She had done her very best to keep her family as clean as possible, but the little boy's feet had healed with dirt still under the skin. When he died of cancer at age 67, his son stood by the bedside. The nurse said, "I wonder why the bottoms of his feet are black?" His son said, "It is all right. He is carrying the soil of the plains with him, even to his grave." (Bryant 1972b)

According to the above story, the widowed mother brought the family through the trek west to safety. Another account states:

> While Sarah Jane Matthews and her husband were crossing the plains with a handcart company, the husband developed arthritis

> to the extent that he could not ford the streams and rivers without a great deal of pain. Sarah carried him across the remaining streams. This is a literal example of supporting the priesthood. (Card 1971)

Though this story is recounted somewhat tongue-in-cheek, it nevertheless points to the fact that in story after story, pioneer women emerge as some of the strongest characters in the narratives. One good sister lost her husband soon after the trek to Salt Lake had begun, and three of her six children died on the way. The first year in Salt Lake Valley, the three remaining children were caught in a storm and froze to death. "This would seem to be the end of the story," said the narrator, "but this woman went on to get married again and start her life all over. She never gave up" (Anderson 1967a). Contemporary Mormons, both women and men, could scarcely find greater examples of courage to face present challenges than is to be found in these stories of rugged pioneer women who never gave up.

NATIVE AMERICANS

Once in Utah, the Saints faced new dangers from the original inhabitants of the region. Though the pioneers had encountered Native Americans on the trek west, few accounts in the archive give details of these encounters. Once the pioneers had arrived in Utah, however, numerous stories developed recounting struggles between settlers and Native Americans. Though the Mormons probably treated the Native Americans better than did most western settlers and consequently had fewer violent encounters with them, the events that have caught the fancy of later storytellers have been the hostilities and conflicts. These narratives are full of dramatic intensity and once again characterize the pioneers as bold and heroic. Unfortunately, they also paint an uncomplimentary and dehumanizing picture of the Native Americans. Told entirely from the settlers' point of view, the narratives refer to Native Americans again and again in pejorative terms, as "bucks" or "squaws," and depict them as less than fully human—vicious, depraved, dirty, lazy, smelly, and stupid. One can only wonder how some of the stories discussed below might sound told from the perspective of the Native Americans.

Many stories of Indian raids and ruthless murders closely resemble accounts of the savagery perpetuated against the Mormons in Missouri a few decades earlier, suggesting that the Saints at times viewed both Missourians and Native Americans in a similar light. For example, one of the Missouri persecution narratives telling of an attack on the Saints at Haun's Mill states:

> It was at the time of the Haun's Mill episode, and during this time some of the Saints had a warning before the disaster struck. H. Lee's mother put him into or under a huge grate in the fireplace

> just before the mob came into her house. They [the mob] saw the mother with the baby, and they killed his mother by shooting her. They took the baby and bashed him against the stone fireplace until his brains were running out. All this was witnessed by this young boy. (Bryner 1970)

A narrative from Sanpete County tells of a local massacre in almost parallel terms:

> These boys [hired to help with the grain harvest] were just about to this farm, and they could hear these Indians whooping and carrying on, so they got down and crawled through the grass over to where they could see this ranch. The father must not have been at home at that time, and there was the mother and a little boy and then a baby. The little boy had run and hid and got away from them, . . . but they took the mother and tied her across a horse and whipped the horse and made it run with her. They took the baby and swung it around and hit its head on a tree and killed it. Then they set fire to the farm. . . . The way they had put [the mother] . . . on the horse had killed her too. (Blackham 1971a)

In similar narratives of brutality, the Native Americans cut off the arm of a man traveling to his home in Bountiful and beat him to death with it (Ball 1992), completely wipe out a group of settlers on the way to Manti (Blackham 1971b), kill and scalp a young boy herding cattle (Lundell 1974), and kill a father and son from Circleville on their way home from cutting wood, filling their bodies with arrows and then stealing their wagon and oxen (Blackham 1971c).

In numerous accounts, Native Americans attempt to kidnap the children of the settlers, especially if the children are fair haired. But they display their assumed depravity most clearly in accounts of how they treat other Native Americans, sometimes children kidnapped from other tribes, sometimes their own:

> Granddad . . . was out working in the field one day and looked up, and two buck Indians had a little Indian girl they had stolen from another tribe, and they made him understand they wanted to trade the girl for some of Granddad's prize heifers he had secured to help build his herd. Granddad hesitated, and they placed her head on a chopping block and indicated they would chop her head off unless Granddad gave them the heifers. To save her life, he went along with their request. (Larsen 1974)

In one instance in Cache Valley, an Indian father threatened to kill his own daughter if a family of settlers would not allow him to exchange her for food. The settlers took the little girl in and raised her as one of their own. When she was fifteen, her father came back after her. "She refused to go with him. She said that she loved her white parents better than her parents who would trade her off for food" (Woodhouse 1975).

Intrepid fighters themselves, the Native Americans in some stories are claimed to have greatly admired white men who resisted their attacks with fierce courage. According to one account, "a stage driver from Eureka was surrounded by warring Indians. He valiantly held them off for a great while, but was finally . . . captured. After he was killed, the braves cut out his heart and ate it because they wanted some of his great courage" (Roberts 1974). According to other accounts, the Indians actually released, rather than killed, dauntless foes.

But even more than they admired brave men, the Native Americans supposedly respected feisty pioneer women who would stand up to them with fire in their eyes. In narratives describing such encounters, the pioneer housewife is not unlike her predecessor in Missouri, who, as in the following story, fearlessly confronted mobsters:

> The Saints knew they were in danger, so it was not unusual for Grandmother to have her gun close by when she was alone. One day two men came up to the door and said they were supposed to collect all of the weapons and they wanted her gun. She looked down the barrel at them and said, "All right, but I intend to unload it first." They rode away and didn't make any attempt to take it by force. (McCauley 1971a)

In a similar fashion, as the following three narratives indicate, spunky Utah pioneer women stood their ground against marauding Indians:

> My grandmother was a little teentsy woman only about five feet tall and real light, and she wouldn't take guff from anybody. One day when she was baking bread, a buck Indian came just as she was taking a loaf out of the oven. I guess he asked for some, but when she said no, he said he'd take it anyway. Well, she was building up a fire and had put the poker and fire shovel right in the fire while she talked. Now the Indian was only wearing a little breech cloth and when he went to take a loaf, she jerked the red-hot shovel right out of the stove and smacked him on the bare behinder. He pulled his knife and said, "I'll kill you." She took her shovel and said, "I'll burn you," and chased him out of the house. (Sabin 1961)

> The husband [of a newly settled farm] had gone off to get supplies. The wife and children were left by themselves. One night some Indians came and started bothering them. Finally the Indians camped right out in front of the cabin. The wife could not sleep because she knew the Indians were planning to kill her and her family. She got

> on her knees and prayed; after that she knew what she must do. She gathered her children, marched outside and spread their bedding out right in the middle of those Indians. She got her children to kneel down and had a family prayer. Then they all crawled into bed and slept as much as they could under the circumstances. The next morning the Indian in charge told her they were planning on killing her and her family, but when they saw how brave she was they decided not to. (McDonald 1984)

> One evening as a certain woman was finishing milking the cows and making cheese in the milk house, there suddenly appeared at the door a small band of Indians. These Indians were very fierce looking and demanded to have the milk and cheese which was there. This pioneer lady, being a fiery-tempered woman, refused to give these Indians what they wanted. Instead she grabbed an axe which lay nearby and began swinging it around her head warning the Indians that the first to attempt to steal the milk and cheese would be very sorry. After contemplating their situation for several moments the Indians began to shrink back away from this woman and toward the door leading to their safety. The woman kept brandishing her weapon, threatening these intruders, and even sermonizing to them, saying that if they had come to her and asked in a gentle manner for something to eat she would gladly have given them what they requested. The Indians left. Later, however, they returned, this time in a different spirit. They asked the woman in a polite manner for some milk and cheese. She gave it to them, and from then on the Indians were very friendly to this "heap brave white squaw." (Rees n.d.)

In some of the stories, resourceful pioneer women move beyond winning respect of the Native Americans through plucky acts of courage and instead diminish their humanity by reducing them to buffoons. In one account, a housewife sicced her dog on Indians who had come begging for bread, causing them to flee in terror (Blackham 1971d). In another, a girl hid from approaching Indians in a flour barrel. Unable to breathe, she emerged from the barrel a ghastly white just as her unwelcome visitors burst into the house. They "took one look at her, thought she was a spirit sent to punish them, and they hurriedly backed out of the door and galloped away on their ponies" (Easten n.d.). And in still another example, a plucky pioneer girl turned a threatening Native American into a complete fool:

> [This family] lived quite close to the hills and Indians were camped quite close to the foothills. This girl was washing; she had a washing machine that was an old wooden one that had a wheel that would

> turn. This Indian brave came down and he had long braids. He came down and he started acting smart to her and talking smart to her and she couldn't understand him. He wanted different things that she had here at her home. . . . When she wouldn't give them to him, he grabbed her and started throwing her around. She grabbed one lock of his hair, his braid, and hurried and put it into the wringer and wound it up tight and fixed it so it couldn't run back, and then she turned and fled while he was tied to the wringer. (Blackham 1971e)

After relating an account of a battle in Diamond Fork Canyon between settlers and Indians who had stolen the settlers' cattle and scalped and cut off the right hand of one of their men, one storyteller added, "The men were called out on such occasions many other times to fight for their land and protect their families" (Anderson 1967b). I have no reason to doubt this story. Battles did occur, with casualties on both sides. But the statement gives not the slightest hint that the Native Americans who had occupied these valleys before the arrival of the Saints might also have been fighting for their land and to protect their families. Nor do any of the stories berating the Native Americans for begging for food suggest that they might occasionally have been reduced to such action because they had been driven from their homes and hunting grounds.

In defense of the pioneers and especially of those who have kept narratives about them alive, I should add that most people who tell the stories do not necessarily do so to deprecate Native Americans; they tell them to illustrate the heroism of their ancestors in taming this land and establishing a new Zion. But in order to achieve these ends, the settlers had to displace the area's original inhabitants. Stories that depict these inhabitants as savage, dishonest, and shiftless have made the task seem more justifiable. Unfortunately, even today the stories have helped keep alive attitudes that might otherwise have disappeared long ago.

A NEW LAND

Fortunately, an occasional story presents the Native Americans in a favorable light. In one story, for example, when the food supply of a southern Utah family was exhausted, a group of Native Americans appeared on the scene. They demanded food. When the mother, whose husband was absent, protested that they had none, the Native Americans opened a sack of clover seed, thinking it was flour, and began eating. They found it so bitter they spit it out and then left. The next morning, the mother "found fresh deer meat at the front door. The Indians had felt so sorry for the children having to eat nasty clover [that] they gave them something good to eat" (George 1982).

This account leads us to the third category of popular pioneer stories—those illustrating struggles to survive in an inhospitable physical environment, where not only the Native Americans, but the Saints as well suffered severe deprivation. These narratives are in many ways similar to the tales of hardship and struggle experienced by the Saints on their trek west, except now the suffering arises not from the difficulties of the journey, but from trying to survive in a hostile land at journey's end. Once again, the tellers of these tales find in them examples of courage and fortitude we would do well to follow in our contemporary world. The stories are, as one narrator points out, "monument[s] to pioneer virtue" (Carson 1973a). Many of the stories, like the following, tell of both severe hunger and self-reliance:

> Things got really hard. There would be lean years on the farm, but . . . [this fellow's] dad would never accept charity or help of any kind. One day he was so hungry because he would share what he had with the children that he fainted in the store. Everyone thought that that was such willpower and remarkable that a man . . . rather than accept charity would be so hungry that he would pass out in the store. They fed the family, and the next year things were better and he paid it all back again. He always paid his tithing, and he wouldn't take charity either. (Carson 1973a)

Other stories tell how the pioneers suffered from lack of material goods and from the harshness of frontier living:

> When Grandma Gurr was a child, her mother told her of the hardships endured by those who settled in Orderville. They had no houses, so the settlers had to dig holes in the ground. These they covered with brush. When it rained they had to leave, and she said as soon as it would start to drizzle, the people would begin to pop up like prairie dogs. They were all very poor and could not afford shoes, so in the winter they would take a hot board with them when they went to school. They would run as fast and as far as they could, and then they would put the board down and stand on it to warm their feet and then begin over again. Granddad Gurr was sixteen before he had a pair of shoes. (McDaniel 1972)

And again:

> My grandfather . . . raced over those hot desert rocks [at Rockville, Utah] on feet that had grown tough as shoe leather, and a good thing too, for he had never had a pair of shoes. It must have been icy enough in midwinter that he had to have makeshift shoes along with all the other makeshifts, for the hot, dry land produced little, and they were very poor. (McCauley 1971b)

Numerous stories tell of heartbreak caused by sickness and death. One narrative tells how a couple lost two children to diphtheria and then had to remain isolated so others would not catch the disease:

> Nobody could go to the home and help take care of the sick. The poor mother and dad had to [care for them], and finally the children died. . . . Some of the . . . young fellows in the town went and dug the grave in the cemetery. Then they had to go stand on the other side of the fence clear away, while the parents put the two children in boxes. They had to build the boxes themselves and dress the children's bodies. They put them into the boxes all by themselves, took them down to the cemetery in their own wagon all by themselves, and put them in the grave—the mother at one end and the daddy at the other—and covered them over so no one else could get close to the plague. . . . Then the mother and daddy got in the wagon and drove home all alone. (Carson 1973b)

This story demonstrates, says the collector, how the people carried on "in the face of great personal sorrow" (Carson 1973b). The clear implication is that in the struggles we face in our lives we should do likewise.

During the pioneer era of hardship and trial, one major narrative cycle rose to prominence—stories of the Three Nephites, those ancient Book of Mormon disciples of Christ who were granted their wish of "tarrying in the flesh" until the second coming of the Savior to "bring the souls of men unto [Christ]" (3 Nephi 28: 9). Throughout the second half of the nineteenth century and still today, narratives have circulated throughout the Mormon West telling of one or more of these disciples appearing to the pioneers and assisting them through difficult times.

Though the stories are interesting for their own sake, for our purposes they provide further insight into what contemporary Mormons perceive to have been the major trials in the pioneers' lives. The narratives cover a broad range of subjects, but their main themes roughly parallel those already illustrated in the stories cited above—struggles with the harsh natural environment, with illness, and with grinding poverty. Three examples will have to suffice. In the first, a Nephite helps a man escape death in a severe snow storm; in the second, two Nephites heal the child of a woman isolated from adequate medical assistance; in the third, a Nephite provides material assistance to a widow and her impoverished family.

> This story was told to me by my father about his uncle, reported as having occurred in the 1880s during the time when settlers from Sanpete County, chiefly Fountain Green and Fairview, were moving over the mountain to settle Emery County. Circumstances had required Uncle Milas to cross over the mountain on foot, since the majority of the people didn't have . . . riding horses in those times.

As he got on top of the mountain, a storm hit, the temperatures dropped, it became very cold. He was unable to move on and unable to find much in the way of shelter, and he realized that unless he could find some and build a fire he would freeze. He did find some sort of sheltered place and attempted to start a fire but was unable to get one going successfully. The wood was damp and the wind and things just generally prevented the fire from burning. He was becoming more and more desperate, more and more hopeless of success. At last he did succeed in getting a tiny little ember going—a small flicker—but it was evident that it was not going to catch on. In fact it was dying out when suddenly someone stepped up behind him and threw something from a bucket onto the fire which made it immediately blaze up and begin to burn the wood vigorously. Uncle Milas turned about to see who had done it since he hadn't been aware of anyone else anywhere near him, and there was no one there. And he searched and called and was unable to find the person. And he always interpreted it as having been one of the Three Nephites who had helped him in a time of need. (Geary 1968)

There was a lady that had a child that was very sick, and she didn't live very close to neighbors. She was alone with the child—her husband wasn't home at the time. She was afraid the child was going to die, and she prayed earnestly that help could come some way to her, and she knelt down and prayed. Shortly after, there was a knock came to the door, and there was a man standing there at the door. He said he had been told to come there, that she had a sick child. He had a partner with him, and if she liked they would come in and administer to the child. She told him she would and didn't give it a thought that he was a stranger. . . . The two men came in and administered to the child. The child was healed almost instantly. She asked them to come in and sit down, but they couldn't stop. But her child was made well. She didn't see where they went. She thought the two men were the Nephites. She never did know where they went. (King 1945)

My aunt, who lived in Rock Point, Summit County, Utah, was left a widow with a large family. She just wondered how she was ever going to manage, and one day an elderly man came to her home and asked for bread. She said, "Oh, I wonder what I'm going to do! I just have this big family and all." But anyway she gave him a meal and brought him in and fixed him up, and when he left he said, "Sister, you'll be blessed. You'll never see the bottom of your flour bin." And she looked for him when he went out the door, and she couldn't find him anywhere. And she always felt that this visit was from one

> of the Nephites. She had looked and looked and not any of the other neighbors had ever seen him. And she said as long as she lived she never did see the bottom of her flour bin. (Browne 1969)

In this last story, the Nephite gives assistance to the widow because, following the teachings of the Savior, she willingly shares her last meager provisions with a stranger. This pattern is followed again and again throughout the Three Nephites canon. The Nephites come to the assistance of those who, in spite of overwhelming hardships, strive to live gospel principles. As the stories continue to circulate among us today, they testify that those of us who follow the examples of our valiant pioneer ancestors will be similarly blessed.

The last two stories given above are interesting for another reason: the subjects are women. Indeed, in story after story the righteous person a Nephite visits is a woman—in many instances a woman struggling to care for her family by herself, because her husband is dead, on a mission, or simply away from home working. These are strong women, tough women, women who do not waver in the faith and who willingly sacrifice themselves for the benefit of their families. For women struggling today to overcome different but equally challenging obstacles, the stories encourage faithful perseverance as they face their trials.

Other pioneer women emerge from a variety of non-Nephite narratives who also serve as role models, but for other reasons—not just because they are faithful but because they are plucky, resourceful women with take-charge attitudes. One good widowed sister, for example, worked hard to support her children by taking in washing. She was thrilled when a neighbor gave her a sack of seed peas one day in exchange for her work. She carefully prepared the hard, sagebrush-covered ground for planting, made furrows, and then, on hands and knees, placed "each precious seed the right distance apart." When she had completed the task, she stood up satisfied, turned around, and discovered that their old rooster had followed closely behind and had eaten every pea. She did not wring her hands in despair. She immediately killed the rooster, reclaimed and replanted the peas, and then ate the tough old bird. When summer came, she and her children enjoyed many meals from the pea patch (Strong 1965b).

In another instance, a sister in Spanish Fork used her old copper clothes boiler until it finally wore clear through and was completely useless. New boilers were available only in Salt Lake City. Her husband was too busy plowing to make the trip to buy a new boiler, and because the family horse was being used in the plowing, the sister could not make the trip herself by buggy. Undaunted, she

> walked the sixty miles from Spanish Fork to Salt Lake City, bought a copper boiler, and carried it sixty miles home. This in itself was an impressive feat, even in those rugged pioneer days. But the thing that made the 120-mile hike really amazing was that when she made that grueling journey, . . . [she] was seven months pregnant. (Walker 1964)

CONCLUSION

As I look back over the stories discussed in this paper, I am aware that they seldom picture the routine events of everyday life in pioneer Utah. To be sure, they tell us of the hardships endured and of the faith and unyielding courage to withstand these hardships. But they do not tell us what the people ate, what they wore, how they made their food and clothing, how they built and furnished their homes, how they educated their children, how they entertained themselves, how they worked, how they worshiped. My grandmother, the wife of a homesteader in Idaho, baked eight loaves of bread for her large family every other day; my mother felt she had successfully passed the rite of passage to womanhood when she first cooked for threshers all by herself; my grandfather followed the yearly agricultural cycle of dry-land wheat farmers. Such details do not appear in these pioneer stories.

Discussing how the stuff of ordinary life gets transformed into legend, folklorist Richard M. Dorson writes:

> There would be little point . . . in remembering the countless ordinary occurrences of daily life, so the legend is . . . distinguished [from regular discourse] by describing an extraordinary event. In some way the incident at its core contains noteworthy, remarkable, astonishing, or otherwise memorable aspects. (1962, 18)

Freshly baked bread appears often in pioneer stories: Native Americans come begging for it; Nephites deliver it to starving missionaries. But the baking of the bread or the cooking for threshers or the planting and harvesting of crops does not seem noteworthy, remarkable, or astonishing enough to have made its way into the stories we tell of our pioneer ancestors. We prefer instead dramatic stories of conflict, struggle, and heroic action.

And this observation takes us back to the point made at the outset. We have remembered the past in terms meaningful to us in the present. We have taken the actual events that gave rise to the stories discussed in this paper and, through the process of communal re-creation, have dropped some details, embellished some, and added some. In the process, we have created narratives that reflect ourselves—our values and attitudes—at least as much as they do the events described.

This is certainly not a process unique to Mormons. I have spent considerable time studying nationalistic movements. Many scholar-patriots, in attempts to create for their countries a national spirit and a sense of national purpose, have sought in the stories of their people's past historical models for what they want the nation to become in the present. Speaking of this process as it relates to living history exhibits in our own country, Mark Leone observes:

> As a visitor, you take all this folklore and all this symbol mongering and imagine yourself to be the native of Williamsburg or Mesa Verde. . . . And because the data are relatively mute . . . , they are then more easily made to give the messages of those who do the reconstructing. . . . The tourist [at Williamsburg] does not really become immersed in the real eighteenth century at all; he is spared the shock of the filth, degradation, and misery common to that era, and is led into a fake eighteenth century, a creation of the twentieth. While in this altered frame of mind he is faced with messages—the reinforcement of standard modern American values like those surrounding the myths of our own origin as a nation—that come out of today, not two centuries ago. (1973, 130-131)

What Leone describes comes close to the process we follow as we tell and retell, and in the telling create and re-create, the stories of our pioneer past. I would not use Leone's word "fake." I see nothing pernicious, or even conscious, in the communal re-creation of our past in folklore. I would use instead the word "constructed." The stories give us a constructed past, a mythical past, a past shaped, as Leone suggests, in terms of our contemporary values, in terms of what we want ourselves to be today.

In saying this, I wish in no way to detract from or diminish the importance of our pioneer heritage. My own roots are too firmly embedded in that heritage for me ever to disparage it. Of my eight great-grandparents, six of them were early converts to the Mormon church from Denmark, England, and Wales. Four of them were part of the exodus from Nauvoo in 1846. Three of these four remained in Winter Quarters, while the fourth marched with the Mormon Batallion. All six of them crossed the plains before the coming of the railroad, one dying on the trip. Four of them crossed in wagon trains, two of them in a handcart company. One of them participated in the united order experiment in Brigham City. Another participated in the skirmishes designed to delay the advance of Johnston's army. All of them played important roles in establishing Mormon communities in Utah. The blood of the pioneers courses through my veins, and I am immensely proud of these ancestors. My regard does not change the fact that the stories many of us have grown up hearing construct a picture of Utah's past that focuses on the heroic and leaves in shadow the living, breathing human beings, with all their human foibles, who have made possible our being here today. If we have in our folk narratives created a picture of the past that is in large measure the image of what we value and want to become, what is that picture? With the exception of those narratives that reflect and continue to strengthen demeaning stereotypes of our Native American brothers and sisters, it's a pretty good picture. In the stories we find both women and men who, inspired by their unwavering faith in the restored gospel, live always by their principles. We find men and women who will not be swayed from their course by persecution, the ravages of nature, unrelenting poverty, illness, or death. We find women and men who, no matter what trials this life may bring, believe that, if they persevere, in the end all really will be well. I have the feeling that if my pioneer fathers and mothers were shown this picture they might smile a bit and then say, "Well, we weren't quite like that, but we hope you will be."

Documenting Folklore

A series of serendipitous events led me to Bert Wilson's Introduction to Folklore class in fall semester 1977, and by the end of the semester I wanted to be a folklorist. I succeeded and became the first permanent archivist in the BYU Folklore Archives, since renamed the William A. Wilson Folklore Archives. Like so many others, I owe my profession to Bert's influence. Bert once told me that he sometimes thought he should have been a full-time archivist rather than the myriad of roles he played throughout his career. I'm glad that wasn't the path Bert chose. For despite his innate ability to document and catalog folklore, Bert himself would be an archivist's nightmare—no one term defines him or his contributions. To identify Bert as a master teacher inadequately states his ability to instruct and guide students. To characterize him as an excellent scholar still minimizes his passion for the discipline of folklore studies. To emphasize his respect for the archiving and documenting of fieldwork—particularly student fieldwork—fails to show how teaching, scholarship, and archiving work together in Bert's contribution to the field and to the training of his students. As the archivist in the Wilson Folklore Archives, I find my work revolves around the philosophies outlined by Bert; "Documenting Folklore" almost serves as a blueprint for my career. The article shows that Bert Wilson is more than a skilled writer and teacher—he is an archivist. Bert's love of archives may be traced to solitary late night walks through the halls of the Finnish Archives when he researched there as a Fulbright Scholar. What began as a pile of boxes in Bert's office has blossomed into two major folklore archives; Bert was instrumental in founding both the Fife Folklore Archives and the Wilson Folklore Archives. Using a numbering system partially derived from the Finnish system, Bert developed a method of cataloging folklore that allows for endless variants while still imposing order. As students who have worked in the Fife and Wilson archives have progressed in their careers, Bert's system has influenced other archives as well. He has contributed significantly to the role of university folklore archives around the United States.

Published in *Folk Groups and Folklore Genres*, 225–54, ed. Elliott Oring (Logan: Utah State University Press, 1986). Reprinted by permission of Utah State University Press.

This article also states Bert's reasons for teaching beginning folklore students how to collect, document, and archive folklore, specifically so they will "look more analytically at the folklore which surrounds them than they might have otherwise." Further, the article explains that archiving collected folklore with contextual data allows the researcher to more fully understand the experience of the collector and the informant. For Bert the importance of students' documenting folklore is twofold: first, for their experience in observing and understanding folklore, and second, for the resulting traditional items preserved in archived collections. Bert sees folklore archives not only as repositories but also as laboratories. In his classes students contributed their own fieldwork to the archives and also visited and read what other students submitted. As a teaching technique, Bert would explain a concept, then follow with a student-collected item, including the context, to reinforce the principle to be taught. As a result students would learn the concept and also become familiar with collected items and how they contribute to scholarship. Archive materials were used not only for research but as a class text as well.

While "Documenting Folklore" prepares students to submit fieldwork findings so that they will be of benefit to archival researchers, the article also provides an excellent functional definition of folklore that can be easily understood by new students so they can recognize and understand the lore that influences their lives. Bert's classic statement in this article that folklore is "things people make with words (verbal lore), things they make with their hands (material lore), and things they make with their actions (customary lore)" finds its way into many lectures defining folklore. A skillful storyteller, Bert knows the value of a good tale, exemplified by the opening dinner party story about the "poisoned" cat. By looking at how folklore functions socially and culturally in his own experience, Bert also invites students to see the significance of what they are collecting and helps them to better understand the importance of folklore in everyday life.

—*Kristi A. Young*

NOT LONG AGO I ATTENDED AN INFORMAL DINNER PARTY WITH A NUMBER of faculty members and spouses. Midway through dinner the associate dean of my college said, "Bert, tell us some folklore." I replied that I would rather experience folklore than tell it. He looked at me blankly for a moment and then turned his attention to the obviously more intelligent faculty member seated across the table. They were soon engaged in an animated discussion of Southeast Asians who kill and eat their own dogs as well as those of their unwary neighbors. A few minutes later, as we complimented our hostess on the excellent fish she had just served, her husband, a fine poet and an even better storyteller, told us of another serving of fish at another dinner party in his native Wales. An up-and-coming young businessman and his wife, friends of a relative of our host, had thrown an elaborate party which they were sure would guarantee the husband's entry into the elite business circles in their community. A few minutes before the guests arrived, the family cat jumped on the table and ate a hole in the beautifully prepared and garnished salmon which was to serve as the dinner's main course. Horrified, the wife threw the cat outside and camouflaged the hole with parsley and other condiments. The party was a success—no one discovered the damage. Convinced that a good reputation among his colleagues was now assured, the husband bade farewell to the last guest and then walked outside, where he discovered the cat dead by the driveway. Mortified, he called everyone who had attended the party, confessed that they, with the cat, had evidently eaten spoiled fish, and urged them to rush to the hospital to have their stomachs pumped. The next morning, as the husband was contemplating his ruined career, his neighbor came by and apologized for having run over and killed the cat the night before. So as not to bother the dinner guests, he explained, he had quietly placed the cat by the driveway and waited until morning to tell what he had done. The story both shocked and amused the people at our dinner party. Most of these aspiring professionals felt genuine sympathy over the tragedy that had befallen the aspiring businessman. I smiled at my wife but said nothing.

The next day I photocopied a story called "The Poisoned Pussy Cat at the Party" from Jan Brunvand's *The Vanishing Hitchhiker: American Urban Legends and Their Meanings* (1981), and copied an entire article from *Western Folklore* (Baer 1982), which discussed widely told stories about Southeast Asians stealing and eating dogs. On a piece of paper, I scribbled, "See what I mean!" and sent the note and the photocopied pieces to the associate dean. He replied that he did now see and that in the future he would be careful what he said around me.

More than almost any other subject, folklore must be experienced directly in actual life, as I experienced these narratives, to be properly understood. In twenty years of teaching, I have discovered that my students can listen to my lectures, can read assigned books and essays on the subject, and can still leave the course not understanding folklore unless they have encountered it in the actual settings in which it is performed. I encourage students to achieve this end by keeping their eyes and ears open to what is going on around them—even to pay close attention to dinner party talk; and I make sure they do this by requiring them to submit, first to me and then to the university archive, folklore they have collected themselves. Writing up these collections carefully enough to help potential archive users understand the substance and significance of the material submitted requires students to look more analytically at the folklore which surrounds them than they might have otherwise. The byproduct of this collecting, of course, is the development of folklore archives to support folklore research. But the main benefit is the increased understanding that comes to the students themselves.

If you are a beginning collector in search of this understanding, you will want to work closely with your teacher or with the archivist to whom you will submit your work. What follows is designed to supplement, not supplant, what they tell you. As you face for the first time the somewhat bewildering task of actually collecting and documenting some of the subject matter you will study, you must develop fairly clear notions about where to collect, what to collect, how to collect, and how to write up your data.

THE TRADITION BEARERS

The essays in this book should have taught you that the study of folklore seldom leads to the strange and exotic, but rather to much of what you have already known and experienced but not recognized as folklore. The essays should also have shown you that folklore is transmitted through time and space, not just by old, rural, uneducated, and ethnically different people, as is often believed to be the case, but by the doctor next door, by the fellow computer programmer at work, by the members of your religious congregation, by your younger brothers and sisters, by friends at a dinner party, and often by yourself. To collect folklore, then, you needn't pack your bags and head for some exotic place (as exciting as that might be); the lore you are after may be no further away than your workplace, your church, your mother's kitchen, your sister's playground, a casual gathering of friends, or your own memory.

As you try to decide where and from whom to collect, think of the different social identities (shaped by the social groups to which you belong) that make up your own personality. You are probably a student. You may belong to a religious group and live in a constant swirl of religious traditions and religious legends. You may have learned to view the world through ethnic or immigrant eyes. You probably have hobbies. You may already belong to an occupational group and may have learned much of what you must know to succeed not from job manuals but from traditional knowledge passed from person to person at work. You may live in a small, homogeneous community. You belong to a family. You have been a child and may still have close ties with children. Think for a moment of the rhymes, the chants, the songs, the games, the riddles, the superstitions, the traditional rules of conduct, and the taboos that you could collect from these youngsters with little difficulty. Other groups you are familiar with share equally rich lore. Though it is possible, and often rewarding, to collect from members of social groups different from your own, the price you will have to pay to establish rapport, win trust, and avoid violation of cultural taboos may be too high for the beginner. You will probably be more successful if you will do your first collecting among people you know. Once you have mastered collecting techniques and gained a better understanding of folklore in general, then you can turn your attention to people whose lifestyles and worldviews differ from your own.

Folklorists customarily refer to the people from whom they collect, whether from their own groups or not, as "informants"; some prefer a more deferential word like "consultants." What you should remember, whatever term you use, is that the people sharing their knowledge with you are the tradition bearers and should be treated with respect. That means you must never collect from them in secret and without their permission.

THE TRADITIONAL WORLD

As you think about the particular social group from which you wish to collect, try to determine what is traditional within that group. What are the behavioral consistencies and continuities? Ask yourself as many questions as you can: Are there rites to initiate new members? Are there superstitions and taboos connected with the group? Are there stories of group heroes or antiheroes? Are there jokes and anecdotes that ridicule outsiders with whom group members must carry on social exchange (doctors versus patients, for example)? Are there jokes about members of subgroups within the same larger social organization (doctors versus nurses)? Do group members wear distinctive clothing, eat distinctive food, use a distinctive and often highly specialized vocabulary? Is there a traditional code of conduct? Are there ways of punishing violators of the code? And so on.

You may find it useful to divide the folklore these questions will call forth into three broad categories: things people make with words (verbal lore), things they make with their hands (material lore), and things they make with their actions (customary lore). Such a division is, of course, highly arbitrary, but it does help order the materials of folklore and get you thinking about what you could most profitably collect. The following lists drawn from these categories suggest some, but certainly not all, the folklore awaiting the collector's hand:

Things people make with words (verbal lore): Ballads, lyrical songs, legends, folktales, jokes, proverbs, riddles, chants, curses, insults, retorts, teases, toasts, tongue twisters, greetings, leave-takings, autograph-book verses, limericks, graffiti, epitaphs.

Things people make with their hands (material lore): Houses, barns, fences, gardens, tools, toys, tombstones, foods, costumes, and things stitched, woven, whittled, quilted, braided, and sculpted.

Things people make with their actions (customary lore): Dances, instrumental music, gestures, pranks, games, work processes, rituals, and community and family celebrations such as weddings, birthdays, anniversaries, funerals, holidays, and religious ceremonies.

Many forms of folklore, of course, overlap these categories. For example, a song is an item of verbal lore and a quilt material lore, but the singing of the song and the making of the quilt are customary practices. In many folklore events, all three media merge. At a birthday celebration, the making and decorating of the cake are customary practices, and the cake itself is an item of material lore; the singing of the birthday song is a customary practice, and the song is an item of verbal lore. What this means, as we shall see, is that you really can't, or shouldn't, collect individual forms of folklore isolated from the other forms that surround them. You can, obviously, record only the words and music of a birthday song, but if you do not describe the setting in which the song is performed, including at least a brief description of the other forms of folklore also present, your recording really will not help you or a potential archive user properly understand the significance of the song in the lives of its performers.

COLLECTING FOLKLORE

This brings us to the issue of how actually to collect the folklore, how to record it so that archive users will recognize the importance of the lore to those who express it.

You will probably do a better job of collecting if you are fortunate enough to be present when folklore is performed naturally, without any prompting from you. Sometimes this happens by accident, as it did with me at the dinner party. More often you can arrange to be present where you know the kind of folklore you are interested in is likely to occur—at a bridal party, for example, where you will collect wedding or shower games. At times you may be able to bring a number of people together who will probably generate the lore you are after. If you arrange a skiing party, you will surely hear a lot of skiers' lore before the evening is over.

The value of this kind of "participant observation" is that you have the opportunity to observe firsthand what sparked the performance of a particular item of folklore, how successful the performance was, and what impact it had on the audience (including the impact it had on you). When you write up the event for submission to the archive, you may first want to interview other members of the audience for their responses to the performance, but, if you have observed carefully, most of what you need to describe of the social setting will already be in your own head.

The difficulty with this kind of collecting is that in many instances you will not be able to record the actual performance as it occurs. You can, of course, set up a tape recorder in advance at a bridal shower or a skiing party and record what takes place there. But if you hear a good story at a dinner party, you will have to go back to the narrator later and ask him to tell you the story again. When you do this, you may want to bring along a couple of people who have not heard the story before so the narrator's retelling will be as spontaneous as possible.

Much of the collecting you do will be by "direct interviewing" from the beginning. Once you have decided what kind of lore you wish to collect, then you must determine which people are most likely to possess the information you are after. As you collect using this method, you will be collecting folklore not from firsthand observation but from other people who were firsthand observers—from somebody else who has been at a bridal shower, skiing party, or dinner party. In this instance, you will have little trouble recording the folklore but will have to work much harder to get the necessary contextual background. You will have to elicit from the person who was present at the folklore performance what you would have observed had you been there yourself.

Don't hesitate at times to interview yourself. Without reaching far into memory, you should remember all kinds of folklore events in which you have taken part. You may never be able to discover completely how a folklore performance affected someone else, but you do know how participation in folklore events affected you. If you were once initiated into a fraternal order, you cannot only describe the initiation, but also tell how it made you feel. Some of our best contextual data come this way.

As you begin to gather material, you should understand at the outset that you can't record *all* the information every potential archive user may one day need to interpret a body of lore. This is why serious folklorists, while using archive data, will collect much of their material in the field—it's the only way to get exactly what they want. But you can record enough data to make your document useful. No matter what kind of lore you collect, you should always ask yourself a number of important questions. First, what is there about this lore that is pleasing? What makes it artistically powerful, or persuasive? Second, how does the lore function in the lives of the people who possess it? What needs does it meet in their lives? Third, what does the lore tell us about the values and attitudes of individuals and the groups to which they belong?

The Art of Folklore

In many ways the performance of folklore could be called an exercise in behavior modification. Through the things people make with their words, hands, and actions, they attempt to create a social world more to their own liking. When they tell a story, or make a quilt, or perform an initiation ceremony, they are usually attempting, through the power of artistically successful forms, to influence the way people act, including at times themselves. We cannot hope to understand the artistic impact of these forms unless they are recorded as precisely as possible as they live in actual performance.

Verbal lore: To capture the art of verbal lore you should, where possible, record your material with a tape recorder, especially free narrative forms in which the wording and presentational style may change strikingly from telling to telling. It is possible to take down material with pen or pencil, but this usually impedes the performance and brings you a truncated bit of reality. The following tape-recorded "scary story," told by an exuberant fourteen-year-old girl at summer camp, captures the essence of the real narrative with an exactness seldom matched in handwritten recordings:

> There was these couples that ran away from home to get married, and they were driving out on the desert, and all of a sudden he ranned out of gas, and she says, "Well, I told you to get some gas at that last town, but you just wouldn't listen."
>
> And he goes, "Well, I'll walk back and get some." And he goes, "Now lock all the doors and windows, because they've heard about this hook man who goes around the desert trying to kill people." And he goes, "Now lock all the doors and windows and don't let it open for anyone or anything that you hear."

> And so she locked them all and started listening to the radio. And she heard more about that hooked man that went around killing people. And so she got really scared. So she turned it off and she fell asleep. And during the night she woke up and she heard a scratching sound. And, and she got kind of worked up about that and so, so she just went back to sleep. And all of a sudden she woke up and she was wondering what woke her up. And there was that hook man outside, and he was sitting there trying to get in the car. And she just kind of got really scared and everything, but she didn't dare try to get out of the car or move. And so she fell asleep just sitting there.
>
> And so, when she woke up again he was gone, but there was still that swishing and thumping sound kind of on the roof of the car, but she didn't dare open it.
>
> Pretty soon she was getting worried about her boyfriend because he hadn't come back all night. And so she fell asleep again because she was really tired.
>
> And pretty soon a cop came—it was in the morning—and he sat there knocking on the windows. And she woke up and she saw the cop and, and he goes, "Open the door."
>
> And so she opened the door.
>
> And he goes, "What do you know about this?"
>
> And she goes, "Know about what?"
>
> And he pointed in this tree above their car—they parked by a tree. And there was the guy, there was her boyfriend hooked to the tree, and he'd been all clawed up by that hooked man.

One of the values of the tape recorder is that it frees you to write down information which *should* be recorded on a note pad, information about the circumstances of the storytelling situation: the setting in which the story was told; the nature of the audience; movements and hand gestures made during the telling; responses and promptings of the audience; everything, in short, to help the reader of your document not only hear the story but also visualize the setting in which it was related.

While the collector of the above item claimed to have recorded it word-for-word as it was told, I suspect that a few false starts and an occasional "uh" were edited out. Many collectors of oral documents, in fact, encourage editing. Folklorists do not, at least not for the archive document. It should be recorded just as it was spoken. If one later wishes to edit the piece for publication, at least the original remains available for scrutiny in the archive. Above all, when you prepare a document for archive submission, be sure to tell whether the item recorded is a verbatim transcription, an edited transcription (tell the extent of the editing), a close (but not totally accurate) shorthand recording, or a paraphrase of the original.

Good transcriptions are hard to make from unclear tape recordings. You should understand that you needn't be an expert or own expensive equipment to get a satisfactory recording. You must, however, use a machine with a separable microphone (in-machine microphones record mostly the whirring of the drive belts), keep the microphone within a foot of the speaker's mouth, and avoid touching or moving the microphone wire during the recording (each stroke of the wire will be transmitted to the tape).

Material lore: Beginning folklore collectors seldom focus on material lore—not because the things people make with their hands are any less worthy of study, but because accurately documenting them is a difficult task, not easily achieved by the novice. This is not to say that if you are interested in ranch fences, quilts, barn styles, or sculpted gravestone motifs, you should not set out to document them. But you should realize that the task will not be particularly easy.

To help archive users understand what is artistically pleasing about the artifacts you document, you must begin with accurate pictures of the objects. Occasionally, you can record these pictures with line drawings just as you can occasionally record verbal lore with a pencil. I have seen excellent sketches of folk toys—rubber guns, sling shots, clothespin pistols, handkerchief dolls, cootie catchers—which vividly depict these objects. But in most instances, you will need to record material culture with a camera, and a good one at that, preferably a 35mm, single-lens reflex camera which can be set for varying light intensities and distances.

You may take either color slides or black-and-white prints. Just as your sound recordings will reveal narrative texture, so too must these pictures display the stylistic and textural features of the artifacts being photographed. That means you will need to take a number of shots of the same object. If you were documenting a quilt, you would want a photograph of the entire quilt so that the overall design would be clear; you would take a close-up of individual blocks in the quilt; and you would want a still closer shot of the needlework in the block. If possible, you would also take pictures of different stages in the quilt making, from assembling the quilting frames to removing the quilt at its completion; and, because material objects are made to be used, you ought to get a picture of the quilt on the bed for which it was made.

Through your photographs, you should give an accurate view of material artifacts as they exist in actual life. To do this, you will have to do more than take pictures. You will need also to submit written texts that explain in considerable detail what appears in the pictures. A photograph of a well-crafted saddle, for example, without an explanation of its different parts and their functions, will be of limited value.

Customary lore: If the pleasure derived from verbal and material folklore comes principally from hearing and seeing, the artistic satisfaction derived from customary lore results primarily from participating in action. Customary practices range broadly across the full spectrum of human activity, but they tend to focus on ceremonies and festive events which tie people more closely to their family, ethnic, religious, occupational, and regional groups; on rites of passage which move people through transitional stages of life such as birth, puberty, marriage, incorporation into new social groups, and death; and on work processes which make easier and more enjoyable the hours people spend earning their bread.

Customary lore is a good place to begin collecting because you will often have to go no further than your own memory and because attempting to understand the significance of the traditional activities which make up your life will help you discover significance in the practices you collect from others. The following excerpt from a Swiss-American student describing Swiss Independence Day (August 1) in her Minnesota community should stir memories of important ceremonial events you could record from your own life:

> Between one and two hundred Swiss-Americans will gather at one of the homes (lately, my family's) and sing traditional songs, play traditional music, dance, eat bratwurst, good Swiss bread and cheese, and drink wine. As the sun sets, the highlight of the evening is reached. A huge bonfire is lit, and everyone gathers around it to soak up its warmth and glow and to sing late into the night—until the fire has died down to a pile of glowing coals.
>
> The creation of this bonfire is a task undertaken with care and great enthusiasm. The men build it, using scrap lumber and carefully balancing and arranging them teepee style till the structure is about 10–15 feet high. The lighting of it is made to be spectacular (with the help of gasoline) and worthy of the long "oohs" and "ahhs" it inevitably gets.
>
> The bonfire is a very old tradition in Switzerland for celebrating Independence Day. Neighborhoods and towns will get together to create one. It is important for the Swiss in America to continue to celebrate the day in this way, for the very reason of being so far from their homeland. The closeness, the oneness, the nostalgic comfort that building and standing around the fire fosters is an important binding force among the Swiss-American group.

When you collect customary practices, the camera will once again serve as a useful tool to record steps in processes like branding cattle, felling trees, preserving food, playing games, and celebrating Christmas. But you must, above all, observe keenly and describe accurately the action itself and the interplay of people involved in the event described. The following description of a fraternity birthday celebration, witnessed for the first time by a new pledge, catches in exemplary fashion both the actions and the joyful spirit of the occasion:

> After everyone had finished dinner, one of the brothers started to sneak away from the table, at which time another brother yelled out that it was that guy's birthday. Everybody grabbed him and

dragged him into the living room (he didn't fight too hard). Everyone was having a fun time of it. They put the guy face down on a table and then carried out the following rite, which I have recorded as I witnessed it:

Every brother got the chance to paddle the birthday brother. The paddles were the ones given by the pledges to their Big Brothers. [This point needs further explanation.] Every brother had a favorite paddle and talked about how each one was most effective at inflicting pain (much to the dismay of the birthday brother). The brothers got their chances alphabetically. They were allowed one swat apiece, but the swing was only allowed from the wrist (so as not to do much damage). A painful swat could still be achieved by most. Most of the swatters would put up the act that they were about to wail on the birthday brother. Some of them would, but others would take it easy and just let the paddle flop down. When hit hard, the swattee would cry out pledges for vengeance. When hit softly, he usually called the swatter a gentleman and gave him sincere thanks. After everyone got their chance, somebody gave the birthday brother a beer. Then they all started singing the following song while they shook his hand:

Happy birthday to you; happy birthday to you.
Happy birthday dear _______; happy birthday to you.
May you live a thousand years.
May you drink a thousand beers.
Get plastered, you bastard; happy birthday to you.

After the song, everyone joined in the following cheer:

Rah, rah, rah, Phi Kappa Tau!
Live or die for Phi Kappa Tau! Rah!

Meaning and aesthetic judgments: As you record data to help the archive user better understand the meaning or artistic significance of the material collected, try to give the tradition bearer's own point of view, not yours, of why something is meaningful or aesthetically pleasing. People who sing working songs, braid hackamores, and ritually celebrate the birth of a child know what pleases them and what does not. And if you ask the right questions, they will tell you.

This is not a particularly easy task. If someone tells you a moving family story about her grandparents keeping the bodies of children dead from the flu in the woodshed until the weather finally warmed enough in the spring to dig the frozen ground, and you respond by asking, "What does that story mean to you?" you will probably be considered both stupid and bad-mannered. But if you can get her talking about the occasion on which she heard the story, those on which she tells it, and her reasons for telling it, you should gain a fair notion of what the story *means* to her. Similarly, if you can get a quilter to tell you why she chooses certain colors for her patterns, a housewife to explain why she arranges food on the table in a given way, a rancher to explain why he prefers to rope calves for branding instead of using a cattle chute, you will have recorded at least some aesthetic judgments. These judgments, to be sure, are usually shaped by the tradition bearer's larger community or social group, but the group aesthetic can be generalized only after the responses of numerous individuals have been documented and archived.

You will discover that while the people you interview, like everyone else, make artistic judgments on formal criteria (the pleasing interrelationship of parts), they also judge folklore creations on functional and associational grounds. A rawhide rocking chair that does not "set well," or does not rock (function) properly, will not be judged artistically successful by the craftsman and his community, no matter how handsome it might appear to the outsider. Similarly, folklore which does not call forth the proper associations will probably not be valued as much as that which does. Children insist on celebrating Christmas the same way each year because doing so brings forth pleasant memories of Christmases past. A housewife continues to use the same decorative pattern in her pie crusts, not because the pattern itself particularly pleases her but because she learned it from her mother as a child and almost feels her mother's presence as she now decorates her own pies.

When I asked a quilter one day which of all the wonderful quilts she had shown me she liked best, she picked out one which to me seemed no more distinctive than the rest. She then explained that she had made the quilt while recovering from an arthritis attack and had hurt more during the quilting than she ever had before. The quilt reminded her of her triumph over pain—and was therefore beautiful. A young woman in my folklore class, expecting her second child and experiencing considerable discomfort, collected and submitted a joke which she found especially funny. It was a joke about a pain machine that supposedly transferred the pains from a woman in labor to the father of the child. The night the baby was due, the doctor hooked husband and wife up to the machine and, as the labor intensified, gradually turned the machine up to its limit. The wife's pains disappeared, but for some reason the husband felt no discomfort himself. The baby safely delivered, the husband returned home, opened the door, and found the milkman dead on the kitchen floor. I thought the joke passingly funny because of the cuckolding of the husband and because of the surprise ending. My student commented, "I found this joke to be very funny. It is funny because it demonstrates to women that men cannot stand as much pain as a woman even though they think they can." As you collect and document folklore, you must discover, through careful questioning, the *tradition bearer's view* of why the quilt is beautiful or the joke is funny.

The Social Function of Folklore

Folklore persists through time and space because the things people traditionally make with their words, hands, and actions continue to give pleasure and satisfy artistic impulses common to the species. Folklore persists also because it continues to meet basic human needs. This means that to properly document folklore you will have to record not just a proverb, or a recipe, or a game, or a story about a poisoned cat at a dinner party, but also the social settings in which these items were performed—not just what was said or made or done, but also the circumstances that generated the performances and the participants' responses to them. The following description of a recitation of a traditional rhyme points the direction you should take:

> Sara [age 62, the collector's maternal aunt, a Swedish immigrant] currently babysits small children in her home for a living. She enjoys her work because she is always around children and always says that she's just a kid herself.
>
> Sara is one of the funniest ladies I've ever known. She's always joking about how she's going on a diet and that we won't even recognize her when we see her next. She has a lot of funny rhymes and a poem for every occasion.
>
> One Thanksgiving Day (last year) she came to Idaho for dinner in Pocatello. We were all just finished with dinner and everyone was letting out their moans and groans from eating too much. Nobody was saying too much at the time because of the agony of bloating ourselves. We were all family members, my mom and dad, some of my sisters, and about three cousins. The little incident that happened wouldn't have been nearly as funny if a couple of our friends (nonfamily members who are considered "high class") had not been there.
>
> What happened was that Sara let go with a *loud* burp. I quickly looked over to see the expressions on the faces of the "high class" friends. It was a little embarrassing for us all, but Sara really smoothed things out well when she said this little rhyme immediately afterwards:
>
> It's better to burp and bear the shame,
> Than not to burp and bear the pain!
>
> After she said it, we *all* had a good laugh, even the two friends who normally wouldn't laugh at such a thing.

Note what the collector has told us in this description. We know a little about Sara's personality; we know what the occasion for the gathering was; we know who was present and something about the way they related to each other; we are aware of the embarrassment caused by the burp; we learn how Sara dealt with the embarrassment through reciting a traditional rhyme; and we learn what impact the recitation had on the others.

Because of what the collector has told us about the social setting in which the rhyme was used, we can now move beyond the rhyme, which by itself could be dismissed as an interesting bit of trivia, toward a better understanding of the way folklore, skillfully used, can help people affect the social environment to their own advantage. One description of one rhyme will not bring us to this end, but enough good descriptions of enough folklore performances will. Again, this is the function of an archive, to keep on file the folklore you collect until enough of it is available to move from descriptions of individual folklore performances to generalizations about folklore's larger social uses.

Just as you should let those from whom you collect interpret their folklore, so, too, should you allow them to comment on their reasons for performing it. I once listened to a tape-recorded story of a family supernatural legend in which the narrator became so emotionally involved in the story that she broke into tears. When the narration ended, the collector, evidently remembering that she was supposed to record information about her informant's attitude toward her narratives, asked, "Now, do you believe the story?" The woman was highly offended, and rightly so. Of course, you will want to know what the tradition bearers believe about their material, but if you will listen and observe their performances carefully enough, and if you will get them to describe the social settings in which they have performed, or might perform, their lore, then you won't have to ask boorish questions to get your information. Certainly in the following illustration there can be little doubt about the attitude of the tradition-bearer, a rodeo cowboy, toward the tradition he describes:

> Many competing cowboys like myself believe and practice this rule whenever competing in a rodeo. The belief is that if you have ever been injured in a certain piece of clothing, whether it be a pair of stockings, Levis, or a shirt, then this article of clothing has been cleansed of bad luck and now every time you wear it, it shall bring you luck.
>
> I got in a fight on a Friday night several years ago, and I was beat rather badly by my opponent. But I was to compete in a jackpot rodeo on the following morning, even though I hurt everywhere. So I took the opportunity to wear a pair of "Wrangler Jeans" that I had been beat up in the night before, feeling that it would be a good omen. And I won the jackpot with one of the classiest bareback rides I have ever made.

The Cultural Background of Folklore

Perhaps the most difficult data to collect is that which places folklore in its larger cultural context. And in this instance, collecting from your peers may be a disadvantage, primarily because the tradition bearers from whom you collect will probably speak a cultural language you already understand; and further, trapped by your mutual understanding, you may feel little need to explain the language for the cultural outsiders who may one day study your collection. For example, the following supernatural legend from Mormon tradition will be rich in meaning for most Mormons but may make little sense to non-Mormons:

> This man and woman was going through the temple doing work for the dead, and they got out to Salt Lake, and they had kids. And at the last minute the babysitter didn't come, and so they had to take their kids to the temple with them. And they were standing outside the temple waiting to get in, and they didn't know what they were going to do with their kids. There was no one around there they could leave them with, and they didn't know what they were going to do with them. While they were standing there, this strange man and woman came up to them and introduced themselves and said they would tend their kids while they went through the temple. The man and woman tended their kids, and the couple went in and did work for the dead, and that couple tending their kids turned out to be the couple they did the work for. When they came out of the temple, the man and woman were no longer there.

The individual who collected this narrative submitted it to the archive with the name of the teller attached plus a brief description of the storytelling setting, but with no information to help the non-Mormon user of the archive understand what is really happening in the story and happening in the minds of those who tell and listen to it. He should have included a statement something like this:

> Mormons believe they have an obligation to save not only themselves and, through missionary work, their neighbors, but also all their kinsmen, who have died without benefit of gospel law. Thus, they seek the names of their ancestors through genealogical research and then in their sacred temples vicariously perform for these ancestors all the saving ordinances of their gospel. In this particular narrative, the couple evidently came "out to Salt Lake" to participate in temple activity because one of the church's limited number of temples is located there. The man and woman who tend the baby are spirits of the dead who have probably long been waiting for saving ordinance work to be performed on their behalf. In a neat turn, the deceased husband and wife take care of the physical needs of the baby while the baby's parents attend to their spiritual needs. A story like this will be considered very sacred to many Mormons and should be treated with respect.

As any Mormon readers of these lines will know, we could still say a good deal more about this story, but the above information should place it in a cultural context making it at least partially intelligible to non-Mormons.

As you record cultural data for your folklore documentation, you should always ask what behaviors, ideas, and concepts people bring to the social setting in which a folklore performance takes place. And then you should include your answers to these questions in your document. What attitudes about Southeast Asians, for example, did the member of the dinner party bring to the discussion of Southeast Asians eating dogs? What feelings about the importance of national heritage did Swiss-Americans in Minnesota bring to their celebration of Swiss Independence Day? What concept of salvation did the teller of the temple story bring to his narration?

If you are collecting from members of your own group, you may already know the answers to these questions and can pull from your own head the information necessary to make the folklore clear to an outsider. If you are not a part of the group, you will have to get this information by learning as much about the group as possible before you begin collecting and then by asking the tradition bearers themselves to explain what you do not understand in the folklore they give you. In the illustration above, asking no more than "What's the difference between a temple and a regular house of worship?" and "What is 'work for the dead'?" would probably produce enough information to make the story understandable.

Because the controlling concepts and the value center of any group are, in the final analysis, the composite concepts and values of individuals in the group, you will need to record as much information as possible about the tradition bearers themselves. You should elicit information that relates directly to the lore being collected—ethnic attitudes from people who tell ethnic jokes—but you should also gather general information: sex, age, ethnic ancestry, education, religion, occupation, hobbies, and so on. And it's probably better to record too much than too little, since you can't know the uses to which your collections might be put in the future. Writing down the occupation of a teller of sexist jokes may seem unnecessary at the moment of collecting, but to the researcher who will one day use your material to study sex role attitudes of different male occupational groups, such information will prove crucial.

THE FOLKLORE DOCUMENT

Once you have brought together the kinds of data discussed in the sections above, your final task will be to write up your material for submission to the folklore archive. You should visit the archive to see where your collections will finally be located, to glimpse the range of materials filed there, to gain a better understanding of the contribution you can really make through careful work, and especially, to review the documentary forms used by the archive. In the absence of specific requirements from the archive or from your instructor, you may want to use the format below (a format used, in varying degrees, by a number of university archives). Remember that your ultimate goal is to capture on paper what took place in a particular folklore performance. Let the format be your servant, not your master. Follow it as closely as possible, but alter it if necessary to meet the demands of the material collected.

1. In the upper right-hand corner, in three lines, put the name of the informant, the place the lore was collected, and the date it was collected. If you submit lore culled from your own memory, write "Myself" for the informant's name and then record where and when you learned the lore.

2. In the upper left-hand corner put the form of folklore collected and, when possible, a title for the lore which suggests its content.

3. Three spaces below the title, at the left-hand margin, write "Informant Data:" and then give general biographical information about the informant and any details, including personal comments, which would give a clearer picture of the informant's relationship to and understanding of the folklore recorded. If you are your own informant, give the same kinds of details about yourself as you would for someone else.

4. Three spaces further down, at the left-hand margin, write "Contextual Data:" and then give both the social and cultural context for the folklore.

Under social context describe the circumstances under which you collected the folklore and under which your informant originally learned it, focusing, as already noted, on such things as the people present when the folklore performance occurred, the circumstances that generated the performance, the way people present participated in or influenced the performance, and the impact of the performance on them. Be sure to indicate if the folklore is normally performed at specific times and before certain people (at family reunions, for instance, or before women only). Other methods failing, you can often get good information about the social uses of folklore by asking for a description of a hypothetical context in which the informant might tell a particular story or take part in a particular ritual. Under cultural context, give information about the informant's culture which would make the folklore understandable to outsiders.

5. Three spaces further down, at the left-hand margin, write "Item:" and then present the folklore collected. Be sure to tell how the lore was recorded and to what extent the words on paper faithfully follow or depart from those of the informant.

If you collect folksongs, try to record both words and music. Put at least one verse directly under the music.

If you submit line drawings or diagrams of steps in an action (finger games, for example), test the accuracy of these drawings before you submit them; see if a friend can perform the actions you have illustrated in the drawing.

If you collect folk speech, or jargon, explain the words and expressions submitted and use them in sentences which communicate the meaning.

If you submit photographs or slides, clearly identify each one and key it to the accompanying written document.

6. In the bottom right-hand corner, give your name and age, your home address (including street number), your school address if you wish, your

university (if applicable), the course for which you are submitting the folklore (if applicable), and the semester or quarter and year (if applicable).

Each folklore document submitted to the archive, then, should contain the following:

Genre	Name of the informant
Title	Place the folklore was collected
	Date the folklore was collected

Informant Data:

Contextual Data:
Social Context:
Cultural Context:

Text:

Your name and age
Your home address
Your school address
Your school
Course number
Semester/quarter and year

The three examples given below (drawn from Utah State University and Brigham Young University folklore archives) follow the format quite closely: each does a reasonably credible job of describing the folklore submitted, although each could be improved.

The collector/informant of Sample #1 describes well enough the hunting practice he witnessed, but does not comment on its impact on him personally, something he could easily have told us since he serves as his own informant. How does he feel about hunting in general? Does he share the attitude of his companions about the manliness of the sport? What kind of verbal teasing accompanies the shooting of the clothing? Did others (insiders) in the party who failed to bag a deer shoot up their clothing? How did they seem to respond to the ritual? Was he, an outsider, treated differently from them? Did he actually shoot his own hat or coat? How did this make him feel? Did he wear the wounded article of clothing during the year? When and where? How did this make him feel? Did he go hunting again?

(Sample # 1)

Hunting Custom	Myself
"Shooting Hunting Clothing"	Spanish Fork, Utah
	October 1979

Informant Data:
Walter Jones was born in Richland, Washington, on July 8, 1960. His father was in the military and moved around the country a lot. Walter's background is basically western. His family origins are northern European. He is a member of the LDS (Mormon) church. Walter is married and is a junior at Brigham Young University.

Contextual Data:
Walter attended BYU back in 1978 and 1979, before entering the armed forces. He lived with a family in Spanish Fork, Utah, and became very close to them. During the month of October, Utah holds its annual deer hunt. The family in Spanish Fork participated in the hunt the same way as most residents of the state, with much enthusiasm. The family invited Walter to participate, and he went along. He had never been on a deer hunt and was ignorant of the great fervor that surrounds it. He and a few others in the hunting party did not shoot a deer and had to go through the punishment described below. The members of the group are a hardy bunch who pride themselves on being very manly. Not bagging a deer is considered not manly, and the person committing the sin is humiliated as a means of punishment. The evidence of humiliation is worn throughout the year to prompt the individual to do a better job in hunting next year.

Item:
If, at the end of the deer hunt, a person hasn't killed a deer, he must take off his hat or coat and lay it on the ground. He is then ordered to shoot the article of clothing and put it back on. When you wear the hat or coat, then everyone will know that you didn't get a deer. The only way to earn the right to wear a good hat or coat is to shoot a deer the next hunt.

Walter Jones
373 N. 400 W.
Provo, Utah
Brigham Young University
English 391 Fall 1985

The collector of Sample #2 records not only a belief (superstition), but also a story (in the informant's own words) about the belief. Whether the informant has actually "gotten over" the experience related we may never know, but at least we know, through her excellent little narrative, how it once affected her behavior. Beyond the narrative itself, we do not learn much about the informant and the role of folk belief in her life and in the rural Mormon community where she lived. For people who may have never seen anything but a gas or electric clothes dryer, the collector probably should have explained "leaving clothes out on the line."

(Sample #2)
Belief
"Diapers on Clothesline"

Chris Sorenson
Logan, Utah
Feb. 5, 1983

Informant Data:
Chris Sorenson, 51, was born (1932) and raised in Roosevelt, Utah. She is an active member of the Mormon church. She has two children and four grandchildren. She presently owns and manages a dress shop. She has a heart of gold and would give anything to her family if she thought it would make them happy.

Contextual Data:
Chris said she heard this a long time ago, when she was about seven. What happened made a big impression on her. She says she knows the event could not really have happened, but it took her a long time to get over it. This is what she said, taken down in shorthand as she spoke:

"When I was little, people told me that if anyone left their clothes out on the line over New Year's Eve, someone in their family would die during the year. One year me and a few of my friends were talking and one of them said, 'I don't believe it, and just to prove it, I'm gonna leave ours out.' In those days we used to have to leave the clothes on the line for quite a few days before they were dry, especially during the winter. Anyway, this girl left their clothes out over New Year's, and a few months later her brother died. This made a really big impression on me. For many years I'd call around to everyone in the family on New Year's Eve and remind them to get their clothes in."

Item:
If you leave your clothes on the line on New Year's Eve, someone in the family will die the coming year.

Mary Sorenson
234 Maple
Logan, Utah
Utah State University
Hist 423 Winter 1983

The collector of Sample #3 gives fairly good information about the social setting but very weak information about the cultural background. He describes the informant's religious feelings and activity, though he does not explain how someone of Jewish ancestry happens to be a Mormon. He describes the natural setting in which the informant told his story, elicits a good statement of the contexts in which the informant would recount the story, and gets at the intensity of the informant's feeling about the story, partly through an ill-advised question which brought informative results. He should also have asked the informant to describe the circumstances under which he originally learned the story. Further, since the collector is Mormon himself, and was a participant observer during the narration, he should have said something about his own response to the event.

The collector tells us almost nothing about the culture that shapes and gives meaning to the narrative. What are a mission (a two-year proselytizing endeavor), an elder (an office in the lay priesthood), a ward (a local congregation), a sacrament meeting (the weekly ward meeting in which the sacrament ordinance is administered and certain members are assigned in advance to give inspirational talks), and the Nephites (ancient American followers of Christ who, according to Mormon tradition, wander the earth helping the faithful in time of need)? Why does the collector call this account a Nephite story when the word "Nephite" is not mentioned in the narrative itself?

Finally, the collector has not just relied on his memory of the story told in the church meeting but has correctly gone to the teller later and had him tell the story again. Unfortunately, he has not recorded the story on tape, and we are therefore denied a verbatim transcription.

(Sample #3)
Legend — Chad Newman
"Nephite Story: Missionaries Rescued" — Pasadena, California
September 1970

Informant Data:
Chad Newman is my brother-in-law. He was born in Pasadena, California, in 1948 and has lived there all his life. He is currently in electrical engineering at Utah State University in Logan, Utah. He is of Jewish ancestry, but no one in his family practices Judaism, and all but his father are active members of the Mormon church. Chad has not served as a missionary, but he is an elder and at USU lives in the Delta Phi house, built by the church and run by the "returned missionary" fraternity. His home address is 5473 Cheery Pl., Pasadena, California.

Contextual Data:
Chad told this story as part of a talk he gave in sacrament meeting in the Pasadena Ward, as an illustration of the ability of the Lord to

protect those who place their faith in Him and live good lives. As nearly as I could tell, everyone present took the story in the way he intended it. Of course, I can not be sure if they all believed it to be a true story, but Chad himself was completely sure of its veracity. I later asked him (somewhat ill advisedly, as it turned out) if he really believed it, to his immediate indignation. He said he knew it was true because it had happened to a companion of someone a friend of his had known in the mission field. He said he didn't know very many Nephite stories, so he couldn't be sure if they were all true, but that he very definitely does believe the Nephites are somewhere here on the earth and have a mission to perform such as told in this story. When asked when and where else he would tell this story, Chad said only to people who were members of the church and who would probably believe in the Nephites and understand what their purpose was.

Item:
[I have recorded the story here not exactly as Chad told it in that particular sacrament meeting, but as he told it to me again in September 1970. I took notes as he told it, and it is close to his version, but mainly in my own words.]

Two missionaries in the Canadian Mission were driving home from a discussion meeting one day and there was quite a bad storm going. They were clear out in the middle of nowhere when their car broke down, and they were unable to repair it. They decided that they would just freeze to death if they stayed there, so they got out of the car and started walking down the road. After a couple of hours they were pretty badly frozen anyway and could tell they weren't going to be able to go much farther. Just then they heard a car coming behind them. It stopped and the man opened the door, and they got into the back seat. They were so cold they just laid down on the floor and didn't even look at the man. Finally they came to a service station, and the man stopped the car at the side of the road to let them out. They got out and stumbled over to the station, but they still hadn't really got a look at the man in the car. When they got up to the station, the attendant looked surprised, and asked where they had come from. They said, "From the car that had just stopped out in front." He said, "There hasn't been any car come along here for a couple of hours." They went out to the road and looked, but there weren't even any tire tracks.

Bill Henry
Route 1, Box 212
Moses Lake, Washington

364 E. 8974 S. #7
Provo, Utah
Brigham Young University
English 391 Spring 1971

CONCLUSION

I have not yet documented the story of the poisoned cat that I heard at the dinner party, but I intend to. I have arranged a gathering at my house, have invited my poet friend, and will ask him to tell the story again, this time with a tape recorder turning. If I am then able to follow the instructions I have given above, I will soon turn into the archive a document which may one day prove valuable to a researcher interested in contemporary legends. And I will in the process have increased my own understanding of folklore and its significance in people's lives. Through collecting and documenting folklore, you too can make an important contribution to folklore research and, in the process, increase your understanding of what it means to be human.

Folklore and National Identity

Herder, Folklore, and Romantic Nationalism

When I studied folklore at Indiana University in the early 1960s, Johann Gottfried Herder did not figure at all in the curriculum on the intellectual history of folklore. Constrained by the ideologies of disciplinarity, my teachers dated the history of the field to the nineteenth-century founders of the systematic, "scientific" folklore (the Brothers Grimm, William John Thoms, Julius and Kaarle Krohn, Sven Grundtvig, Francis James Child, E. B. Tylor), with a predisposition toward the Nordic and German scholars who systematized the philological method or to the British scholars who had the good taste to write in English. Earlier works that made it onto the syllabi were included because they represented classic collections of texts that provided important evidence for the history of particular folklore items.

I was first introduced to Herder, rather, as the foundational figure who provided the intellectual charter for Boasian, Americanist anthropology, with its focus on the nexus of languages, texts, and the particularities of culture histories as "the foundation of all future researches." This lead was mentioned in passing in Dell Hymes's first course at the University of Pennsylvania (which I had the good fortune to take), provocatively entitled The Ethnography of Symbolic Forms. I read a few brief secondary sources on Herder in the ensuing years, but encountering Bert Wilson's "Herder, Folklore and Romantic Nationalism" in 1973 was a threshold experience, the true source of an extended engagement I have had with Herder ever since. When I read that article, lights went on all over the place.

First of all, Bert's argument enabled me to see the powerful affinities between folklore and Americanist anthropology, to that point obscured for me by the vigorous foregrounding by folklorists of the critical differences between the disciplines, an essential part of discipline-building rhetoric. When the Herderian foundations of both Boas's program and Krohn's *folkloristische Arbeitsmethode* are recognized,

Published in *Journal of Popular Culture* 6 (1973): 819–35. Reprinted by permission of *Journal of Popular Culture.*

disciplinary divisions of intellectual labor seem somehow less important . . . at least to me, if not to more intellectually disciplined colleagues.

Second, Bert's essay crystallized for me the fundamental intellectual differences between rationalist, Enlightenment-based orientations to folklore as anachronistic leftover from a premodern past, and romantic orientations to folklore as expressions of the *Volksgeist* and the foundation of an authentic polity. Moreover, the article suggested, both conceptions were part of the symbolic construction of modernity.

And third, the article made clear that folklore theory was essentially political, that conceptions of folklore and motivations for its study are not neutral strivings toward disinterested knowledge, but are ideologically founded. Folklore is inevitably about the politics of culture, and the uses and abuses of the concept and the discipline are not simply secondary distortions of some purer intellectual mission.

Bert's essay on Herder and his later book on *Folklore and Nationalism in Modern Finland* (1976a) represent benchmark works in the critical study of folklore's intellectual history, essential reading for all my students. They have certainly shaped my own engagement with the intellectual history of folklore and anthropology, in particular with ideologies of language and oral poetics in the making of modernity and its attendant structures of inequality, culminating in my recent book with Charles L. Briggs, *Voices of Modernity* (2003). My reading of Herder differs in some significant respects from Bert's—I am convinced, for example, that many of the ideas Bert attributes to Vico's influence in fact stem from other sources—but without the stimulus of Bert's work, I wouldn't have pursued the inquiries that have led me to this (and so many other) understandings of what folklore and anthropology are about.

—*Richard Bauman*

> *Methinks I see the time coming when we shall return in earnest to our language, to the merits, to the principles and goals of our fathers and learn therefore to value our own gold.* —Johann Gottfried Herder

ENGLISH-AMERICAN FOLKLORE STUDIES BEGAN AS THE LEISURE-TIME ACTIVity of scholar-gentlemen intrigued by that quaint body of customs, manners, and oral traditions called *popular antiquities*—rebaptized *folklore* in 1846. With the advent of evolutionary anthropology in the second half of the nineteenth century and with its emphasis on folklore items as survivals among the peasants of ancient practices and beliefs, folklore became the object of serious study by scholars like Tylor, Lang, and Gomme. Since then both English and American folklorists have devoted much of their time to the study of survivals and to the historical reconstruction of the past or of past forms of present lore.

On the continent serious folklore studies began earlier and followed a different path. There they were from the beginning intimately associated with emergent romantic nationalistic movements in which zealous scholar-patriots searched the folklore record of the past not just to see how people had lived in bygone days—the principal interest of the antiquarians—but primarily to discover "historical" models on which to reshape the present and build the future. In this paper I shall attempt to show how this marriage of folklore research and nationalistic endeavors occurred and to describe some of its results.

Nationalism is a term not easily defined. Hans Kohn calls it an idea, "a state of mind, in which the supreme loyalty of the individual is felt to be due to the nation-state" (1961, 149). In words of about the same effect, Carlton J. H. Hayes calls it "a fusion of patriotism with a consciousness of nationality" (1960, 2). He defines a nationality as "a group of people who speak either the same language or closely related dialects, who cherish common historical tradition, and who constitute or think they constitute a distinct cultural society" (1926, 5). In other words, the nation-state to which the patriot owes his allegiance is defined according to ethnographic principles. Both as an inspiration for the idea of nationalism and as a means of winning the minds of men to that idea, folklore has served well.

In western Europe and America the rise of nationalism in the late eighteenth century was, at least in the beginning, in line with the liberal and humanitarian philosophies of the Enlightenment. It was precipitated in no small degree by Rousseau's doctrine of popular sovereignty and "by his regard for the common people as the true depository of civilization" (Kohn 1961, 150)—ideas which found their most powerful manifestations in the French and American Revolutions. Adherents of the new nationalistic philosophy looked forward to the day when the entire human community would share in those rights recently won in America and France. To them, as Kohn points out,

> the nationalism of the French Revolution . . . was the triumphant expression of a rational faith in common humanity and liberal progress. The famous slogan of "liberty, equality, fraternity" and the Declaration of the Rights of Man and of the Citizen were thought valid not only for the French people, but for all peoples. (1961, 150)

In central and eastern Europe, however, a different kind of movement—romantic nationalism—developed. In these areas, where the people were generally socially and politically less developed than in the West, national boundaries seldom coincided with those of existing states. Hence nationalism here became a movement not so much to protect the individual against the injustices of an authoritarian state, but rather an attempt to redraw political boundaries to fit the contours of ethnic bodies. To be sure, the adherents of this nationalism took over Rousseau's concept of popular sovereignty, but to it they wedded the idea that each nationality is a distinct organic entity different from all other nations and that the individual can fulfill himself only to the degree that he is true to that national whole of which he is merely a part. Thus individual will became secondary to national will, and service to the nation-state became the highest endeavor of man. In contradistinction to liberal nationalism, romantic nationalism emphasized passion and instinct instead of reason, national differences instead of common aspirations, and, above all, the building of nations on the traditions and myths of the past—that is, on folklore—instead of on the political realities of the present.

The man most responsible for the creation of this romantic nationalism was the German scholar Johann Gottfried Herder (1744–1803) (see Gillies 1945; Clark 1955; Herder 1967–1968). In its beginning stages, romantic nationalism was little more than the wistful dream of scholars and poets who endeavored through constant education and propaganda to kindle the spark of national consciousness in the hearts of their lethargic countrymen. As Kohn points out, they "became the voice and the conscience of their people, interpreting its history or mission and shaping its character and personality." And "always they developed a philosophy of history and society, in the center of which stood their own nation and the principle which was to sum up its idea and faith" (1946, 2). Such a man was Herder, whose philosophy of history not only inspired the German nationalistic movement but, for better or for worse, seems to have served as the foundation for most such movements since his time. By showing the German people why their building a national culture on native foundations was not only desirable but absolutely necessary, Herder formulated a set of principles of nationalism that have generally been held applicable to all nations struggling for independent existence.

Some of the principal tenets of his philosophy Herder took from other sources. In 1768 he received a copy of Michael Denis' *Die Gedichte Ossians, eines alten celtischen Dichters*. The book, a translation of Macpherson's *Poems of Ossian*, contained elaborate notes which had originally been written by Melchiorre Cesarotti for the Italian translation of Macpherson and which had been taken over by Denis, translated, and added to his own work. In these notes Cesarotti had relied heavily on the *Scienza Nuova* of Giambattista Vico—particularly on Vico's ideas about poetry and history. From Vico—via these notes—Herder received two ideas that were to become cornerstones of his own philosophy (Clark 1947, 657–59).

The first of these was the idea of different historic ages, each of which evolves naturally out of the preceding age—in other words, the concept of continuity in history. "All things," said Herder, "rest upon one another and have grown out of another." And again: the fatherland "has descended from our fathers; it arouses the remembrance of all the meritorious who went before us, and of all the worthy whose fathers we shall be" (1967–1968, 5: 565; 17: 319). This idea was soon to have tremendous national significance.

The second concept that Herder took from Vico was that each historical epoch forms an independent cultural entity whose various parts are integrally related to form an organic whole. Applying this concept of culture patterns to the historical stages of individual nations, Herder was soon to argue that since each nation was organically different from every other nation, each nation ought to be master of its own destiny. "Every nation," he said, "contains the center of its happiness within itself" (1967–1968, 5: 509).

From the writings of Charles de Montesquieu, Herder received further support for his concept of independent culture types. From them he also received a new idea—that these culture types are to a large degree determined by the physical environment in which nations are located. "Nature," said Herder, paraphrasing Montesquieu,

> has sketched with the mountain ranges she formed and with the rivers she made flow from them the rough but definite outline of the entire history of man. . . . One height created a nation of hunters, thus supporting and necessitating a savage state; another, more spread out and mild, provided a field for shepherd peoples and supplied them with tame animals; another made agriculture easy and essential; and still another began with navigation and fishing and led finally to trade. . . . In many regions the customs and ways of life have continued for millennia; in others they have changed, . . . but always in harmony with the terrain from which the change came. . . . Oceans, mountain chains, and rivers are the most natural boundaries not only of lands, but also of peoples, customs, languages, and empires; and even in the greatest revolutions of human affairs they have been the guiding lines and the limits of world history. (1967–1968, 13: 37–38)

Herder contended, then, that from the varying circumstances of nations' physical environments had emerged national differences and that these, enhanced over the years by historical developments, had gradually evolved into distinct national units, the organic structures of which he considered to be reflected in what he called national characters, or national souls. "Those peculiar national characters," he said,

> which are so deeply implanted in the oldest peoples, unmistakably manifest themselves in all their activities on earth. As a spring derives its component parts, its operative powers, and its flavor from the soil through which it flows, so the ancient characters of nations arose from family traits, from the climate, from the way of life and education [for Herder education and tradition were synonymous], from the early transactions and deeds peculiar to them. The customs of the fathers took deep root and became the internal prototypes of the race. (1967–1968, 14: 84)

Since no two nations had shared common environments and common histories, then no two nations could share common characters.

Herder next argued that since each nationality was, in effect, created by nature and history, man's duty was not, as the advocates of the Enlightenment maintained, to work for the creation of a common community of nations governed by universal, rational law, but rather to develop each nation along those lines laid down by nature and history. In bold defiance of the Enlightenment, he declared: "Every [nationality] carries within itself the standard of its own perfection, which can in no way be compared with that of others." He insisted that "we do justice to no nation by forcing upon it a foreign pattern of learning." And over and over again he proclaimed that "the most natural state is *one* people with *one* national character." Therefore, nothing seemed to him so unnatural as "the wild mixtures of various breeds and nations under one sceptre" (1967–1968, 14: 227; 13: 384; italics mine).

In advocating this position Herder was again influenced by Montesquieu. In the *De l' esprit des lois* (1748), Montesquieu had argued that the laws of a nation are merely the necessary relations arising from the nature of that nation's social character and geographical environment. Since these factors vary from place to place, there are no universal laws—only national laws. The laws of a nation best suit itself and only by chance can be applied to other nations.

Herder took over this relativistic position and made it a central part of his philosophy. "O, that another Montesquieu," he said, "would enable us to enter into the spirit of the laws and governments on this round world of ours" (1967–1968, 13: 386). Throughout his works Herder himself tried to become this other Montesquieu—though the real Montesquieu may not have agreed with the image—and repeatedly reminded his readers that every nationality must develop in accord with its own innate abilities, in line with its own culture pattern. As Alexander Gillies points out, Herder attempted

> to show and assess the value of what had of necessity to emerge, and to point out the universal moral, for peoples as for individuals, namely that each must fulfill nature's intention, indeed cooperate with her, by achieving what it is possible to achieve in given circumstances. (1945, 87)

For a nation to do otherwise—to attempt to develop on a cultural foundation other than its own—meant breaking the continuity of past development and disrupting the nation's organic unity. The consequences would be the stultification of native cultural forms and ultimately the death of the nation itself. "The stability of a nation," said Herder,

> which does not forsake itself, but builds and continues to build upon itself, gives a definite direction to all the endeavors of its members. But other peoples, because they have not found themselves, must seek their salvation in foreign nations, serving them, thinking their thoughts; they forget even the times of their glory,

> of their own proven feats, always desiring, never succeeding, always lingering on the threshold. (1967–1968, 23: 160–61)

I should emphasize that, as the above quotation indicates, when Herder spoke of self-fulfillment he spoke of peoples, not of people, and of nations, not of individuals. Inherent within his philosophy was the idea that the individual could receive his fullest development only as an integral part of his particular nation. "Since man originates from and within one race," he said, "his development, education, and way of thinking are genetic." Thus "every human perfection is national," and the individual achieves his own salvation only through the salvation of his nation (1967–1968, 14: 84; 5: 505).

Like Vico, Herder sought to explain the nature of a thing by studying its origin. But also like Vico—and like Aristotle—he put the nature of a thing in its end, in its final cause. Aristotle said man was made for life in the city-state. Vico said he was made for civilization. Herder said he was made for humanity (Humanität). "Humanity," said Herder, "is the character of our race. . . . We do not bring it with us ready-made into the world. But in the world it must be the goal of our strivings, the sum of our exercises, our guiding value" (1967–1968, 17: 138).

Herder defined humanity in a number of ways, but in each case, as Gillies says, it was clearly "something of which man alone is capable, and which he must learn to develop for himself in this life" (1945, 80). The important point for our purposes is that Herder believed that humanity was something man could achieve only as a member of a nation (1967–1968, 1: 366; 13: 159, 343, 346; 14: 83, 84, 227) and that nations could arrive at humanity only if they remained true to their national characters, or souls. Each nation, then, by developing its own language, art, literature, religion, customs, and laws—all of which were expressions of the national soul—would be working not only for its own strength and unity, but also for the well-being of civilization as a whole. Each nation had a special "mission" to perform in the progress of man toward humanity—the cultivation of its own national characteristics. "All nations," said Herder, "each in its place, should weave [their part of] the great veil of Minerva" (1967–1968, 17: 212).

But as Herder looked around he was greatly distressed to see that his own land was not fulfilling its mission—was not developing along nationalistic lines. At the close of the sixteenth century, German intellectual life, which had once held such great promise, had begun to decline. By the beginning of the eighteenth century, after suffering through the disruptions caused by the Reformation, the Counter Reformation, and the Thirty Years' War, "Germany was a masterpiece of partition, entanglement, and confusion" (Ergang 1966, 13). The country was divided into 1,800 different territories with an equal number of rulers. There was no unity in commerce and industry, and the air was rife with religious feuds.

Worse still, the people had abandoned their own native cultural forms for foreign models—particularly those of the French. The German nobility, to

Herder's despair, had widely imitated the brilliant court life of Versailles with the unfortunate consequence that French ideas and customs had filtered down to the middle classes and had widened the gap between them and the common people. French was the language of refinement and culture, and the German of the common people was considered vulgar. Those who had to use it padded it with so many foreignisms that it was scarcely recognizable to the lower classes. In literature, matters were equally bad. German writers not only used French as their principal medium of expression; they also based the form and content of their works on French and classical models and extolled the cosmopolitan ideals of the Enlightenment.

All this spelled disaster to Herder. He insisted that Germany must return to her own foundations—and do so immediately—or Germany was doomed. "The remains of all living folk (or national) thought," he warned, "are rolling with an accelerated final plunge into the abyss of oblivion. The light of the so-called culture [Enlightenment] is eating around itself like a cancer. For half a century we have been ashamed of everything that has to do with the fatherland" (1967–1968, 25: 11). He begged his countrymen not to abandon their native traditions in favor of those of other nationalities, but rather to cherish their own ways of life inherited from their fathers and to build upon them. And to those who found delight in aping foreign models, he declared: "Now seek in Germany the character of the nation, the manner of thinking peculiar to it, the genuine mood of its language" (1967–1968, 1: 366).

The point at which Germany had begun to lose the true spirit of its nationality and to ignore its historical antecedents had been, thought Herder, the end of the Middle Ages. At this time native traditions had been interrupted by foreign influences introduced by the Renaissance. To regain its lost national soul, then, Germans would have to return to the Middle Ages—to the point where the break had taken place—and resume their cultural development from there. A healthy, durable culture, Herder repeated again and again, must be built on a native foundation. He did not suggest, I must add, that the Golden Age lay in the past. For him, with his concept of humanity, the Golden Age was in the future. It was just that Germany had unfortunately gotten off the only cultural track that would lead it to humanity, and, for its own salvation, had to be put back on. As Robert Ergang points out, Herder wished to lead his people to the national past, the spring of the national sentiment, "so that they might refresh themselves by clear draughts and then go onward to a great future" (1966, 232).

But how were the Germans to bridge the chasm between the present and the past? How were they to rediscover their lost soul? For Herder there was only one way—through folk poetry.

To understand Herder's concept of folk poetry we must turn once again to Vico. For Vico, mythos equaled history. The first poets, he claimed, were actually historians who spoke in metaphorical language. Later ages distorted and misunderstood their meaning, but originally the poems of Greek mythology were descriptions of actual events. Thus for Vico, and for Herder, who accepted Vico's point of view, poetry could be used to explain history—to get otherwise unobtainable data about past epochs. Applying Vico's thesis to the Bible, Herder concluded that the creation story in Genesis was a glossing dealing with the institution of the Sabbath, that the Song of Solomon was a collection of folksongs of Solomonic antiquity, and that Revelations was, as Robert T. Clark puts it, merely "the historical reaction of the aged Apostle John to the destruction of Jerusalem by the Romans—which John might conceivably have seen—and an application of images from the prophecies and from this terrible event to the Second Coming" (Clark 1955, 163, 255–57, 269). Thus from these Biblical folk poems it was possible to learn a great deal about past events. In the same way, argued Herder, Germans could learn the events of their own history by studying the folk poems that still survived among the peasants.

Still more important, Vico claimed that folk poetry reflected the sociocultural pattern of the society in which it originated. Homer, he said, was nothing more than a projection of Greece—a disguised name for the people. He

> composed the *Iliad* in his youth, that is, when Greece was young and consequently seething with sublime passions, such as pride, wrath, and lust for vengeance, passions which do not tolerate dissimulation but which love magnanimity; and hence this Greece admired Achilles, the hero of violence. But he wrote the *Odyssey* in his old age, that is, when the spirits of Greece had been somewhat cooled by reflection, which is the mother of prudence, so that it admired Ulysses, the hero of wisdom. (1961, 270)

Thus "Homer was an idea or a heroic character of Grecian men insofar as they told their histories in song" (Vico 1961, 269), or, in the idiom of Herder, Homer was the summation of the national soul expressed in the poems of the folk.

This idea—that the national soul, or the cultural pattern, of a people expresses itself best in that people's folk poetry—is found everywhere in Herder. "Poetry," he said, "is the expression of the weaknesses and perfections of a nationality, a mirror of its sentiments, the expression of the highest to which it aspired." Folk poems he called "the archives of a nationality," "the imprints of the soul" of a nation, "the living voice of the nationalities." From them "one can learn the mode of thought of a nationality and its language of feeling" (1967–1968, 28: 137; 9: 532; 3: 29; 24: 266; 9: 530; Ergang 1966, 198, 220). What better place, then, could a man go to discover the soul of a nation than to its folk poetry?

But who were these "folk" poets whose poems were the key to national character? They were, said Herder, those who were organically one with their culture—those most in tune with the national soul. Through the free use of their imaginations and through reliance upon their emotions—instead of their reason—they allowed the creative force of the folk character to work through them and thus became the producers of truly national poetry—poetry which bore the stamp of both the physical and cultural environment in which it had been created. Herder wrote:

> To . . . chain and to interrogate the Proteus which is usually called national character and which manifests itself no less in writings than in usages and actions, this is a noble and fine philosophy. It is practised with greatest certainty in the works of poetry, i.e., of imagination and feeling, because in these the entire soul of a nation reveals itself most freely. (Gillies 1945, 105)

Folk poets, then, were national poets—the agents through whom the true character of a nation made itself manifest.

These folk poets, I must emphasize, did not have to be anonymous, nor did they have to speak from hoary antiquity. For Herder the only requirement was that the folk poet reflect the culture in which he lived. "The most indispensable explanation of a poet," he insisted, "especially is the explanation of the customs of his age and nation" (Gillies 1945, 28). Homer and Shakespeare he considered two of history's greatest folk poets because they had so adequately expressed their own nations in their poetry. Of Homer he wrote, in words strongly reminiscent of Vico, "I consider him the most successful poetic mind of his century, of his nation. . . . But I do not look for the source of his happy genius outside of his nature and of the age that shaped him" (1967–1968, 3: 202). Again he emphasized that the great folk poets of Greece—Homer, Aeschylus and Sophocles—had succeeded because they "wrote with a Greek pen, on Greek faith, for Greece" (1967–1968, 2: 114).

Herder would have been only too glad to turn to contemporary German folk poets to seek guidance for his country, but unfortunately there were none. With the exception of perhaps Klopstock, they had all bartered their German birthright for a mess of French pottage. For this reason it was essential to turn to the peasants, to those Germans who had remained the most unspoiled by foreign influence and who had kept on their lips those songs created by folk poets in the days when German culture had rested on its own foundation. Of these old poets, Herder said, they "are our fathers, their language the source of our language, and their unrefined songs the mirror of the ancient German soul" (1967–1968, 2: 246). In their works, then, lay the road to salvation.

As the above quotation indicates, folk poetry had still another value for Herder: it had retained the national language in its most perfect form. National language was extremely important because, according to Herder's organic view of culture, only through it could one think naturally and respond to and express the national soul. "Every language," he wrote, "has its definite national character, and therefore nature obliges us to learn only our native tongue, which is the most appropriate to our character, and which is most commensurate with our way of thought" (1967–1968, 1: 2; Kohn 1967, 432–33; see also Herder 1967–1968, 1: 366; 2: 13, 19; 17: 286). Therefore, he argued that

> a nation . . . has nothing more valuable than the language of its fathers. In it lives its entire spiritual treasury of tradition, history, religion, and principles of life, all its heart and soul. To deprive such a nation of its language, or to demean it, is to deprive it of its sole immortal possession transmitted from parents to children. (1967–1968, 17: 58)

But, unfortunately, the language of the fathers had been demeaned. Latin and French instruction in the schools and the general use of French by members of polite society had, as has been pointed out, so loaded it down with cumbersome foreignisms that it was hardly recognizable. Only in folk poetry had it retained the pristine beauty found in the literature of the Middle Ages. Hence only to this earlier literature or to folk poetry could the poet wishing to remain true to the idiom of the fathers go for inspiration.

Much of the stimulation for Herder's work with folk poetry came from his reading of Bishop Thomas Percy's *Reliques of Ancient English Poetry* and James Macpherson's fraudulent *Poems of Ossian*, both of which were published in England in 1765. These works—particularly the Ossianic poems—convinced Herder that the earliest Celts, Germans, and Norsemen (at first no distinction was made between these races) had possessed cultural values equal to those of the Greeks (Clark 1955, 144, 194–95). English literature had become great—and consequently also the English nation—because it had developed continuously out of these ancient cultural values. For example, Shakespeare had, believed Herder, based many of his works on ancient popular ballads, stories, and myths (see Gillies 1937). On the other hand, German literature—and so too the German nation—had languished because German poets, unlike the English, had ceased to remain true to their native traditions. Herder said:

> From ancient times we have absolutely no living poetry on which our newer poetic art might grow as a branch upon the national stem. Other nations have progressed with the centuries and have developed on their own foundations, . . . from the beliefs and tastes of the people, from the remains of the past. In this way their literature and language have become national. The voice of the people has been used and cherished, and they have in these matters acquired a much larger public than we have. We poor Germans have been destined from the beginning never to be ourselves, always the lawgivers and servants of foreign nations, the directors of their fate and their bartered, bleeding, impoverished slaves. (1967–1968, 9: 528)

It was in emulation of the success of the English, then, that Herder began his campaign to revive his nation's past and to make it the basis for a new German literature and a new German way of life. The first and most important step in this campaign was to collect and publish the surviving folk poetry—"to make available," as Gillies says, "the lost treasures of the past as a foundation for future writers to build upon; to bring about in contemporary Germany a set of literary conditions similar to those of Elizabethan England, out of which new Shakespeares and Spensers might grow" (Gillies 1945, 52). With the taking of this step, European folklore scholarship was officially begun.

Herder made one of his first pleas to collect folklore in 1773 in an essay called "Auszug aus einem Briefwechsel über Ossian und die Lieder alter Völker" (1967–1968, 5: 159–207). The essay awakened an immediate interest in folklore and inspired G. A. Brüger to write his *Herzensguss über Volkpoesie*, published in 1776. Then in 1777 in his essay "Von Ähnlichkeit der mittleren englischen und deutschen Dichtkunst," Herder wrote a moving call to arms:

> Great empire! Empire of ten peoples, Germany! You have no Shakespeare. Have you also no songs of your forebears of which you can boast? Swiss, Swabians, Franks, Bavarians, Westphalians, Saxons, Wends, Prussians—have all of you together nothing? The voice of your fathers has faded and lies silent in the dust. Nation of heroic customs, of noble virtues and language, you have no impressions of your soul from the past?
>
> Without doubt they once existed and perchance still do, but they lie under the mire, unrecognized and despised. . . . Lend a hand then, my brothers, and show our nation what it is and is not, how it thought and felt or how it thinks and feels. (1967–1968, 9: 530–31)

In typical form, Herder set an excellent example for his countrymen by answering his own call. As a young man he had begun collecting folk poems and had continued the practice over the years. In 1778 and 1779 he published part of these poems in his now famous *Volkslieder* (after his death retitled by his editors *Stimmen der Völker in Liedern*). This work, along with his continued admonitions to save the nation's old literature, finally overcame the opposition of those who looked with scorn on songs of the "common" people, and folklore collecting began in earnest.

Two of the first to respond to Herder's call were Friedrich David Gräter and Christian Gottfried Böckh who, inspired by Herder's writings, founded a periodical called *Bragur, ein literaisches Magazin für deutsche and nordische Vergangenheit*, which was dedicated to the collection and publication of folklore. In the ensuing years others joined the cause. In 1803 Ludwig Tieck published *Minnelieder aus dem Schwäbischen Zeitalter*. From 1805 to 1808 Clemens Brentano and Achim von Arnim published three volumes of folksongs entitled *Des*

Knaben Wunderhorn: alte deutsche Lieder. In 1807 Josef Görres published the results of his studies of almanacs and old storybooks. In 1812 Jacob and Wilhelm Grimm edited ancient fragments of the *Hildebrandslied* and the *Weissenbrunner Gebet* and then from 1812 to 1815 published their famous collection of folktales, *Kinder-und-Hausmärchen*. In 1815 they brought out a volume of the Poetic Eddas and from 1816 to 1818 published *Deutsche Sagen*, an analysis of the oldest Germanic epic tradition. Jacob Grimm's attitude toward his material is typical of the period and shows the strong influence of Herder. He wrote:

> Having observed that her Language, Laws and Antiquities were greatly underrated, I was wishful to exalt my native land. . . . Perhaps my books will have more influence in a quiet happy time which will come back some day; yet they ought to belong to the present too, which I cannot think of without our Past reflecting its radiance upon it, and on which the Future will avenge any deprecation of the olden time. (Grimm 1883, iv)

From the time of the Grimms on, folklore collecting continued unabated and with increasing enthusiasm.

As Herder had hoped it would, the folk poetry revival moved German literature away from the rationalism and cosmopolitanism of the Enlightenment, which Herder believed had led to a sterile uniformity, and based it on the irrational and creative force of the people. He had once said that unless our literature is based on the folk, "we shall have no public, no nation, no language, and no poetry of our own. . . . We shall write forever for chamber scholars and disgusting critics from whose mouths and stomachs we get back what we have written" (1967–1968, 9: 529). But now the longed-for day had arrived. Men like Novalis and Fichte steeped themselves in folk traditions and wrote literary *Märchen* and ballads. And the young Goethe, who was to set the tone for many others, learned from Herder that German literature, to become great, must derive its inspiration and form from the poetry which had survived from the nation's own past. At Herder's insistence, Goethe even collected folksongs and, as Gillies says, "learned to listen through them to the voice of nature from which they sprang" (1945, 19).

The first literary men to follow Herder's footsteps were the members of the *Sturm und Drang* school. Like Herder, they revolted against the authority of the Enlightenment and stressed spontaneity and originality, and, also like Herder, they considered the folk the principal source of genuine poetry. To them creative genius and *Volk* became almost synonymous. Shortly after the turn of the century the Romanticists also focused their attention on the folk. Under the leadership of men like Friedrich Schlegel, who was strongly influenced by Herder, they turned to the literature of the past—to medieval and to folk poetry—to find ideals for the present and future. And on the basis of this material they created a body of literature which—so they believed—once again expressed the national soul, a literature to which a people seeking its national identity could turn for strength and inspiration.

We realize today, of course, that the past to which the followers of Herder turned was, for the most part, a mythic past, that the great and noble nation they wished to re-create was in the main the product of their own fruitful imaginations. But the important point to remember is that the people involved believed that there had once been such a Germany. And believing so, they made it so—that is, they actually created a new nation in the image of what they thought the old one had been. Looking back at this period some fifty years later, T. Benfey assessed the role folklore had played in the creation of this new Germany:

> The recognition of the great value of the German folk song wakened an interest in the other creations and expressions of the German folk soul. With equal zeal, legends, fairy tales, manners and customs began to be investigated, collected, and studied. The influence of the folk soul upon the other fields of human development—law, state, religion, all forms of life—was recognized and traced. From this, assisted by many other factors, there arose not only an entirely new conception of the history of civilization, but above all a reverence and love for our people, such as had long been lost in Germany. The recognition that the individual must be rooted in his own people, that he must feel himself at one with it and with its spirit, and that only on this sod must he ripen to independence, blossomed into full consciousness, into shape and into active life. It became evident where they had erred and what ignominious consequences the lack of patriotism had incurred. The feeling of duty toward the nationality grew strong with the love for it. The whole people became engrossed in the idea of marshalling all its powers to regain the independence so nearly lost and to make secure its nationality by means of the re-establishment of its unity. (1869, 318)

The work of Herder had not been in vain.

The seed of nationalism planted by Herder bore fruit in many lands. The concept that each individual nation could contribute to the progress of humanity only by developing on its own cultural foundation was eagerly accepted by underdeveloped ethnic groups in central and eastern Europe. It meant "that each could feel a messianic quality within itself" (Gillies 1945, 129). Herder did all he could to engender this feeling and to make these groups nationally conscious, particularly by encouraging them to cultivate their own national literatures. In *Volkslieder* he again set the example by publishing folksongs from many other lands in addition to his German songs. In 1803 he announced his intention to publish a new collection of folk poems which were to be arranged according to nationality and which, he hoped, would further the cause of humanity, but he died before he could complete the project. Throughout his life he insisted on the right of each nation to determine its own destiny in accord with its own innate potentialities.

Perhaps Herder's influence was strongest among the Slavs, whose origins he idealized and whose folk poetry he greatly admired. He frequently urged the collection of this poetry, along with old customs and traditions, that the gap between past and present might be spanned and that the Slavic nations might then go on to a glorious future. Herder's works were published in the Slavic countries in both the original German and in translation and were instrumental in stimulating Slavic patriotism. As A. Fischel says, Herder is justly called "the real father of the renaissance of the Slavic peoples," for he "was the creator of their philosophy of culture. They saw the course of their historical development up to the present with his eyes, they drew from his promises the certainty of their future high destiny" (Ergang 1966, 261).

The Slavs responded to Herder's call to action with great enthusiasm. A few examples will illustrate. In 1822 the Slovak Jan Kollar, who had studied at Jena and was thoroughly acquainted with Herder's philosophy, preached nationalistic sermons in Budapest. He pleaded for the creation of a common Slavic literature and urged the scattered peoples to unite and fulfill their mission. In 1834 and 1835 he published two volumes of folksongs. From 1823 to 1827 another Slovak, Pavel Josef Šafařík, published folksongs and in 1826 brought out his *Geschichte der slawischen Sprache and Literatur*. In 1822 the Czech Frantizšek Ladislav Čelakovský, a great admirer of Herder, published a collection of folksongs from the Slavic peoples. Like his teacher Herder, he claimed they expressed the true spirit of the Slavic nationality. In Serbia, folksongs were collected by Vuk Karadžić, and in Poland by Kazimierz Bordziński. Folk poems of the Cashubians, Ruthenians, and Ukrainians were also collected and studied. All this activity led to a literary nationalism which became pan-Slavic in scope. In Slavic lands, then, as in Germany, patriots sought goals for the future in their past; and they sought their past in their folklore.

But Herder's influence was by no means confined to Germany and to the Slavic countries. In Finland, which had become united with Russia in 1809, Herder's philosophy became the guiding light for a small group of patriotic intellectuals who, concerned over the possibility of a forced Russification of their language and culture, turned to their past to find strength for the future. One of this group said, in words that sound as though they were copied directly from Herder:

> No independent nation can exist without folk poetry. Poetry is nothing more than the crystal in which a nationality can mirror itself; it is the spring which brings to the surface the truly original in the folk soul. (Wuorinen 1931, 69)

Another argued that if Finns would collect their folk poems and work them into an organized whole "a new Homer, Ossian, or *Niebelungenlied*" might be the result; and, "exalted, the Finnish nationality, in the luster and glory of its own uniqueness and adorned with the awareness of its own development, would arouse the admiration of the present and of the future" (Gottlund 1817, 394). In 1835 Elias Lönnrot fulfilled this prophecy with the publication of the epic *Kalevala*, which he created from his huge collection of folk poems. In the following years, Finnish patriots attempted to restore to the Finnish people, who had been divided and suppressed by years of foreign domination, the national characteristics and cultural values depicted in the epic.

In Norway, during the middle of the nineteenth century, much the same story was repeated. For centuries the country had been under either Danish or Swedish domination. Now it was time, argued a small group of romantic nationalists, for Norwegians to be Norwegians. The influence of the Enlightenment and the infiltration of foreign influences had, they believed, corrupted large sections of the population, causing them to abandon native traditions and to lose contact with the national Idea. Only among the peasants, who were considered the custodians of the national character, could the traditions of the fathers be found. Hence it was to these traditions that the nation must turn for its salvation. Oscar J. Falnes sums up the feeling of the time with phrases that bear the strong imprint of Herder:

> No part of the peasant's heritage gave such adequate expression to nationality as his literary tradition; it was considered preeminent in this respect partly because it was related so intimately to the folk character. The folk tales, it was said, had "grown organically" from within the peculiarity of each people, they were the clearest revelation of the folk spirit. The folk-literature having sprung from the people's "innermost uniqueness" belonged "to us and to no one else"; in it was enshrined the "soul of the nation." (1933, 250)

To recapture this national soul and to put the country back on its own cultural foundation, scholars began seriously to collect and publish folklore. From 1841 to 1844 P. C. Asbjørnsen and Jørgen Moe published their collection of folktales, *Norske Folke-eventyr.* In 1845 and 1848 Asbjørnsen published a collection of fairy tales and folk legends, *Norske Huldre-eventyr og Folkesagen.* And in 1852 L. Lanstad published his famous collection of folk ballads, *Norske Folkeviser.* These works were generally received with enthusiasm, particularly by the press, and helped convince the people that Norway had had a glorious past and that by reviving the spirit of this past the nation could have an equally glorious future. To this task the nationalists dedicated themselves in the years to come.

Though Herder himself is now remembered mostly by specialists, his philosophy of history lives on. The list of nations in which this philosophy has inspired, or is still inspiring, romantic nationalistic movements could be greatly extended, but in each case the story would be about the same. Whenever nations turn to their folkloristic past to find faith in themselves and courage for the future, they are following lines laid down by Herder.

That romantic nationalism is, by definition, a folklore movement should by now be obvious. As we have seen, Herder taught that each nation is by nature and by history a distinct organic unit with its own unique culture; that a nation, to survive as a nation, as well as to contribute to the development of humanity as a whole, must cultivate this national culture, developing it along lines laid down by past experience; that the total cultural and historical pattern of a people—the national soul—is expressed best in folk poetry; and that should the continuity of a nation's development be interrupted, the only road to salvation lies in collecting the folk poetry surviving from the time of the break, using it to restore to the nation its national soul, and thus making possible its future development on its own foundation.

Romantic nationalists, then, like English-American folklorists, have studied folklore items as survivals from the past. But while the latter have been content merely to work out historical reconstructions based on these survivals, the former have attempted not only to reconstruct the past, but also to revive it—to make it the model for the development of their nations. Having once achieved their goals, they have often moved on to other endeavors, but their past accomplishments have remained to inspire other dependent nations seeking historical justification for their separatist policies. Consequently the same stirring phrases about glorious national pasts and noble destinies that once moved Europeans to action are today to be heard echoing throughout Africa and Asia. Those who see folklore not just as a body of tradition to be classified and catalogued but also as a dynamic force in the lives of men would do well to study and learn from the nationalistic movements of the past century; for it appears that for some time to come the story of nationalism will continue to be an oft-told story and that folklore will remain one of its most important chapters.

Sibelius, the *Kalevala*, and Karelianism

In this engaging article, William Wilson provides an overview of the social and artistic movement of late nineteenth-century Finland known as Karelianism. The term Karelia (Finnish Karjala) designates both a portion of eastern Finland and a broad expanse of territory east of the border. The eastern region was never part of the Swedish empire, an entity that molded the culture of Finland proper for six centuries. Predominantly Orthodox in faith and possessing a language distinct from (although very closely related to) Finnish, it would seem an unlikely candidate for national epitome. Yet through the epic song collecting efforts of Elias Lönnrot (1802–84), Karelia became the birthplace of the Finnish national epic, the *Kalevala* (1835), and a dominant source of inspiration for artistic and intellectual endeavors thereafter.

As in other national contexts—such as Swedish Dalecarlia, Norwegian Telemark, American Appalachia—Finnish Karelia came to be viewed by the era's scholars, writers, composers, and artists as a treasury of premodern worldview and the epitome of national folk culture, despite its distinctive and at times idiosyncratic features. Somewhat ironically, this embrace of Russian Karelia intensified in the face of czarist Russification efforts at the end of the nineteenth century, as Wilson discusses. Writing in a volume intended for musicologists and music historians, Wilson explores Karelianism as a whole, placing the composer Jean Sibelius within his sociopolitical and historical context as well as within the wider process of intellectuals' use of folk culture for nationalist purposes.

The present article is by no means Wilson's first foray into Finnish folklore or history. His dissertation, which developed into the study *Folklore and Nationalism in Modern Finland* (1976a), examines the role of folklore and folklorists in shaping Finnish political stances toward the Soviet Union, especially during the era of the two world wars. The feelings of kinship toward Karelians across the border—a product of Karelianism as an aesthetic movement—became both a motivation

---

Published in *The Sibelius Companion*, 43–60, ed. Glenda Dawn Goss (Westport, Conn.: Greenwood Press, 1996). Reprinted by permission of Greenwood Press.

and a justification for Finnish military actions in the region. Prominent folklorists took a leading role in shaping the rhetoric of nationalism that pervaded public discourse during the era. Wilson's study raised many eyebrows and provoked some outrage in Finland after its translation into Finnish, and remains a mainstay of folkloristic curricula in the history of the discipline on both continents.

Anticipating Eric Hobsbawm and Terence Ranger's *The Invention of Tradition* (1983), Wilson's book set the ground for the reflexive examination of folklorists' roles in building national images and revealed the degree to which "culture work" holds political and social implications. In a later article, "Partial Repentance of a Critic: The *Kalevala,* Politics, and the United States" (1987a), Wilson tempers his analysis somewhat by commenting on the surreptitious ways in which sociopolitical agendas can emerge in public sector folklore work, such as that he has been involved with personally in the state of Utah. Folklorists can become more *products* than *shapers* of the wider cultural ideologies to which their efforts contribute. This article, again, represents a seminal contribution to the field's discussions of reflexivity, public folklore, and what would eventually come to be called in American politics the "Culture Wars."

The present article largely avoids such reflexive discourse and simply seeks to delineate the Karelianist movement as we see it in figures like Sibelius. In so doing, however, Wilson captures the youthful energy and idealism of Karelianism, sketching at the same time both the interdisciplinarity and the emotional investment that has undergirded elite approaches to folklore—and the field of folklore studies—since the late eighteenth century.

—*Thomas A. DuBois*

DURING THE SUMMER OF 1891, WHILE ENGROSSED IN THE COMPOSITION OF his first major orchestral work, the *Kullervo* Symphony, Jean Sibelius and his friend Yrjö Hirn traveled to the city of Porvoo on Finland's southern coast to meet Larin Paraske, a singer of Karelian folksongs. Born and raised in an area just south of the Karelian Isthmus, Paraske had over the years developed a vast repertoire of Karelian songs, many of them with analogues in Finland's national epic, the *Kalevala.* She had come to Porvoo so her friend and long-time supporter, Pastor Adolf Neovius, could record her repertoire and prepare it for publication. While there, she quickly became something of a celebrity, attracting leading cultural and artistic figures to the city. Some came to encounter an "authentic" representative of the Karelian folk and of the *Kalevala* song country, others came to paint her in native costume. Sibelius came to hear her sing. He listened attentively and made notes on her inflections and rhythm (Tawatstjerna 1976, 1: 97–98; Timonen 1982, 149–52).

What force drew Sibelius and his artistic contemporaries to Porvoo to seek out this unlettered singer of Karelian songs? Why was she an object of such great interest? What was so important about her having come from Karelia? Nearly half a century after the visit to Paraske, Yrjö Hirn looked back at the time and coined the term "Karelianism" to characterize the intellectual current that had moved many in the artistic community to seek their inspiration both from the *Kalevala* and from Paraske's home region, Karelia (1939, 203).

Hirn's term has gained such widespread acceptance in Finland that cultural historians writing for foreigners use it on occasion without bothering to explain its meaning. For example, in a fact sheet published by the Finnish Ministry for Foreign Affairs and designed to acquaint foreigners with the development of Finnish literature, Pertti Lassila writes: "In [the poet Eino] Leino's work neo-Romanticism developed into a national form stimulated by the *Kalevala*, the mythical past of the Finnish people and Karelianism" (1985, 2). Without the necessary background, such a statement will be lost on most non-Finns. To understand the nature of Karelianism, the forces that brought it into play, its connection to the *Kalevala*, the contribution of both to the life and work of Jean Sibelius, and his contributions to them, we must visit, however briefly, certain key events in Finnish history.

By the close of the first millennium of the Christian era, the people we now know as Finns inhabited three distinct and independent tribal, or cultural, regions—Finland Proper in the southwest, Häme in the central part of the country, and Karelia in the east. From these areas, separated at first by great distances, settlement would eventually spread to the rest of Finland. Though the people of these regions had achieved relatively high stages of cultural development, and though they spoke dialects of the same language, they had not coalesced into any sort of unified federation and were thus ill prepared to protect their independence against foreign forces moving into their land from the west and the east.

From the west, in the wake of international trade, came the Swedes and the Roman Catholic Church; from the east came the Russians and the Orthodox church. The conflict that would develop between these two powers for the control of Finland would last for centuries; but by the end of the 1200s, Finland Proper and Häme had fallen under Swedish jurisdiction and the conflict had developed into a struggle over control of the remaining area, Karelia. The battle ended, at least temporarily, in 1323 at the Peace of Pähkinäsaari, when the first of several borders separating Finland from Russia was formally drawn. The border ran from a point near the eastern end of the Gulf of Finland to another point near the northern end of the Gulf of Bothnia. For our purposes, the most important consequence of this border drawing is that it split Karelia in two—the western half, with Finland Proper and Häme, falling under Swedish control and the influence of Western culture, the eastern half falling to Russia (then Novgorod) and Eastern influences.

During the next two centuries, Finland was drawn inexorably into Sweden's political, administrative, and ecclesiastical power structure but managed to maintain a degree of cultural autonomy. As the kingdom of Sweden-Finland moved toward the modern era, that autonomy was quickly eroded. In 1523, the adroit young rebel, Gustavus Vasa, established himself as head of a hereditary monarchy and centralized administrative power in Stockholm. In 1527 he issued an edict breaking the power of the Roman Catholic Church and bringing the Reformation to the realm. Both actions would have far-reaching consequences for Finland. Two in particular concern us.

First, according to Reformation doctrine, one could comprehend the saving power of the gospel only from the direct word of God as revealed in the scriptures. To comprehend that work, of course, one had to have access to it. Thus in the mid-1550s Bishop Mikael Agricola reduced spoken Finnish to letters and, in the ensuing years, began working toward a translation of the Bible. In addition, he and his fellow clergymen began composing the country's first Finnish language religious poetry. The folksongs surviving from Finland's independent and pre-Christian era were at that time still known widely throughout the land and could have provided native models for this developing body of poetry. But these songs were undercut by the Lutheran clergy, who identified the songs with paganism, argued that they had been spawned by Lucifer for the corruption of the people, and set out to replace them with a new poetry based on foreign models (Finno 1583). As literary historian Viljo Tarkiainen has noted, these clerics, with their stilted verses, ignored the rhythms of native poetry and "trampled folksong and its centuries' long traditions to the ground and attempted to place the cultivation of literature and especially of poetic language and form on a completely different foundation, mimicking modern Germanic poetic patterns. . . . Thus began the age of religious literature and the time of foreign imitation which continued essentially the same throughout the period of Swedish rule" (1922, 14).

Second, with the Reformation emphasis on using vernacular languages, Finnish could have replaced Latin as the national tongue had the Finns been an independent nation. But as members of the Swedish realm, they had to yield ground on almost all but religious fronts. Throughout the Middle Ages, many state and judicial affairs in Finland had been conducted orally in Finnish. With the shift to centralized government, written documents replaced oral communications, and mastery of Swedish became essential for anyone seeking public office. From the local parish to the capital city, affairs of state, business, and education were conducted in Swedish, with the result that Finns seeking social or economic advancement had to abandon their native tongue and learn Swedish. In addition, Finns traveled to Sweden and Swedes traveled to Finland to fill administrative posts and in the process linked Finland still more closely to the mother country. By the end of the seventeenth century the political ideal had become "*una religio, una lingua, una lex, lidem mores*" (Jutikkala 1961, 122). By the end of the following century the unlettered common people and public functionaries could no longer understand each other. A Finnish peasant seeking justice in a court of law had to listen to his case argued in a language he did not comprehend.

Against this backdrop of Swedification of Finnish culture and the suppression of native artistic forms, the first stirrings of a national consciousness began to appear. From the mid-1660s on, a small but growing group of academics began to demonstrate that Finns were not just Swedes living on the eastern shores of the Gulf of Bothnia but were a *separate* people with their own distinctive cultural traits. Their efforts culminated in the second half of the eighteenth century in the works of Henrik Gabriel Porthan, who cast the light of his scholarship on the Finnish language, on Finnish history, and on the once-hated folksongs. These scholars, however, were a distinct minority. In the country at large, the upper and lower classes were divided not only by wealth and position but by language and culture as well. The lower classes spoke the language and followed the traditions of their forebears; the upper classes spoke the language and subscribed to the customs of mother Sweden. As a result, almost two different nations lived in Finland, separated from each other, as historian Eirik Hornborg has noted, "in a way that today is difficult to comprehend" (1963, 185).

Porthan died in 1804. In 1808 Czar Alexander I struck an agreement with Napoleon and then ordered his troops across the Finnish border. A year later, 1809, at the Diet of Porvoo, Finland's six hundred-year ties with Sweden were forever severed and the country became a Russian grand duchy. Both sides of a divided Finland now faced a foreign master.

In some ways, Finland's new status put the country into a more favorable position. Whereas Finland had been primarily a Swedish province among other Swedish provinces, now, as an "autonomous" grand duchy, the country had been elevated, as the czar himself proclaimed, to "membership in the family of nations," with its own constitution, carried over from the period of Swedish rule, and its own Diet empowered to act in all ways not reserved to the czar (Jutikkala 1961, 187).

But a group of farsighted Finns, mostly idealistic young scholars at the University of Turku, realized that what the czar had given the czar could take away and that union with Russia, even as a grand duchy, could eventually lead to Finland's absorption into that giant country. They realized also that Finland, lacking the binding ties of a common language, a common history, and a common artistic tradition, was ill prepared to face the Russification of their country that loomed ahead. The only way to resist was to unite their fragmented country into a Finnish Finland. Thus the rallying cry of the Turku Romantics became: "We are not Swedes; we cannot become Russians; let us therefore be Finns" (see Castrén 1951, 160–61).

But what did it mean to be a Finn? How was this country whose native culture had been so compromised by centuries of Swedish rule ever to find its true self? The answer lay in continuing the work already begun by Porthan; and it lay in putting into practice the romantic nationalistic philosophy of Johann Gottfried Herder then making its way to Finland (see Wilson 1973b). According to Herder, a people, to survive as a nation, must avoid all foreign imitation and develop its language usage, its literature, and its history on its own cultural foundation. In these, argued Herder, a nation could discover its national soul, or spirit; only by being true to this spirit could a nation endure. Finally, he argued that when the continuity of a nation's cultural development had been interrupted, as it had in Herder's Germany and as it certainly had in Finland, the only salvation lay in collecting from the common people the folksongs and traditions surviving from the time before the break. From these the collectors could put the nation once again in touch with its true national spirit and thus make possible its future development on its own cultural foundations. Herder's call to arms to his own German countrymen could have served equally well for Finns:

> The voice of your fathers has faded and lies silent in the dust. Nation of heroic customs, of noble virtues and language, you have no impressions of yours out from the past? . . . Lend a hand then, my brothers, and show our nation what it is and is not, how it thought and felt or how it thinks and feels. (1967–1968, 9: 530–31)

For the Finns, returning to the voices of their fathers meant discovering in their folksongs that heroic pre-Christian age when Finns had walked as free men and women on free Finnish soil. Soon sentiments similar to Herder's began echoing through the writings of the Turku Romantics. One of them, studying for a year in Uppsala, wrote home: "No honest Finn can love this thankless, limp, enfeebled, poor Sweden . . . boasting of the heroic deeds of its forefathers. . . . Lord God, how wonderful it would be . . . if we could hope by reawakening the spirit of Porthan to ignite an interest in our history and national language. . . . We are another nation, and our forefathers were as hairy-chested as the Goths ever were" (Heikinheimo 1933, 331). The appeal to awaken the spirit of Porthan was, of course, an appeal to return to folk poetry, or folksong. Another wrote that "antiquities live in the people's chronicles and in their artistic creations, in which they survive from times immemorial"; thus every nation that wished to be true to itself "must return to the furthest roots of all its native power, strength, and energy, to the pure spring of native poetry. Everything must be built on a native foundation" (Arwidsson 1909, 138). And still another, in what would prove to be a prophetic statement, wrote that if Finns would collect their folksongs and work them into a unified whole, "a new Homer, Ossian, or Nibelungenlied" might be the result, and, "exalted, the Finnish nationality, in the luster and glory of its own uniqueness and adorned with the awareness of its own development, would arouse the admiration of the present and of the future." Then, in words that might have been written by Herder, he declared: "Just as an independent nation cannot exist without a fatherland, no fatherland can exist without poetry. For what is poetry except the crystal in which nationality mirrors itself, the spring from which the nation's original feeling arises to the surface" (Heikinheimo 1933, 307–8).

The Turku Romantics stirred national sentiments, later called "Fennomania," that would grow ever stronger throughout the century. Their aims were to unite their divided country, to awaken national pride by exalting Finland's heroic past, to persuade their Swedish-speaking countrymen to abandon their own language and learn Finnish, and to develop artistic traditions that rested on a native—that is, Finnish—foundation. Though some of them began to collect folklore and though their impassioned pleas caught the nervous attention of public officials, the Turku Romantics actually achieved very few of their goals. Many of them, having come from the Swedish-speaking educated classes, could not themselves manage the language they wished to make their own. More important, the evidence supporting their grand claims was so scanty that many of their educated countrymen doubted seriously that Finnish could become the language of sophisticated society or that the Finnish people were capable of developing praiseworthy artistic traditions. Said one of these critics: "Geese all speak the same tongue, it is true, but they do not form a nation. . . . Finnish, as a language, cannot spawn anything but ABC-books" (Jutikkala 1961, 204–5). Another critic wrote, speaking of painting but expressing a typical view of all the arts: "Finland is too cold, too poor, and, let us say without timidity, too uncivilized for the magnificent and colorful flowers, those southern sun maidens, of pictorial art to gain an enduring footing in its snow-covered granite soil" (Valkonen 1989, 7).

The next generation of scholar-patriots set out to provide the necessary evidence. Chief among them was Elias Lönnrot, who proclaimed little but accomplished much and who would carry to completion the work his predecessors had only dreamed of. Like his compatriots, Lönnrot had been educated in the Swedish-language school system, but he had been raised in a Finnish-speaking home and therefore knew the language. He began collecting Finnish folklore during his student days and published small collections of folksongs. After completing medical studies, he moved in January 1833 to the remote inland city Kajaani as a district doctor. From there he trekked countless miles through the sparsely populated country north and east of Kajaani and across the nearby Russian border in Karelia, collecting from these backwoods areas a large store of epic songs no longer to be found in southwestern Finland. These he worked over and over until he had welded them into that unified whole predicted earlier. On February 28, 1835, he mailed the completed work, the *Kalevala*, to Helsinki for publication. Following more collecting trips by himself and others, he published an expanded and revised edition in 1849.

Lönnrot never claimed to have restored the fragmented parts of an earlier epic whole existing in ancient Finland, though he did believe the *Kalevala* reflected the historical unity imposed upon the songs by the events they described. Later research has shown that, though most of the lines in the *Kalevala* come from authentic folksongs, Lönnrot, following the practice of his time, arranged and rearranged them to the extent that the final result would have to be called at least as much the literary creation of Elias Lönnrot as it would the creation of the folk.

No such thoughts were harbored by the Finns at the time of the epic's publication. Here at last was the proof that Finland had a noble and independent past, that ancient *Kalevala* heroes—Väinämöinen, Ilmarinen, and Lemminkäinen—had walked Finnish ground and performed deeds of renown for the fatherland. Here was the proof that the long-disparaged Finnish language could produce works of high literary merit. Here, in short, was the historical warrant for Finland's existence as a nation, the model after which Finland should build its future.

The appearance of the *Kalevala* had an almost magical effect on the Finns. That their downtrodden little nation on the fringes of the civilized world could produce a work comparable to the world's greatest epics became an enduring cause for great pride. "With one stroke," as Yrjö Nurmio has pointed out, the *Kalevala* swept away much of the suspicion with which Finnish had been regarded (1947, 109). The epic provided Finnish nationalists, the Fennomen, all the evidence they needed to resume the course charted by the Turku Romantics before them. In March 1836 J. G. Linsén, chair of the Finnish Literature Society, declared that on the basis of the *Kalevala* the Finnish nation could now say: "I too have a history" (1961, 11). The popular poet Zachris Topelius, Jr. stated: "One people! One land! One tongue! One song and wisdom! From lake to lake, from breast to breast fly the words: From their own fountainheads run Finland's rivers; from its own fountainheads may . . . [Finland's] future run" (Haavio 1949, 250). And the poet Johan Ludvig Runeberg, whose patriotic poetry would match Lönnrot's efforts in raising the national consciousness, declared the *Kalevala* to be nearly the match of the Greek epics and stated that it excelled even them "in the sublimity of its descriptions of nature" and "in its simple beauty" (1835). When the famous German philologist and folktale scholar Jacob Grimm lectured on and praised the *Kalevala*, the Finns, who have always sought the praise of foreigners, found further justification for their rising self-esteem (Wilson 1976a, 43).

The gift Elias Lönnrot had given his people in the *Kalevala* would have far reaching consequences. Motivated by a new spirit of patriotism engendered by the *Kalevala*, many Finnish intellectuals formed societies which bound their members to speak Finnish, and some newly married couples resolved to adopt Finnish as the language of their homes. But official steps would have to be taken before Finnish could ascend to its deserved place as the national language. In 1863 Lönnrot's friend, the powerful political leader Johan Vilhelm Snellman, was able to persuade the czar to sign a language edict granting the Finnish language equal status with Swedish in bureaus and courts of justice when they had direct dealings with the people. In 1883 and 1887 the edict was strengthened to require public officials to speak the language of the districts to which they were assigned. In 1836, Gabriel Linsén had demanded schools for the people who had created the *Kalevala*. At that time, aside from church catechismal schools, there were none. In 1866 a state-supported primary school system was established, and in 1873 a teachers' training school began preparing Finnish language teachers. Shortly after the turn of the century 3,678 primary schools were in operation. Progress in secondary schools was slower, but by the turn of the century Finnish-speaking secondary schools outnumbered Swedish-speaking schools, and the number would continue to grow. With the increased literacy brought about by these schools, a newspaper-reading public developed rapidly. In 1835, the year the *Kalevala* was published, there was only one Finnish-language newspaper in the country. In 1850 there were four, in 1885 thirty-one, and in 1910 eighty-six (Wilson 1976a, 45–48).

To claim that all these advances were a direct result of the publication of the national epic would be to push the issue too far—other forces were at play in the country. But considering the abysmal state of affairs during the first third of the century, these improvements are remarkable. Without the change of spirit brought about by the *Kalevala* and the subsequent rising national esteem, this progress would scarcely have been possible. As folklore scholar Jouko Hautala has pointed out, the *Kalevala* came to the Finnish people "like a gift from heaven," bringing them the most prized of literary possessions—an ancient national epic:

> [It] brought into view a legendary, heroic, splendid past about which there had been no previous knowledge; it showed how a language considered poor and barren had through centuries of cultivation been developed into a dazzling, rich medium for high poetic expression; it offered faith and trust more sorely needed than we can today even imagine. (1954, 115–16)

By the last decades of the nineteenth century then, the hopes of the Turku Romantics for the establishment of a Finnish-language Finland, once hailed as wild-eyed dreaming, had largely been fulfilled. The other dream of the Turku Romantics—for a distinctively Finnish artistic culture—was soon also to be realized.

At the same time the above developments were taking place, and largely as a consequence of them, major advances in the arts were also occurring. The Finnish Literature Society had been founded four years before the publication of the *Kalevala* and had funded some of Lönnrot's collecting efforts. In the following years, other organizations came into being to promote the development of Finnish arts: the Finnish Arts Association in 1846, the Artists Society in 1864, a Finnish opera company in 1871, the Finnish Theatre in 1872, the Finnish Society of Crafts and Design in 1875, the Friends of Finnish Handicrafts in 1879, and both the Helsinki Music Institute, where Sibelius studied, and the Helsinki Philharmonic Orchestra, which promoted his music, in 1882.

M. A. Castrén, the Finno-Ugrian scholar who translated the *Kalevala* into Swedish in 1841 and served as the first professor of Finnish at Helsinki University, once wrote:

> The *Kalevala* . . . which . . . always brings to mind the distant antiquity in which we encounter the original peculiarity of the national

> character of the Finns together with their most ancient religious concepts must be recognized in all respects as a remarkable phenomenon. . . . If I should wish to predict for Finland a future time where her sons, inspired by true patriotism [and] renouncing foreign culture, confess only that to be right which has developed from their own spiritual life and work, I should seek a foundation for these hopes in the *Kalevala.* (Haavio 1949, 241)

In the 1870s and early 1880s, with many of the goals of the Fennomen achieved and with the chill winds of evolutionary and positivistic science having blown in from England, Finland's artistic sons and daughters actually turned away from the *Kalevala* and the heroic past for a season and turned their attention to realistic and naturalistic depictions of the world around them. Two circumstances took them back to their national epic—a neo-Romantic wave in the arts that moved across Europe into Finland and focused attention once again on the past and the beginning of a long-feared attempt to wipe out Finnish rights and assimilate Finland into Russia.

Annoyed by the success of Finnish nationalists and moved to action by his own nationalistic Pan-Slavists, the czar took steps, beginning in 1890, to eliminate Finland's privileged position as an autonomous grand duchy and to incorporate Finland into the mother country. Attempts were made to unify postal, customs, and monetary systems; Finns were conscripted into the imperial army; the Finnish Diet lost the authority to make laws; the judicial system was all but dismantled; and the governor general demanded that Russian be made the administrative language of Finland and that Russian be taught in the schools.

Had such an attempt occurred at the beginning of the century, it would in all likelihood have been carried out without difficulty. But, as historian Eino Jutikkala points out, "the Finland confronting the [current] crisis was incomparably more resistant to alien pressure than she had been during the early part of the period of autonomy. Where before there had been slumbering masses of subjects, there was now a true nation, determined to defend its rights" (1961, 227). The work of the nationalists had not been in vain.

In defense of their rights, the Finns turned once again to the *Kalevala*—to justify their historical right to exist as a nation and to bolster their courage to face present difficulties. The now-thriving newspaper industry took the message to the people, arguing again and again that a nation that had created the *Kalevala* could not perish. "When we think of the great value of the *Kalevala*," wrote one editorialist, "then our breasts swell with pride; and consequently we believe that a nation which was able in early times to create such a work of genius cannot succumb as it fights on behalf of its culture, its language, and its being" (Kansalliseepoksista 1910). In 1907 the poet Eino Leino penned an editorial that typifies the spirit of the entire period:

> The main thing is that the national spirit which appears in it [the *Kalevala*] is the spirit of a free nation and that in reading it we feel ourselves to be free, proud, and independent.... From it there steps before us a nation which is not poor or sick, a nation which enjoys its existence, which sings from the fullness of its heart and whose heart is sensitive, delicate and open to all the beauty in the world. It is no slave nation ... nor is it an upstart nation, but rather a nation which has its own customs, traditions, gods and concepts of life. It is *old Finland*.... The Finnish tongue in the *Kalevala* sounds freely, brightly, and victoriously. It gives a picture of a nation which is sovereign. (Haavio 1949, 264)

But it was on the artistic front that the defense of this sovereign nation depicted in the *Kalevala* primarily took place, for it was believed that the best way to win the sympathy of foreign lands and to resist Russian oppression was to maintain a high level of artistic achievement. Nearly the entire artistic community joined together in an unprecedented manner in the service of a common cause. As Timo Martin and Douglas Sivén note, "all cultural work was understood to be a struggle on behalf of Finnishness, and artists considered themselves the people's interpreters whose task it was to demonstrate Finland's fitness as an independent nation" (1984, 101). They ushered in, in the process, what many have called the golden age of Finnish art and what may have been the golden age of the Finnish spirit as well. According to Aimo Reitala, "the most significant results came about . . . when neo-Romanticism was united with national ideology. This line of development originated from the *Kalevala*. From the national epos came the essential catalyst, and, at the same time, the dream was fulfilled on whose behalf the Fennomen had long struggled" (1987, 18). The earlier nationalists had created a Finnish language culture; the creative geniuses of this era—the writers, poets, painters, architects, musicians—would create a Finnish artistic culture that would generate on a large scale a national self-esteem never before experienced. It would be difficult to overestimate, argues Reitala, the importance of this artistic culture "in creating the conditions necessary for independence" (1987, 11).

As we turn to the work of Sibelius and his artistic compatriots, we must do so against the long sweep of Finnish history sketched above. Theirs was not an idle interest in or a passing fancy with the *Kalevala*. They were engaged in a struggle for their national survival. The *Kalevala* was the book that had brought to life ancient, independent Finland and would now provide historical justification for their nation's continued existence as well as models on which to pattern their own behavior. It was the book whose songs had kept alive memories of those former days of glory through centuries of foreign rule and through attempts to erase the name Finland from the map. It was the book that had elevated the Finnish language to a language of culture and had prepared the way for Finland's entry into the family of civilized nations. And it was the book, in this time of great need, whose heroes and heroines could be brought to life once again in the paintings, musical works, and literary compositions of contemporary Finnish artists.

Sibelius, one of the most important of these artists, was no pulpit-pounding nationalist. Indeed, his biographers have often played down nationalistic impulses in his work. But even had he wished to do so, he could scarcely have escaped the patriotic sentiments to which he had been exposed much of his life.

That exposure began during Sibelius's school days in the city of his birth, Hämeenlinna. Born into a Swedish-speaking family, he began his education in a Swedish-language school but then, at the age of eight, was placed in one of the newly founded Finnish-language elementary schools. He later attended one of the best Finnish-language secondary schools in the country, a "showpiece" of the Fennomen (Tawaststjerna 1976, 1: 17). There he studied under Arvid Genetz, an ardent student of Finnish culture under whose tutelage Sibelius, according to his own account, became attached to the *Kalevala.* "In my home and its neighborhood," said Sibelius in an interview with A. O. Väisänen, "I heard only Swedish, but Finnish folklore had a remarkable infectious strength. And the Kullervo legend first captured my imagination" (1921, 77).

During his musical studies in Helsinki from 1885 to 1889, Sibelius became acquainted with the aristocratic Järnefelt family, vigorous defenders of the Finnish language. A good friend of the three artistic Järnefelt sons and greatly taken by their sister Aino, whom he would later marry, Sibelius spent much time at the Järnefelt home, which had become a center for discussions of nationalist cultural and political issues and where Sibelius was drawn more firmly into the Finnish camp.

Sibelius continued his studies in Berlin from 1889 to 1890. While there he attended a performance of his countryman Robert Kajanus's *Aino* Symphony and became aware, as he later told Karl Ekman, "of the wonderful opportunities the *Kalevala* offered for musical expression" (1936, 88). Sibelius returned to Finland in the summer of 1890, became engaged to Aino Järnefelt, and then left for an additional year's study in Vienna. There he began work on the *Kullervo* Symphony, whose principal character had fascinated him during his secondary school years. His letters to Aino during that period reveal an increasing interest in everything Finnish. He encouraged her to write to him in Finnish and said: "It is a good thing that you love the language, and things Finnish; I can understand you so well." Later he wrote: "I am reading my *Kalevala* diligently, and I feel I already understand Finnish so much better. . . . *Kalevala* seems a quite modern work to me. It reads like pure music, theme and variation" (Lampila 1985, 5).

In turning to the *Kalevala* for inspiration, Sibelius was not simply satisfying a personal fancy but was acting in full harmony with the spirit of the times. The kind of growing attachment Sibelius was feeling for the epic was, according to an 1890 newspaper editorial, the sentiment all Finns should be feeling. "So dear is this work to us," stated the article, "that it should be on every bookshelf" because "our nation's ancient songs, compiled in this work, will forever awaken nobleness and patriotism in the rising generation, . . . will show that our little Finnish nation is a separate independent nation among many others, a nation which has its own task in the great work field of humanity" (Silmäys Kalevalaamme 1910). Years later Eino Leino, summing up the feeling that had developed at this time, argued that honoring the *Kalevala* "is to us Finns the same as honoring one's own deepest being" and that for a Finn to ridicule the *Kalevala* would be akin to sinning "against the Holy Ghost" (1917, 1–2).

Sibelius would never have used such flamboyant language; but neither was he about to sin against the Holy Ghost. On his return from Vienna in 1891, he became closely associated with and embraced the ideals of the Young Finland circle, a group of nationalistic artists, musicians, poets, writers, and political activists who were associated with the newspaper *Päivälehti* (founded in 1889), who were intensely engaged in the development of Finnish arts as a hedge against Russian tyranny, and who, as Ekman notes, "had made up their minds to draw inspiration for their art from the source of Finnish nationalistic enthusiasm" (1936, 108). That source was often the *Kalevala.* From the performance of his first major work, the *Kullervo* Symphony, in 1892, to the completion of his last major effort, *Tapiola,* in 1926, Sibelius, motivated in part by the ideals of his Young Finland compatriots and by his own love for and pride in his country, returned to the *Kalevala* again and again for subject matter for many of his compositions: *The Boat Journey; Hail, O Moon; Lemminkäinen Suite* (including *Swan of Tuonela* and *Lemminkäinen's Return*); *Origin of Fire; Kyllikki; Pohjola's Daughter; Luonnotar; Song of Väinö.*

Very few of Sibelius's works were overtly nationalistic. With the exception of *Finlandia,* the *Karelia Suite,* and perhaps the final movement of the *Second Symphony,* his works do not consciously stir patriotic feelings. Indeed, aside from the titles, listeners may find little direct connection between the compositions and the epic on which they are presumably based.

But for many the titles may have been enough. As least as important as the contribution of national sentiment to Sibelius's work was the contribution of his work to the development of that sentiment. The references in the titles to events and characters from the *Kalevala* would have caused Finns to *perceive* the compositions as purely Finnish in character, and that perception would have raised their national consciousness. Indeed, the enthusiastic response of the packed house to the premiere of the *Kullervo* Symphony may have resulted as much from pride in a native son's having given musical form to the national epic as from the artistic merit of the work itself. Many years later, in a reader used in the primary schools, Helmi Krohn unwittingly illustrated that very point: "Jean Sibelius is the creator of Finnish national music, for no one has been able as has he to interpret with musical compositions the Finnish people's deepest spiritual life. . . . He more than anyone else has made Finland's name known abroad and with his work has also shown the world that in our barren land an original and powerful art can blossom" (1931, 38). It is interesting to note that for Krohn, and surely for many Finns, Sibelius was important for the same reason the *Kalevala* was often deemed important: both had made Finland's name known abroad. It seems hardly surprising, then, that in 1935, during the centennial celebration of the publication of the national epic, the prestigious *Kalevala* Society would name Sibelius its first honorary member.

Almost the entire artistic community worked hard to bring Finnish art to full bloom, and, as noted, many of its leading figures attempted to do so by focusing attention on the national epic. As a result of their efforts, their countrymen soon encountered the *Kalevala* at every turn. They read about it in the press; they viewed it in the paintings of Akseli Gallen-Kallela; they witnessed it in the *Jugendstil* architecture of Eliel Saarinen; they met it in the *Whitsun* poems of Eino Leino; and, of course, they heard it sounding clearly in the music of Jean Sibelius. They even recognized it in names chosen with increasing frequency to christen their children—"Aino," "Väinö," "Ilmari," "Kalevi," "Kyllikki"—or bestow on their places of business—"Sampo," "Pohjola." Before 1890, Finnish scholars had constructed a picture of Finland's ancient and independent past based on Lönnrot's *Kalevala*. Now the general public developed a picture of that past based primarily on artistic interpretations of the epic. And partly as a result of these creations, what had in reality never really existed would come finally into being—a Finnish Finland.

We have come a long way in our attempt to understand the significance of Sibelius's visit to Larin Paraske. As an authentic singer of songs similar to those from which Elias Lönnrot had compiled the *Kalevala*, Paraske would clearly have caught the attention and won the admiration of Finnish artists and it would have made good sense for Sibelius, working on his first *Kalevala* composition, to have visited her and listened to her sing. But the importance of Paraske's having come from Karelia remains unexplained.

When Lönnrot published his 1835 edition of the *Kalevala*, he subtitled the work *Old Karelian Poems from the Ancient Times of the Finnish People*. The title makes clear two important points: first, that Lönnrot had, as he stated in his introduction to the epic, collected many of the songs from the remote regions of "Finnish and Russian Karelia" (1993, 39), where a thriving singing tradition still existed especially on the more primitive Russian side of the border, and, second, that the songs would throw light on Finland's ancient past. In other words, the road to that past led through Karelia to the *Kalevala* and from there to the heroic cultural foundation on which Finland wished to reconstitute itself. Though scholars would argue over the exact place of origin of the *Kalevala* songs, by the end of the century, the *Kalevala*/Karelia connection would become an article of faith moving artists in the Young Finland movement to action.

In 1835, however, most Finns knew little, if anything at all, about the *Kalevala* song country. Lönnrot's subtitle to the epic, his explanations in the introduction, and especially his Karelian travel narratives published in the popular press began to raise Karelian consciousness throughout the country. Other actions would soon follow. A new generation of folklorists, awakened by Lönnrot to the national importance of the work, tramped the Karelian backwoods once again, collecting still more songs. They were followed by linguists, ethnographers, and naturalists whose studies placed understanding of the area on a more solid footing and whose travel narratives intensified public interest.

One of the most important of these travel accounts was A.V. Ervasti's popular *Muistelmia matkalta Venäjän Karjalassa kesällä 1879* (Recollections from a Trip in Russian Karelia during the Summer of 1879). In 1873 Ervasti had written a colleague: "The same blood flows in their [the Karelians'] veins as in ours; we are one people, given birth by one mother. What's more, we citizens of the grand duchy owe them an eternal debt of gratitude; through them the Finnish people's—that is, mainly our—reputation has spread throughout the world, for the *Kalevala* is their deed" (Sihvo 1973, 190). In his *Recollections* Ervasti came back to this same theme, stressing repeatedly that the Karelians east of the border were Finns, not Russians. "We are speaking here," he insisted, "only of Finns and of Finnish lands" (1880, 141).

Under the persisting Herderian doctrine that national boundaries should coincide with cultural and linguistic boundaries, under the newly arrived neo-Romantic emphasis on the past, and driven by the need to establish a national cultural identity as a protection against Russian assimilation attempts, the Ervasti-style linking of Finland and the *Kalevala* to Karelia received its fullest artistic expression in the decades immediately preceding and following the turn of the century, in the works described above. When he coined the term "Karelianism" to describe this period, Yrjö Hirn argued that *Kalevala* pursuits and Karelian pursuits had become inseparable, that they were, indeed, the same thing. "Lönnrot and his followers," said Hirn, "had, after all, collected the richest harvest of old heroic poems from Karelia. It was natural, therefore, to conclude . . . that the cradle of the Finnish national poetic work was to be found in Karelia and that Karelia had been the stage for the events sung about in the *Kalevala*" (1939, 203).

If, as it was believed, the world brought to life by the *Kalevala* was still to be found in Karelia and if it were true that in order to be successful, Finnish artists would have to situate their depictions of the epic in that world, then learning as much about Karelia as possible would become vitally important. To know and understand the *Kalevala*, one had first to know and understand Karelia, the land of its birth. Such a need would explain Sibelius's trip to Porvoo to hear Larin Paraske sing her *Karelian* songs. More important, it would explain why in the following years Karelia would become almost a Finnish holy land, the center of Finnish nationality, to which Finnish artists would make sacred pilgrimages.

In 1890 the *Päivälehti* ran a stirring editorial:

> What success might that artistic work enjoy whose material was taken from the place where the *Kalevala* has been sung and where lives that people who to the present day have preserved the Karelian

> "character" which elsewhere has been lost or corrupted! How many fine nuances in our old poetry might be cleared up if an artist's keen eye would place before us the environment in which the singers have lived and from which they surely have received strong influences themselves! To be sure, in this matter ethnography has been a great aid to our imaginations. But work tools, dresses and ornaments are dead things and have negligible influence. We need flesh and bones, light and shadows; we long to see so called moods of nature, fully living people. In a word: Karelia's artistic side is what we would like to experience. (Valkonen 1989, 52–53)

In response to this clarion call, members of the artistic community began trooping into Karelia to imbue themselves with the spirit of the *Kalevala*. The painter Akseli Gallen-Kallela, who has been credited with beginning the Karelianism movement, was already in Karelia, on his honeymoon, when the *Päivälehti* article appeared. In the summer of 1892 Sibelius followed Gallen-Kallela's example and, with a stipend from the Finnish Literature Society to collect folksongs, took his new bride to Karelia. Gallen-Kallela visited the region again that same year, as did the sculptor Emil Wikström, the artists Eero Järnefelt and Pekka Halonen, and the fiction writer Juhani Aho. In 1894 architects Yrjö Blomstedt and Viktor Sucksdorff made the trip; they were followed in 1896 by the poet Eino Leino. From 1892–1895 Into K. Inha traveled the Karelian paths Lönnrot had once walked and photographed the scenes and people that would appear in his popular *Kalevalan laulumailta* (From the *Kalevala* Song Lands) and would bring Karelia vividly alive for those not able to visit the place (Inha 1911). In 1921, Sibelius's brother-in-law, Eero Järnefelt, looked back at this time and characterized the nationalistic fervor that dominated the period:

> During that time of great enthusiasm we young artists rushed like explorers . . . to seek subject matter for our paintings from our own people and landscapes; and like youth always, we believed we had found the Finnish nation and its landscapes, the *Kalevala* and Kanteletar [Lönnrot's collection of lyric songs] completely anew. They were for us like an untouched wilderness mysteriously lighted. (1921, 94–95)

Also in 1921, in somewhat less dramatic tones than those of his brother-in-law, Sibelius recalled his Karelian travels:

> In the summer [of 1892] I left with my wife for Karelia. The trip took us to Korpiselkä and Ilomantsi. I met Petri Shemeikka [a well-known folk singer]. When he stepped toward me from the dim corner of the cottage, he seemed magnificent. He sang too. I also

> heard the playing of the kantele. . . . A great love overpowered me during that trip and is still strong in me. (Väisänen 1921, 77)

To what extent Sibelius's experiences in Karelia directly influenced his musical compositions is difficult to say. In 1893 he composed the *Karelia Suite*, incidental music accompanying a series of historical tableaux based on Karelia's past, as part of an effort to strengthen cultural ties between Karelia and Finland. According to Sibelius's biographer Erik Tawaststjerna, this was thought to be "the most effective way of meeting Russian cultural penetration, and as such it clearly engaged Sibelius's sympathies" (1976, 2: 145). In 1909 he made a second trip to Karelia, and the powerful nature scenes he encountered at Lake Pielinen would be imprinted on his *Fourth Symphony* (ibid., 2: 130–32). But it was surely that "great love," which overpowered him on his first trip to Karelia, that on numerous occasions led Sibelius back to the national epic in search of themes and narrative cores that he would then develop according to his own lights.

In the eyes of the general public, the compositions that resulted, along with the creations of Sibelius's artistic kinsmen, not only established the strong Finnish identity necessary to withstand Russian pressure; they also situated that identity in Karelia where, far from corrupting foreign influences, illiterate singers had preserved the testament of Finland's past glory.

The cultural awakening that occurred following Lönnrot's publication of the *Kalevala* had primarily reached the intelligentsia who, once awakened, had laid the foundation for future national development. The second cultural awakening that occurred at the turn of the century, building on that earlier foundation but brought now to full power by the golden age of Finnish art, with its strong emphasis on the *Kalevala* and Karelia, reached most of the nation. And this nation, having now found itself, would survive Russian oppression and in 1917, despite internal social upheaval, declare itself independent.

In the years following independence, Karelianism became still more political. In 1920, at the Peace of Tartu, Finland and Russia agreed to maintain their existing border. This meant that the part of Karelia assigned to Russia centuries ago by the Treaty of Pähkinäsaari, the part where Lönnrot had reaped his richest harvest of epic songs, would remain in Russian hands. During the 1920s and 1930s Karelianism would become a movement intended to wrest East Karelia from Russian control and join it to Finland in a Greater Finland united by blood, language, and cultural traditions. But that is another story.

In a rousing speech given on *Kalevala* Day (the annual celebration of the publication of the epic) in 1922, E. N. Setälä, a prominent cultural and political leader in newly independent Finland, looked toward Greater Finland, but his words can serve also as a summary of the period we have just reviewed:

> How could anyone who works in the fields of Finnish science and art, or who works in politics for the preservation and strengthening of Finnish independence and freedom, be cool towards Karelia,

> which has given such a thrust to Finnish cultural independence and freedom that without it the Finnish nation would not be the nation of culture and most certainly would not be the independent nation it now is. . . . "Kalevala Day" is Karelia Day. Let us all rise from our places, let us devote a moment of silence to the memories which take us back centuries and millenniums to the Finnish nation's ancient life; let us devote a moment of quiet thought to that tribe which has given so much to Finland. . . . Glory to the *Kalevala*! Glory to Karelia! (1923, 11–12)

As Setälä's words suggest, the Karelianism movement looked both backward and forward. It looked back through the *Kalevala* "to the Finnish nation's ancient life" to see what Finland had been in order to discover what Finland could become. In that endeavor, Jean Sibelius, who has become a Finnish national symbol as important as the national epic to which he gave musical voice, played a more important role than he himself may have ever realized.

Folklore, Nationalism, and the Challenge of the Future

Whether on Finnish nationalism or Mormon popular expressions, William A. "Bert" Wilson has moved as gracefully as any folklorist between the romantic and the critical motivational poles of folklore study. On the one hand, folklorists participate in a celebration of disempowered voices, marginalized peoples, and the everyday. On the other hand, folklorists engage in critiques of power, confronting hegemonic discourses and dominant representations. Bert challenges us to think about the role of folklore in the creation of power while also asking us to remain hopeful in the human condition as we celebrate diversity. If anything, Bert remains honest—honest in reporting the achievements and ironies in a group's folklore and honest with himself in appreciating and holding ambivalence for that same folklore. In this piece, which was a plenary address of a special conference on folksong sponsored by the Archives of Latvian Folklore, he makes bare both his honest suspicion and optimism in folklore.

There is an interesting tension presented in this paper between the danger in folklore's power to persuade and impose, and the promise of folklore to empower and liberate. In his work on Herder and Finnish nationalism, Bert implies that scholars must pay attention to the interplay of art and politics. What makes Herder's model of using the poetic "national soul" to cultivate sentiments of attachment and legitimacy of the nation so dangerous is more than simply how national identities can be pitted against each other. The danger lies in how people can be persuaded by folklore forms to participate in acts of domination and aggression, or minimally, persuaded to essentialize difference and imagine themselves in superior positions. As Bert reminds us, what makes this model even more dubious is that such nationalisms do not emanate out from the "people," but represent scholarly constructs of imagined pasts driven by ideological agendas in the present, imposed on "others" and the "people" themselves.

But Bert also sees promise in folklore, because it has proven to empower dependent and suppressed groups as they seek independence and because it may prove

---

This paper was delivered in a plenary session of the conference "Folksong: Text and Voice," sponsored by the Archives of Latvian Folklore at Riga, Latvia, September 24, 1994.

to liberate the "human spirit" and help us find a "common humanity" amidst our divisive national differences. This promise in folklore must be tempered with two cautions, however. First, both the oppressor and the oppressed, the dominant and the marginalized, can use folklore for their own purposes. Second, the empowering of one group too often leads to a new suppression of other groups within a nation (e.g. by gender, class, ethnicity, religion) and without (e.g. other territorial groups). Bert appreciates that national boundaries are always messy, crosscutting and blurring salient group formations, and that internal homogeneity within is a fiction. He proposes then that we can at once promote the multicultural and think beyond nationalism to a shared humanity.

I share in Bert's critical gaze and romantic optimism, but it is now time to rethink two contemporary implications. First, too much emphasis on the spurious, or constructed, nature of national identities may neglect how people share a history of making and reproducing images and forms that are experientially meaningful. To over-emphasize the fiction of identity formation may represent a new form of colonization, because it neglects how folklore serves many oppressed peoples as their cultural capital for resistance and it perpetuates domination by undercutting the oppressed's counter-rhetoric. Second, national identity formations can hardly maintain themselves with two seemingly contradictory contemporary forces: globalization and fragmentation. Globalization has created transnational and multinational identities while fragmentation has rekindled old divisions within nation-states or allowed new identities to form in new territorial and cultural spaces. This intersection of the global and the local often operates independent of old nationalisms. Understanding the "challenge of [this] future" will be a challenge to folklore scholarship in the early twenty-first century. This does not mean nationalism will no longer prove a powerful construct, but folklorists will need to waver between complex poles as Bert has done to illuminate the power of folklore in these global changes.

—Phillip McArthur

We mark this year the 250th anniversary of the birth of Johann Gottfried von Herder. I was first brought to a study of Herder because I was curious to know how the scattered groups of people living in Finland at the beginning of the nineteenth century, speaking separate dialects and feeling precious little kinship with each other, could have possibly coalesced by the end of the century into a people unified enough to resist terrific Russian assimilation pressures and two decades later actually become an independent nation. My quest for answers led me to certain key ideas of Herder that were making their way to Finland shortly after Finland became a Russian grand duchy in 1809 and that had direct applicability to circumstances prevailing at the time.

First, Herder taught that each nation is a distinct organic unit created by its own peculiar environmental and historical circumstances and different, therefore, from all other nations. The organic structures of these units were reflected in what Herder called national characters or national souls.

Second, Herder taught that a nation could not survive as a nation and could not contribute to the progress of humanity as a whole unless it remained true to its national character; it must cultivate its own native cultural and artistic traditions along lines laid down by past experience. "Each [nationality]," declared Herder, "carries within itself the standard of its own perfection which can in no way be compared with that of others." Again and again he declared that the most natural state was one people with one national character. Therefore, nothing seemed so unnatural to him as the "wild mixing of various breeds and nations under one scepter" (1967–1968, 14: 227; 13: 384). To introduce foreign elements into a unified organic nation, into the body politic, would, he believed, ultimately lead to the death of that nation.

Third, Herder taught that the cultural and historical pattern of a people—the national soul—is expressed best in its language and particularly in its folk poetry, the loftiest expression to which language could aspire. "Poetry," said Herder, "is the expression of the weaknesses and perfections of a nationality, a mirror of its sentiments, the expression of the highest to which it aspired." Folk poems he called "the archives of a nationality," "the imprints of the soul" of a nation, "the living voice of the nationalities." From them one could "learn the mode of thought of a nationality and its language of feeling" (1967–1968, 18: 137; 9: 532; 3: 29; 24: 266; 9: 530). Clearly, then, if one wanted to live in harmony with his own nation, to capture its spirit and make it his own, one must do so by absorbing its poetry and living in accordance with its spirit.

Finally, Herder taught that should a nation's continuity with its past be broken, as had been the case with Germany following the Middle Ages, and had certainly been the case of Finland during six hundred years of Swedish rule, the only hope for salvation lay in collecting from the peasant population the old poems surviving from the golden age of the past and then using them to restore to the nation its national soul and to develop its future national progress on a native foundation.

Motivated by these dogmas, a generation of young Finnish scholar-patriots, Elias Lönnrot chief among them, began trekking the Finnish hinterlands, collecting the folk poems which Lönnrot would in 1835 combine into the national epic, the *Kalevala*. The publication of the *Kalevala* would inspire two national awakenings—the first following the appearance of the epic, the second occurring at the end of the century, when Finnish artists, musicians, poets, and writers turned to the *Kalevala* for the inspiration necessary to create a truly national art. Both awakenings, combined with other forces, would lead eventually to Finnish independence in 1917.

Similar nationalistic movements, of course, developed elsewhere in Europe and later in Africa and Asia. Whenever dependent or suppressed peoples have sought in their folklore historical justification for their separatist policies, they have followed lines laid down by Herder (Wilson 1973b). Today, with the breakup of the former Soviet Union and with nations constituting or reconstituting themselves, the old dogmas are coming back into play.

As we turn our attention to these movements, it is essential to remember at least three things: First, the terms "national identity," or "ethnic identity," do not originally derive from the people nor are they the result of natural law. They are, rather, scholarly constructs, or, as folklorist Roger Abrahams has suggested, "powerful fictions" (1993, 5), created by the intelligentsia in order to move the people in directions the intelligentsia wish. Second, to move the people in these directions, the intelligentsia must teach them to recognize, value, and shape their lives according to these constructs. Third, the ends which proponents of national or ethnic identity serve are always ideologically motivated. Considering these circumstances, those engaged in national movements carry a heavy burden of acting in morally responsible and humane ways.

Some today consider all nationalistic movements bad. I do not hold that view. In 1835, the year the *Kalevala* was published, Finnish-speaking citizens, the bulk of the population, could not hear their own legal cases tried in court in their own language; social and educational opportunities and advancement were open only to those who spoke Swedish (there were no Finnish-language schools); and only one Finnish-language newspaper was being published. By the turn of the century, these conditions had been dramatically reversed. Finnish had been given equal status with Swedish, and public officials were required to speak the language of the districts to which they were assigned. Shortly after the turn of the century, 3,678 Finnish-language primary schools were in operation, and Finnish-speaking secondary schools outnumbered Swedish-speaking schools. By 1910, eighty-six Finnish-language newspapers were being published. At that moment, Finnish nationalists could look back at their efforts to improve the lot of their countrymen with justifiable pride (Wilson 1976a, 26–66).

But during the twentieth century, nationalistic movements and the folklore scholarship that supports them have frequently moved in unfortunate directions—directions Herder could not have envisioned. Time will allow only brief mention of three of these.

First, in pursuit of national ideals, we have too often kept our eyes riveted on the past and have ignored present realities. In 1815, the ardent Finnish nationalist Adolf Ivar Arwidsson turned to folk poetry in an attempt to find "a more natural and more pure tongue" (Heikinheimo 1933, 120–21); a few years later he urged that the old folk poetry be collected so that "we might be able to create new temples to the art of the fatherland on this native foundation." "Antiquities," he said, speaking of the old poetry, "live in the people's chronicles and in their artistic creations, in which they survive from times immemorial." Thus every nation that wishes to be true to its own character "must return to the furthest roots of all its native power, strength, and energy—to the pure spring of native poetry. Everything must be built on a native foundation" (Arwidsson 1909, 67–68, 138).

This view, that the past is always better than the present, has led to a number of unhappy results. In my own country, those who have studied immigrant communities have too often focused only on those "pure" old forms brought to the United States from the immigrants' countries of origins. Speaking of this approach to the study of Finnish American traditions, Yvonne Lockwood writes: "For many decades scholars researched only the folklife of the Old Country and the remnants or survivals of early immigrant life. The alterations and adaptations in immigrant culture to forms that suited the United States context were actually regarded as poor copies of 'pure' Old Country culture" (1990, 5). Consequently, the rich cultural forms resulting from immigrant traditions adapting to an American environment have been ignored—and both our scholarship and our understanding have suffered.

A similar attempt to focus on the untainted past can be seen in UNESCO's efforts to preserve and safeguard folklore. According to Lauri Honko, who has summarized UNESCO's work for the *Newsletter* of the Nordic Institute of Folklore, "the cultural and psychological reaction in the western industrialized countries" to the pains brought about by developments in our technological, electronic world "has been regionalism and a return to old tradition" (1982, 2). We should, of course, study the old traditions but in the context of the contemporary technological world. To do otherwise is akin to studying immigrant traditions in the United States without paying any attention to the American environment in which they are enacted. Like it or not, we live in an electronic, technological world that is here to stay. Our task should be to focus on all our citizens, not just those living on the margins of modernity; we should identify the traditional forms they have borrowed, adapted, and generated in response to the circumstances of their lives and then demonstrate how these forms, like older forms of folklore, fulfill human needs common to us all.

In any attempt to capture the past through folklore study and to make that past the pattern for contemporary society, we should remember, as postmodern criticism has taught us, that we never actually capture reality in language; we construct it. Narrators of the past do not give us objectively accurate portraits of what really occurred in earlier times but rather stories shaped by their own personalities and forged in response to present needs. Their narratives, therefore, are often more akin to fiction, in the best sense of the word, than to history. That is, they are creative interpretations of the past that may in the final analysis tell us a good deal more about the narrators themselves than about the events they describe. As a result, they seldom provide adequate models for the building of modern states.

And that leads me to my second concern with folklore-based nationalistic efforts. In 1921 the prominent Finnish educator E. A. Saarimaa repeated for his fellow teachers a sentiment that had persisted throughout the entire nationalistic movement: "The national significance of our folklore," said Saarimaa, ". . . entitles it to a prominent position in the national literature studied in our secondary schools. But particularly the fact that our nation's individuality is best revealed in this poetry makes learning it important. The nation's soul is nowhere reflected so clearly as in its almost collectively created poetry. And one of the most important tasks of the secondary school is to acquaint the students with their own nation" (1921, 1–2). It may be true that folklore captures the soul of a people, but it is equally true that the image of that soul reflected in folklore is also a constructed image, a reflection not necessarily of an objective reality but rather of the ideological predisposition of the individual holding the mirror. That is something we must always remember when anyone tries to move us to action by encouraging us, as loyal citizens, to conform to a behavioral pattern suggested by our folklore.

Such attempts occurred in Finland between the world wars, when propagandists from both sides of the political spectrum insisted that the *Kalevala*, a work supposedly sprung from the hearts of the people, reflected their own particular points of view and then argued for diametrically opposed courses of action—the political right to generate in the citizenry a militaristic posture and to argue for an expansionist foreign policy that included annexing East Karelia into a Greater Finland; the political left to counter the ideology of the right and to argue for a classless, communist society (Wilson 1976a, 118–203). In 1956 Finland's President J. K. Paasikivi, architect of Finland's postwar foreign policy, wrote: "The East Karelian issue, though it was a daydream with no realistic foundation, has greatly damaged us and our relationship with the Soviet Union. It stimulated mistrust of us. This [East Karelia] enthusiasm awakened in the Soviet Union greater attention [to Finland] than has been thought" (1959, 7). At the negotiating table, the Finns would at war's end pay a dear price for the Greater Finland dream, a dream based in part on a questionable interpretation of the national epic.

My third concern with nationalistic pursuits that draw support from folklore study relates directly to current attempts to establish, or re-establish, national governments in lands formerly under control of the Communist empire. In 1817, the energetic Carl Axel Gottlund, in words that bore the clear imprint of Herder, declared: "Just as an independent nation cannot exist without a fatherland, no fatherland can exist without poetry. For what is poetry except the crystal in which nationality mirrors itself, the spring from which the nation's original feelings rise to the surface" (Heikinheimo 1933, 307–8). In a nation whose people comprise a reasonably homogeneous population, such a sentiment may make sense. But few such nations exist today. In most Eastern European lands, and indeed in much of Europe, different ethnic groups reside within the same national boundaries. In the passage cited above, Paasikivi attributed much of the excessive Greater Finland fervor to ideas promulgated earlier by Finnish nationalist J. V. Snellman. In words that have proven more prophetic than either Paasikivi or Snellman could have possibly imagined, Snellman declared: "As broadly as the Bulgarian language is spoken just as broadly should national Bulgaria extend. . . . As broadly as the Serbian language is spoken should Serbia extend" (Paasikivi 1959, 6).

As we all know, those geographic spaces where Serbian is spoken are also occupied by other peoples. And we all know the terrible price being paid as one or another of these peoples attempts to establish its hegemony. Speaking to this issue recently, Roger Abrahams states:

> Attempts to redress historical dislocations can lead to struggles for self-realization that resuscitate arguments developed during the formative period of earlier nation-states. In these struggles, we witness the revival of the notion of fatherland that maintains a confrontational stance vis-à-vis conquering regimes seeking to subject various groups to marginalization or expulsion. . . . The recent history of much of Eastern Europe shows that one people's nationalism can be transformed into the means by which other peoples are disenfranchised. (1993, 5)

In this day of ethnic cleansing, disenfranchising, and ethnic warfare, the old models clearly no longer work. If we are to avoid the horrors already developing, we must adopt at least two seemingly different but mutually supporting stratagems.

First, we must develop a multicultural approach that finds strength in diversity and leads us to enrich our lives by learning to value and appreciate the cultural heritages of all the people living within our national boundaries—an approach Herder himself may have favored, since he cherished the cultural traditions of all peoples. Speaking of circumstances in his country, Australian folklorist Keith McKenry states:

> The folklife of Australia comprises a diverse body of living traditions . . . which we have inherited not only from earlier generations of Australians but also from our forebears in other parts of the world. These traditions run deep, giving each of us our sense of cultural identity, yet binding us together as Australians and giving us a basis for sharing, as members of Australia's rich multicultural society. (Honko 1988, 6)

In my own country, the United States Congress has passed an American Folklife Preservation Act that stresses the same principles. Among other things it states:

> The Congress hereby finds and declares—(1) that the diversity inherent in American folklife has contributed greatly to the cultural richness of the Nation and has fostered a sense of individuality and identity among the American people; (2) that the history of the United States effectively demonstrates that building a strong nation does not require the sacrifice of cultural differences. (1976)

Following the ideals stated here, the Folk Arts Program of our National Endowment for the Arts has attempted to identify, study, and bring to public attention the cultural heritages of all our people. I am not trying to impose an American model on anyone, but the decision to value rather than to combat difference seems a much safer course in today's perilous world.

Finally, we must seek in the differing cultural heritages of our neighbors not just those features that separate us from each other but also those which unite us—not just those traditional behaviors arising from our national or ethnic uniqueness, but those given birth by our common humanity, by our common human struggle to endure. Clearly, folklore is shaped by the groups that perform it and thus keep it alive; as a result, it can increase our understanding of and sympathy for these groups. But as we seek to understand these different peoples through their folklore, we should remember that in the final analysis folklore is cut from the marrow of human experience. For me, the great value of the *Kalevala* is that it illuminates not just the Finnish spirit but also the human spirit. Like all good literature it confronts again and again those enduring human problems which have neither time nor place. As I read the *Kalevala* I do not have to be a Finn to be moved by the hapless Kullervo's desperate question to his mother: "Will you mourn for me, my mother, / When you hear that I am dead?" And I do not have to be a Finn to weep with his mother as she responds: "You don't know a mother's mind, / Understand a mother's heart. . . . / I will flood the house with weeping, / Making waves upon the floorboards; . . . / What I cannot bear to weep, / Cannot bear to weep in public, / I will sob out in the sauna, / Weep in secret in the sauna, / Overflowing bench and platform" (Lönnrot [1849] 1984, 253).

Properly understood, then, the folklore of different nationalities and different ethnicities will, to be sure, help us understand what it is to be Finns, or Americans, or Japanese, or Latvians, or Russians. But it will also help us realize what it means to be human beings.

Finns in a New World

A Folkloristic Perspective

Rephrased as a question, the title of this address could easily have been announced as "How do Americans form identities?" While Wilson is dealing in this paper particularly with the contemporary situation of Americans of Finnish ancestry, his analysis of the connection of cultural expressions to feelings of ethnic belonging could be applied to other groups. As with his other studies, however, he is careful to ground issues of identity in the distinctive historical and cultural experience of specific groups and recognize that differences often emerge.

The question might be begged as to why ethnicity often takes priority as an important identity. The U.S. Census's surveys of ethnic ancestry in 1990 and 2000, for example, revealed that more than 90 percent of Americans claimed at least one ethnic ancestry, and many wrote in several. Concerned as a folklorist with the dynamics of tradition, Wilson points out that this ancestry becomes an identity through participation in cultural traditions, and individuals intentionally make decisions about their level of participation. Hence, Wilson uses the concept of Finnishness, as other scholars have used Jewishness or Irishness, to indicate an expression or feeling of belonging. Wilson interprets it colloquially as "a sense of who you are." This "-ness" fits in with views of modernity in which people have emotional or spiritual ties to an identity, even in the absence of "objective" criteria of living in community with others of the group, speaking the language, having an ethnic name, or being born in the country of origin, and so on.

As an American Studies scholar, Wilson also recognizes that individuals in a diverse society such as the United States may have several cultural identities that they express simultaneously. A wrinkle Wilson adds in his discussion is the

---

This paper was a keynote address given at the conference on "The Making of Finnish America: An Ethnic Culture in Transition," sponsored by the Immigration History Research Center at the University of Minnesota. It was published in *Kalevalaseuran Vuosikirja* [*Kalevala Society Annual*] 72 (1993): 182–95. Reprinted by permission of the Kalevala Society.

modern tendency to "consume" identities in the form of purchasing ethnic displays rather than through cultural performance, which we normally associate with "expression." Therefore he addresses the ways that Americans of Finnish ancestry gain and maintain ethnic identity, especially if they are several generations removed from the country of origin. He reminds his audience that this identity is often a new hybrid born of the American experience and traditions are invented to reinforce the "Finnish American" image. Forces are at work in the formation of identity to claim authenticity for one's ethnic identity by revitalizing traditions viewed as ancient and authentic, and simultaneously to create traditions anew to keep one's identity vital and modern.

From his study of Finland, he points out that perceptions of what is ancient and authentic in the home country can often be deceiving, which is a reminder of how perceptual identity as a cultural process can be. Understanding this process leads Wilson to consider the impact of folklore's symbolism of authenticity. His plaint that many Americans of Finnish ancestry valorize the ancient and miss the opportunities for meaningful cultural experiences in the context of modern society references what Alan Dundes called the "devolutionary premise in folklore theory." This premise that he criticizes is that folklore decays through time, and therefore the item in contemporary society is inferior to the ancient original. Following the devolutionary premise, a bias is implied against "progress" in theorizing culture. Rather than bemoaning that old folklore, and by extension Finnishness, is dying out, Wilson's "folkloristic perspective" is that folklore is continuously being created and should be appreciated for how people strategically use it to give a sense of themselves.

For Wilson's related writing on issues of identity, see "A Sense of Place or a Sense of Self: Personal Narratives and the Construction of Personal and Regional Identity" (2000) and "On Being Human: The Folklore of Mormon Missionaries" (1981). For his views of national identity and romantic nationalism, see *Folklore and Nationalism in Modern Finland* (1976a); "Herder, Folklore, and Romantic Nationalism" (1973b); and "Richard M. Dorson's Theory for American Folklore: A Finnish Analogue" (1982). For the discourse on "devolution" and "evolution" in folklore theory, see Alan Dundes's "The Devolutionary Premise in Folklore Theory," (1969); William A. Wilson's "The Evolutionary Premise in Folklore Theory and the 'Finnish Method'" (1976b); and Elliott Oring's "The Devolutionary Premise: A Definitional Delusion?" (1975).

—*Simon J. Bronner*

As I approach the subject of this essay, "Finns in a New World," or, perhaps better, "The Making of Finnish America," I must do so humbly, realizing that not a drop of Finnish blood flows through my veins. This is not to say that I am unaware of Finnish American issues. After all, I have been married to a Finn for thirty-four years and have followed the activities of Finns in my home state of Utah, where scores of Finns arrived before and after 1900 to work in the mining industry. Still, I readily admit that I am an outsider, denied by lack of Finnish birthright license to speak as one having authority about what it means to be a Finnish American. This gives me considerable pause since I have learned that, while Finns are fully capable of self-criticism, they have not always happily accepted the criticisms of others.

For example, in 1902, on the occasion of Elias Lönnrot's one hundredth birthday, the Swedish scholar K. B. Wiklund published articles on the *Kalevala* in both Sweden and Germany, pointing out what Finnish folklorists had known for some time but what the general Finnish population would not fully grasp for some years to come—namely, that Finland's national epic, while based on Finnish folklore, was the literary creation not of the Finnish folk but of Elias Lönnrot and that it had been composed not in some distant antiquity but in the 1800s at Lönnrot's work table. The Finnish popular press responded to this attack on the integrity of the *Kalevala* with vigor. An editorial writer in *Uusi Suometar*, a leading nationalist newspaper, angrily declared:

> That scientist [Wiklund] who serves Uppsala University, [and] who in his two publications has particularly wanted to oppress the Finns, knows well how to serve other than scientific ends. And now the sourness he has sown is spreading in Germany—it has already pretty well poisoned Scandinavia; it will move from Germany to France, to England, and so on; and in a few years no foreigner will any longer believe that the Finnish nation has its own national epic.
>
> But that must not happen! Dr. Wiklund's doctrine offends the national self consciousness of every Finn. It damages those good opinions which the educated in foreign lands hold about our people. Therefore, our scientific and professional men must pick up the pen and prove this "Wiklundism" to be without doubt a fabricated scientific lie. [W:nen 1901: 2]

In what follows, I will do my best not to fabricate any scientific lies. I would like to draw a few parallels between my ongoing study of Finnish Finns in search of their identity and Finnish Americans in search of theirs. I come to my subject as a folklorist who has spent some years studying the Finns' attempts to discover in their folk culture what earlier was called the national spirit, or national soul, and what we would today refer to as the national identity.

On February 28, 1835, Elias Lönnrot sent the manuscript of what was to become the *Kalevala* to Helsinki to be published. From that time Finns have celebrated February 28 as *Kalevala* Day. I am currently studying how these celebrations have been observed in Finland over the last century. The first major celebration was held in 1885, fifty years after the publication of the first edition of the *Kalevala*, the last major commemoration in 1985, one hundred years later. During the century separating these two commemorative events, dramatic changes have occurred in Finland. In 1885, many of the goals of the

Finnish nationalists had been achieved: Finnish had joined Swedish as an official language; Finnish-language schools had been established; and a Finnish-language press was growing stronger. Twenty-five years later, in 1910, these advances were about to disappear under the heavy hand of intensifying Russian oppression. In 1935, twenty-five years after that gloomy period, Finland was now an independent country, boldly claiming its place among the family of nations. Fourteen years later, in 1949, on the one hundredth anniversary of the publication of the second edition of the epic, Finland, after fighting two devastating wars with the Soviet Union, was struggling with all the resources it could muster not to become another Czechoslovakia. In 1985, once again proud, independent, and prosperous, Finland celebrated its national epic with a gusto that echoed throughout the world.

I am attempting to learn how "to read" changing *Kalevala* Day celebrations, to discover in them responses to shifting cultural/political aspirations and thus to view them as keys to understanding what has been going on in the country at any given moment. One could draw obvious parallels between the *Kalevala* Day celebrations and the recent FinnFest USA celebrations held in the United States. I will return to this subject later. First I wish to address more fundamental similarities lying at the heart of my research and at what I perceive to be the core of Finnish American studies.

In 1809, after some six hundred years of Swedish rule, Finland became a grand duchy of Russia. Torn from their cultural ties with mother Sweden, opposed to the possibility of Finland's absorption into Russia, and inspired by the tenets of romantic nationalism moving into the country from the continent, young Finnish intellectuals took the first steps toward the creation of a Finnish Finland. Their rallying cry became: "We are not Swedes; we can never become Russians; let us therefore be Finns" (see Castrén 1951, 160–61). But what did it mean to be Finns? Separated from each other by regional differences and speaking different dialects, average Finns of the time had no concept at all of "Finnishness." It remained for the nationalistic intelligentsia, therefore, to create that concept for them. One of these young nationalists, on a visit to Sweden in 1818, wrote home: "No honest Finn can love this thankless, limp, enfeebled, poor Sweden, . . . boasting of the heroic deeds of its forefathers. . . . Lord God, how wonderful it would be . . . to ignite an interest in our history and national language. . . . A Finn should no more praise the Goth's manhood. We are another nation, and our forefathers were as hairy-chested as the Goths ever were, even though they were not such famous pirates" (Abraham Poppius, in Heikinheimo 1933, 331). Another wrote: "Just as an independent nation cannot exist without a fatherland, no fatherland can exist without poetry. For what is poetry except the crystal in which nationality mirrors itself, the spring from which the nation's original feelings rise to the surface" (Gottlund 1817, 397–98).

These statements, and others like them, were the clarion calls that sent Elias Lönnrot and his disciples scurrying through the Finnish hinterlands to collect the old epic poems, pure and undefiled, that would eventually result in the publication of the *Kalevala*, the work which would serve, at least originally, as the source book for a pure Finnish history, a pure Finnish language, a pure Finnish literature, and, based on these, a pure Finnish national character, or identity (Wilson 1976a, 26–61).

What was this national character like? What did it mean to be a Finn? The answer to that question pretty much depended on the needs of the moment. The image of the Finnish past and of the Finnish national character supposedly reflected in the old folk poetry very often was shaped more by the political predispositions of the scholars holding up the mirror than by the poetry itself. Thus in the years following the publication of the *Kalevala*, as public schools and the popular media exercised more and more control over the thinking of the people, the folk poetry was used to further every cause imaginable; and the protagonists of the epic who emerged from its poetic lines were viewed as everything from peaceful hunters and tillers of the soil to mighty warlike heroes eager with the sword to win honor and glory for the fatherland.

This is a process, by the way, that has not ended. I recently watched a Finnish television program deploring the devastation of the forests in East, or Soviet, Karelia. One of the arguments used against this destruction was that these forests should be preserved because Elias Lönnrot had once trekked through them collecting the core of the ancient Finnish folk poetry. And new causes will continue to develop. As current demands for restoration to Finland of Finnish-Karelian lands annexed by the Soviets during World War II continue to intensify, I will watch eagerly to see if the *Kalevala* will be used to justify such restoration, just as it was used between the world wars and during the first months of the Continuation War to justify the annexation by the Finns of Russo-Karelian lands that had never belonged to them (Wilson 1976a, 137–61, 181–95).

Three issues are central here to my research and, I believe, to those studying Finnish Americans. First, the terms "national identity" or "ethnic identity" do not originally derive from the people but are, rather, scholarly constructs. They are created by the intelligentsia in order to move the people in directions they wish. Second, to move the people in these directions, the intelligentsia must teach them to recognize, value, and shape their lives according to these constructs. Third, the ends which proponents of either national or ethnic identity serve are almost always ideologically motivated.

In his study of Swedish Americans, folklorist Larry Danielson has identified four stages, beginning with unconscious ethnicity and ending with conscious ethnicity, that many immigrants go through (1979). In the first stage, immigrants are unconsciously ethnic—that is, they continue to do things in the old ways simply because they know no other ways; their language, their foodways, and their kinship relationships remain what they were in the Old World. In the second stage, the immigrants continue many of the old traditions but are now aware that these are different from surrounding cultural practices and that they themselves are different because they persist in these traditions.

In the third stage, the children and grandchildren of immigrants consciously put off the old ways—that is, they abandon their parents' and grandparents' language and customs and become as thoroughly American as possible. In the fourth stage, having been awakened by the intelligentsia to the value of their heritage, the descendants of the earlier immigrants consciously try to revive the old ways, though in a manner that does not produce for them the discomfort experienced by their forebears.

It is the conscious ethnicity, of course, that captures my interest and relates most closely to my own research and to the issues I have identified above. By the time Finnish Americans have become consciously ethnic, they have usually become better educated and more prosperous, thereby becoming more susceptible to educational and promotional efforts aimed at them; they have, as a result, learned through the popular media and through the efforts of Finnish American organizations who they really are; motivated in part by what Aili Flint calls the "nostalgia factor" (1985, 5), they have sought the source of their identity in older customs or in practices borrowed from mother Finland; and they have begun to incorporate some of these practices into their own lives, above all as proud symbols of their ethnic heritage. In other words, they have followed just about the same roads as those traveled by their kinsmen in Finland in the late nineteenth and early twentieth centuries.

This revival, or discovery, of ethnic heritage can take many forms. I will concentrate on two. First, there is usually an attempt to take pride in one's past by recovering the immigrant experience through recording the reminiscences of older members of the community. This is the approach Michael Loukinen takes in his two films, *Finnish American Lives* (1984) and *Tradition Bearers* (1987), as he focuses in the first on the patriarch of a three-generation Finnish American family and in the second on traditional Finnish American craftspersons. In both films the emphasis is on *the way it was* rather than on *the way it is.* While the subjects of the films live in the present, they primarily tell stories of the past—of life in the Old Country before immigrating, of the trip to America, and of hardships endured during the first years in this country.

The Finnish Americans presented in these films are treated with great sympathy and quickly win viewers' admiration. Stories like the ones they tell are extremely important. As Barbara Kirshenblatt-Gimblett points out, such reminiscing can be "life-sustaining" for older people in general and for immigrants in particular. "Reminiscence," she says, "which is part of the vital process of self-integration at the end of a very long life, can span almost a century in some cases, and can compensate for the partial and restricted experiences of later generations." Telling stories of the past can thus become "essential to personal as well as cultural survival" (1983, 41).

Still, there are certain cautions those of us who study these stories should exercise. Postmodern criticism has taught us that we do not capture reality in language; we create it—or, in the jargon of the day, construct it. Narrators of the past do not necessarily give us accurate portraits of what really occurred in their earlier lives but rather stories forged in response to present needs. Their narratives, therefore, are often more akin to fiction, in the best sense of the word, than to history. That is, they are creative interpretations of the past that may in the final analysis tell us a good deal more about the narrators themselves than about the events they describe.

Also, as we present the reminiscences we have recorded, we should resist the temptation to cast them in an overly romantic sheen. Listening to the dulcet tones of "Kotimaani onpi Suomi" or of Kantele music sounding in the background as narrators in Loukinen's films tell their stories, or looking at pictures of Kantele players taken not in those areas from which most Finns emigrated but in East Karelia, may give the films a romantically artistic flavor but will not do a great deal to enhance their historical veracity.

The second form of conscious revival of ethnicity is closely related to the first. It seeks the source of ethnic identity either in "pure" old artifacts or in "authentic" Finnish art forms borrowed from modern Finland.

Though contemporary Finnish folklorists and ethnographers have happily moved in new directions today, this search for old or authentic cultural forms has, as I have already suggested, deep roots in Finland itself. For example, as early as 1702 Henricus Florinus published a collection of some 1,600 proverbs, hoping to find in them, he said in the introduction to the collection, "many an old, pure Finnish word" (1702, Preface)—that is, words not corrupted by foreign influence. In 1815 the ardent nationalist Adolf Ivar Arwidsson began collecting Finnish folk poetry in the hopes of finding in them "a more natural and more pure tongue" (Heikinheimo 1933, 120–21); a few years later he urged that the old folk poetry be collected vigorously so that "we might be able to create new temples to the art of the fatherland on this native foundation." "Antiquities," he said, speaking of the old poetry, "live in the people's chronicles and in their artistic creations, in which they survive from times immemorial." Thus every nation that wishes to be true to its own character "must return to the furthest roots of all its native power, strength, and energy—to the pure spring of native poetry. Everything must be built on a native foundation" (1909, 67–68, 138).

In these phrases, three important concepts are clearly evident: that the old is always better than the new; that pure and undefiled language and cultural artifacts are always better than admixtures resulting from the blending of two or more cultures; and that national, or ethnic, identity, must therefore be built on a pure and uncorrupted native foundation.

These ideas did not die easily. As late as 1943, the renowned Finnish folklorist Martti Haavio published *Viimeiset runonlaulajat* (The Last Poem Singers), whose title clearly reflects Haavio's distaste for what he called the "gaping emptiness" ([1943] 1985, 363) of his own modern world and his enormous admiration for the last of the great singers who had kept alive the older, purer forms of folk poetry for the blessing and benefit of contemporary Finland. Commenting on the scores of scholars, artists, musicians, and literati who had been inspired by earlier writings to troop into Karelia at the turn of the century to imbue themselves with the spirit of the *Kalevala* song lands, he wrote:

> Undoubtedly, many of them were disappointed because a pilgrim who departs with too high expectations will hardly ever see miracles. And, furthermore, the time of miracles had passed in Karelian lands. Those golden years, spoken of in those books with such unrestrained enthusiasm, belonged to an unreturnable past. As early as 1906, O. A. Haiari wrote the funeral address for the former Border-Karelia when he said: "The backwoods are decreasing in Border-Karelia, and the twilight of fairy tales is disappearing from them. A new generation hears the jingling of cow bells there where the hunter once charmed the forked-antlered cattle of Tapiola. The piercing sound of the factory steam pipes sounds where before the whistle of a bear echoed. At the edge of the wilderness village, where the women once recited incantations at the roots of a holy sacrificial pine, there towers now the ridge beam of a new elementary school." ([1943] 1985, 160)

According to Yvonne Hiipakka Lockwood, a similar predilection for the romantic past has characterized Finnish American studies: "For many decades," she writes, "scholars researched only the folklife of the Old Country and the remnants or survivals of early immigrant life. The alterations and adaptations of immigrant culture to forms that suited the United States context were actually regarded as poor copies of 'pure' Old Country culture" (1990, 5). Such a predilection can be seen in both of Loukinen's films, in which the idea predominates that the old ways are best—from speaking the Finnish language, to playing the accordion, to making twine for spinning, to tying a sauna vihta (sauna whisk). In *Finnish American Lives*, the son of the old Finnish immigrant says: "Anybody can make a vihta, but he [the speaker's father] ties it like the Finlanders do in Finland." When the old man dies, his passing, like the passing of Haavio's last singers, seems to symbolize the disappearance of a culture that will make the world ever poorer for its loss.

Ironically, when Finnish Americans have broken away from the older cultural forms, their doing so has brought sharp criticism from some Finns, who evidently judge the merit of Finnish American expressive forms according to their correspondence with Finnish cultural practices. As Marsha Penti points out, the FinnFest USA festival held in Berkeley in 1986 brought an angry response from a reporter for the *Ilta-Sanomat* [Evening News], who entitled his article covering the event "American Finnishness Dancing into the Grave: Folk Dance Orgies Under the Palm Trees." Deploring the absence of "pure" Finnish cultural forms in the celebration, he wrote: "The festival which has swollen to almost a folk dance orgy is at the same time a rehearsal for a funeral: the number of Finnish-speaking American Finns is decreasing in tempo with the departure of the elderly: only a folk costume and kantele are left in the closet" (Penti 1990, 18). Here again is the old longing for the pure forms of the past. In some ways, the reporter's statement is not much different from Haavio's lamenting the departure of the last singers of the old epic songs.

These FinnFest USA festivals move us to a slightly different but still related concern—an emphasis now, not so much on pure survivals from the past as on "authentic" Finnish, as opposed to Finnish American, cultural forms. As Marianne Wargelin points out in her article "Ethnic Identity for Sale,"

> Finnish American ethnic festivals today consider the sale of Finnish import items *de rigueur*. The Finnish gift shop owners fill tables and rooms to overflowing with merchandise to sell. The national Finnish ethnic festival, FinnFest USA, vigorously promotes its tori [market place], where festival attendees can browse among Finnish goods in "the heart of FinnFest." Interestingly, when FinnFest USA first started in 1983, its tori was a space for Finnish American crafts: rag rugs, straw items, and sauna vihtas (bath whisks). In 1984, the tori mixed gift shop sales with crafts. In 1985, the gift shops began to dominate the tori, and they have ever since. . . . After eight FinnFests, Finnish American crafts are difficult to find in the tori. (1990, 34)

It is probably true, as Penti argues, that, in spite of its Finnish-based component, the FinnFest celebration

> is a particularly useful vehicle for identity assertion and formulation. FinnFest attendance in itself can be a way of heightening identity awareness. The typical festival goers are enthusiastically excited by the possibilities of meeting old and making new friends with whom they are united by bonds of ethnicity. (1990, 18)

It is probably also true, as Wargelin points out, that "Finnish American consumers confirm that they see purchases of these Finland-made products as acts of ethnic identity" (1990, 34). As one whose own home is full of Finnish design objects purchased in Finland by my Finnish American wife, it would be something less than admirable for me to deplore the purchase of such objects by other Finnish Americans.

Still I find troubling Penti's statement that FinnFest "is an artificially created event which appeals to Finnish Americans of diverse backgrounds and is promoted by twentieth century marketing tactics" (1990, 16). However valuable for its participants and however conducive to the development of ethnic pride, FinnFest still strikes me as an imposed popular-culture event, highly orchestrated, that must of necessity ignore regional and cultural differences, even if it is celebrated in a different geographic area each year.

This attempt to homogenize all Finnish Americans into a unified whole with a common ethnic background is akin to efforts of nineteenth-century Finnish romantic nationalists to create from multiple regional and cultural groups a unified Finnish nation. Such efforts certainly can produce, and have produced, laudable results. But without proper restraints, they can also pretty badly distort reality.

Finnish Americans, after all, are not all alike. It seems crucially important, therefore, to discover how in different communities with different historical backgrounds they have chosen to live their lives and how they choose to celebrate themselves—how they wish to present themselves to each other and to the general public and, in the process, say, "This is who we are." I have no quarrel with what the FinnFest organizers do in their festivals or with what Michael Loukinen does in his films. I am troubled more by what they do not do.

I would like to see in the festivals and in films about Finnish Americans examples of *Finnish American* practices and customs representing a merger of different ethnic cultures and resulting from varying geographical and historical circumstances. According to Lockwood, because culture is always changing in response to present circumstances, one should give up the old notions of the pure and the authentic and realize that "Finnish American culture is not the same as culture in Finland, that it is not simply 'a diluted version' of what existed, or exists, in the homeland, and that it is a creature of its own making" (1990, 4–5).

This strikes me as excellent advice. What pursuits of the older, purer forms of Finnish cultural practices or of contemporary Finnish artistic expressions like Iitala glass or Marimekko design share in common is the notion that whatever originated in Finland in the past or has been created in Finland in recent years is somehow superior to cultural artifacts created and shaped by the historical experiences of Finnish Americans. Anything "made in Finland" is therefore qualitatively better than anything produced here—a notion that the romantic nationalists of yesteryear would have understood perfectly well.

Let me return for a moment to Martti Haavio's *The Last Poem Singers* and to his statement about the disappearance of an earlier Finnish culture. Quoting Haiari, Haavio sorrowed over the loss of elk hunters, of a bear's whistle, and of a sacrificial tree and over their replacement by cowherds, factory whistles, and a schoolhouse. I have no quarrel with Haavio's desire to preserve a record of the last singers of songs and of the culture that produced them; indeed, we owe him a great debt of gratitude for having done so. But what about those cowherds, those factory workers, those school children? Weren't they also important? Didn't they also have a culture? Shouldn't that culture also have been studied? Wouldn't such study have taught us just as much about life in Karelia in particular and about the human condition in general as the exploration of the lives of the old singers?

I hope my comparison is obvious. Don't Finnish Americans also have independent cultural traditions separate from those of their ancestors? Aren't those cultural traditions equally important? Shouldn't they be studied and valued? And, most important, shouldn't they be seen as the principal sources of contemporary Finnish American identity? In the creation of this culture, says Lockwood, Finnish Americans have "both adopted new ways and adapted old ways of life to fit their new cultural and social context" (1990, 5). What that means is that scholars must learn to look for and at Finnish American life in ways they have may not have looked before.

A good example of a cultural expression born on American soil and having precious little to do with anything in Finland is St. Urho's Day, a day celebrated with gusto by some Finnish Americans and deplored with a matching vehemence by others. I would certainly like to know what there is in the character of certain Finnish Americans that causes tales of a fictitious saint who once saved the Finnish grape crop from destruction and thus preserved the country's wine production to excite them far more than do events sponsored, let us say, by the Knights and Ladies of Kaleva, seeking in the *Kalevala* a common Finnish heritage. I will never learn the answer to that question, however, if I become too preoccupied with the survival of earlier Finnish practices.

Cultural *adaptation* is probably a more common process than the adoption of completely new forms like St. Urho's Day. In the Scofield coal-mining community in Utah, once occupied by scores of Finns, one will find numerous Finnish saunas invisible to the observer accustomed to the frame and log saunas brought to Michigan, Wisconsin, and Minnesota from the Old Country. Utah Finnish miners, cramped into small houses often not their own, had to put their saunas wherever they could find a place for them—in coal sheds, in tool houses, and on back porches. During a day I spent photographing these saunas, I was amazed to open the door of a nondescript, un-sauna-like shed and then to walk into a room that was in almost all ways similar to saunas I had known in Finland. According to Carolyn Torma, "Finnish-American architecture which most closely resembles Old World models is regarded as the most 'ethnic'" (1990, 28). Again, anyone operating from this perspective, anyone looking for "pure" old forms, would have missed these Utah saunas, which played as important a role in the lives of the Scofield miners as have the more traditional saunas in the lives of immigrants in the Upper Great Lakes areas.

Much of this cultural adaptation is what Barbara Kirshenblatt-Gimblett calls cultural "recycling"—that is, practices originating in the Old World assume new functions in their new environs (1983, 42). An excellent example of this recycling would be the celebration of Laskiainen at Palo, Minnesota, as documented in the film entitled *At Laskiainen at Palo, Everyone is a Finn* by Elli Köngäs Maranda, Marsha Penti, and Thomas Vennum (1983). At first glance, the film is what the Finns would probably call a *sekamelska*, a confusing mixed-bag of just about everything. The annual celebration, which was begun in 1935, does retain some elements of the original Finnish practices, such as sledding down hills and eating pea soup; but it also contains just about everything else—from a royal festival queen with an honor guard carrying hockey sticks to women dressed in Finnish national costumes and displaying Finnish crafts; from cheese making to the construction of a Lapp village; and from traditional bleeding practices to cure illness to clog dancing to the tune of "Oh, Them Golden Slippers." The newspaper reporter from the *Ilta-Sanomat* who was so confused by the Berkeley FinnFest USA festival might well lose his mind were he to attend Laskiainen at Palo.

Laskiainen, or Shrovetide, which has been celebrated broadly across Finland, goes back to medieval Catholic practices that have merged with pagan calendar customs. The name of the celebration comes from the verb *laskea*—"to descend" or "to go down"—and did not mean, as Y. H. Toivonen has demonstrated, to descend hills, as on a sled; rather, it meant to descend into the forty-day fast period beginning Lent. The word for Easter, *Pääsiäinen*, came from the verb *päästää*—"to let loose" or "to release"—indicating a release from the fast at the end of Lent (Vilkuna [1950] 1968, 54).

In Finnish peasant society, the hundreds of different customs surrounding Laskiainen, or attached to the day, have been far more important than the religious observances. These customs, as Kustaa Vilkuna has noted, have focused primarily on the world of women—especially on the division of labor falling to them. Why, for example, did the women cook pea soup, and make it as greasy as possible? Because, says Vilkuna, after the soup was eaten, "the more grease glistened on fingers and in the corners of mouths the better the pigs would fatten in the summer [and] the cows would give milk, and the more butter the housewives would be able to churn and the more ham they would be able to cure" ([1950] 1968, 55).

Since the making of linen was a crucially important task carried out by women, it was important for them to do all they could to assure a good flax crop during the summer. A large number of homeopathic practices to produce such crops were, therefore, attached to the observance of Laskiainen. The following examples from Jouko Hautala's *Vanhat merkkipäivät* (The Old Red-Letter Days) are typical: "On Laskiainen you were to comb your hair nine times so that beautiful flax would grow in the summer. Every time you combed your hair you were to stand on a chair so that the flax would grow tall." "If you sweep the floor nine times on Laskiainen, the flax will grow well; and if you carry the sweepings far away, the flax will grow tall." "On Laskiainen, the women wore white clothing in order to get white flax." "On Laskiainen, if the women folk let their hair down, then the flax will grow tall." "On Laskiainen Eve when you went to bed, if you threw yourself onto the bed from a standing position, then [in the summer] the flax would remain standing and would not lie flat." "In the evening the younger people went sledding and the further the sled coasted, the taller grew the flax the following summer. Sliding down the hill, they shouted, 'Tall flax, Tall flax'" (Hautala [1948] 1974, 74–75, 83, 80, 75, 81, 96).

This last example brings us at last to the one of the few "authentic" features of Laskiainen, besides eating pea soup, that have persisted in Palo, Minnesota—sledding or sliding down hills. But even that practice has changed rather dramatically. While it is true that in Finland the younger people enjoyed coasting down hills, adults also, and especially women, participated in the sledding very seriously. Often they used as sleds the platforms of spinning wheels, the connection between the spinning wheels and flax and linen being obvious. And occasionally they followed a practice which, if revived at Palo, would certainly enliven the occasion even more. I quote from Hautala: "If tall flax was desired, then on the morning of Laskiainen the woman of the house had very early to slide down a certain hill on her bare bottom" (Hautala [1948] 1974, 97).

In Finland itself, many of the old customs have died out. Some families will still eat pea soup and Laskiais-pulla, and the children, often in outings organized by their schools, still enjoy sledding. But that's about it. Very few people participating in these practices will be aware of the once prevalent homeopathic magic connecting them to success in women's work. In Palo, the wide array of Laskiainen customs has all disappeared. But, as opposed to the celebration in Finland, a dazzling display of new practices with no connection to Laskiainen has been added.

Some will say, "Why, these things are not Finnish at all!" And they will, of course, be right. The practices are not Finnish; they are Finnish American—or at least Palo, Minnesota, Finnish American. Community based, community organized, and community run, Laskiainen at Palo reveals the spirit and the ethnic identity of Finnish Americans living there many times better than any attempt to revive or keep alive the old ways ever will. As Marsha Penti states, "*Laskiainen* [at Palo] is an example of folk festival creativity at its best. American Finns have not only had to, but have wanted to, adapt their celebratory life" (1990, 16). Or, as Barbara Kirshenblatt-Gimblett might say, they have "recycled" Old World culture to reveal what they consider most important about their lives in their new homeland.

One more issue needs brief discussion. I earlier suggested that those who seek to identify, teach, and advocate either national or ethnic identity are always ideologically motivated. I see nothing wrong with that so long as we acknowledge the motivations that move us to action. Too often we do not.

Archeologist Mark Leone, speaking of living history exhibits, states:

> As a visitor you take all this folklore and this symbol mongering and imagine yourself to be the native of Williamsburg or Mesa Verde. . . . And because the data are relatively mute . . . , they are then more easily made to give the message of those doing the reconstructing. . . . The tourist [at Williamsburg] does not really become immersed in the eighteenth century at all; he is spared the shock of the filth, degradation, and misery common to that era, and is led into a fake eighteenth century, a creation of the twentieth. While in this altered frame of mind he is faced with messages—the reinforcement of standard modern American values like those surrounding the myths of our own origin as a nation—that come out of today, not two centuries ago. (1973, 130–31)

Archeology in the service of national goals is not particularly offensive, says Leone, but what is offensive "is the archeologists' unawareness of this . . . function" (1973, 133). Leone is speaking of living history presentations, but what he says can apply equally well to the search for ethnic identity and to attempts to promulgate that identity through publications, films, and festivals.

So I ask again: how aware of, or how forthright about, their motivations are those engaged in these activities? When in 1978 I did fieldwork for the American Folklife Center in Paradise Valley, Nevada, documenting ranching customs of the area, I soon discovered a number of cracks in paradise. I was told by my supervisor that if I included negative statements in my report, he would edit them out. We cannot, he said, give negative impressions in a study funded by the public and made available to the public, including the people of Paradise Valley. In ethnic studies, it may also be common practice to focus on the smiling aspects of traditional culture and to "edit out" the rest.

The romantic nationalists in Finland tended to view the past as a golden age in which only heroic action occurred. Individuals seeking their ethnic roots often yield to the same temptation. I have some trouble believing, for example, that the early Finnish Americans were quite as heroic as they appear in some presentations. In the minutes book of the Vuoriston Tähti [Star of the Mountains], one of the Finnish temperance societies operating in Utah around 1900, it is fascinating to watch human foibles coming constantly to the fore. In one instance, members of the society reveal that a committee was being formed to visit the former financial secretary and to reclaim from him the society's funds. Further, I have difficulty believing that different groups of immigrants—Church Finns, Red Finns, Temperance Finns—lived together in harmony, bound together by the common ties of blood, language, and national origin. In her *Defiant Sisters: A Social History of Finnish Immigrant Women in Canada* (1988), Varpu Lindström-Best moves beyond the smiling aspects of immigrant life and brings to light such unpleasantries as suicide, bootlegging, and prostitution—circumstances later generations in search of their ethnic identity, and imbued with feelings of ethnic pride, are not always willing to acknowledge. In a similar vein, Carolyn Torma points out that a too heavy emphasis on the brighter side of Finnish immigrant life may also have distorted the study of Finnish American material culture. Unwilling to look at the underside of the immigrant experience, scholars have, she argues, focused on safe buildings like saunas and have ignored structures tinged with controversy. She states, speaking of a historical preservation program:

> Buildings which might reflect conflict or unpopular views are often overlooked. Not surprisingly, buildings which might represent the historic Finnish-American radical movement are almost completely absent from this list of [historical preservation] sites. This selectivity of political points of view is common throughout the preservation program. (1990, 29)

Of particular importance here is the question of what agendas are being served in Finnish American festivals—from community-based events like the celebration of Laskiainen, to grand events sponsored by Knights and Ladies of Kaleva, to the broader national FinnFest USA festivals. From my study of *Kalevala* Day celebrations, it is clearly evident that as political and national needs change, the celebrations of the *Kalevala* also change to reflect and reinforce current aspirations. And they are also shaped by the cultural/political ambitions of the organizations sponsoring them.

For example, in the grandiose 1935 celebration held in Helsinki, the speaker of Parliament, Kyösti Kallio, proclaimed:

> As we think of our nation's past and of its time of wandering in the wilderness, when in unbelievably primitive circumstances it managed to preserve itself, we can come to no other conclusions than that it had been able to endure and to maintain life by the aid of the hope and faith which are characteristic of it and which are contained in our folk poetry. And that same hope in the future prompts and obligates us more purposefully than in the past to perform our duty. An essential part of this duty is the continuing study of our antiquity. (1936, 60)

At the same time, across the border in Soviet Karelia, *Kalevala* celebrations were also held, though the language used there was somewhat less restrained than were the measured words of Kallio. Titles of articles appearing in the popular press give some indication of the tenor of the times: "Folklore and the Imperialistic Aims of the Finnish Bourgeoisie," "The Attempts of the Finnish Bourgeoisie to Force the *Kalevala* into the Service of Nationalism and Chauvinism," and "To What End has the Finnish Bourgeoisie Used and Is Now Using the *Kalevala*?" One impassioned editorialist wrote:

> Thousands of Fascist students have been sent throughout the land to arrange *Kalevala* celebrations, that is, to whip up anti-Soviet feeling. . . . The Finnish bourgeoisie have come to the egocentric conclusion that they can without hindrance soil and desecrate the best products of the people's creative ability and force them into the service of their plundering and national oppression. (Leppänen 1935)

I could go on, but there is little need. The point is that the cultural symbols on which national and ethnic identity are based can be used for a variety of ends and that it is therefore important to stand aside now and then to take a calm, detached look at the causes being served.

Though I still consider myself an amateur in the study of the Finnish American experience and though that experience is not part of my own Idaho, Mormon, and western heritage, I nonetheless hope that by drawing parallels between my studies of Finnish nationalism and the studies of those devoted to Finnish American ethnicity, and that by highlighting some of the strengths and pitfalls inherent in both, I will at least have raised issues worth thinking about.

As I have written this paper, my thoughts have kept drifting back to earlier conversations between myself and my Finnish American son-in-law. From the day he first began courting my daughter, I began trying to persuade him to use the Finnish pronunciation of his surname—Jämsä. He steadfastly resisted all my importuning, calling himself instead Ralph Jam-sa. Finally, I realized that I was trying to force him back into what I have been cautioning others to avoid—an adherence to old, pure linguistic or cultural forms. For my son-in-law, his name, as he pronounced it, symbolized both his Finnish ancestry and his American experience; and it was foolish of me to try to change that. He had learned to look to himself and to the experiences of his Finnish American family for the principal sources of his identity and had discovered instinctively what Yvonne Hiipakka Lockwood has stated so nicely: "People in the United States who trace their origins to Finland are neither American nor Finnish; rather, they are Finnish Americans" (1990, 5).

Folklore, Religion, and Who We Are

The Concept of the West

And Other Hindrances to the Study of Mormon Folklore

Throughout Bert Wilson's essays, articles, and talks, there runs a constant emphasis on the importance of the individual regardless of geography or religion. This clearly reveals a deep understanding of his own religious ethos and the universal nature of religion as a cultural force, regardless of where it is situated. In "The Concept of the West," Wilson argues that to understand the folklore of expressive religious behavior, "We must begin with the religious individual, with *homo religiosus*." As folklorists or others who may be interested in religious behavior, he suggests that "our aim should be to discover what it means to be human and religious." The editors who initially published the following article noted that "[Wilson] unearths entrenched assumptions and gives us new perspective on the purported impact of geography on religion and vice-versa" (see Stewart 2000, 6). The Mormons are seen, Wilson reminds us, "not only as a religious group, but also as a regional group," and that presents a complex hindrance to the study of Mormon folklore. As Wilson notes, Mormons are a worldwide organization. They are both urban *and* rural, hierarchical *and* bottom-up, fixed *and* dynamic, mechanical *and* organic, controlled *and* creative. In short, individual Mormon interpretation of the belief system is as varied as any other religious, cultural, or folk group, and Mormon folklife and behaviors occur in differing cultural settings internationally.

In this article, Wilson quotes Jack Santino's essay entitled "Catholic Folklore and Folk Catholicism," (1982), because of an intriguing argument that Wilson both supports and expands. Santino suggests looking at "the circumstance of being Catholic" as "an aspect of a larger phenomenon, that of Catholicism, which is itself a cultural force." Mormonism is also a cultural force, and Wilson compares the circumstance of being Catholic with the folklore of Mormon missionaries. Referring to his "On Being Human" article, also included in this volume, Wilson

---

Published in *Worldviews and the American West: The Life of the Place Itself*, 178–90, ed. Polly Stewart et al. (Logan: Utah State University Press, 2000). Reprinted by permission of Utah State University Press.

states, "[Missionaries] serve in different regions throughout the world and in each region develop a body of lore peculiar to that location, but by the circumstance of being Mormon missionaries and participating in common experiences, they have developed a body of lore that shapes their identity and binds them together, no matter in which part of the globe they might have served." Wilson then shares Santino's lament that the lore of being Catholic, or of being Mormon, has been insufficiently studied, and he advocates the study of "folklore that comes into being simply by virtue of individuals' being religious, no matter where they are found." He encourages us, therefore, to shift our emphasis from the narrower study of folk religion to the broader, more inclusive, and ultimately more rewarding study of religious folklore.

Wilson suggests that we must expand our vision in regard to studying Mormon folklore "from the past to the present, from the rural landscape to the urban centers, and from the West in general to the faith and commitment that give unity and direction to Mormon life." The Mormon belief system is a scaffolding upon which its adherents throughout the world build their lives, but the cultural contexts of their lives vary according to experience, time, and space. Wilson argues, therefore, that Mormon lore and the lore of other religious individuals need to be studied in the context of "the swirl of stories that has surrounded us since we were born—stories we listen to or tell about the events of everyday life and about the worlds we occupy," a sentiment he expressed in the article "Personal Narratives: The Family Novel."

In his essay "On Being Human," Wilson reminds us that "generalizations . . . must be used with care; no one individual will ever fit the generalized pattern completely, and this behavior, though it may have taken on a distinctive Mormon coloring—or, in our case, a Mormon missionary hue—may not be peculiar to Mormons or missionaries at all but rather to people everywhere." The key to Wilson's methodology that combines individual experience and generalized understanding is contained in his article "Personal Narratives: The Family Novel," where he states, "I can't imagine that you will be overly interested in my particular family, but by showing you how such stories have operated there perhaps I can lend you new lenses to look at the ways they operate in your families." By articulately showing us "hindrances to the study of Mormon folklore," Wilson again opens rich avenues and directions for the study of the religious folklore throughout the world—by reminding us to study first "that splendid and worthy object . . . *homo religiosus*," regardless of the physical environment.

—*Jacqueline S. Thursby*

ALTHOUGH THE STORY OF MORMON FOLKLORE IS CONSIDERED BY MANY scholars to be inextricably connected with the story of the American West, to read either of these stories as an inevitable part of the other is to read both of them wrong. But associating Mormons with the West is only one of the hindrances to the proper interpretation of Mormon folklore. Over the years such interpretation has been impaired by two separate emphases in folklore and historical studies—first, by a lingering adherence to Robert Redfield's notions of the little (or folk) tradition versus the great (or urban) tradition and, second, by the persistence of the environmental-determinism theories of Frederick Jackson Turner and, especially, of Walter Prescott Webb. Both of these approaches have stopped us from adequately examining what is most important not only in the study of Mormon folklore but in the study of religious folklore in general—that is, the nature of religion itself.

Beginning in the 1930s, Redfield attempted to draw distinctions between what he called "folk" and "urban" societies by viewing folk societies as unsophisticated, homogenous, conservative, agrarian (or rural) enclaves isolated from a surrounding sophisticated, heterogeneous, dynamic, city environment (1930; 1941; 1947; 1955). It would be a mistake to tie Redfield to the nineteenth-century advocates of unilinear cultural evolution. Still, they shared points in common—especially their situating folklore among the rural and unlettered common folk isolated by these circumstances from the more progressive and educated urban world.

These ideas have strongly influenced students of religious folklore in America, particularly those who have focused on what William Clements has called "the folk church." The folk church, says Clements, "constitutes the basic unit in American folk religion" (1983, 139; 1974; 1978). Drawing in part on Don Yoder's well-known distinction between official and unofficial religion (1974), a distinction bearing strong Redfieldian imprints, Clements argues that the folk church is characterized by an "orientation toward the past, scriptural literalism, consciousness of Providence, emphasis on evangelism, informality, emotionalism, moral rigorism, sectarianism, egalitarianism, and relative isolation of physical facilities." More important for our purposes, the folk church, like a Redfieldian or especially a nineteenth-century folk community, exists "outside the main currents of American culture," "often in direct antithesis to the establishment churches" and "mainline religion" and flourishes along this more sophisticated society's "social, economic, political, and even physical margins" among "peripheral social groups," "low-income economic groups," "politically disenfranchised groups," and "people on the wilderness frontier" (Clements 1983, 1139).

Others have employed the same distinction between folk and mainline churches. In *Powerhouse for God* (1988), for example, Jeff Todd Titon, citing both Yoder and Clements, defines folk religion "as religion outside of the 'official' or established or normative religion." "So long," he continues, "as the definition of the folk church turns on the 'folk' as a group outside the power structure . . . I am certainly happy with that folk-cultural definition. . . . 'Outside the power structure' is admittedly vague, but it suggests differences in wealth, status, education, and most of all economic and political impact among insiders and outsiders" (1988, 144, 149). In their excellent *Diversities of Gifts: Field Studies in Southern Religion* (1988), Ruel W. Tyson, James L. Peacock, and

Daniel W. Patterson bring together a group of essays focusing on what they call "independent Protestants," groups very much like Clements's folk churches. The essays, they tell us in their preface and epilogue, are "studies of Southern religious life, but not of the highly organised and self-publicizing denominations like the Southern Baptists, Episcopalians, Presbyterians, or United Methodists." They are instead groups that "have no national bureaucracies and do not house their faiths in uptown churches" and that "choose not to conform to mainstream models." These churches tend not to attract the wealthy and have no "large-scale hierarchical or associational organization." Members of these churches, who "favor preaching inspired by God directly" and are "suspicious of education in seminaries . . . tend to locate on country roads, mountain ridges, or side streets rather than on the main street or in wealthy suburbs" (1988, xi, xiii, 205).

In *God's Peculiar People: Women's Voices and Folk Tradition in a Pentecostal Church* (1988a), Elaine Lawless eschews some of the above distinguishing features of folk religion but still adheres to what is central in Clements and in Tyson, Peacock, and Patterson—that is, to independent religious enclaves, Redfield's little communities, characterized by the absence of an established hierarchy and of fixed theological and liturgical forms. "Folk religion," Lawless insists, "must be recognized as a traditional religion that thrives in individual, independent religious groups that owe little allegiance to hierarchical [read 'mainline'] powers" (1988a, 3).

In spite of a certain irreverence that may have crept into what I have just said, I do not object to the studies I have referred to. These are admirable treatments of southern fundamentalist and Pentecostal groups. But I do object to the part being made the standard for the whole—to the model applied to these investigations of small-scale southern religious groups becoming the pattern for other studies of American religious folklore.

The main problem with this approach is that it excludes from serious study the vibrant traditions of those uptown churches. For example, in 1984 Lawless wrote:

> The Mormon religion could never be considered a "folk religion"; its standardized, hierarchical make-up prevents the emergence of the more performative modes and variation typical of folk religions. And Mormonism is not a sub-religion or sect, a fringe element of any main-line American denomination; there is no element here of little society to larger society of which Robert Redfield speaks. (79)

What do we do, then, with the religious folklore of Mormons, Catholics, Episcopalians, and other established religions, religions that are not little societies? Clements urges the study of "parallels" to folk religious traits "among mainline religious groups" (1983, 139). Others follow suit. For example, in the syllabus of his course in folklore and religion given at Utah State University in

1988, Steve Siporin stated: "We will explore folk religions and part of 'major' religions that owe their continuity and dynamism more to the practices and beliefs of their members than to the writings of institutional leaders"—that is, Siporin's students would study only those parts of official religions that approximated folk religions. In the syllabus to her course in folk religion given the same year at the University of Missouri, Lawless was unequivocal: "This course will focus on various religions that have been identified by folklorists as 'folk religions,' that is religions that owe very little, if any, allegiance to an official, hierarchical governing body. . . . We will also be identifying 'folk' practices which survive in mainstream, official religions." Lawless then promised to study Mormons for their "'folk' religious qualities."

In recent years, some progress has been made in looking at religious traditions from a broader perspective than that of folk religion. In *Handmaidens of the Lord: Pentecostal Women Preachers and Traditional Religion* (1988b), Lawless still referred to folk religion and still cited Redfield, but subsequent books (1993; 1996) show no evidence of the term or the Redfield citations. Lawless still teaches a course in folk religion and introduces the course with readings from Yoder and Clements. To her credit, though, she asks students in a midterm examination to "develop an argument that outlines the pitfalls of attempting to define a 'folk religion'or a 'folk church.'" The question suggests that she and her students are taking a critical, questioning approach to these concepts. In another course, Religious Expression and Folk Belief, Lawless moves away from folk religions per se and explores phenomena occurring cross-culturally, such as the nature of verbal art, performance, and ritual and belief. Siporin, in his current folklore and religion class, still states that he and his students will "explore precisely those dimensions of religion that lie outside organized, formal religious systems." But his selection of course texts like Mireca Eliade's *The Sacred and the Profane: The Nature of Religion* (1959) and Victor Turner's *The Ritual Process: Structure and Anti-Structure* (1969) suggests that this class will also examine religious phenomena cross-culturally. To the extent that other folklore courses across the country follow these models, these are encouraging approaches. But they do not go far enough. There is nothing wrong, of course, in studying independent Protestants, folk religions, or folk churches. But we must not look at all religious traditions in formal vs. informal or institutional vs. noninstitutional terms. We must understand that the formal, hierarchical religious institution may itself be the source of much folklore.

In 1982, Jack Santino, in an intriguing essay entitled "Catholic Folklore and Folk Catholicism," recommended an approach that could, if adopted, produce rich results in the study of organized or mainline religions. In addition to studying "folk Catholicism" (the lore of enclaved groups), Santino argued, researchers should focus on the lore in Catholic communities that results from the circumstance of being Catholic. "I am more interested," he wrote, "in seeing [the St. Francis phenomenon] as an aspect of a larger phenomenon, that of Catholicism, which is itself a cultural force." He continued:

> In addition to popular culture and folk Catholicism, there is another aspect to this corpus of material: the shared, expressive, traditional culture of mainstream American Catholics, members not of Redfield's little, or folk, society, but his great society, people who, although they may be members of an urban ethnic group, share with other Catholics of different backgrounds, not their ethnicity, and more than simply the name of their religion. They also share tales of parochial school education, of nuns and priest, beliefs, legends, and cosmology, perhaps even sharing worldviews and behaviors which are the result of processes informed by all of the above. . . . Perhaps we are better served by the study of Catholic material in ethnic, regional, urban, and familial studies of folklore. It is my experience, however, that Catholics share a body of lore that transcends those categories, that is recognizably based in the experiences of Catholicism in America and can be most profitably approached as the expression of that experience. (1982, 97, 100)

Reading these lines, I think of the lore of Mormon missionaries. They serve in different regions throughout the world and in each region develop a body of lore peculiar to that location, but by the circumstance of being Mormon missionaries and of participating in common experiences, they have developed a body of lore that shapes their identity and binds them together, no matter in which part of the globe they might have served (Wilson 1981).

Santino laments that the kind of lore to which he would direct our attention "has been neither delineated nor studied by folklorists" (1982, 99). I share his lament. We need to move from the narrow concept of *folk religion* to the broader concept of *religious folklore*—that is, to folklore that comes into being simply by virtue of individuals' being religious, no matter where they are found. We do not, or should not, talk about folk occupations or folk regions. Rather, we focus on occupational or regional folklore—folklore arising from the circumstance of working at different occupations or of residing in different places. In like manner, we should shift our attention in religious studies to the lore that arises, not just from enclaved groups, but from the circumstances of practicing religion.

In American folklore study in general, we have been able to move from agrarian to urban worlds without neglecting the former, from peripheral to mainline society, discovering in the process that folklore does not just survive in the city but that the city itself generates folklore. It is time to make such a move in religious folklore studies, to see the institutional church, like the city, as a generator of folklore, to recognize what we know to be true in other areas of folklore research—that is, that folklore is common to the species, not just to those living on the margins of modern society. In spite of their churches' hierarchical structures and mainline status, Baptists, Episcopalians, Presbyterians, Methodists, Catholics, and Mormons have generated religious traditions as profoundly significant as those found among independent Protestants. If we can do nothing more than reduce the lore of these established churches to parts of the larger official religion or identify in their lore folk religious elements or parallels to so-called folk religions, then we will have taken a giant step backwards in our attempt to understand the religious behavior of our fellow beings.

In the case of Mormons, the problem of proper interpretation is made more acute by the fact that Mormons are seen not only as a religious group, but also as a regional group. Thus, the Redfieldian notion of the isolated enclave separated from mainline culture once again hinders understanding, this time, paradoxically, because Mormons are seen as belonging to the periphery.

Though Mormon folklorists had been writing about their religious culture for some years, Mormon folklore was brought to the attention of a larger American and international audience by Richard M. Dorson, who in 1959 published his popular *American Folklore* and included "Utah Mormons" in his chapter on "Regional Folk Cultures," arguing that they were one of the five richest regional folk cultures in America (1959, 113–21). Identifying these regional enclaves as "minority cultures," he stated:

> Such nooks and byways resist the relentless forces of change and mobility in contemporary American life. In place of mass culture, they represent folk cultures, whose roots and traditions contrast oddly with the standardized glitter of American urban industrial society. In the folk region, people are wedded to the land, and the land holds memories. . . . These folk regions become important reservoirs of traditional lore. Much of their folklore will be common to other parts of the country and to other countries, but they stand out in the density and abundance of their oral tradition. (1959, 75)

In 1964, in *Buying the Wind: Regional Folklore in the United States*, Dorson reinforced this notion by including Utah Mormons among the major groups surveyed (497–535). Dorson's view is not quite survivalist, though it comes perilously close. It defines regional, and therefore Mormon, culture as agrarian and conservative, in contrast to a dynamic urban society. As a means of understanding contemporary Mormons the statement is entirely misleading since the overwhelming majority of Mormons today live in cities.

If Dorson fell short of the mark in characterizing Mormons, John Greenway missed it completely. In 1964, the same year Dorson published *Buying the Wind*, Greenway, then editor of the *Journal of American Folklore*, added another element to the definition of this regional group—evolutionary backwardness—and thus harked back not to Redfield, but to Redfield's nineteenth-century predecessors. "Folk to me," he said, "means a phase in the evolution of culture from primitiveness to civilization, and a folk society is a homogeneous unsophisticated group living in but isolated from a surrounding sophisticated society by such factors as topography, economics, race, and, as in the case of the Mormons, religion" (1964, 196). Five years later, in 1969, Greenway began his *Folklore of the Great West* with a lead essay on the Mormons, in a section he called "The Good Old Days." In the introduction to the book, Greenway defined not just Mormons but other western groups as culturally backward islands, "separated enclaves" surrounded by progressive mainline American culture. "Since advance lies with numbers in the evolution of culture," he argued, "such dissident groups are condemned to fall backward, the faster for their coherence" (1969, 3).

Thus in the eyes of at least some leading folklorists, both Mormons and other western groups have been viewed as somewhat romantic peasant communities that fit nineteenth-century concepts of folklore. And to a certain degree that idea persists. For example, in 1988 Hector Lee, speaking of the Mormon and western studies of Austin Fife, wrote:

> Because this is a region of spectacular scenic beauty that appeals to tourists, and a milieu that fosters highly advanced educational systems in a modern environment impressively replete with the latest electronic sophistication, it is easy to overlook the fact that there has always been and still is a solid bedrock and thick underlying vein of traditional lore here, which gives a special character to the social structure of the area. (1988, xvi)

That Lee felt constrained to explain that even in an educated, modern, urban society folklore could actually exist suggests that we still have some way to go in our understanding of the nature of folklore in general and of Mormon folklore in particular.

Other sources in historical/cultural studies have also contributed to misleading interpretations of Mormon folklore. In 1893 Frederick Jackson Turner published his famous essay "The Significance of the Frontier in American History." In opposition to the older view that social institutions evolve like germ cells, without reference to environment, he claimed in this and subsequent essays that environment has significantly shaped the course of cultural development. The most important feature of the American environment, he argued, was the presence of an area of free land on the western edge of a constantly advancing frontier. As settlers poured into this free land west of the frontier, they were changed into the ruggedly independent, self-reliant, freedom-loving characters we have liked to call American (Turner 1920).

It would be tempting to see the Mormon migration to the Great Basin in these terms. Consider the following story collected in 1924 from an old pioneer woman whose family had pushed and pulled their meager possessions across the plains in a handcart because they could not afford a team and wagon:

> We were six in family when we started—father, my stepmother, two brothers, a sister sixteen years of age and myself. It seems strange

> that there were more men and boys died than there were women and girls. My two brothers died on the way, and my father died the day after we arrived in Salt Lake. The night my oldest brother died there were nineteen deaths in camp. In the morning we would find their starved and frozen bodies right beside us, not knowing when they died until daylight revealed the ghastly sight. I remember two women that died sitting by me. My mother was cooking some cakes of bread for one of them. When mother gave her one of them she tossed it into the fire and dropped over dead. I remember distinctly when the terrible storm came, and how dismayed the people were. My stepmother took my little brother and myself by the hand and helped us along the best she could while sister and father floundered along with the handcart. How we did struggle though that snow, tumbling over sage brush and crying with cold and hunger.
>
> When we camped they had to scrape a place to camp on, and not much wood to make a fire with. The food rations became scarce—there were four ounces daily for an adult and two for a child, and sometimes a little piece of meat. Oh! I'll never forget it, never!
>
> When we arrived in Salt Lake we were taken to the assembly room and the people were asked to take as many of us into their homes as they could take care of. My father and mother were taken to one place and my sister and I each to another. I did not see my father again—he died the next day. . . . I did not stand on my feet until the sixth of March. I lost the first joints of six of my toes. My step-mother then carried me twelve blocks to [a] man's home who had been a friend of father's. Mother would carry me as far as she could, then she would put me down in the snow. Then we would cry a little while and go on again. (Ricks 1924)

It would be easy to see this story as an excellent example of the American character forged by the frontier experience—the resolve to keep struggling forward in the face of desperate odds, to stop and cry for a while but then to get up and go on again, to rub one's bruises after being thrown from a spirited horse but then to get on and ride again, to mourn the loss of the *Challenger* astronauts but then to put another shuttle into space. And maybe it is. Mormons themselves, who are as susceptible to nationalistic propaganda as anyone, may see the story in that light today.

But for most of them it will carry other messages. It will remind them that their ancestors were on the plains suffering terribly not to fulfill some grand dream of American manifest destiny but because they had been denied their constitutional rights to worship as they pleased, because their prophet Joseph Smith had been murdered, because the governor of Missouri had issued an order calling for the extermination of all Mormons in the state, and because they had been driven from their homes in Illinois to begin an exodus that would stretch over several decades. Hardly the stuff of patriots' dreams. What's more, the Mormon westward migration and settling of the Great Basin, far from being an exercise in rugged individualism, was one of the most successful communal and communitarian movements since Moses led the children of Israel to the Promised Land.

Turner argued that it was not a specific place but a constantly moving frontier that had shaped American character. In 1931, in *The Great Plains*, Walter Prescott Webb modified this view by claiming that geography itself (that is, place) was an important determiner of culture. The Great Plains, said Webb, had three primary characteristics—they were flat, treeless, and arid. Any land west of the Mississippi possessing at least two of these features would significantly determine the life lived there. The Great Plains environment, he said, "constitutes a geographic unity whose influences have been so powerful as to put a characteristic mark upon everything that survives within its borders." And again, "The historical truth that becomes apparent in the end is that the Great Plains have bent and molded Anglo-American life, have destroyed traditions, and have influenced institutions in a most singular manner" (1931, vi, 8). In a similar vein, Richard Dorson, who fixed Mormons in Utah, was to add in *American Folklore*: "Each regional complex contains its own genius . . . depending upon the historical and ethnic and geographical elements that have shaped its character" (1959, 75).

In 1942, eleven years after the appearance of *The Great Plains*, western novelist Wallace Stegner published his influential *Mormon Country*; the same year historian Nels Anderson published *Desert Saints: The Mormon Frontier in Utah*. Both books identified Mormonism not just as a religion but as a place, a western place. Other histories followed, such as Gustive O. Larson's *Prelude to the Kingdom: Mormon Desert Conquest*, in 1947, and Leonard J. Arrington's monumentally important *Great Basin Kingdom: An Economic History of the Latter-day Saints, 1830–1900*, in 1958—not the Mormon Kingdom, nor the Kingdom of God, but the Great Basin Kingdom, a western geographical kingdom.

This notion of geographic determinism sounds clearly in the titles of Austin and Alta Fife's *Saints of Sage and Saddle: Folklore among the Mormons* (1956), and Thomas E. Cheney's *Mormon Songs from the Rocky Mountains* (1968). Fife especially saw himself as a regional folklorist, his Mormon studies being only part of a larger effort to understand the West. The title of Hector Lee's *The Three Nephites: The Substance and Significance of the Legend in Folklore* (1949) is less revealing, but Lee, a friend of Stegner's, clearly saw the legends as part of the pioneer West, useful, he said, as a means of understanding "pioneer concepts, attitudes, and impulses" (126). And he frequently used Stegner's term, Mormon Country (1949, 9; 1988, 15).

Though all these works at times rise above their titles and tell us things about Mormons having little to do with the West, the public perception of Mormons places them squarely in the center of the West. This is clear from the dust jacket and cover illustrations on the two editions of the Fifes' *Saints of Sage and Saddle.* The 1956 edition, published by Indiana University, shows a bearded westerner—a rifle in one hand, a tablet with mysterious inscriptions in the other—and a rural village in the background. The University of Utah's reprinting of the book in 1980 shows a ragged family trailing a wagon train across a barren western landscape.

Without question, this landscape does play a part in contemporary Mormon lore. For example, Three Nephite stories in which one of the eternal wanderers introduced to us by the Book of Mormon comes to the aid of a family whose car has broken down miles from anywhere are understandable only if one appreciates western distances. But the main function of the landscape is to provide a resonant background. The principal focus is elsewhere, on a God who will intervene to save the lives of the faithful. Consider still one more story:

> A dear L.D.S. [Mormon] lady left her small family in Phoenix to go to the temple in Mesa. While she was in the middle of a session, she got a strong feeling that she should go home—that something was terribly wrong. The feeling wouldn't go away, so she told the temple president and asked him what she should do. He said, "Have no fear. You are doing the right thing by being here. All is well at home." So she continued the session. She hurried home when she was through and found her six-year-old daughter in bed. She asked her daughter if something was wrong. She told her mother that she had left the house while the babysitter was busy with the other children and had gone out by the canal near their house. While she was playing, she slipped on some grass and fell in. She couldn't swim, and the canal is deep. Many people drown this way. But a lady all dressed in white came along just then and got her just before she would have drowned. The lady set her on the bank and made sure she was okay. The little girl asked the lady who she was because she knew that the lady didn't live near by. So, the lady told her what her name was. The lady who saved the little girl was the lady whom the mother had done work for in the temple that day. (Wright 1975)

Barre Toelken, who studies water lore and symbolism in western and Mormon lore, is interested in this story because the themes of water and irrigation make their way into sacred narrative (1991). He is right, of course, but to really comprehend this story one must probe the depths of deeply-held Mormon beliefs, beliefs I haven't space to detail fully here. Briefly, Mormons believe that saving gospel ordinances must be performed in the flesh. Since their deceased ancestors have not had this opportunity, Mormons seek out the names of these ancestors through genealogical research and then vicariously perform these ordinances for them in sacred ceremonies in their temples. The session mentioned in the story would be an occasion for performing these ordinances.

To believing Mormons, this story speaks many messages. It encourages them to persist in the search for their ancestral roots; it testifies to the validity of temple ordinances; it suggests that God is a caring God who will protect them in time of need; it stresses the importance of the family and strengthens family ties; it gives them hope that these ties will continue beyond this life. In one narrative situation after another, these messages are brought forcefully home by an artistic performance of the story designed to move listeners to action and are made all the more powerful by the narrative symmetry in which two lives are saved at the same moment—the physical life of the young girl and the eternal life of the rescuer, the mother serving as the link between the two. Surely, no one would argue that the performance of the story is any less powerful because it occurs in a church with a fixed theology and an established hierarchical structure. And one would hope that no one would demean those who tell the story by referring to it as a folk religious element surviving in an established church.

The story has little to do with the West and even less to do with untenable notions of cultural evolution or of isolated cultural enclaves. Anyone who would understand the West must, of course, pay heed to the Mormon role in settling and developing that important part of our country. But the emphasis should probably be more on the impact of the Mormons on the West than of the West on the Mormons. Especially is that true today when most Mormons do not live in the West. Of today's ten million Mormons only ten percent live in Utah, and over half of all Mormons live outside the United States and Canada (Hart 1997). Therefore, any attempt to describe the contemporary Mormon ethos as a result of western landscape will be doomed to failure.

If we are ever to understand Mormons by examining their folklore, we must turn our eyes from the past to the present, from the rural landscape to urban centers, and from the West in general to the faith and commitment that give unity and direction to Mormon life. And we must finally discover behind Mormon folklore typical human beings coming to terms through their lore with enduring life and death questions that know neither temporal nor cultural boundaries.

As folklorists, our aim should be to discover what it means to be human; as folklorists interested in religious behavior, our aim should be to discover what it means to be human and religious. Lawless argues that in our attempts to understand religious folklore we should begin with what is traditional within a particular religion (1988a, 4). I would argue that while we may end with what is traditional, with those expressive religious behaviors we call folklore, we must not start there. We must begin with the religious individual, with *homo religiosus*. Until we work our way back through the cultural overlays of the physical environment, until we discover the generative force that lies behind both highly structured liturgical ritual on the one hand and spontaneous witnessing of the spirit on the other, until we get back to religious individuals in both uptown churches and on mountain ridges, until we comprehend their need for security, their quest for meaning, their desire for the continuance of what they cherish most, until we get there, all our efforts, to quote an old book, may be little more than sounding brass or tinkling cymbals.

And when we get there, when we have worked our way through folk churches, through established churches, through the intricate relationships between canonized dogma and resulting folk expression, through Pentecostal brothers and sisters, through saints of sage and saddle, we will discover at last, standing alone, that splendid and worthy object of our study—*homo religiosus.*

THE STUDY OF MORMON FOLKLORE

An Uncertain Mirror for Truth

Although my associations with Bert Wilson have a timeless quality, I know that our friendship was greatly deepened by the opportunity for long talks as we participated in the Fife Folklore Conference at Utah State University in 1979. Bert, his scholarly work, and our long conversations that summer are a part of who I am and how I try to think about folklore, especially the religious and spiritual dimensions of the topic that so interest both of us.

This article, "The Study of Mormon Folklore: An Uncertain Mirror for Truth," became part of a fascinating, and, to some extent, troubling set of experiences that Bert and I shared more than a decade ago. These experiences showed how the scholarly bias for objectivity conflicts with attempts to introduce personal reflexivity into religious studies. In 1989, Bert and I were invited to be part of a panel on "Reflexivity in the Study of Belief," presented at the annual meeting of the American Folklore Society. For this panel, Bert chose to expand on the themes raised in "The Study of Mormon Folklore," originally given as a Christensen Lecture at Brigham Young University. In his panel paper, eventually published as "Folklore, a Mirror for What? Reflections of a Mormon Folklorist," (1995), Bert noted that scholars, like their informants, shape their expressions in response to social pressures, "to please and meet the expectations of those who will read our publications or view our presentations" (15). Bert tackles central issues of belief study, specifically the ways that folklorists' values and expectations shape their description of belief and its cultural aspects.

Both essays, therefore, reflect Bert's growing awareness of how his own depiction of Mormon folklore had been shaped by scholarly expectations to produce an account he came to feel was not inaccurate, but incomplete in important ways. He notes in both papers that Mormon folklore scholars (including himself) had not attended to the many stories about people who devote themselves to the service of others, which are just as much a part of Mormon oral tradition as are tales of

---

This paper was delivered as the Brigham Young University College of Humanities P. A. Christensen Lecture, February 17, 1988. It was published in *Dialogue: A Journal of Mormon Thought* 22 (1989): 95–110. Reprinted by permission of the Dialogue Foundation.

the supernatural. To illustrate this point, Bert described his moving experience in Finland when he joined another man in blessing a blind, elderly woman who was having back trouble. The woman thanked Bert for blessing her with peace. Realizing the deep importance of such experiences, and their frequent recounting in Mormon oral tradition, led him to question the balance of his own past accounts of Mormon religious folklore.

In the "Mirror for What?" paper, Bert provided some clear examples of the scholarly pressures leading to the imbalance that favors supernatural events over common acts of service. In one example, a prominent folklorist, on hearing Bert's intention to include more such everyday material, said to him, "You're not going to collect those, are you? Those things are everywhere." When a colleague used the "Uncertain Mirror" article in a seminar in folklore and religion, both the colleague and her students commented on the lack of supernatural events that would identify the Finnish blessing story with more common expressions of religious folklore. His colleague said, "Basically you had a warm fuzzy feeling which told you that you were comfortable with being a Mormon" (see Wilson 1995, 18). That warm fuzzy feeling, the students had thought, was personal and religious but not folklore. I would suppose that had the Finnish woman instantaneously received her sight or been suddenly healed of her bad back, the status of folklore might well have been achieved. Similar responses of confusion followed our first attempt to publish the panel papers in a scholarly journal. After reviewers read the papers, Bert's approach and "insider" status earned his paper the epithet of "testimonial," while my paper was deemed appropriate for a 1950s-era parish newspaper. As noted, I eventually published the panel papers when I was guest editor of *Western Folklore.* But these initial responses show the high stakes involved in attempting reflexivity, especially when core beliefs and values are involved.

Indicative of Bert's approach to belief studies and scholarship on Mormon folklore, the two papers I have discussed are reflexive accounts of being a Mormon folklorist who studies Mormon culture. "Uncertain Mirror" is addressed to a nonfolklorist Mormon audience and "Mirror for What?" to a non-Mormon folklorist audience. Both essays were directly subjected to the pressures of bias toward scholarly objectivity that Bert describes and challenges. In our work on religious folklore, Bert and I assert that personal commitments cannot be eliminated; they can only be made explicit and controlled for. Bert's essays, and some of the reactions to them, illustrate so forcefully that when personal commitments are expressed reflexively then some members of the academy question the validity of the scholar's voice in preference for an objective and neutral stance. The result in terms of religious studies is a kind of one-way mirror, to stay with Bert's reflective image. The believer's commitments are revealed to the observer, but the observer's side of the glass is dark and offers no reflection. The only antidote to the blinding effects of this stance is the kind of honest reflexivity that Bert offers us, and a commitment to the value of a diversity of views rather than approaches rooted in the now untenable assertion that there is a single, neutral view that scholarship can claim.

—David J. Hufford

WHEN I BEGAN GRADUATE WORK AT INDIANA UNIVERSITY IN 1962, I HAD NO intention of studying Mormon folklore.[1] Indeed, my only experience with that subject had been mild shock when my English Romanticism professor, Orea Tanner, referred to stories of the Three Nephites as "folklore." I had come to IU to pursue a much more serious end—to learn as much as possible about Finnish folklore as a necessary prelude for my intended study of Finnish literature. But then I met Richard M. Dorson, head of the Indiana University Folklore Program and the dean of American folklore study. Relying on the works of Mormon folklorists—Thomas Cheney, Hector Lee, and Austin and Alta Fife—Dorson had written a chapter on Mormon folklore for his very popular text, *American Folklore* (1959); he lectured on Mormon folklore in his survey courses; and he made sure his students paid attention by asking questions on the subject in doctoral examinations.

When I arrived in Bloomington, he was delighted to have a real Mormon in his program and soon set me the task of studying my own cultural heritage. During the fieldwork class I took from Dorson, I turned to Mormon faculty members and graduate students at the university and collected and annotated forty legends of the Three Nephites. Professor Dorson was amazed to discover that Mormon folklore could be collected outside Utah, and I was hooked. A shortened version of this collection became my first publication in a professional journal (1969); and, though I have continued to study Finnish folklore and literature, I have from that time to the present devoted much of my energy to collecting and trying to understand the folk literature of the culture that produced me.

In the classes I have taught at Brigham Young University and Utah State University since completing my study at Indiana in 1967, I have required students to collect, interpret, and submit to the archives folklore they have encountered in their own lives. Though they have been free to collect whatever they wish, many, probably believing that following their professor's enthusiasms is the better part of valor, have turned their attention to their own Mormon traditions, with the result that the archives at both USU and BYU are brim full with Mormon materials. The slim file of Three Nephite narratives I collected at Indiana University now contains about fifteen hundred separate stories; the missionary collection John B. Harris and I have brought together includes well over five thousand items; and these are only parts of the whole. The total Mormon collection contains thousands of separate items, mostly narratives—a database large enough, I trust, to warrant my making some generalizations and suggesting some directions for future research.

Before trying to draw a picture of the Mormon world that emerges from narratives in the folklore archives, I must make a few statements about the premises that underpin the work of most folklorists.

First, the people who possess a body of lore—that is, the folk—are not, as was once thought, unlettered, mainly agrarian people bound together by some kind of psychic unity that stretches relatively unchanged across cultural boundaries and from age to age. This concept of "the folk," which, unfortunately, some historians writing about Joseph Smith's magical practices still adhere to, is both outdated and misleading, and any research conclusions based on it should be accepted with great caution, if at all.

Who then are the folk? We all are. Each of us has a number of social identities—for example, I am a father, a college teacher, a Democrat, a westerner, and a Mormon. When I am with people who share my Mormon identity and in a social context that brings that identity to the fore, my other identities will be at least partially suppressed and I will think and act in traditionally prescribed ways, in ways similar to those in which other members of my group will think and act. As we relate to each other and to our Mormon world, we will attempt to manipulate the social environment to our advantage by generating, performing, and transmitting "lore," by communicating, that is, through traditional forms ranging from the stories of inspiration and courage we recount about our pioneer ancestors, to the advice and comfort we give to a friend mourning the death of a loved one, to the jokes we tell about our bishops. Again, this is a process we all participate in. We are all the folk.

Second, narratives shared by members of a like-minded group serve as a mirror for culture, as a reflector of what members of the group consider most important. Thus the stories we Latter-day Saints tell provide valuable insights into our hopes, fears, dreams, and anxieties. This is so for the simple reason that folklore depends on the spoken word for its survival. Like all people, we tell stories about those things that interest us most or are most important to us. Each individual Latter-day Saint is in some ways different from all other Latter-day Saints, but if a story does not appeal to a sufficient number of us to keep it alive, if it does not somehow relate to what I have called our "value center" (1973a, 48–49)—a consensus center of attitude and belief that ties us all together—it will either be altered by the tellers to make it conform to that value center or it will disappear. Those stories that continue to be told can serve, therefore, as a barometer of our principal concerns at any given time. If we want to understand Mormon hearts and minds, we should pay close heed to Mormon oral narratives.

Third, storytellers themselves recount their narratives not to help scholars better understand what is important to them but rather to satisfy their own ends and meet their own needs. A Mormon missionary who tells his junior companion about another missionary who decided to test his priesthood power by ordaining a post to the priesthood and then was struck dead by a bolt of lightning does not tell that story to satisfy intellectual curiosity. The story does reflect the Mormon conviction that God will not be mocked and is useful, therefore, to the student of Mormon belief; but the missionary tells the story primarily to persuade his companion, and to remind himself, that if they don't want to be zapped by lightning they had better take serious things seriously. In other words, folklore has significant functions for both tellers and listeners.

Finally, every telling of a story is in some ways an exercise in behavior modification, an employment by the narrator of a rhetorical strategy designed to persuade the audience to accept a certain point of view or to follow a certain course of action—to convince one's fellows, for example, that ordaining posts to the priesthood is not a very healthy practice. Few storytellers would consider themselves artists, but they know that if they are to encourage the righteous or reform sinners they must make their stories artful—that is, they must imbue them with power. There are, of course, good and bad storytellers just as there are good and bad creative writers. The principal difference between successful oral and written storytelling lies not in the artistic merit of the works created but in the methods of composition. The writer achieves artistic power by carefully arranging words on the written page. The speaker of tales, in a dynamic process that cannot adequately be captured on the written page, achieves the same end by responding to an active audience. It is this interplay between teller and listeners which in the final analysis will give shape, meaning, and power to the story created. The art of folklore, therefore, lies not in the tale told, but in the *telling* of the tale. Some of the stories I will turn to now, reduced to paper, may seem fairly pedestrian; but in actual performance many have had the power to move listeners to laughter or to tears.

If a dreadful holocaust were somehow to destroy all Mormon documents except those in the BYU Folklore Archives, what sort of picture of our contemporary Mormon world would a future generation of scholars, using only these surviving manuscripts, be able to draw? From the manuscripts, they would discover, first, that we have ennobled our pioneer past and made it a model for present action; second, that we see ourselves as actors in a cosmic struggle between the forces of good and evil; and, third, that in spite of the seriousness of this struggle, or perhaps because of it, we have developed the saving grace of easing tensions by laughing at ourselves and sometimes at the system we live under. In what follows, I offer a brief glimpse of each of these constituent parts of our Mormon world as revealed in folklore.

Every culture has its own creation myths—a body of narratives explaining how the social order came into being and providing models after which people in the present should pattern their behavior. People from all cultures tend generally to believe that the first way of doing things was the best way; therefore, when they struggle to solve contemporary problems, they seek answers in the primordial reality reflected in their origin narratives. Jews and Christians turn to the Bible, Communists to the words and deeds of Marx and Lenin, Americans to stories of their founding fathers, and Latter-day Saints to accounts of their pioneer ancestors.

From the outset, our Mormon forebears found themselves in sharp conflict with established American society. Their insistence that only they possessed the "correct" way to salvation, their tendency to establish political control in the areas they settled, their attempts to establish a theocratic state, and, later, their practice of polygamy engendered the hostility of their fellow citizens, who drove the beleaguered Latter-day Saints from New York to Ohio to Missouri and, finally, to Illinois, where in 1844 Joseph Smith paid a martyr's price for his vision of the kingdom of God restored. Two years later Brigham Young led the Saints out of the United States in search of peace and refuge in the mountains and deserts of territorial Utah. There they struggled to overcome an unfriendly natural environment, colonized the Great Basin, sent out missionaries to gather in the elect, and set themselves single-mindedly to the task of "building up" a new Zion in preparation for the second coming of the Savior.

Out of this cauldron of struggle and conflict were forged many of the stories we still tell today, stories that inculcate in both tellers and listeners a great sense of appreciation for the sacrifices of these first Latter-day Saints and a determination to face present difficulties with equal courage.

Perhaps the most gripping cycle of stories has to do with the migration west in the years between 1846 and the coming of the transcontinental railroad in 1869. Many who took part in this migration traveled in covered wagons; others, who could not afford wagons, pushed and pulled their meager supplies across thirteen hundred miles of prairies and mountains in homemade two-wheeled handcarts. The stories resulting from this experience tell of hardships endured on the trip and of the fortitude of the people who could suffer loss of almost all they held dear and still continue the journey. In almost every instance, the stories remind generations of Mormons raised on the stories the debt of gratitude we owe those who prepared the way for us, persuade us to hold fast to the church for which they paid such a dear price, and encourage us to face our own trials with similar courage and to press on and on in whatever tasks we may be given in building up the kingdom. The following two stories are typical:

> After spending a year at Winter Quarters, this handcart company continued the arduous journey west. Faced again by another hellish winter and accompanying starvation, disease and death, the ill-fated handcart company became smaller and weaker. First, Sister Anderson's great grandfather died. A day later the youngest daughter died, leaving Sister Anderson, a son, and a daughter to survive. In the desperation of starvation, Sister Anderson and other members of the handcart company boiled boots and saddles to make rawhide soup, which, miraculously, was their sustenance until help and provisions met them and safely took them to the Salt Lake Valley.

> The McCareys were among the several thousand Mormons who lost all their worldly possessions in the tragic mid-winter exodus from their beloved homes in Nauvoo. With little food and scant protection from the elements, they suffered greatly from hunger and disease at Winter Quarters and during their long migration to

> Salt Lake City. Yet on reaching the Platte River crossing, they were still in sufficiently good condition to kneel together and thank the Lord for getting them through the worst part of the journey.
>
> During the river crossing cholera broke out among the members of the company. The terrible disease raged throughout the camp. Dozens died. It was necessary for James McCarey to assist in digging graves for the victims. James was a willing worker and finished three graves that October morning, even though he began to feel a little ill as he started the third. A short time after the last grave was completed, James was dead from the effects of cholera. His young daughters Victoria and Mary helped their mother wrap him in an old blanket, place him in the grave, and cover him with the dirt he had spaded up two hours earlier.

The teller of this story, the great-great-grandson of one of the little girls who helped bury her father, will not easily turn from the faith his ancestor died for.

Some of the most heroic figures in the trek west were the women, who, far from being subservient to the men, stood gutsily for their own rights, as in the following story, and can also serve as models for contemporary women.

> Those women who crossed the plains, walking all the way were brave people, enduring many hardships. But one of our great-grandmothers was also very stubborn. They had loaded up their wagon and started to come west. But when they came to the point where they had joined up with a company and were to cross the Mississippi River, grandfather decided they would have to lighten the wagon. So he told grandmother she would have to leave her big beautiful copper kettle and her large feather mattress. These two items were the only things she took of her especially treasured household goods. So she refused to leave them behind. At that, grandfather took them out of the wagon and laid them by the roadside, but grandmother sat right down beside the mattress and the kettle and declared that she would not go without them. If they were left, she would stay behind. So the frustrated men took the wagons and drove off, but she remained behind. In the face of this resistance, grandfather relented and came back to get her. They decided that she could take the kettle and the mattress if she emptied out the feathers. This was all right because she could always fill the tick with new feathers when they settled a new farm. And with everything settled they continued on their way.

Once safely across the plains and established in their Great Basin communities, the Mormon settlers continued to experience hardships and convert them into stories as they endured severe winters, dry summers, failed crops, swarms of crickets, attacks by unfriendly Indians, and arrests and jailings by federal officers for practicing polygamy. Some faltered and lost the faith that had brought them there, but many were sustained in their struggle to conquer the western wilderness by a belief, a belief clearly evident in the stories, that they were engaged in a cause that could not fail. Individuals might fail, but the new Zion would not.

As the pioneer era passed, the world in which Mormon stories circulated changed markedly. But the telling of stories continued unabated. The reason for this is that the generating force behind Mormon storytelling was not the persecutions of the church nor the hardships of frontier life but rather the theological beliefs of the people. The external world may have changed, but these beliefs remained, and continue to remain, constant. Most of us still hold fast to the visions of Joseph Smith, we still believe that only through the restored gospel can the world be saved, and we still believe we have a sacred obligation to take our message to the world. Thus in a changed physical world but inspired by the same deeply held convictions, stories continue to play a significant role in Mormon life.

In many ways, the roles of these stories in our New Zion are similar to those played by accounts of remarkable providences in the Bible Commonwealth American Puritans once established in their new land. In 1694 the Puritan divines Increase and Cotton Mather and the Fellows of Harvard College instructed the New England clergy to record the remarkable providences that would show the hand of God in their lives. They said:

> The things to be esteemed *memorable* are specially *all unusual accidents*, in the heaven, or earth, or water: All wonderful *deliverances* of the distressed: *Mercies* to the godly; *judgments* on the wicked; and more glorious fulfillment of either the *promises* or the *threatenings* in the Scriptures of truth; with *apparitions, possessions, inchantments*, and all extraordinary things wherein the existence and agency of the *invisible world* is more sensibly demonstrated. (Mather [1702] 1853, 2: 362)

This passage seems not unlike instructions Mormons are given on how to keep a Book of Remembrance. Puritans and Mormons alike have told stories to illustrate the hand of God or the influence of Satan in all things, to bring vividly alive the dramatic conflict in which the powers of good and evil struggle for mastery of our souls.

Perhaps our most frightening stories, as I can testify after collecting a lot of them, are those in which Satan or his evil spirits attempt to take control of our bodies to thwart the work of the Lord—to hinder a missionary from going tracting, for example, or a convert from joining the church, or a bishop from carrying out his duties. In most of these stories the evil spirit is exorcised by prayer or by the power of the priesthood. But in some instances the spirit cannot be exorcised because the possessed individual courts disaster by seeking out the devil: "A girl from Torrence, California," for example, "was playing with a [Ouija] board. She asked by whom the board was controlled. The reply came back, 'The Devil.' An undescribable force picked her up and slammed her against the wall. The jolt of the slam damaged her spine. She is now paralyzed from the waist down."

In another story, known widely in the mission fields, a young elder actually prays to the devil:

> [A story] had been going around the mission field about an elder who decided that he would test the powers of Satan. So he decided that he would pray to him. He left his companion and went into the closet that was in their apartment. His companion, after missing him, noticed that the closet door was open only about an inch, and so he walked over to the closet and tried to open up the door and couldn't get it open. And he called the mission president, and the mission president came over with his assistants, and together all of them pried at the door. And finally when they got it open, the elder was kneeling in prayer, but he was up off the ground about two feet, suspended in air. And so they immediately administered to him, and he fell on the floor, dead.

In other versions of this story, the praying elder is slammed against the wall, instant death the result; in another story, the missionary is found in bed, burned from one end to the other; in still another the shell of a body remains, but the insides have been cooked out. Logically, these stories make little sense; one would expect the devil generously to reward those errant individuals who turn to him in prayer, but instead he kills them. Logic notwithstanding, the narratives serve as forceful warnings that one does not provoke the powers of hell with impunity.

In a number of stories, Satan seeks to destroy church members not by possessing their bodies but by enticing them to sin. These cautionary tales, and their number is legion, show what happens when one surrenders to the alluring powers of evil. One example will have to do:

> A missionary had been on his mission for twenty-three months and had served a very honorable mission, been an assistant to the mission president and held every leadership position in his mission. He had been successful in baptizing many people into the church. But one night he and his companion were cooking dinner and when they got ready to eat they discovered they were out of milk. This one elder told his companion he would be right back; he was going to run to the store on the corner and get some milk. Both of them thought that since the store was only a block away

> there would be no problem. But on the way, somehow a neighbor woman enticed the elder into her house. He then committed an immoral act with this woman, was excommunicated, and was sent home dishonorably from the mission field.

Narratives like this are similar to those war stories in which the protagonist is killed on his last bombing raid or on his last patrol just before his scheduled return home. Both sets of stories emphasize that one is never safe (from an enemy's bullet or from the sexual enticement of the world) and that one must therefore be constantly on guard to the very end.

Almost as frightening as stories of the devil's terrible actions are those in which a vengeful God wreaks havoc on the enemies of Zion. In their book *Carthage Conspiracy*, Dallin Oaks and Marvin Hill write: "A persistent Utah myth holds that some of the murderers of Joseph and Hyrum Smith met fittingly gruesome deaths—that Providence intervened to dispense the justice denied in the Carthage trial. But the five defendants who went to trial, including men who had been shown to be leaders in the murder plot and others associated with them, enjoyed notably successful careers" (1975, 217). The myth Oaks and Hill refer to is that perpetuated principally by N. B. Lundwall's oft-reprinted *The Fate of the Persecutors of Joseph Smith* (1952); the popularity of this book suggests, unfortunately, that Latter-day Saints are as capable as anyone of taking uncharitable and unchristian pleasure from the discomfort of those who oppose them.

But perhaps the issue is more complicated than that. One of the best ways to prove the validity of a cause is to prove that God is on one's side. Thus Mormon tradition is replete with accounts of God fighting Zion's battles. Consider, for example, the following story:

> There was a preacher in Yakima, [Washington], who hated Mormons and the Mormon church. Because of his constant efforts, the man became well known for his feelings. One Sunday he delivered an unusually fiery speech against the Mormon church in which he denounced Joseph Smith as a liar and the Book of Mormon as a fraud. In his closing remarks he stated that if everything he said wasn't true the Lord should strike him dead. After the services, he walked out of the church and fell dead upon the lawn.

A spate of stories tells how the Lord pours out his wrath on those who oppose or abuse missionaries. In these accounts, the elders, following biblical example, shake dust from their feet and thereby curse the people who have treated them ill. The Lord responds to the missionaries' actions in a dreadful manner. In Norway a city treats missionaries harshly; they shake dust from their feet, and the city is destroyed by German shelling during the war; after the war the repentant townspeople invite the missionaries back. Throughout the world, other cities that have mistreated missionaries suffer similar fates. Towns are destroyed in Chile by floods, in Costa Rica by a volcano, in Japan by a tidal wave, in Taiwan and Sweden by fire. In South Africa a town's mining industry fails, in Colorado a town's land becomes infertile, and in Germany a town's fishing industry folds.

Individuals who have persecuted missionaries may also feel God's wrath. An anti-Mormon minister loses his job, or breaks his arm, or dies of throat cancer. A woman refuses to give thirsty missionaries water and her well goes dry. A man angrily throws the Book of Mormon into the fire only to have his own house burn down. In one story, widely known, two elders leave their temple garments at a laundry, and when the proprietor holds them up for ridicule, both he and the laundry burn, the fire so hot in some instances that it melts the bricks. In all these stories the implication is clear: the church must be true because God protects it and its emissaries from harm.

If the wrath of God is kindled by outsiders who attack the church, as these stories would suggest, it is still more easily aroused by church members who fail to do their duty or who engage in blasphemous acts. A large number of stories, in which Cotton Mather would certainly find evidence of the "judgments on the wicked," teach us to do right by showing what will happen if we don't. In Idaho, the wayward son of a stake president consecrated a glass of beer; he passed out immediately, fell into a coma, and died a few days later. In 1860 Brigham Young dedicated "Salem Pond," a new irrigation project, and promised that no one would die in the pond if the people refrained from swimming on Sunday; the eight people who have since drowned there were all swimming on Sunday. In southern Utah, a young man refused a mission call; about a month later he died in an automobile crash. And, as I have already noted, a missionary who attempted to ordain a fence post or, depending on the version, a Coke bottle, a broomstick, a fire hydrant, or a dog, was struck dead. All these stories attempt to inculcate in the listeners the moral appended by the narrator to the following account:

> This is a story about two South American missionaries—I don't remember who told it to me. As the story goes, the two missionaries were in a place where the people didn't like them very well at all. And . . . [these people] decided that they'd get rid of 'em quick and had some kind of poison food that they fed them. I don't remember what it was, but I think it was some kind of poison meat. And the missionaries blessed it and ate it and didn't die from it. And all the people were very impressed, ya know, and told 'em what happened and said, "Truly, you must be men of God," ya know; and they got a lot of converts from it. They went to another town and decided that they would try the same thing. And so they said, "See now we can eat poison meat, and we won't die." And they ate it, and they died. And the moral that I got from it, from the person who told me, was that "Thou shalt not tempt the Lord thy God."

Listening in one sitting to all these stories—to accounts of evil spirits and of the judgments of God on the unrighteous both within and outside the church—can be a pretty grim experience. Fortunately, the bulk of Mormon folklore falls under what Cotton Mather would have called, "Mercies to the godly." Stories that fall under this heading testify to the validity of the gospel in a positive way by showing the rewards that come, or will come, to those who live righteously. A number of these stories simply recount the advice, comfort, and protection individuals receive for individual problems. But many of them cluster around and mirror major emphases in the church—missionary service, genealogical research, and temple work.

The following four stories stress these themes. The first one illustrates the protection worthy missionaries may receive in dangerous situations; the second story ties missionary labors into the important task of binding the hearts of the fathers to their children; the third story demonstrates the kind of help those intent on turning the hearts of parents and children toward each other may receive in their genealogical research; and the fourth account stresses attending the temple to perform saving ordinances (do temple work) for the dead:

> [A missionary was assigned to New York City.] And they had a lot of gangs and stuff, and they were in a bad part of town. And they were in teaching a family, and when they came out there was a gang waiting to beat up these missionaries. And the missionaries got really scared and ran to the car and got in it . . . , and it wouldn't start. Meanwhile, the guys with the chains and the knives were starting to get closer and closer to the car. So they got real scared, and the one says, "Well, let's have a prayer." So they said the prayer and turned on the ignition, and sure enough, the car started up and they took off. And they got about five or ten miles away or so—anyway they decided to find out why the car wouldn't start, and they got out, and they opened the hood, and there's no battery. That's the story this girl told in my Book of Mormon class.

> One family said they would never be baptized but that they would listen to what the missionaries had to say. The elder had faith that if he lived right the family would accept the gospel, so he set their baptism date for two weeks away. After the family had been given the sixth and final discussion, they were still not willing to be baptized. The missionaries asked them if they could have a word of prayer and return tomorrow. When the prayer was finished and they looked up, the man was crying. While they were praying he didn't want to close his eyes, for behind the missionary he saw his [deceased] father. He asked them. "What does this mean?" The missionary explained to him about work for the dead—baptism and other ordinances. The man and his family were baptized.

> [A group was sitting together talking after a session in the Los Angeles temple. One woman said] that she'd gone as far in her genealogy as she could and she couldn't do anything else; she'd just reached a dead end. So while the group was sitting there and they were talking about genealogy and such, . . . a little old lady with gray hair came up. She was carrying a briefcase, and she sat down in the group, and everybody thought everyone else knew her. You know, she'd just joined the group, and so then all of a sudden, a few minutes later they noticed . . . she was gone. But she'd left her briefcase. So they picked it up and tried to talk to the temple workers and see if anyone had seen her or knew where she went—tried to find her, and they couldn't. So they decided, "Well, maybe if we open the briefcase, then it'll have her name or something in it, and we can locate her that way." So when they unlatched the briefcase, undid the fasteners or whatever, it just flew open, you know, because it was so filled with papers and things, and the pressure was pretty great. And it turned out that the information that was on the papers was this lady's genealogy who'd remarked to the group that she'd gone as far as she could go.

> A man and his wife were leaving Tooele, Utah, on their way to an evening session at the Salt Lake Temple. As they were late, they debated whether to take time out to pick up the elderly man who was walking on the road ahead of them. Upon deciding to stop, the white haired man thanked them as he got into the car. He then told them he knew that they were on their way to the temple and that they should do all the temple work they could as time is short and the blessing of temple work would be taken from us as time runs out for this life. They turned around to question the man further, but he was nowhere to be seen, and the back seat was empty.

In all these stories there is what I would call an "if/then" structure. If the Lord really saved the missionaries from the gang, if the investigator's father really appeared to him, if the frustrated genealogist's family data were really given to her in a remarkable way, and if the elderly hitchhiker really declared that the time to complete temple work was very short—if all these events really happened, then missionary work, genealogical research, and temple work must be true principles; and if they are true principles, then we should more diligently seek to obey them; and if we seek to obey them, then the Lord will bless us, protecting us from harm and guiding us to success as good finally conquers evil.

Heroic though it may be, this struggle between good and evil can wear us down a bit—especially those of us painfully aware of our own imperfections in a society that demands perfection. Some crack under the pressure, but most of us make it through, primarily because of our convictions, but partly because we, unlike the Puritans, have learned to laugh at ourselves and at the system that controls us. Consider, for example, the poor bishop who must urge his people on to a standard of conduct he seems not capable of reaching himself.

> There was a Mormon bishop in a small Utah town who, like all Mormon bishops, worked so hard at his calling that he never had time for his own activities. One Sunday, when the pressure had gotten unbearable, he decided to skip meeting and go golfing. This he did and had quite an enjoyable time. Upon returning home, however, he found his town had vanished. A bit bewildered, he went to his house where he found a note tacked to his door. It read: "Sorry we missed you. —Enoch."

Or consider another bishop who must commit himself to an ideal world while pragmatically learning to deal with the real world:

> A bishop who was conducting a church building fund in his ward preached a sermon from the pulpit one time about being blessed for contributing to the building fund. After his sermon, a member came up to him and said, "Bishop, that was a damned fine sermon." The bishop replied, "Brother, you had better watch the swearing." The member continued, "Yes sir, Bishop, that was such a damned fine sermon that I gave an extra $650 for the building fund." The bishop paused, then said, "Yes, brother, it takes a hell of a lot of money to build a church."

Or consider the long-suffering Relief Society president:

> A Catholic priest, a rabbi, and a Mormon bishop were bragging about how much their various congregations believe them. So they decided to test a member of each faith to see which one would believe a strange thing. They went to a Jew's home. "Hello, Mrs. Goldstein; I'm a holy cow," said the rabbi. "Oh, come on," said Mrs. Goldstein, "you're a lot of strange things, but I know you're not a holy cow." So they went to a parishioner's home, and the priest said, "Hello, Mrs. Florentin; I'm a holy cow." "Oh, father," she said, "I know you're not a holy cow, but come on inside anyway." So they went to a Relief Society president's house with whom the bishop had had many meetings. He knocked on the door. As soon as she saw who it was, she exclaimed, "Holy cow, is that you again?"

Or consider, finally, the poor stake president in the following story:

> At a stake conference in Idaho once the stake president was sitting up on the stand, and somebody else was talking. The stake president noticed three people standing up in the back because they didn't have a seat. He proceeded to attract the attention of one of the deacons to have him go get three chairs. He was motioning, signaling "three" with his fingers, moving his lips wide and slow, mouthing the words "three chairs." But the deacon still hesitated. The stake president kept it up, getting more insistent all the time and finally said, "Come on, get up." So the deacon finally dragged himself up [in front of the congregation] and said: "Rah, rah, rah, stake president!"

If there is any central figure in Mormon folk humor it is not J. Golden Kimball—who today belongs more to popular culture than to folk culture—or any of the revered, and sometimes frightening, general authorities. The central figure is the beleaguered bishop, his counterpart, the Relief Society president, and occasionally a high councilor or stake president—in other words, people not too different from you and me. If we have not already become the very leaders the jokes poke fun at, we are likely to do so if we mind our manners. These leaders are bedeviled by the same problems that plague us. Hence there is a more affectionate feeling toward the objects of Mormon humor than there is in the anticlerical jokes of many other groups. As we laugh at the jokes, we are perhaps laughing more at the circumstance of being Mormon than at the imperfect bishop or stake president. We are laughing, that is, at ourselves—and through that laughter finding the means to deal with stresses that might otherwise be our undoing.

This, then, is the Mormon world scholars of a future age would discover if they were to turn to the materials in the folklore archive and to publications based on those materials. In this world, people take great pride in their pioneer heritage and seek in the heroic deeds of their founding fathers and mothers models of conduct for the present day; they see themselves engaged in a struggle between good and evil and attempt to encourage proper behavior by recounting faith-promoting stories, or remarkable providences, of the tragedies that will strike the wicked and of the rewards that await the righteous. And when the burdens of their religion sometimes weigh too heavily upon them, they seek to ease the pressures by laughing at both themselves and at the system in order to face the new day with equanimity.

But is this an accurate picture? To answer this question we must consider carefully the nature of folklore inquiry. As I said at the outset, folklore is an unfailing mirror of what is most important in a society. The problem is that what the nonspecialist sees in that mirror will be what the scholar chooses to collect and study. In defining legends, Richard M. Dorson once wrote: "There would be little point . . . in remembering the countless ordinary occurrences of daily life, so the legend . . . is distinguished [from regular discourse] by describing an extraordinary event. In some way the incident at its core contains noteworthy, remarkable, astonishing or otherwise memorable aspects" (1962, 18). But in far too many studies, what is considered memorable has been determined not by the people who tell the stories, but by those who collect and study them. Thus while folklore remains a true mirror for culture, the cultural reality reflected in a published work depends very often upon the predisposition and presuppositions of the scholars holding the mirror. (And that, of course, is true also for historical and sociological studies of Mormon culture.)

In 1948 Austin Fife wrote in the *Journal of American Folklore*:

> The roots of the theology of divine intercession are so deeply implanted in the Mormon folk mentality that forces for the cultural absorption of Mormonia into the current of intellectual life have, at best, made only superficial penetration. The integrity of the philosopher and the objectivity of the man of science are in Utah as a thin crust over a pie of spiritualism and propitiatory ritual still hot from the oven. Humanists and scientists of Mormonia are compelled either to bury their ideals in speechless serenity or to resort to a fantastic set of mental calisthenics in order to appear to accommodate their beliefs to the spiritualistic impulse of their environment. Failing this, they must depart Zion to take refuge among the Gentiles, for the time has not yet come when they may aspire to become prophets in their own land. (1948, 30)

Now I would argue that this statement is not overburdened with scholarly detachment and that the sentiments expressed there would have to shape the images reflected in Fife's Mormon folklore study—that is, in his mirror for Mormon culture. When he and his wife Alta published *Saints of Sage and Saddle: Folklore among the Mormons* (1956) eight years later, much of the anger evident in this statement had disappeared, but enough of it remained to color at least the tone of the writing through which some of the data were presented in the book.

But I am concerned here not so much with the Fifes, whose enduring contributions to Mormon and American folklore studies are incontrovertible, as with my own work, with the research and writing I have conducted in Mormon folklore for the past twenty years. Once again, does the picture I have drawn give an accurate view of Mormons? Two months ago I might have answered, "Yes." After all, the picture does capture principal concerns in the church, the reality of Satan, the need for constant vigilance in adhering to gospel principles, the importance of missionary work to save the living, and of genealogical research and temple work to save the dead. But, in spite of all this, I must now answer the question, "Only in part."

During the Christmas break, my wife, Hannele, and my son and I visited Hannele's mother in Finland. The night before I returned I had my own remarkable experience, which I recorded in a letter to a friend:

> Hannele's mother has excellent home teachers. One of them keeps her driveway clear of snow, and the other takes her and an even older blind sister to church each Sunday. The day before I left Finland this good blind sister, Sister Vassenius, was having problems with her back and asked her home teachers to give her a blessing. One of them couldn't make it, so the other asked me to join him. We went into her darkened old home, where she still lives alone, in spite of her blindness and eighty-eight years. He anointed, and I blessed. I heard no voices, saw no visions, witnessed no miracle—except the miracle of heart touching heart. When I finished, she stood up, put her arms around me, and thanked me for blessing her with peace. And I realized, perhaps better than I have for a long time, that what I had just experienced was the essence of the gospel. The gospel's not to be found in intellectual discussions about God's omniscience, nor in scholarly debates over the nature of Joseph's first vision or over whether or not he used a divining rod. It's to be found in the homes and hearts of the Sister Vasseniuses throughout the church, where people take seriously the Savior's injunction, "Come unto me, all ye that labour and are heavy laden," and as a result find rest to their souls. I wish the missionaries who brought Sister Vassenius into the church long years ago could have been there to witness this fruit of their labors, to see the gospel they had preached bring light to blind eyes and joy to a tired heart.

As I sat on the plane the next day thinking of this experience, I recalled another good Finnish member whose husband had been a chain-smoking alcoholic who in a drunken stupor had thrown up all over the rug the first time the missionaries visited but who gradually turned his life completely around and embraced all the virtues he had once scorned. His wife told me, "Before the missionaries came, my life was hell on earth; now it's heaven." "If experiences like these are at the heart of what it means to be Mormon," I wondered—at the heart of that value center I talked about—"why aren't they a part of Mormon folklore?" And then I realized that, of course, they are—they have just not been collected and studied. I have probably told the story of the alcoholic's conversion a hundred times; and I have heard a hundred stories like it. Yet rarely have I attempted to collect that kind of material.

During my first year in graduate school at Indiana University, I reviewed the Fifes' *Saints of Sage and Saddle* in Professor Dorson's seminar on theory and technique. In the main, I praised the book—and it deserves praise; but I also criticized what struck me as the work's exaggerated emphasis on the supernatural at the expense of any discussion of Mormon moral and spiritual values and of the motivating principles of sacrifice and service which I knew from experience were essential parts of being Mormon. I wrote:

> The missionary returning from the field will probably tell of a healing or two he has witnessed and of a miraculous conversion he has had a part in, but primarily he will talk about the change of character he has observed in the lives of those who have accepted the gospel. He will tell many stories about people who have abandoned their own interests to devote themselves to the service of others. These stories are just as much a part of Mormon oral tradition as are tales of the supernatural, and no survey of Mormon folklore is complete without them. (1963, 5)

When I wrote those lines, I feared that Professor Dorson would attack me for being a narrow Mormon apologist. Instead he wrote on my paper: "Splendid appraisal and statement of unnoticed Mormon traditions." As I continued Mormon folklore research in the coming years, I should have followed my own instincts; I should have followed Professor Dorson's counsel and turned my attention to these unnoticed traditions. When I left Indiana, I did break new ground in my studies of Mormon folk history (1973a and 1979), of the contemporary era (1976), of Mormon humor (1985), and, with John Harris, of missionary lore (1981 and 1983b); but in my work with Mormon traditions in general I let myself be too easily influenced by what folklorists generally have considered to be memorable in religious folklore—that is, with dramatic tales of the supernatural rather than with the quiet lives of committed service that I knew really lay at the heart of the Mormon experience.

Mormon supernatural stories do indeed exist in rich abundance (sometimes too rich for my taste). And they do play the roles I have described. But they are only part of a larger, more important, whole. The picture I have drawn here is not inaccurate; it is simply incomplete or, perhaps better, not quite in focus. It is, therefore, an uncertain mirror for truth. Fortunately, scholarship is usually a self-correcting process. The task for future Mormon folklore study will be to enlarge the picture, and to bring the images reflected in it into sharper focus.

I wish to end this essay on a personal note. I attended Indiana University under a National Defense Education Act Fellowship that paid more than I had been earning as a full-time faculty member at BYU and made possible my completing a second major in Uralic-Altaic Studies and picking up an additional minor in anthropology. At the time I made a private vow to pay back to the American public in service the debt I owed them for making my education possible. I have genuinely tried to do that through my teaching, through my involvement in public folklore programs, and especially through my research and writing. By studying closely one group of human beings—the Latter-day

Saints—I have hoped to discover the universal truths manifested in specific ethnographic facts and thereby to increase awareness of and sympathy for the human condition in general.

During this past semester, after suffering strength-sapping bouts of ill health and carrying a heavy administrative assignment, I found myself thinking, "You've published some twenty articles on Mormon folklore now. Maybe it's time to bring the best of these together in a book and then to stand by at last and, as Robert Frost might say, watch the woods fill up with snow." Then came my trip to Finland. Rejuvenated now by three weeks away from the office, with my earlier commitment always in memory, and with new research designs for making the study of Mormon folklore a more certain mirror for truth swirling through my mind, I guess I'll have to let the woods go for a while, or let them fill up with snow without my being there to watch. I still have promises to keep, and miles to go before I sleep.

NOTE

1. All items of folklore cited in this paper are located in the Brigham Young University Folklore Archive, Provo, Utah.

On Being Human

The Folklore of Mormon Missionaries

Only a week before I received the invitation to write this introduction, two faculty members who are team-teaching an introductory class about world arts and cultures queried me. Their course concerns concepts and perspectives in the intercultural, interdisciplinary study of art, aesthetics, and performance. Among other matters, it examines the performative representation of cultural identity. The instructors sought articles outside their own fields that students should read. Immediately I recommended William A. (Bert) Wilson's "On Being Human: The Folklore of Mormon Missionaries." It deals as much with behavior, performance, and culture as it does with the lore of a particular religious identity. The piece is imminently readable; Bert is a marvelous storyteller and a fine writer. Based on a huge quantity of recorded data, personal experience, and years of reflection, this essay contains numerous insights about the nature of narrating and its impact on people's emotions, behavior, and interactions.

I met Bert Wilson at Indiana University. He was completing his graduate studies in the Folklore Department as I was beginning mine. His book *Folklore and Nationalism in Modern Finland* (1976a), which grew out of his dissertation, remains the best study of the use of folklore in nationalistic movements. When we first met we talked about his interest in Mormon folklore. He was dissatisfied with earlier works. Either the publications consisted largely of documentation without analysis or, written by outsiders, the interpretations were inadequate and inappropriate. As a practicing Mormon, Bert has an "emic" or insider view of the traditions. He was a missionary to Finland. He has participated in some of the lore that he reports and analyzes in his publications.

Two major streams of scholarship appear to have influenced Bert's interpretation of the traditions presented here. One is a behavioral perspective, which

---

This paper was delivered as the 64th Annual Faculty Honor Lecture in Humanities at Utah State University on November 18, 1981. It appeared the same year in a lecture series booklet published in Logan, Utah, by Utah State University Press. Reprinted by permission of Utah State University Press.

embraces a performance studies approach. When he writes about stories being framed with beginning and closing markers and with a stylized manner of performance (including gestures, rhythmical speech, shifts in intonation, and ceremonial language), he draws upon ideas propounded by Roger Abrahams, Richard Bauman, and others who (like Bert himself) contributed to the analysis of verbal art as performance. When he dwells on "the *telling* of a story" during which the narrator and listener together shape the form and meaning, and on the unique circumstances in which the narrating occurs, he relies largely on the work of Robert A. Georges, who helped develop a behavioral orientation in folkloristics. This perspective eschews the study of "texts" in favor of concentrating on communication and social experience in the context of specific events. A result is the greater understanding of expressive behavior as, in Bert's words, "an artful rendering of significant human experience." This is particularly apparent in Bert's moving examination of his mother's narrating, which he writes about in "Personal Narratives: The Family Novel," included at the conclusion of this volume.

Functionalism, too, inspired the present article. This can be seen in the latter part that analyzes four sociocultural and psychological consequences of the lore of Mormon missionaries. In addition to its obvious entertainment value, Bert writes, the lore functions to create a sense of group solidarity, let off steam as a form of coping and silent rebellion, promote conformity to accepted standards of conduct, and develop an image of a world in which the missionaries may succeed (eventually emerging as victorious). William R. Bascom discusses several of these in "Four Functions of Folklore" (1954). He contends that folklore enables people to escape in fantasy from repressions imposed upon them by society, validates culture by justifying its rituals and institutions, inculcates behavioral norms, and applies social pressure in order to maintain conformity to accepted patterns of behavior. A paradox arises according to Bascom: while folklore appears to play a vital role in transmitting and maintaining a culture's institutions and enforcing individual conformity to behavioral norms, at the same time it provides socially approved outlets (wishful thinking, letting off steam) for the repressions imposed by the institutions. Bert examines this paradox more fully in an essay titled "The Paradox of Mormon Folklore" (1976c).

All of us are influenced by the writings of others. When I penned the introductory essay in a volume that I edited on the Finnish national epic, I drew heavily upon Bert Wilson's book about folklore and nationalism in Finland (see Jones 1987b). His articles on Mormon traditions evince the intellectual rigor possessed by his study of Finnish nationalism. Each is well written and insightful; all stand as the best that has been published on the subject.

Two other matters should be mentioned. The concept of "folk group" has often been bandied about since Alan Dundes proposed it in the mid-1960s (based on the notion of "a folk" as opposed to "the folk" articulated by Richard M. Dorson in *Bloodstoppers and Bearwalkers* ([1952] 1972). Bert Wilson, in the present essay, is one of the few scholars to have ever pointed out some of the concept's flaws (for yet others, see Blumenreich 1974).

Second, Bert Wilson is both a devout Mormon and a folklorist specializing in the traditions of Mormons. While his insider status yields important ethnographic insights, it poses challenges. As Bert indicates, the concept of "the folk" is outmoded in folkloristics (although it is still used by some scholars in other fields). To speak of Mormonism as "folk religion," which some in the past have done, is both inaccurate and offensive. Bert had to clarify for himself the difference between official church teachings and what could be identified as "folklore," that is, traditions learned informally and engaged in by people in firsthand interaction. When he addresses an audience of Mormons, he takes care to differentiate between the two. This need is even greater when he speaks or writes to non-Mormons lest they view adherents to this religion as somehow "strange," and as "different" from themselves. As Bert makes apparent in his writings, it is the ability and propensity of all of us to describe something that happened (to "tell a story"), to ritualize, and to experience the sacred in our everyday lives that makes us human, that is, members of a common species regardless of other identities that we might assume or be ascribed. In engaging in folklore, Mormons express their humanity—just as the rest of us do.

—*Michael Owen Jones*

NOT LONG AGO, I WAS ASKED TO ENTERTAIN SOME OF MY COLLEAGUES AT A faculty gathering by telling stories about J. Golden Kimball, that crusty old Mormon divine who salted his sermons and public statements with a liberal sprinkling of cuss words and earthy metaphors.[1] Because I know a fair number of these stories and enjoy telling them, I agreed. The event was a tolerable success. At least most people laughed, and no one threw brickbats. Still, as I drove home, I wondered if I had not done more harm than good. I had, I feared, simply strengthened the notion, held by many, that the study of folklore might provide interesting material for after dinner speeches but certainly could not be expected to increase our understanding of the human condition.

I would like to rectify that impression. The night I told J. Golden Kimball stories, I played the role of folklore performer. Now I will play the critic. My argument will be that the performance of folklore—whether it provides us with delight and amusement or causes us to fear and tremble—is one of our most fundamental human activities. The study of folklore, therefore, is not just a pleasant pastime useful primarily for whiling away idle moments. Rather, it is centrally and crucially important in our attempts to understand our own behavior and that of our fellow human beings.

To defend this thesis, I will share with you some of the insights my colleague John B. Harris and I have gained from studying the folklore of Mormon missionaries. Some ten years ago, Professor Harris and I began collecting missionary folklore, mostly from recently returned missionaries attending Brigham Young and Utah State Universities. The results of our efforts now fill eleven volumes—a database large enough, we believe, to at last warrant some generalizations. I would prefer to move directly to a discussion of this data, but I have learned from past experience that if we hope to arrive at any common agreement tonight, we must first come to some general understanding of what folklorists study.

In brief, folklorists study people, the "folk," who in face-to-face interactions with other people attempt to control the circumstances of their lives by generating, performing, and transmitting "lore," by communicating, that is, through traditional forms ranging from the songs they sing and the stories they tell to the ways they celebrate their birthdays and prepare their food.

The people who generate, perform, and transmit this lore are, among others, readers of this essay. When the term folklore was coined in 1846, the "folk" were thought at that time to be unsophisticated, unlettered peasants—the *vulgus in populo*—people living mainly in rural areas, isolated from the more civilized members of society and carrying in their collective memory survivals, or relics, of earlier, primitive customs and usages. This notion held sway throughout the nineteenth century and through much of this one; indeed, it has not yet completely faded. For many, the term *folklore* still conjures up images of European peasants spinning tales of olden times or of Appalachian hillbillies strumming happily away on their banjos.

By midcentury, however, most folklorists had begun to hold a more realistic view. They came gradually to understand that folklore can help us understand not just the past but also the present, that folklore flourishes in urban industrial centers as well as in the agrarian countryside, and that all of us—sophisticated and unsophisticated alike—possess folklore and participate in folklore processes. As a result, they began to speak not of *the folk* but of different *folks*, that is, of different folk groups isolated from the rest of society and bound together by such circumstances as age, occupation, religion, ethnicity, and regional habitat. And they began to study such diverse groups as children and senior citizens, airline hostesses and medical doctors, Amish and Catholics, westerners and southerners—and even such people as Mormon missionaries, who could be defined as an occupational subgroup within the larger Mormon religious group.

Though certainly an advance over the older view of the folk as peasants or quaint rural people, this newer concept, which dominates much of American folklore research today, is not without problems. First, it stereotypes people, failing to take into account differences and assuming that what is true of one group member will be true of them all. Second, it focuses on what is unique to a particular group rather than on what members of the group share in common with other people. As a result, folklore study, which above all else ought to be a humane discipline, fails at times to acknowledge our common humanity and serves, or can serve, as a divisive rather than a uniting force in society.

To counter these problems, some folklorists have begun to speak not of different folk groups but of different social identities. For example, I am a Mormon, but I am also a father, a teacher, a Democrat, an Idahoan, a tennis fan, a photography nut, and so on. To assume that one can know me fully simply by identifying me as a Mormon is to assume too much. It seems safer to say that in certain situations my Mormon identity will become dominant and my other identities will be forced into the background, though never fully suppressed—that is, even in my most intense Mormon moments, I will not cease entirely to be a Democrat, and conversely, when I play the role of Democrat, I will not cease to be a Mormon. In those situations in which my Mormon identity becomes dominant, I will think and act in traditionally prescribed ways, in ways somewhat similar to those in which other Mormons will think and act when their Mormon identities are dominant. This being the case, one should be able to observe these Mormon ways of thinking and acting and then say something about the nature of Mormon behavior in general. Generalizations, however, must be used with care; no one individual will ever fit the generalized pattern completely, and this behavior, though it may have taken on a distinctive Mormon coloring—or, in our case, a Mormon missionary hue—may not be peculiar to Mormons or missionaries at all but rather to people everywhere.

From this point of view, Mormon missionaries are not uniquely missionaries. Each elder or sister is a composite of the identities he or she has brought to the field; no two are exactly alike. However, unlike the rest of us, who are constantly changing roles (and therefore identities), missionaries play the same role for the duration of their missions. Occasionally, and often to the displeasure of their leaders, some of the missionaries' other identities will come to the fore; but for the most part, from the time they are called to the field until they are released one-and-a-half to two years later, these young people are engaged full tilt in missionary activity. Even in those moments when they are not directly involved in proselyting efforts, they must at all times, day and night, be accompanied by at least one other missionary companion, a circumstance that reminds them constantly of their missionary role. They thus afford us an excellent opportunity to observe the behavior of people whose shared identity persists for a sustained period and to discover what is unique and what is universal in that behavior.

Presently, some thirty thousand missionaries, most between the ages of nineteen and twenty-three, serve in all areas of the free world and in some not so free. One could argue that the geographical spread of these missionaries and the cultural differences in the lands in which they serve preclude the development of a folklore widely known to most of them. Such an argument overlooks the nature of missionary work. Though in the past this work was somewhat loosely organized and missionaries, once called to the field, were left pretty much to their own devices, this is not the case today. The work is now tightly structured, highly programmed, and routinized. Missionaries in Japan, Finland, Argentina, and Los Angeles will follow essentially the same schedule, participate in the same activities, and abide by the same rules as missionaries throughout the system. Though regional differences will obviously occur, it is possible to identify a missionary lifestyle that has produced a common folklore.

This folklore has evolved over time from day-to-day interactions of missionaries facing similar problems and involved in similar social situations. As they have participated in typical activities (such as door-to-door "tracting" or holding discussions in the homes of investigators), or as they have experienced recurrent events (such as facing hostile crowds or witnessing some people accept their message and join their church), they have developed somewhat similar responses and attitudes to the circumstances of their lives, and they have told stories and participated in activities that embody these attitudes and that give them a sense of control in a world not always friendly. The more they have told these stories and participated in these activities, the more they have formularized them into recognizable patterns. As they have continued to face problems and find themselves in social situations similar to those that have occurred in the past, they have sought resolutions in these now traditional stories and activities—or, in other words, in their folklore.

No matter what form this folklore takes—song, tale, customary practice—the performance of it will almost always be an act of communication, an act through which the performer attempts to persuade the audience, and sometimes him- or herself, to accept a certain point of view or to follow a certain course of action. These performances might be called exercises in behavior modification. They may entertain us, but they also change us.

Obviously, not all communicative acts aimed at persuasion are folklore. We can distinguish those that are by at least three identifying features that "frame" them, or set them off, from the regular flow of communication.

First, folklore is framed by the use of beginning and closing markers. When we hear someone say, "Once upon a time . . ." or "Say, did you hear about . . . ," we know that regular conversation is about to be interrupted by the telling of a tale. When the narrator says, "And they lived happily ever after" or "And that really happened," we know that the telling has ended and that regular discourse will begin again. The markers that signal the beginnings and endings of other folkloric communications may be subtler, but they nevertheless exist; when we pick up the appropriate signal, we know what will follow.

Second, folklore is framed, as I have already noted, by a recurrent and clearly recognizable structural pattern. For example, the basic structure of Mormon legends of the Three Nephites is this: someone has a problem; a stranger (usually an old man) appears; the stranger solves the problem; the stranger miraculously disappears. A story may have more to it than this—the person visited may be tested by the old man before being helped—but it must have these elements. Any story incorporated into the Nephite cycle will be adjusted to make it conform to this pattern. The process is similar to a writer's attempt to develop his or her personal experience into a short story. To be successful, the writer must distort the experience to make it fit the requirements of form. Missionaries telling their own experiences do the same thing. The experiences are real enough, but the missionaries must distort, or at least carefully select, the details of these experiences to make them fit the narrative forms traditional in the mission field.

Third, stories are framed by a stylized manner of performance. Stylistic devices include such things as gestures, body language, rhythmical speech, musical sounds, shifts in intonation, and the use of ceremonial language. When someone tells a J. Golden Kimball story and imitates Kimball's high-pitched nasal voice, the performer is using a stylistic device.

Folkloric communication, then, can be distinguished from other forms of communication by beginning and closing markers, by recognizable structural patterns, and by stylized presentation. These distinguishing features, of course, warrant our calling folklore what literature itself is generally considered to be—an artful rendering of significant human experience. In at least one important way, however, folklore differs from literature. No matter how much advice a poet may get from colleagues and no matter how he or she attempts to shape the lines to communicate effectively with a specific audience, once the poem is completed and committed to print, the exchange between poet and audience ends. Each person may respond differently to the poem and may interpret it differently. But the words themselves, as they appear on the printed page, will ever remain the same.

With folklore, there is no printed page. There is only the performance in which a song is sung, a tale told, a ritual enacted. The song, tale, or ritual are parts of the whole, but they are not the whole itself. The performance is the whole. The markers I have discussed above do not set off a story; they set off the *telling* of a story, a telling whose form and meaning are shaped by teller and listener alike as each responds to and gives feedback signals to the other. Thus in a very real sense, the telling is the tale, the singing is the song, the enactment is the ritual. The artistic tensions that develop as one reads a poem occur primarily between the reader and the lines on the written page and only indirectly, through these lines, between the reader and the poet. The artistic tensions that develop in a folklore performance occur directly and dynamically between listener and performer. We can record part of the performance and print it in a book as a folklore text, but in doing so we give readers only a mutilated bit of reality. The real art of folklore and the real meaning of folklore lie only in the performance of folklore.

For example, when a group of missionaries is faced with a problem that needs solving—what to do, for instance, with a recalcitrant elder (a male missionary) who will not do his duty or who may have committed an unworthy act—one of the missionaries will assume the role of storyteller, or performer. Looking to the wisdom handed down from the past and therefore considered to be of special value, he will begin to tell of an earlier missionary who behaved in a similar way and suffered the wrath of God as a result. His listeners may not know the particular story being told, but they will know its form and will recognize the values the teller is attempting to uphold. They will expect him both to stay within the narrative bounds dictated by tradition and at the same time to perform well enough to excite their sympathies and persuade, or attempt to persuade, them to accept his point of view. In other words, they will judge the competency of his performance. As they do so, they will send signals as feedback. He will then adjust his storytelling accordingly, manipulating the form and especially the style of his presentation to make it as artistically powerful, and therefore as persuasive, as possible. If he is successful, he will reform the sinner, or at least he will persuade fence-sitters not to follow the sinner's example. As we skim rapidly over a number of examples in this essay, we should remember that behind each of them lies this kind of performance.

Clearly, no two missionary folklore performances will ever be the same, even if the same story is told in both. The time and place of telling, the nature of the audience, the skill of the teller, the reason for the telling—all these will combine to make the form and meaning of each performance unique to that performance. Still, while each performance is different from every other one, each is also similar to others. From performance to performance, through time and space, there will be consistencies and continuities in the products of these performances (the stories, songs, customs, and language usages), in the ways missionaries express themselves, and in their reasons for doing so. These are the focus of our study.

To understand the significance of these consistencies and continuities in the lives of missionaries, we must look closely at the circumstances under which missionaries generate folklore and especially at the uses to which they put it. I will look at four of these. Each is different from the others, but in each we find missionaries attempting to maintain a sense of stability in an unstable world.

The first use missionaries make of folklore is to create an esprit de corps, a sense of solidarity among themselves. When a brand-new, nineteen-year-old elder, a "greenie," arrives in some distant mission field, frightened, feeling very much an outsider, and wondering if he should catch the next plane home, the first folklore he is likely to encounter will probably be directed against him. For example, in Norway, when a new missionary arrived, seasoned elders

> sat him down in a chair; they fixed a light above him, and they interrogated him about his moral life. When he volunteered the information that he had kissed a girl before, they let him know that he was completely washed up as far as his career goes in the mission. He would always be a junior companion, never be allowed to lead a discussion. And he believed the whole thing.

In London, England, new missionaries were told to save their bus ticket stubs for a halfpenny rebate per ticket. The greenies saved drawers full of these—some, following instruction, even ironed them—only to learn later that they were totally worthless. In Texas, a senior companion instructed his new junior companion how prayers were to be offered in the mission:

> "Now, Elder, out here we pray an awful lot. If we had to repeat these prayers all the time we'd spend most of our time on our knees

> and never have time to do the Lord's work. Instead, we have all the prayers numbered." With that the two slid to their knees and the senior volunteered to say the prayer. "Number 73," he prayed, and jumped into bed, leaving the new missionary in a crumpled mass on the floor.

In Norway, a senior companion, after going through essentially this same ritual, prayed, "Lord, number 10 for me and number 35 for the greenie." In Spain, greenies and senior missionaries prepared to eat a first dinner together:

> The zone leader asked one of the older elders to say the blessing on the food. They all bowed their heads, and the elder very seriously said, "Number 9, Amen." While the poor new missionaries were still recovering from that, the zone leader looked at the elder who had said the prayer and just as seriously retorted, "Elder, you always say the same prayer."

Sometimes church members, posing as someone else, usually an investigator, have joined the senior missionaries in these pranks. In Norway again, the missionaries asked a greenie:

> "Do you have your first discussion?" And he said, "I have it. I've been studying it. I learned it when I was down in the mission home." And they said, "Okay, you've got to have it good, 'cause we're giving it tonight." So they went—four of them—over to this house to give it—the discussion. And, of course, it wasn't really an investigator; it was a member. And they said, "This man is very musically inclined, and it gets a little bit mundane talking to him all the time. He likes us to sing him the discussions." And so they started out singing the first two lines of the first discussion, and then he said, "Hit it!" And so the new elder proceeded to sing the rest of the discussion in Norwegian.

In California, a senior companion offered to demonstrate to his new greenie how he succeeded in placing copies of the Book of Mormon in people's houses. The two of them knocked on a door. A woman answered, and the senior companion threw a book past her into the house and then ran, leaving the greenie to stammer out an explanation to the irate woman. The woman turned out to be the bishop's wife "and all worked out right in the end." In Germany,

> a senior companion had a married friend who was coming through Germany on his honeymoon. He was just about to get a greenie, so he arranged a party with all the missionaries in the district to welcome him. He also arranged to have his married friend act as

> a companion to another missionary at the party. At the party they arranged to have the greenie find the supposed missionary kissing a girl, who in reality was his wife. They didn't tell the poor greenie that it was a joke until he had been on his knees in fasting and prayer for three days.

I could continue this way for the rest of this paper. The easiest missionary folklore to collect is this kind of prank played by seasoned missionaries, sometimes in collusion with members, on naive, unsuspecting greenies. When we first began to uncover these practices, we seriously wondered about the dedication of "ministers of the gospel" who would participate in such frivolous activity. Then a couple of our informants taught us what we should have known all along. One of them, a fellow who had protested to us that no such pranks had ever been played on him during his mission, later came to Professor Harris's office, laid his head on the desk, and sobbed, "I was never really a part of the missionaries; now I know that I had no jokes played on me because I was not accepted." Another young man told me that when he arrived in the Philippines, the first meal he was served in the mission home was made up of all green food served on green dishes on green linen to remind him of his greenness. "I felt like I had been baptized," he said. And this is exactly what these pranks are—baptisms, or initiation rituals. The missionary who had never been accepted by his fellows had not been initiated. People who must work closely together, who must depend on each other in a common struggle against an alien world, must, if they are to succeed, develop camaraderie and a sense of community. Through the initiation, the new missionary, the outsider, is incorporated into the system. In scriptural terms, he puts off the old man, the greenie, and puts on the new man, the seasoned elder. He now belongs. He is first abused in some way; through the abuse he is humbled; as he recovers from the experience, usually through shared laughter, he becomes one with the group. "I felt kind of dumb at first," said one greenie, "but it was kind of fun after it was all over." Another commented, "It took me a while to cool down, but afterward we laughed for days about the whole thing." Still another, who had been subjected to praying by numbers, said, "It took me a minute to figure it out, but after I did they all laughed and had a [real] prayer. We did it a few weeks later to some new elders." In this last instance, the new missionary, only just initiated himself, soon began to initiate others and thereby was brought still more tightly into the system. Most missionaries participate in these pranks, then, as a means of establishing and maintaining a sense of community among their members.

Other folklore practices also contribute to this sense of community. A greenie newly arrived in the field will often hear his companions speaking a language he does not understand. A junior companion is not just a junior companion—he is "little brother," "the young one," "boy," "the slave." The senior companion, on the other hand, is "the boss," "the pope," "the chief," "sir." The girl back home is "the wife," "the lady in waiting." The rejection letter from this girl is "the Dear John," "suitable for framing," "the acquittal," "the Big X." The mission home is "the zoo," "the Kangaroo court." Investigators are "gators," "our people." Good investigators are "goldies," "dry Mormons." Investigators who are not interested in the message but like to talk to missionaries are "professionals," "gummers," "lunchy," "the punch and cookie route." The Book of Mormon is a "bomb" (BOM). Baptisms are "tisms," "dunks," "splashes," "payday." Tracting is "bonking on doors," "self-torture." The tracting area is "the beat," "the jungle," "the war zone." Good missionaries are "spiritual giants," "rocks," "nails." Aspiring missionaries are "straight-arrow Sams," "cliff climbers," "pharisees." Bad missionaries are "screws," "hurters," "leaks," "liberals." The mission president is "the man," "Big Roy," "the head rhino." A returned missionary is "a reactivated makeout," "an octopus with a testimony." And so on. No missionary, of course, will know all of these terms. But almost all will know some of them or others like them. They have been generated over time as missionaries have characterized the circumstances of their lives in specialized language—in missionary slang or argot. When we asked missionaries why they used this language (and they use it most when they are by themselves—never with investigators and seldom with mission leaders), the most common response was that it creates a feeling of self-identification with other missionaries. It contributes, in other words, to that sense of community the initiation pranks help to establish. Once a greenie learns it, he no longer is a greenie, an outsider. He is now a missionary. He belongs. He speaks the language.

But this is not the only use of this language. The second most common response to our question was that the language was a means of letting off steam, a kind of "silent rebellion." One missionary replied, "It was about the only thing we could say that wasn't programmed." In this unprogrammed language, spoken in casual conversations, missionaries have found a means of dealing at least in part with pressures imposed by the system. A missionary who can laugh at his beat-up bicycle ("the meat grinder"), at his food ("green slop"), at his apartment ("the cave"), and even at chafing rules is likely to be much more effective than one who broods over these circumstances. If he can laughingly call his tracting area "the war zone," he is likely better to survive the battle.

Sometimes, however, the laughter makes nonmissionary Mormons uncomfortable. Many of them do not particularly enjoy hearing the Book of Mormon referred to as a "bomb" ("How many bombs did you place today, Elder?"); nor do they like to hear baptisms called "splashings" or "dunkings." But these people do not have to see their names on a comparative list each month showing the number of books placed, and they do not have to struggle to meet a baptismal quota. The missionaries are simply dealing with pressures in one of the ways open to them—by smiling through language at what might otherwise be their undoing. It is quite clear from our data that most missionaries admire the good elders, "the giants," and dislike the bad ones, "the screws." Yet for the missionary who never quite succeeds as well as he would like, who never leads the mission in baptisms, it is sometimes comforting to view those who do as "climbers" or "straight-arrow Sams." Similarly, when a small group of missionaries refer to the mission president as "Big Roy" instead of "President Jones," they are not setting out to overthrow the authoritarian structure of the mission; they are simply reminding themselves that the authority who presides over them—fearsome as he sometimes appears—is also a man.

The second way missionaries use folklore, then, is to cope with the pressures resulting from submitting to the way of life and to the sometimes nagging rules prescribed by mission authorities. This fact is even more evident in some of the stories missionaries tell. Consider the following:

> Two missionaries were stationed in Zambia (formerly northern Rhodesia) and were doing their normal missionary work. After a while, they decided to split and take off into the Congo. Their chapel was only forty miles from the Congo, and Leopoldville, where all the revolutionary excitement was going on, was not much further away. So they devised a plan—to make out their weekly reports to mission headquarters two weeks in advance and give them to their landlady, who in turn would send one in each week at an appointed time. By this means, the missionaries would have two free weeks to venture into the wilds of the Congo. All this would have gone well, except the stupid landlady sent the report for the second week in first and the report for the first week second. That spilled the tomatoes, and the mission president caught them.

This is one of the most widely told stories we have collected. The details can change. The landlady can send all the reports in at once to save money. The place the elders visit will depend on the mission: from Brazil they go to Argentina, from Chile to the Easter Islands, from Italy to Egypt, from Norway to Scotland, from Germany to Yugoslavia, from Okinawa to Hong Kong, and from parts of the United States to other parts of the United States. In all cases, however, the structure is the same: the missionaries prepare activity reports for several weeks in advance and leave them with the landlady; the missionaries take an unauthorized trip; the landlady sends the reports in out of sequence (or all at once); the missionaries are caught.

In somewhat similar stories, missionaries enter a sporting event against mission rules—a surfing contest, an auto race, a ski race, a bronco ride—and win. They are photographed; the pictures are published by the press; and the mission president sees them. In still others, missionaries participate in an event outside mission boundaries, like a World Series game, and somehow manage to appear in front of a TV camera just as their mission president sits down to watch the evening news.

Though many missionaries disapprove of the actions in these stories, most enjoy the stories. One of them said he enjoyed the mixed-up-report narrative "because missionaries don't do that kind of thing, and these guys did." That's exactly the point. Good missionaries do not do what characters in the stories do. Yet they delight in telling the stories. Why? Again, the missionaries themselves provide answers. One of them, who had been an assistant to his mission president told me, "Those of us who were straight, who kept the rules, had to tell stories like these to survive." Another assistant to the president said, "You would always like to do something like that yourself, and you kinda admire someone who has the guts to do it." A third missionary, in what is also a good description of a storytelling performance, commented perceptively:

> This [an unauthorized trip story] was told to me as a true story by my first companion while we were out tracting one day. If you spend eight hours a day just walking around knocking on doors, you gotta have something to do, and it's nice weather, and you wish you weren't doing it [tracting], and you start telling stories. It's escapism. It took a long time; he embellished it and dragged it out so we could waste a lot of time with it. Then we'd daydream and think about where we'd like to go if we took a vacation.

In other words, some missionaries tell these stories because the characters in the stories do for them what they cannot do for themselves—take a vacation, at least in fancy, from the rigorous life they must pursue each day of their missions. The characters in the narratives do not, I stress, provide models for the missionaries to emulate. Most missionaries know that to behave in such a way would be destructive to both themselves and the missionary system. The wayward missionaries in the stories, as Roger Abrahams has suggested of other such trickster heroes, are not models for conduct but rather "projections of desires generally thwarted by society" (1966, 321–62). The trickster's "celebrated deeds function as an approved steam valve for the group; he is allowed to perform in this basically childish way so that the group can vicariously live his adventures without actually acting on his impulses." In other words, as one of our missionaries said, "The elders told stories like this just to relieve the monotony, so you could just imagine what it would be like without getting in trouble for [doing] it."

The third way missionaries use folklore is to persuade themselves and their companions to conform to accepted standards of conduct. Through dramatic narrations that tell of God and Satan intervening in their lives, missionaries attempt to show what punishments will befall the erring and what rewards await the righteous. The message of the unauthorized trip stories we have just considered is ambiguous. Since the wayward elders are always caught, the narratives could be told to warn missionaries to stay in line. Sometimes they are. Normally, however, like trickster tales in general, such tales are told as amusing stories, as stories designed to provoke laughter. The accounts of supernatural punishments and rewards, on the other hand, are told in dead seriousness.

For missionaries who dishonor their priesthood and engage in sacrilegious acts, the wrath of God is quick and sure. One widely known story, recounted throughout the mission system, tells of elders who, as in the following account, are struck dead for testing their priesthood power by attempting to ordain a post or a Coke bottle or an animal: "Two missionaries were messing around, and they decided to confer the priesthood on a dog which they saw on the street. Before they could complete the ordinance, a bolt of lightning came and struck the dog and the two elders, and it *zapped* them."

Ironically, it is usually Satan rather than God who punishes the missionaries for their wayward conduct. In one rather terrifying cycle of stories, a missionary attempts to strengthen his testimony of Christ by seeking first a testimony of Satan. In Denmark, much to the horror of his companion, a missionary began one night to pray to the devil.

> He proceeded to pray, hour after hour; his companion had gone to bed and left him on his knees praying for a manifestation, or wanting to see the Devil in person. And so, as the story goes, he finally . . . made enough noise so his companion woke and went to the window and saw a black figure on a black horse coming down the road toward their apartment. And they were up at least two stories, and this particular individual, as the story goes, jumped out of the window.

Another telling of the story, this time from Norway, ended this way:

> He looks over to the bed where his companion has gone to bed finally, and he's completely dead from his appearance, and there's a black figure on a white horse in the room, who is laughing. And then it just kind of fades away, until there's nothing and the companion's dead.

In many tellings of the story, the nonpraying companion summons the mission president for help. Usually when they enter the room by breaking down the door, they find the praying elder suspended in the air, his hair sometimes as white as an old man's. In one account, when they open the door, the suspended elder's body is slammed against the wall, instant death the result. In another, they find the bed pinned to the ceiling with the missionary dead between bed and ceiling. In still another, the elder is in bed, burned from one end to the other. In some instances, the shell of a body remains, but the insides have been cooked out.

Since not many missionaries are likely to pray to the devil, these stories are probably told and retold because of their evocative and symbolic power. They can be seen as warnings against evil in general. Numerous stories, however, do relate to specific missionary rules and regulations and are told to inspire proper adherence to them. For example, a photograph taken of an elder swimming, against mission rules, showed a black figure hovering near the swimmer.

A Brazilian missionary refused to sleep in his temple garments because of hot weather: "When his companion woke in the morning, he found the errant elder pressed into the wall so hard that he could hardly pull him off. The elder was obviously dead from being mashed into the wall." In Oklahoma, two missionaries, one with a broken arm, attended a fundamentalist revival against mission rules. The preacher healed the missionary's arm, but as a result, the elder was possessed by an evil spirit. When the mission president cast out the spirit, the elder's arm broke again. In other stories, missionaries are either killed or tormented for violating a variety of rules: experimenting with spiritualism, playing the Ouija board, swimming, boating, dating a girl, playing rock music, arguing with companions, not staying with companions, or sometimes simply not working hard enough. In actual performance, these stories have an emotional impact I cannot begin to communicate here. I have listened to them, and they have frightened me. Missionaries who participate in the telling or hearing of them will not lightly violate mission rules.

If the missionaries' God is a wrathful God, he is also a generous God, amply rewarding those who do his will. Stories demonstrating this point are so numerous I cannot begin to survey them here. Three brief examples will have to suffice:

> A couple of missionaries in Iceland were coming back from an appointment when their car went off the road into a ditch. They knew that if they stayed in the car they would freeze to death and no one could see them. So they started down the road hoping to find someone on that deserted road. Along came a man in a truck and got them inside just as they began to freeze to death. He dropped them off at the apartment, and before they could thank him, he was gone. And there were no tire tracks in the freshly fallen snow.

> There were two elders who were tracting, and one woman invited them into her home and said she was looking for a true church. And she fed them. They made an appointment to come back and teach her some time later. As soon as they came back, and she saw who they were at the door, she invited them in and said, "I want to be baptized," without even talking to them. And they asked her why, and she said that she had read that the true servants of the Lord could eat poison things and they would not be harmed. And then she told them that what she had fed them last week had been poison.

> A missionary and his companion one time decided to take a little bike ride through the countryside, and they just kept going and going and going, and got farther out into the country. And finally they came to this little farm. It was so late that they couldn't leave, so the couple were very, very, very nice, and in fact, they even vacated

> their own bed and gave it to him and his companion, and they slept on the floor. And as it turned out, they were converted—the whole family.

The first two stories deal with the very real dangers missionaries face on the highways and at the hands of the frequently hostile people they must try to convert. The telling of these stories provides some relief from the fear engendered by these circumstances. For example, the teller of the missionaries-in-the-storm narrative said that the story shows how "the Lord really watched out for missionaries." The teller of the poison story, a mission leader, used it as "a faith-promoting experience of what can happen if elders honor their priesthood and do their jobs properly." The message of both is clear: do your duty and the Lord will protect you. The third narrative belongs to a category I call last-door stories. In these, missionaries are led to, or are impressed to knock on, just one more door, behind which always lives a future convert. Again the message is clear: no matter how discouraged you are, no matter how many doors have been slammed in your face, if you will trust in the Lord, keep trying, and knock on that last door, you will eventually succeed.

All of the stories we are considering here—whether of punishments or rewards—follow what I call an anxiety-reducing formula. In the performance of such a story, the narrator will "name," or identify, a recurrent problem (a missionary who seems possessed by an evil force, for example, or a hostile community that threatens the safety of the missionaries); the performer will seek in the traditional stories available to him accounts of similar problems solved in the past; applying the wisdom gleaned from these stories, he will suggest a behavioral resolution to the present difficulty (don't break mission rules or work hard and trust the Lord). Missionaries who participate in such performances will have their fears allayed, will gain a sense of control over a threatening environment, and will thus be able to work more effectively.

The final use to which missionaries put folklore is one that in some ways subsumes all the others. In this instance, missionaries tell stories to persuade themselves that, in spite of massive evidence to the contrary, they may eventually emerge victorious. The largest number of narratives here are the conversion stories I have just alluded to, stories that tell of missionaries bringing converts into the church and that provide hope to so-far unsuccessful elders. But in many narratives, the missionaries do not win converts; they just win—they get the best of a hostile world that has seemingly conspired against them. For example, a missionary who has been tormented again and again by animals will delight in the following account:

> He went to this discussion. The lady's cat was always bothering him. This cat just kept coming in and would attack everything on the flannel board [the board missionaries use for demonstrations]. He came up close to him and this elder just kinda reached down

> and flicked it on the bridge of the nose. Didn't mean to hurt the cat but it killed it. It dropped on the floor and the lady was out of the room at the same time, so they curled it around the leg of the chair. And he sat and petted it all through the rest of the discussion. The next time they went, the lady mentioned the cat was dead.

Most of these stories have to do with missionaries getting the best of smart alecks they encounter while tracting, For example, when a jokester says, "I hear you guys believe in baptism by immersion," and throws a bucket of water on the elders, one replies, "Yeah, and we also believe in the laying on of hands," and then he "cools him." When a nosy lady snickers, "I hear you Mormons wear secret underwear," a sharp elder responds, "Well, isn't your underwear secret?" Or "Ma'am, there's nothing secret about our underwear. If you'll show us your underwear, we'll be willing to show you ours." When a red-headed Norwegian woman fumes, "I know what you guys do. You come over here to get all the women and you take them back to Salt Lake City and sell them," the missionary replies, "That's right. We just sent a shipment off last week. In fact, we had ten with red hair, and lost one dollar a piece on them." When a woman asks the missionaries at her door if it is true that all Mormons have horns, the new junior companion replies:

> "Yeah, as a matter of fact I just had mine clipped in Salt Lake just before I came out here." And she says, "Really?" and he says, "Yeah, you can feel the little bumps right here on my forehead." And so she put her hand on his forehead, "Well, I don't feel anything." And he said, "Not even a little bit silly?"

In one instance that recalls the story in which missionaries were poisoned as a test of their power, two missionaries called on a Protestant minister.

> He said, "Gentlemen, I have here a glass of poison. If you will drink this poison and remain alive, I will join your church, not only myself but my entire congregation." And he said, "If you won't drink this poison, well, then I'll conclude that you are false ministers of the gospel, because surely your Lord won't let you perish." And so this put the missionaries in a kind of a bind, so they went off in a corner and got their heads together, and they thought, "What on earth are we going to do?" So finally, after they decided, they went back over and approached the minister and said, "Tell you what—we've got a plan." They said, "You drink the poison, and we'll raise you from the dead."

In these stories, the missionaries gain victory over their adversaries through the skillful use of their own wits. In other stories, when the opposition is keener, they are not equal to the task and are forced to bring the Lord in to fight the battle for them. In these accounts, following biblical example, the elders shake dust from their feet and thereby curse the people who have treated them ill. The Lord responds to the missionaries' actions in a dreadful manner. In Norway, a city treats missionaries harshly; they shake dust from their feet, and the city is destroyed by German shelling during the war. Throughout the world, other cities that have mistreated missionaries suffer similar fates. Towns are destroyed in South America by wind, in Chile by floods, in Costa Rica by a volcano, in Mexico by an earthquake, in Japan by a tidal wave, in Taiwan and Sweden by fire. In South Africa, a town's mining industry fails; in Colorado, a town's land becomes infertile; and in Germany, a town's fishing industry folds. Individuals who have persecuted missionaries may also feel God's wrath. An anti-Mormon minister, for instance, loses his job, or breaks his arm, or dies of throat cancer. A woman refuses to give missionaries water, and her well goes dry. A man angrily throws the Book of Mormon into the fire only to have his own house burn down. In one story, widely known, two elders leave their garments at a laundry, and when the proprietor holds them up for ridicule, both he and the laundry burn, the fire so hot in some instances that it melts the bricks.

I do not admire the sentiments expressed in these stories, but as a former missionary who has been spat upon, reviled, and abused in sundry ways by people I only wanted to help, I understand them. I still remember standing on doorsteps after being stung by cruel, biting rejections, and muttering to myself, "Just wait, lady. Comes the judgment, you'll get yours." I would not have "dusted my feet" against anyone; few missionaries would. But many savor the victories that are theirs when they participate in performances of these stories, performances that persuade them that God is on their side and will help them carry the day. For a moment at least, the world bent on thwarting their intentions to save it seems conquerable.

In one of our stories, a newly arrived missionary goes into the bathroom each morning, lathers his face richly, and shaves with great care. His companion, growing suspicious, checks the razor and discovers the greenie has been shaving without a blade. In a missionary song, a parody of "I am Sixteen Goin' on Seventeen," a senior companion sings to his greenie:

> You are nineteen, going on twenty
> Now greener than a lime,
> And you have learned the twelve discussions
> If you are on the dime.
>
> Totally unprepared are you
> To face the world of men,
> Timid and scared and shy are you
> Of things beyond your ken.

You need someone older and wiser
Telling you what to do.
We are twenty-one, some of us twenty-two.
We'll take care of you.

In studying missionaries, we must keep always in mind that we are dealing with untried, indeed often unshaven, young men—nineteen and twenty—who in their first real encounters with the outside world are placed in circumstances that would try the mettle of the best men. In spite of J. Golden Kimball's quip that the church must be true, otherwise the missionaries would have destroyed it long ago, these young people function remarkably well. Few of them crack under the enormous pressure they face each day.

I am not foolish enough to argue that the missionaries endure only because of their folklore. They endure primarily because they are committed to their gospel and convinced of the importance of their work. But that conviction is constantly bolstered and maintained by the lore they have created. As we have seen, through the performance of this lore they develop a strong esprit de corps; they relieve the pressures imposed by the rulebound nature of the system; they channel behavior down acceptable paths; and, most important, they develop a picture of a world that can be overcome.

That world, of course, is very often the world missionaries want it to be rather than the one it is. A performance of folklore is much like a game. In it missionaries create a world similar to but nevertheless separate from the one in which they live. And in that fictive world they play the roles and face the problems that will be theirs in the real world. If the performance is successful, the fictive world and the real world for a moment become one, and missionaries leave the performance with the belief, or at least the hope, that problems faced and solved there can be faced and solved in similar ways in real life. They are a little like the ballad hero Johnny Armstrong, who, mortally wounded, leaned on his sword and shouted encouragement to his men:

Saying, fight on, my merry men all.
And see that none of you be tain;
For I will stand by and bleed but awhile,
And then will I come and fight again. (Child 1884, 3: 367–68)

Missionaries bleed. But they come back to fight again. The significance of folklore performance is that it helps them keep up the fight.

In all of this there is nothing unique to Mormon missionaries. The problems faced by missionaries are not just missionary problems; they are human problems. A missionary who tells a new junior companion to save worthless bus ticket stubs is not much different from a boy scout who sends a tenderfoot on a snipe hunt or a logger who crams a greenhorn's lunch bucket full of grasshoppers. The world is full of greenies who, to function adequately, must first be initiated. Other people besides missionaries, then, must develop a sense of community, must deal with pressures imposed by the systems they live under, must encourage proper behavior, and must come at last to believe they can subdue the world. What missionaries share with others is not so much common stories or practices but rather common reasons for performing them—common means of achieving these ends. From studying the folklore of missionaries, or railroaders, or college professors, we will, to be sure, discover what it means to be a missionary, a railroader, or a college professor. But if we learn to look, we will discover also what it means to be human.

NOTE

1. A full bibliographic survey of the rich sources lying behind the ideas presented here is beyond the compass of this paper. The following authors and their works have helped shape my thinking and will serve as a good beginning for one wishing to pursue the subject further: Roger Abrahams (1966, 1968, 1972, 1976, 1977), Richard Bauman (1975), Dan Ben Amos (1971, 1975), Alan Dundes (1977), Robert A. Georges (1969, 1978, 1979, 1980), Michael Owen Jones (1981), Barre Toelken (1976, 1979). All items of folklore cited in this paper come from the Harris-Wilson Missionary Collection, Utah State University Folklore Archives, Logan, Utah.

The Seriousness of Mormon Humor

My first foray into humor studies occurred when I tried to make sense of the humorous repertoire of a particular group that—not unlike the Mormons—was shaped by dramatic historical events and possessed a distinct ideology. In that and subsequent studies, I came to understand that while humor served to entertain and to lubricate social interaction, it was also a significant form of expression. Important messages were conveyed through jokes, wisecracks, and anecdotes. Humorous expressions offered insights into the concepts, concerns, and values of individuals and groups. For more than three decades now, I have heeded Bert Wilson's admonition that jokes are something to be taken seriously.

Wilson's lifelong involvement in the religion and culture of Latter-day Saints—as participant, observer, and analyst—has permitted him to produce detailed records and rich understandings of Mormon life and experience. Eschewing study of the central doctrines and institutional practices of the faith to focus on the stuff of everyday living—the folklore—he has been able to offer, both to the outsider and insider, a glimpse of what it means to be Mormon. Mormon humor is not the least of this stuff of everyday life, and Mormon humor has a direct bearing on Wilson's larger project of understanding what it means to be human.

Religion, for the most part, has not been kind to humor. The early rabbis condemned jesting and laughter as did the church fathers. Rabbi Akiva said, "Jesting and levity accustom a person to lewdness." Saint John Chrysostom asked, "Christ is crucified and doest thou laugh?" Those fixated on the world-to-come have little sympathy for the distractions of the world in which we live. In this respect, the Church of Jesus Christ of Latter-day Saints is no different from any other. Salvation is a serious business and the institutions, offices, and practices that ensure salvation merit reverence—not ridicule.

This paper was read at the Sunstone Theological Symposium in Salt Lake City on August 23, 1984. It was published in *Sunstone* 10 (1985): 6–13. Reprinted by permission of the Sunstone Foundation.

But a church is not simply a bundle of beliefs and ritual practices. It is organized for and by people, and those people, whether they like it or not, must work out their salvation in this world. Thus, as examples in this article demonstrate, a bishop, who is supposed to be a wise and effective leader, an inspiration to his ward, can be a fool or philanderer. It is not that he *is* a fool or philanderer (although humor can be directed at particular individuals). But because the bishop is human, he can be. Any organization, whatever its goals, must depend upon people who are inept, foolish, or weak—at least some of the time. This is, perhaps, the most fundamental incongruity that conditions religious humor: the irreconcilability of the ideal and the real, the quest for perfection within a material world.

Humor very much depends on a keen apprehension of this world and its ways. And humor, with all its dependence on exaggeration and absurdity, is very much attuned to balance—not extremes. It is the repertoire, however, that is significant in establishing this balance, not the individual joke. For every joke that seems to target the overly pious, there is a joke that targets the sinner and backslider. For every joke that focuses on the overly rigid and unwavering bishop, there is a joke about the bishop who compromises doctrine all too freely. For every joke about a Relief Society president with extensive sexual experience, there is a joke about a saint who is incapable of recognizing even the most blatant sexual allusion. The joke is a kind of *reductio ad absurdum* that tells us when a particular line of thought or behavior goes beyond the pale. A repertoire of jokes delimits the boundaries of a world within which the ordinary, aware, and reasonable person can be expected to think and live.

Anthropologist Melford Spiro, in trying to reconcile Burmese *nat* spirit cults—with their attentions to the exigencies of everyday life—and the philosophical doctrines of Theravada Buddhism, suggested that it was the *nat* cults that allowed Buddhism to retain its exalted, systematic, and uncompromising nature. The *nat* cults addressed the here-and-now and allowed village people to confront the world in which they were forced to live. Consequently Buddhist doctrine did not have to bend itself to the necessities of the everyday. It seems to me that religious humor often serves similar ends. As Wilson says in this article, "The jokes remain as clear markers of central issues in the society, as a barometer of those concerns engaging the minds of the people at any particular moment." In the face of impenetrable doctrines and extraordinary demands, religious humor may remind struggling saints that they must make their way in this world, and remind them that this world is also with them.

—*Elliott Oring*

SOME TIME AGO A FRIEND OF MINE, TALKING TO A PROFESSOR OF HISTORY, SAID he thought the historian and I were working somewhat similar ground—to which the historian replied, "No, we do legitimate history, not folklore.[1] Why, you should see some of the things Wilson studies. He even takes jokes seriously." I do indeed. And I hope to win others to this conviction.

Perhaps even scholars with a little more vision than this particular historian have failed to take either Mormon literary or folk humor seriously because they have believed that no such humor exists. As Richard Cracroft has pointed out, "one must search far into the first half of the twentieth century before turning up any intentionally sustained published humor" (1980, 31). Not until recent times, in novels like Samuel Taylor's *Heaven Knows Why* (1994) or in shorter pieces like Levi Peterson's "The Christianization of Coburn Heights" in *Canyons of Grace* (1982) do we find much *written* evidence that Mormons have been anything but the stolid, unsmiling souls the rest of the world has believed them to be.

Nor is there in the folklore record—at least in the folklore record made available to us through the work of earlier scholars—much evidence to give a happier picture. The reason for this is simple. Just as earlier Mormon writers attempted to give literary expression to the clearly serious struggle to establish the kingdom of God in the western wasteland, so too did the first students of Mormon folklore seek out the folk expressions generated by that struggle. Thus in the first, and still most important, major study of Mormon folklore, *Saints of Sage and Saddle: Folklore among the Mormons* (1956), Austin and Alta Fife devoted one deliciously funny chapter to the trickster hero J. Golden Kimball but filled the rest of the book with solemn and miraculous accounts in which the Saints, aided by God and his angels, struggled to overcome both themselves and a frequently hostile world.

It is not surprising, then, that Leonard Arrington—one historian who does take jokes seriously—addressed Brigham Young University students on "The Many Uses of Humor" and, following the Fifes, said: "The humorous tradition of J. Golden Kimball stories is in marked contrast to the bulk of Mormon folklore, which is dominated by tales of miracles and the supernatural—all serving the didactic function of teaching that God still actively intervenes in the lives of men. . . . Revelatory self-directed humor concerning the weaknesses and special difficulties of Mormons is rare." But then, perhaps troubled by this doleful view of Mormon folk tradition, Arrington added: "A study [by Lucile Butler] of humorous stories told among Ephraim, Utah, residents suggests that perhaps a much larger body of Mormon folk humor could be gathered . . . were we to take the time to gather it" (1974).

Captivated by tales of angels, Nephites, and devils, then, collectors of Mormon folklore have in the past not taken the time to collect that large and vibrant body of jokes which Mormons tell and have probably always told each other about each other—with the result that the scholarly world still tends to view Mormons as a rather dour and pious lot, seldom given to laughter at their own imperfections and human foibles. During the past fifteen years my students and I have attempted to remedy this situation by collecting and depositing in folklore archives at least some of the Mormon jokes and anecdotes Arrington hoped someone would gather. This paper is a first, albeit hesitant, attempt to come to terms with this material.

At the outset, there are three points to note about these jokes. First, many Mormon jokes are Mormon by adoption rather than by birth. As folklorists know, much folklore is not culture-specific—that is, though the lore may thoroughly reflect the values, attitudes, anxieties, and beliefs of a cultural group, that lore itself may have originated elsewhere, may have at one time been taken over by the group, and then may have been reshaped to reflect the group's cultural contours and express its dominant concerns. So it is with Mormon jokes. These jokes are Mormon not because of where they came from but because of the uses to which they are put and because of what they reveal about the narrators. Most joke tellers, I should add, have no idea that the jokes they tell are not originally Mormon. It is the spoil-sport comparative folklorist who points this out.

The second point to observe is that the J. Golden Kimball cycle is not the heart and center of Mormon humor. While it is certainly true that this cycle is, or at least has been, the creation of the Mormon folk, it is also true that J. Golden is well on the way to becoming a popular hero rather than a folk hero. The folk legacy record by Hector Lee (1964); the book *The Golden Legacy* (1974), by Thomas Cheney; the one-man show, "J. Golden," written by James Arrington and starring Bruce Ackerman; the feature column in *Sunstone*, "J. Golden Nuggets," by James N. Kimball—all these have pulled the crusty old man away from traditional culture, where knowledge is passed along in face-to-face interactions among small groups of people, toward popular culture, where knowledge is disseminated in a one-way communication from the cultural taste-makers to large groups of people by means of the popular media.

If there is any central figure in Mormon folk humor it is not J. Golden Kimball or any other general authority of the church—except occasionally Brigham Young, whose straight speaking, association with polygamy, and safe distance in the past make him the object of some jokes. The central figure instead is the beleaguered bishop, his counterpart, the Relief Society president, and occasionally a high councilor or the stake president—in other words, leaders at lower levels of authority than the revered and fearsome general authorities. Unlike the general authorities, these leaders are nameless—partly because they represent folk types rather than specific individuals, and mainly because, as lay leaders, they represent you and me. Most of us, if we keep our noses even partly clean, may well become the very leaders we make fun of; what's more, many of us already face some of the same problems that now bedevil these leaders. There is in many of these jokes, therefore, a more affectionate feeling toward the objects of the humor than there is in the anticlerical jokes of other groups. Consider the following three stories:

> It seems that a bishop and his two counselors were all stranded out in the desert and just didn't know what they were going to do. Then they noticed a lamp lying there in the sand. They picked it up and rubbed it, and out popped a genie. The genie said each one

> of them could have one wish. The second counselor said, "I wish I was home by my swimming pool drinking a big glass of lemonade." Zap, and he was gone. The first counselor said, "I wish I was home sitting in front of the TV with a big glass of orange juice." Zap, and he was gone. And the bishop said, "I wish my two counselors were here to help me decide."

> A bishop who was conducting a church building fund in his ward preached a sermon from the pulpit one time about being blessed for contributing to the building fund. After his sermon, a member came up to him and said, "Bishop, that was a damned fine sermon." The bishop replied, "Brother, you had better watch the swearing." The member continued, "Yes sir, Bishop, that was such a damned fine sermon that I gave an extra $650 for the building fund." The bishop then said, "Yes brother, it takes a hell of a lot of money to build a church."

> There was a Mormon bishop in a small Utah town who, like all Mormon bishops, worked so hard at his calling that he never had time for his own activities. One Sunday, when the pressure had gotten unbearable, he decided to skip meeting and go golfing. This he did and had quite an enjoyable time. Upon returning home, however, he found his town had vanished. A bit bewildered, he went to his house where he found a note tacked to his door. It read: "Sorry we missed you. —Enoch."

Here, in each of these jokes, is a bishop not unlike ourselves. He must make decisions he does not feel prepared to make; he must commit himself to an ideal world while pragmatically learning to deal with the real world; and, after all the work he does to help others achieve their salvation, he may fail to make the grade himself. As we laugh at these jokes, then, we are perhaps laughing more at the circumstance of being Mormon than we are at the imperfect bishop. And thus it is with much Mormon humor: the targets of the jokes, ostensibly someone else, are really ourselves.

A third point to consider about Mormon jokes is that, contrary to the expectations of many, humor growing out of the Mormon experience will not always reveal a united people, sharing a common identity and viewing the world through similar eyes. While the same Mormon jokes will often be told by members from all segments of Mormon society (the only limiting factor being the intelligence necessary to understand the humor), there is no uniformity of belief about the appropriateness of these jokes. About the only thing clear from the data is that some Mormons frequently tell Mormon jokes and find them greatly amusing, that some never tell the jokes and find them offensive, that the bulk of Mormons range somewhere between these two extremes, and that it is almost impossible to know which Mormon will fall into which of these categories. Folklore, we should remember, is communal but not stereotypical; that is, it is kept alive by members of a particular community but does not characterize every member of the community.

According to folklorist Elliott Oring, it is strong emotional involvement which causes some of us not to appreciate our humor. "Appreciation of humor," says Oring, "may . . . require a measure of emotional distance from the subject matter of the humor. Often concepts, philosophies, personalities, or societies may be disparaged in a joke and should these be the focus of intense emotion, humor may not be experienced. The communication may be regarded as a slander rather than as humor because the hearer is unable to achieve sufficient emotional distance" (1981, 54). If what Oring says is true, then one would expect important and sacred Mormon concepts, philosophies, and personalities not to be the objects of humor, at least not among the faithful. Or one could argue that, when the jokes are told, they may be seen as a measure of the psychic distance a Mormon is able to put between himself and the teachings of his church. A few examples from each of the main themes in Mormon humor will reveal whether Oring's principle holds true.

When a three-year-old Mormon boy and a little Catholic girl once sneaked away to a pond behind the boy's house and stripped to the buff to go swimming, the boy looked at his naked companion and exclaimed, "Gosh, I didn't know there was such a difference between Mormons and Catholics." The difference Mormons perceive between themselves and members of other faiths is usually of quite another nature. One of the principal causes of contention between Mormons and their neighbors is the Mormon insistence that Mormons alone possess the complete truth, the only way to salvation, and that all other churches are in error. Out of this belief is often born a smug self-righteousness that is evident in jokes Mormons tell about their dealings with people of other faiths. For example, when a public school teacher asked a little Mormon boy in her class what he would be if he weren't Mormon, he replied, "Embarrassed!" Another time

> two young deacons were very excited about their priesthood lesson which was about baptism. They decided to practice the baptismal service after Sunday School. They went to one boy's home and found the mother cat and her kittens to practice on. The kittens were first because they were smaller and easier to handle, but when they tried to immerse the mother cat, they had quite a bit of difficulty. Finally they gave up in despair, and one of the young boys suggested that they just sprinkle the mother cat and let it go to the Devil.

And still another time

> three ladies on a bus began talking about Mormons. One lady said, "I live where it's 50 percent Mormon and I hate it because I can't

> ever do anything. I want to move." The second lady said, "Well I live where it's nearly 80 percent Mormon and I want to move to a place where there aren't any so I can have some fun." Then the third lady said, "I live in Utah and that's almost all Mormon. I can't ever do anything fun without being looked down on. I want to go someplace where there aren't any Mormons." Just then a man sitting in front of them, who was a Mormon, turned around and said, "Why don't you all go to hell! There aren't any Mormons there!"

But alongside these anecdotes exists another body of jokes in which Mormons poke fun not at others but at the notion that Mormons alone are destined for salvation. For example, according to an anecdote that made the rounds several years ago,

> President Kimball sent out messages for all members of the church to meet on Temple Square for an important message. The Tabernacle, the Assembly Hall, and the Salt Palace were full, and people were all over. President Kimball got up and said: "Saints, I've got some good news and some bad news. First the good news. We have just received a telegram from Western Union; the Millennium is here. Christ arrives in two days. Now for the bad news. We're all supposed to meet at the Vatican."

In the most frequently collected joke in the USU archives, St. Peter conducts a group of people on a tour through heaven and shows them where the different churches are located. As they pass one room, St. Peter says, "Shhh! Quiet! Those are the Mormons; they think they're the only ones here."

A second major theme in Mormon humor has to do with money. Scarcely a year goes by that someone in the national press does not write an exposé on the great wealth of the Mormon church. In the church itself, members, who are asked to pay a full tithing as well as contribute to the missionary fund, the building fund, and the welfare fund, feel at times, as one wit put it, that the letters LDS really mean "Lay Down the Silver." Or when they see the statue of Brigham Young in downtown Salt Lake, back to the temple and hand outstretched toward Zion's National Bank, they may feel there is some justification in the jingle, "There stands Brigham / Like a bird on a perch, / With his hand to the bank / And his back to the church." They chuckle when they hear that the Mormon skyjacker was finally apprehended because he aroused suspicion by suddenly paying $50,000 in tithing. They point out that Howard Hughes did not make it into heaven because in his supposed "Mormon will" he left to the church only a sixteenth of his fortune instead of a tenth—a full tithe. And they tell jokes like the following:

> There was recently a local resident whose beloved dog died of a heart attack. Because this man loved his dog so much, he decided

> that it would only be appropriate for the pet to have a church funeral. So the man called upon his bishop and asked him if he could have a funeral service for his loved one in the neighborhood LDS chapel. The bishop replied that this was a highly unusual request and one which would probably not be appropriate for an LDS chapel. The man, greatly disappointed, then asked the bishop whether one of the non-Mormon churches in the area would conduct such a service. The bishop, obviously relieved by this suggestion, said that he was sure that one of them would. The man then asked how much money one of these "gentile" churches would charge for such a service. The bishop replied that he did not have any idea of the possible financial costs. The man, while leaving the bishop's office, casually replied, "Well, that's no problem, friend. You see, I am willing to pay $1,000 for a proper service." The bishop, greatly surprised by this statement, jumped up and said, "Wait, brother! Wait! Why didn't you tell me before that your dear pet was a Latter-day Saint."

Not only are members expected to donate money to the church, they are also expected to give great amounts of time. There is considerable truth to the jingle: "Mary had a little lamb. / It grew to be a sheep. / Then it joined the Mormon church / And died from lack of sleep." As every Mormon knows, with a lay clergy and with each member expected to accept "calls" in the church to be a Sunday School teacher, a scoutmaster, a secretary, and so on, a visit from the bishop seldom betokens a social visit but rather another call to duty. Especially is this true when the bishop visits the Relief Society president, the woman in the ward to whom the bishop turns most frequently for help on projects. Thus the following story:

> A Catholic priest, a rabbi, and a Mormon bishop were bragging about how much their various congregations believed them. So they decided to test a member of each faith to see which one would believe a strange thing. They went to a Jew's home. "Hello, Mrs. Goldstein; I'm a holy cow," said the rabbi. "Oh, come on," said Mrs. Goldstein, "you're a lot of strange things, but I know you're not a holy cow." So they went to a parishioner's home, and the priest said, "Hello, Mrs. Florentin; I'm a holy cow." "Oh father," she said, "I know you're not a holy cow, but come on inside anyway." So they went to a Relief Society president's house with whom the bishop had had many meetings. He knocked on the door. As soon as she saw who it was, she exclaimed, "Holy cow, is that you again?"

Though there is no direct statement of it, there is at least a slight hint of impropriety in this joke, in all the visits the bishop has been making to the home of the Relief Society president. In other stories there is more than just a hint. For example, one Sunday in Idaho an old farmer stood up in testimony meeting and laconically said:

> Well, it's been a right good week. No dead pigs. Corn's in. Cows milked. Few flies, but that ain't so bad. Yep, everything was goin' along right fine, up until last night—when Ma went out and committed adultery.

This brings us to the third major theme in Mormon humor: sex. There seem to be fewer jokes in this category than in others; still, there are too many of them to be ignored. One of the perplexing problems with these jokes is that in many of them some authority figure, usually the bishop or Relief Society president, is guilty of violating the very law he or she is most concerned with upholding, the law of chastity. Perhaps the church's very strict sexual code makes the violation of the code the most effective way of deflating authority figures by making them, as Freud would say, seem inferior or ridiculous. However, as already noted, these figures are very often simply ourselves, struggling with the same problems we must face. The number of excommunications in the church for sexual offenses suggests that the struggle is real enough. These sexual jokes may be one of the few socially acceptable ways of talking openly about this forbidden subject.

Sometimes, in the face of temptation, the bishop in these stories is naive, or sexually unaware:

> A Mormon bishop was hunting deer in the mountains around Salt Lake City. He came into a clearing, and there on the ground was a beautiful woman without any clothes on. "Are you game?" asked the bishop. "I sure am," came the suggestive reply. So the bishop shot her.

More often, faced by this same temptation, the poor bishop succumbs:

> There was a new Mormon bishop who looked like Dean Martin. One day he went around visiting the ladies in his ward. Each time he would knock on the door, the lady would answer, "Dean Martin!" The bishop would say, "Oh no, I'm your new bishop." Finally he came to a door that was answered by a beautiful young girl who was nude. She said, "Dean Martin!" The bishop sang, "Everybody loves somebody sometime. . . ."

Sometimes it is the bishop's good helper, the Relief Society president, who is the butt of the joke:

> Last summer at Bear Lake a young man of little modesty decided to get in a little nude sunbathing. He walked naked along the beach until he felt tired, so he lay down on the warm sand and soon fell asleep. As he was sleeping, the Logan ladies' Relief Society moved onto the beach for their annual picnic. They all sat down near the sleeping man, but did not notice him. Eventually the man woke up and looked around in fright at all these ladies. Not knowing what to do, he grabbed a brown paper bag that was lying nearby, pulled it over his head, and ran past the ladies toward his car. After the shock wore off, the women began to wonder who this man was. One lady turned to the others and said, "Well, I could tell it wasn't *my* husband." Another one said, "I had a good look and could tell that it surely wasn't my husband." Another one said that she didn't recognize the man either. Finally the Relief Society president spun around and said, "Ladies, I had a good look too, and I'm sure he isn't even in our ward."

On one occasion,

> a woman in St. George, Utah, had a set of triplets and two sets of twins. A church authority visited the area for stake conference, surveyed the woman's offspring, and exclaimed, "Good heavens! Do you get multiple births every time?" She replied, "Oh no. Most of the times we don't get anything."

Though Mormons are sternly warned to avoid pre- and extramarital sex, they recognize, as this last joke suggests, the importance of sex in marriage. They do not believe that children are conceived in sin. Thus, according to tradition,

> Brigham Young was coming across with a pioneer wagon train, and they got close to the Great Basin area. He sent a scout out ahead to see what it was like. And a little while later the scout returned—he was racing back on his horse and saying, "It's there! It's terrific! There's a beautiful lake and it's a paradise. All we can do is fish and make love all day long!" And then Brigham Young turned to him and said, "Well, salt the lake."

There is some hint, however, that Brigham Young's wives may not always have approved of this view:

> As Brigham Young's wagon pulled over the ridge into the Salt Lake valley, Brigham Young's wife was standing looking into the valley. Brigham Young came forward and said the now-famous line, "This is the place!" To which his wife haughtily replied: "This is neither the time nor the place, Brigham."

But while sex in marriage is generally perceived as all right, Brigham's wife notwithstanding, the main purpose of sex is still thought by the faithful to be the production of offspring. Thus in Utah, which has the highest per capita birthrate in the nation, it is not unusual to hear riddle-jokes like this: "Did you hear that the state bird is going to be changed?" "No." "Yeah, from the seagull to the stork." Question: "How can you tell if you are at a Mormon wedding?" Answer: "The mother of the bride is pregnant." Nor is it unusual to hear people make jokes like the following, jokes that make fun of, or negate, Mormon reproductive capacities: "My wife is a big fan of the pill. She eats them like candy. The other day she had taken a number of them and then went to her church duties. While she was there, she sneezed and sterilized the whole thirty-first ward Relief Society." In another story,

> a young girl was sent away to BYU by her parents, and at the end of her first semester she came back home telling her parents that she had to drop out of school because she was pregnant. Her parents were astonished, to say the least, that their daughter with such a fine Mormon upbringing could have this happen to her. They immediately asked her if the boy didn't intend to do the right thing and marry her. To which the girl replied, "Oh Mother, I couldn't marry him! He smokes."

The reference here, of course, is not just to sex but to the Mormon Word of Wisdom, the health code that prohibits use of tobacco, alcohol, coffee, and tea. Jokes about the Word of Wisdom comprise the fourth main theme in Mormon jokelore. Mormons hold ambiguous attitudes toward this teaching. Some think it is greatly overemphasized at the expense of more important principles, hence the joke just cited. Others secretly wish they could occasionally indulge in such pleasures, hence the following joke:

> Some members of a civic organization were making plans for a social. For the party the refreshment committee decided to serve liquor as part of the refreshments; but when it came time for the party, the refreshment committee noticed that the invitation committee had invited several clergymen, and they were in attendance. This presented a problem because they didn't want to serve liquor with the clergy present. Since they were having watermelon for dessert, they decided they would open one watermelon and drain all the juice from it and then fill it back up with liquor for their own use. But as you would expect, the watermelons got mixed up, and they discovered that the watermelon with the liquor in it had been served to the clergymen. They looked to see what was taking place. The Catholic priest was eating his watermelon like there was nothing wrong with it; the Baptist minister was also enjoying his.

> Then they noticed the Mormon bishop. He was likewise enjoying his watermelon, and he was saving the seeds and putting them in his pocket.

Some Mormons take a cynical view of the Word of Wisdom, questioning the sincerity of those who abide by its principles. For example, "Why should you always take at least two Mormons on a hunting trip?" Answer: "Because if you take only one, he'll drink all the beer." Still other Mormons willingly obey but feel uncomfortable when they must explain to non-Mormons why they can't drink the cup of coffee offered them in friendship. These Mormons will take painful pleasure from the following joke:

> One day St. Peter was repairing the gates of heaven and a Catholic priest who had just died came to get in. "It'll be a few minutes before you can enter," St. Peter said, "The gates are broken. You can go over there and have a cup of coffee while you wait. . . ." Not long after, a Protestant minister who had just died approached St. Peter to enter heaven. "You'll have to wait a while while I fix these gates," St. Peter said. "Just go over there and have some coffee." The minister joined the priest. Soon a Mormon bishop who had just died came up to St. Peter and wanted to get into heaven. St. Peter said, "You'll have to go to hell. I don't have time to make hot chocolate."

The fifth, and final, category of Mormon humor is represented in all these jokes—antiauthoritarian humor. Mormon anticlerical stories are legion but space will allow only a few more examples:

> At a stake conference in Idaho once the stake president was sitting up on the stand, and somebody else was talking. The stake president noticed three people standing up in the back because they didn't have a seat. He proceeded to attract the attention of one of the deacons to have him go get three chairs. He was motioning, signaling "three" with his fingers, moving his lips wide and slow, mouthing the words "three chairs." But the deacon still hesitated. The stake president kept it up, getting more insistent all the time and finally said, "Come on, get up." So the deacon finally dragged himself up [in front of the congregation] and said: "Rah, rah, rah, stake president!"

> There was once a group of Mormons who went to Russia on a tour. . . . About the third day there, three people were arrested for spying. They just happened to be a Relief Society president, a bishop, and a high councilor. The Russians first brought in the Relief Society president and gave her the last wish of her life. . . . She was granted

> [her wish of listening to a tape of the Mormon Tabernacle Choir] and then killed. The Russians then brought in the high councilor, and he was asked for his last wish. He replied that he had a talk prepared for that Sunday and would like to stay alive till Sunday so that he could give his talk. He was then put back into his cell until Sunday. It happened that when the bishop was brought in to see the Russians, he heard what the other two had wished for. When asked what he would like for his last wish, the bishop simply replied, "I would just like to be killed before I have to listen to that high councilor on Sunday."

> During sacrament meeting one Sunday, the bishop noticed that too many of his ward members were sleeping. After the last speaker was done, the bishop got up and in his indignation began to really shout at the congregation . . . about how they should be coming to church to receive the Spirit and how they couldn't do that if they were sleeping. He finished off quite emphatically by shouting, "Now, all of you who don't think you'll go to hell for sleeping through church, stand up!" One of the offending brothers had managed to sleep through all of the bishop's tirade except for the last two words. When he heard the command to "stand up!" he immediately jumped to his feet. The whole congregation was rolling on the floor. The brother looked around pretty bewildered and said, "I don't know what we're voting on, bishop, but you and I are the only ones for it."

The final joke comes from my ancestral country, Malad, Idaho, where the bulk of the original Mormon settlers were Welsh and where any Scandinavians were in a distinct minority:

> A certain bishop [a Welshman] noticed some contention between a Welshman and a Danish brother in his congregation, so he called the good Danish brother into his office and said, "What's the problem between you and Brother Jones?" The Danish brother replied: "Veil, dat old Velshman called me a Danish s. of a b. Now vouldn't dat make you upset vith him?" The bishop replied, "No, it wouldn't bother me at all; I'm not Danish." Whereupon the Danish brother defensively asked: "Veil, den, vat if he called you dat kind of s. of a b. vat you are?"

In Mormon joke after Mormon joke, as in these just cited and in many I have given above, an LDS authority figure has the props knocked out from under him, is sworn at, or is made to look ridiculous. Though I am by no means a slavish follower of the safety-valve theory of humor, it seems clear that many of these jokes grow out of the tellers' attempts to live more comfortably within an autocratic and pervasively authoritarian system. For a moment, at least, the tellers humanize and make less fearsome those who control their lives.

In light of this fact, do Mormons exemplify Oring's notion that excessive emotional attachment to certain concepts, doctrines, and personalities prevents appreciation of jokes on these topics? Yes and no. The major themes in Mormon jokelore are not just random clusterings of stories; they parallel instead central issues in the Mormon church: the unique and divine calling of the church, the law of tithing, the law of chastity, the Word of Wisdom, devotion to duty, and unquestioning obedience to authority. Most believing, active Mormons will certainly have a heavy emotional investment in these ideas. Yet some of these believing, active Mormons will find the jokes immensely funny, and others will consider them offensive, bordering on sacrilege. Pleas by both Richard Cracroft and Leonard Arrington for a renaissance of Mormon humor and statements by them that this humor can serve healthy restorative functions, enabling Mormons to deal with the frailties of both themselves and their leaders, oversimplify the issue. Clearly, for some Mormons, Mormon humor serves this laudatory function. For other Mormons it can serve dysfunctional or destructive ends.

It would be a mistake to assume, then, as folklorists and others often do, that what is true of one Mormon will be true of them all or that most Mormons will respond in similar ways to the telling of Mormon jokes. It is impossible to stereotype Mormons. Each person must be viewed as an individual in some ways separate and distinct from all members of the group.

It would also be a mistake to develop any monistic interpretation of the function or meaning of the jokes. For example, within a few days after the revelation granting blacks the priesthood June 8, 1978, a spate of "blacks and the priesthood" jokes spread rapidly along Utah's Wasatch front, as many will remember. Most of these were in the form of riddle-jokes. "Have you heard that they've taken the Angel Moroni off the Salt Lake Temple?" "Yes, they're replacing him with a statue of Louis Armstrong." "Have you heard that we've raised tithing to twelve percent?" "Yes, the extra two percent is to pay for busing." According to Richard Cracroft these jokes were "a sign of healthy adjustment to a sudden change in a long-standing uncomfortable condition" (1980, 36). Richard Poulsen, on the other hand, observed in an address to the American Folklore Society that the jokes afforded "an opportunity for Mormons to express the fact that an accepted pattern (of supposed racial tolerance) has no necessity" and added that the joke-telling gave Mormons a twofold victory: "victory over the threat of disruption in the status quo (by black inroads in the sacred), and victory over those who have imposed the pain of change (prominent leaders of the Mormon church)" (1988, 30). Which of these interpretations is accurate? Both of them, of course. The jokes themselves have no intrinsic meaning that we have only to discover and then we will know the truth. They have only the meanings perceived in them by the tellers and listeners, meanings depending on where the jokes are told, by whom, and to what ends. Or they have the meanings imposed upon them by their interpreters—in this instance Cracroft and Poulsen. From these interpretations we may well learn more about Cracroft's and Poulsen's own personal views of Mormon culture than we will about the culture itself.

Does this mean, then, that Mormon jokes are of little consequence in gaining insight into Mormon society? Of course not. Legend scholar Linda Dègh has shown us that while belief in legends like the stories of the Three Nephites may range from absolute belief to absolute disbelief, the legends themselves remain, in Degh's words, as "sensitive indicators" of conditions within a society (1973, 8). So it is with jokes. The opinion of whether Mormon jokes are funny or are in poor taste will range from one extreme to the other. But the jokes remain as clear markers of central issues in the society, as a barometer of those concerns engaging the minds of the people at any particular moment. As we discover those things that move some Mormons to laugh the hardest or provoke others to righteous anger, we may learn in the process to recognize those things most Mormons feel most deeply.

NOTE

1. All items of folklore cited in this paper are located in the Fife Folklore Archive, Utah State University, Logan, Utah.

FREEWAYS, PARKING LOTS, AND ICE CREAM STANDS

Three Nephites in Contemporary Mormon Culture

Part of Bert Wilson's appeal as a human being, scholar, and friend lies in his character as a no-nonsense *homo religiosus*; Bert is down-to-earth, objective, and not given to unbridled fantasy. It is his very reasonableness in writing about religious folklore that makes him trustworthy for the outsider and a fair representative of the insider. His voice has opened not only Mormon religious folklore but religious folklore in general to many readers and suggested research possibilities and fresh kinds of knowledge to new generations of scholars.

"Freeways, Parking Lots, and Ice Cream Stands" offers both a permanent contribution to humanistic scholarship and an important moment in the evolution of Wilson's thinking as a folklorist. Indeed, the effect of Bert's contribution has been so complete that some readers may be surprised to learn that the vitality of Three Nephite legends was ever in doubt. However, the discovery that Nephite legends were not just a "fading survival" was a significant realization, with a much larger message. Something Bert and a few others were gradually bringing into full awareness in the academic world was that religion *itself* was not a fading survival. Some folklorists and other scholars, either following Wilson's lead or developing similar ideas independently, shifted scholarship to describe how and why religious folklore functions in the daily life of modern people, not to expose the innocence, naïveté, quaintness, or ignorance of "folk religion" as earlier folklorists had explicitly or implicitly done. These scholars have contributed to the dignity and respect accorded those "for whom," in the words of Joshua Trachtenberg, "religion is no bare logical exercise, no social doctrine or philosophical or even theosophical system, but a sorely needed source of strength" (see Trachtenberg 1942, 173).

This paper was delivered as a dinner address at the Sunstone Theological Symposium in Salt Lake City on August 29, 1987. It was published in *Dialogue: A Journal of Mormon Thought* 21.3 (Fall 1988): 13–26. Reprinted by permission of the Dialogue Foundation.

This article, for all its import, also represents a particular moment in Wilson's thinking and engagement with Mormon folklore. His initial article on the genre, "Mormon Legends of the Three Nephites Collected at Indiana University," (1969, 3–35), mainly compiled and annotated legends from his own collection. In this article, Wilson analyzes the function of the stories in the lives of Latter-day Saints; he considers how the Three Nephite legends help tellers and their audiences find meaning and overcome difficulties. Later, he took another step and realized that he and other scholars had unintentionally overemphasized Three Nephite stories in their scholarship. As exemplified in this article, these stories were dramatic, miraculous, and uncanny, and thus satisfied the outsider appetite for the exotic, the colorful, the exceptional. And that, Wilson realized, was the problem: a folklorist needs to resist the exceptional—the audience-pleasing—and seek out the typical if he or she is to represent truly a culture *as it sees itself.*

Seven years after this article, Wilson wrote, "We shape our data not to reveal the essence of the material we have collected, but to please and meet the expectations of those who will read our publications or view our presentations" (see Wilson 1995, 13–21). Although this article provides an important shift to understand function in Wilson's study of Mormon folklore, later articles included in this volume show attempts to move beyond only the supernatural elements of Mormon storytelling. The Three Nephites ultimately led Wilson away from themselves to autobiographical narratives of conversion, to a dry, self-effacing Mormon sense of humor, and to stories of thoughtful acts of service—the truly common and most widespread instances of Mormon folklore.

—*Steven Siporin*

In the 1892–93 issue of *The Folk-Lorist*, a publication of the old Chicago Folk-Lore Society, the Reverend David Utter, from Salt Lake City, published a short piece entitled "Mormon Superstition." He recounted Mormon beliefs about Indians, summarized briefly the contents of the Book of Mormon, and then told how, according to this book, three of Christ's new-world disciples called Nephites had been allowed to remain on earth until the Savior returned again. "Many of the saints now living," wrote Reverend Utter,

> tell that they have, at different times, seen one or more of these three immortal "Nephites." A daughter of Brigham Young, now a good Unitarian, has told me that her father told, with great and solemn pleasure, of an interview that he had with one of these remaining apostles in Liverpool, when he was there on a mission. The apostle met him at the chapel door, an old man with a long gray beard, made himself known, and spoke many encouraging and helpful words. (1892, 83, 76)

So far as I know, this was the first reference in a scholarly publication to what has become one of the best known supernatural-narrative cycles in the

United States—the legend of the Three Nephites. And for over three decades it remained the only reference. Then in 1938, in a short article entitled "The Three Nephites in Popular Tradition," folklorist Wayland Hand once again introduced the Nephite legend to the scholarly community, recounting stories of a mysterious stranger who reportedly had prepared the way for Mormon missionaries in a southern town (1938, 123–29). Hand did not continue his study of the Nephite tradition, but three other folklorists, Austin and Alta Fife and Hector Lee, had also become interested in the legend and had begun collecting stories in earnest. In 1940 and 1942 Austin Fife published "The Legend of the Three Nephites among the Mormons," a groundbreaking collection of fifty-two texts, and "Popular Legends of the Mormons," which contained a summary of the main features of the stories. In describing the Nephites, Fife gave a capsule summary of the legend that has served to the present day:

> In localities of Utah, Idaho, and other states where the Mormon faith is prevalent, one frequently hears accounts of the miraculous appearance and disappearance of kindly, white-bearded old men who bring messages of the greatest spiritual importance, give blessings in exchange for hospitality, lead lost people to safety, and perform various other miraculous deeds. These old men are said by the people to be the "Three Nephites." (1940, 1)

In 1947, building on the work of the Fifes and basing his study on an expanded corpus of 150 legends and their variants, Hector Lee wrote a dissertation on the Three Nephites; in 1949 he published the work as *The Three Nephites: The Substance and Significance of the Legend in Folklore.* In 1956, the Fifes turned their attention to the Nephites once again, devoting a rich chapter to them in their monumental *Saints of Sage and Saddle: Folklore among the Mormons* (233–49).

As important as these works were, knowledge of the Three Nephites reached a national audience primarily through the efforts of Richard M. Dorson, dean of American folklorists and head of the prestigious folklore program at Indiana University. Drawing on the works of the Fifes and Lee, Dorson summarized the Nephite legend in his widely read *American Folklore* (115–18), published in 1959, and again in *Buying the Wind: Regional Folklore in the United States* (500–508), published in 1964.

Mormons, of course, at least those from the Mountain West, have needed no such works to make them aware of the Three Nephites. They know of them directly, sometimes through their own experiences, which they have interpreted as Nephite encounters, more often by hearing Nephite stories repeated in their homes and churches and by telling them to others. I remember well one such storytelling event from my own life.

On a rainy night in early October 1960, a fellow high school teacher and his wife—Ray and Ann Briscoe—were driving me to Salt Lake City. As we dodged through the late-evening traffic, I listened fascinated as Ann told me that on these very roads in recent months an old hitchhiker had hailed rides with Mormon motorists, had warned them to store food for an impending disaster, and had then disappeared miraculously from the back seats of their cars. The hitchhiker was thought to be one of the Three Nephites. I believed the story, partly because of the mood in the car that night, but primarily because I had grown up with stories of Nephite visits and found this account compatible with my past experience.

Two years later, now a graduate student at Indiana University interested primarily in Finnish folklore and literature, I met Richard Dorson, who was delighted to have a real Mormon in his program and who introduced me to the scholarly study of my own tradition. Inspired by his enthusiasm, I turned to Mormon faculty members and graduate students at the university and in 1964 collected from them forty Nephite narratives for Dorson's fieldwork course—seven of them variants of the story I had heard that rainy night in Salt Lake a few years earlier (Wilson 1969, 3–35). Dorson was surprised and pleased to discover that Mormon folklore could be collected outside Utah. And I was hooked—from that day to the present, in one way or another, the Nephites and their stories have been my companions.

As I began collecting Nephite accounts, I expected my work merely to substantiate earlier findings of the Fifes and Lee. I was wrong. Both Austin Fife and Hector Lee had argued twenty years earlier that the number of Nephite accounts was at that time decreasing, and Lee especially believed the legend would not flourish in a more technological and rational age. But my collection showed that the legend was alive and growing, at least among my informants in Bloomington, Indiana. From twenty-one individuals, I easily collected my forty tales in a very short time—and could have collected more had the semester's end not been approaching.

Lee also had argued that while older Nephite stories were still being told, new accounts were not surfacing. According to Lee, the legend developed slowly from 1830 to 1855, grew more rapidly from 1855 to 1875, reached its peak from 1875 to 1900, waned slightly from 1900 to 1925, and after 1925 dwindled to only a few scattered narratives (1949, 31). The stories he had collected were, Lee argued, cultural survivals from the pioneer past and therefore useful primarily as a means of understanding "pioneer concepts, attitudes, and impulses" (1949, 126).

I certainly did collect some fine pioneer narratives. The following is a good example:

> This story is part of the family traditions on my mother's side of the family. It dates back, I believe, to the 1870s when my mother's grandparents lived in the central Utah area, more exactly in the region of Manti. My great-grandfather had a sawmill in the area and often would go up in the mountains to cut trees, and my

> great-grandmother would be left at home with the many children. Well, one time my great-grandfather was away, and great-grandmother was home watching the kids, and it happened that at the time the Manti Temple was to be dedicated. And my great-grandmother wanted very much to go, but she could find no one to watch the children because everyone in the area was going to the Manti Temple dedication. On the morning of the dedication she [was] still sure that she would not be able to go. She met an old man at the front gate, and he said, "Sister Swenson, I see that you'd like to go to the temple dedication. I'm just passing through; let me watch your kids and they'll be all right as long as you're gone. Don't worry." My great-grandmother did not know the man, had never seen him before; but somehow she felt that he was a kindly old man and agreed. And she went to the temple dedication. When she came home from the temple dedication, she met the old man just coming out of the front gate, and he said, "Well, Sister Swenson, you have nothing to worry about," and he walked down the street. And she watched him go, and it seemed that as he just about turned down the path out of sight he met two other old men. And it was felt in the family tradition that these were Three Nephites and one of them had stopped to help my great-grandmother with the children so she could go to the temple dedication.[1]

But I also collected stories far removed from a rural pioneer setting. Consider the following account:

> I heard this from the person it's said to have happened to, which might give it some more importance. The story was related by the owner of the A&W Root Beer stand on the corner of—I think it's State Street and the entrance to Brigham Young University campus in Provo, Utah. He said he was working in his stand one afternoon in the summer when an old man came walking up and asked if he could have something to eat. The man seemed rather poor, and so the owner gave him an ice cream cone and—perhaps something with it. I don't remember. After finishing this, the old man told the owner—he said something like this, "You'll always have all you need if you're generous with what you have and live righteously." The owner of the root beer stand turned to comment to one of his employees in the store, and when he looked back the old man had disappeared. And he said he immediately went outside to look for him, saying that he couldn't have got off in this short of time—it was just a few seconds—and looked all around in every direction up and down the street and couldn't find him. And in relating this story, then, he said that it wasn't possible for him to have walked out

> of sight in that short a period of time from the open space around the drive-in. And so he looked upon this as certainly a visit from a being somewhat supernatural, to say the least. And this seemed the highlight of . . . this fellow's talk in which he came [to stake priesthood meeting] and related this story and also, then, pointed out how he had been closing his stand on Sundays for a long time now and that it hadn't seemed to affect his income. . . . So this seemed to be fulfillment of the promise made that if he was generous and living righteously that he wouldn't be in need.

According to Hector Lee, only five of the stories he had collected occurred after 1925 (1949, 31). But of the twenty-seven individual stories I collected in Bloomington (the other thirteen texts were variant accounts of one or more of these), eight of them, like the A&W story, related events that had occurred in the recent past. This was an important discovery. If what was true of these Bloomington Mormons should prove true of Mormons in general, the Nephite stories could serve not just as a window to the pioneer past, but also as a means of understanding contemporary Mormons coming to terms with the circumstances of modern living.

When I came to Brigham Young University and developed a course in folklore in 1969, I began to test this hypothesis. As part of their course work, students in my classes must always submit folklore they have collected themselves to the BYU Folklore Archives. While I have never required students to collect Nephite stories, many of them have. As a result, a steady stream of Nephite narratives has come into the archive each year, producing, at last count, a rich store of some 1,500 texts, ample evidence, I would think, that the legend is still around.

Dating the events these stories recount is no easy task, because new wine often gets put into old bottles. That is, while the structure of a particular story remains the same, the setting is often changed from pioneer to modern times. For example, one very popular pioneer narrative goes as follows:

> There was a missionary thousands of miles away from his home. He was starving to death. He didn't have anything to eat, so he knelt down to pray. When he finished, a man came to him with a piece of bread covered with a towel. He ate the bread and kept the towel. Months later, when he returned home, he brought the towel to his wife. When she saw it she asked him where he had found her towel. He then related the story to her. She told him that the same day he was starving to death a man came to her door and asked her for some bread. The only bread she had was a piece that she was baking, and because it was fresh, she covered it with that towel. They thought that the man who asked her for bread was one of the Three Nephites.

A modern version of the story goes like this:

> A stranger called at the home of Mrs. John Harris of Roosevelt, Utah, and asked for a meat sandwich. Mrs. Harris's husband was stationed in Korea for the U.S. Army, and a few days later, this stranger presented Mr. Harris in Korea with an identical sandwich to that which his wife had given to the stranger.

It is possible, of course, that these two stories are of independent origin, but it is much more likely that the latter is a modern adaptation of the former. And so it is with many other stories. A horse-drawn wagon tips over and pins a man under a load of wood; a stranger appears from nowhere, rescues the driver, and then disappears. In a modern version of the story the wagon simply becomes a truck.

In spite of the difficulty in dating the stories, careful textual comparisons will show that at least half the Nephite accounts in our collection describe events that occurred after 1925—and a considerable number of them after 1960. More important, well over half the events described in the stories are believed by their tellers to have occurred in modern times. The stories speak to us, then, both of the past, or at least of our interest in the past, and of the present. They are not, as Lee suggested, simply survivals from an earlier nonrational, nonscientific way of thinking but are very much a part of our contemporary world. And while they are delightful stories whose own existence is their best excuse for being, they also provide us valuable information about ourselves. They do this for the simple reason that, like people everywhere, we tell stories about those things that interest us most or are most important to us. Further, because the stories are oral, depending on the spoken word to keep them alive, when a given event ceases to interest us, stories we tell about that event will disappear. Thus by looking carefully at the Nephite accounts and at the dominant themes contained in them, we should be able to discover those issues of central importance at any one time to the church and especially to individual church members.

A few of these issues have grown out of concern over world political situations. For example, in the 1950s, during the tense years of the Cold War and the Korean War, the story I have already mentioned of a Nephite warning of imminent disaster and encouraging individuals to follow church counsel by storing a supply of food, spread rapidly through the Mormon West and became the best-known Nephite account of all time (Wilson 1975, 79–97). The following is a typical example:

> A lady got up [in a testimony meeting] and was quite excited and upset about this. She said that this experience had happened to—I don't remember the relation, a friend of a friend or something. And they had been on their way to the temple and had stopped to pick up a man who was hitchhiking, and they'd talked to him about

> various things. And suddenly he asked them if they had their two-year supply of food, and they said no. And he said, "Well, you better get it because the end is coming, and it's coming soon." And then the conversation turned to other things. And they turned around, and he was gone, just vanished.

During the years this story was circulating, another narrative also gained wide currency. In this account the normally peace-loving Nephites, sometimes followed by a phantom army, entered the Arab-Israeli conflict on the side of the Israelis:

> There was this war between the Arabs and the Jews, and the Jews were outnumbered by hundreds, thousands. They had one cannon, and they had like about ten men, and the Arabs had stuff from Russia, artillery and all sorts of stuff. And the Jews were banging on cans and moving the cannon over here, and they'd shoot it and then they'd move it back and shoot it so the Arabs would think they had lots of men. And they were only fooled for a little while. And then when the Jews had just about run out of all their ammo and they were ready to surrender, then the Arabs, they all threw down their weapons and came walking out waving the white flag and everything, surrendering to these Jews. And the Jews walk out, and there's ten of them. And the Arabs say, "Where's the rest of your men?" And the Jews say, "What do you mean the rest of our men. This is the total company." And the Arab guy who was spokesman for the group said, "Where are those thousands of troops that were just across the hill with the man in white leading them? This man was dressed in white, and he was leading all these thousands of men, and he had a long beard."

In some accounts *three* men in white robes and flowing white beards appear to the Arab generals and warn them to surrender or face annihilation. The story, which originally entered Mormon tradition via the religious press, has been applied to most major Arab-Israeli conflicts—1948, 1956, 1967, and 1973. It has not been collected much in recent years; but considering current geopolitical tensions, it may reappear, assuring Mormons that the Lord is still in charge of events in the Middle East.

Most Nephite accounts are much less dramatic than these and relate not to national or international events, but to the personal problems of individual Mormons. These stories can be grouped into three broad categories.

The first of these has to do with genealogy and temple work. Since salvation depends on family members attending the temple to seal themselves first to each other and then to their deceased ancestors whose names they have discovered through genealogical research, it is understandable that the Nephite canon is replete with accounts of the old men appearing to church members and encouraging them to do their duty. In the genealogy stories, the Nephite, as in the following narrative, usually appears to a faithful individual who has worked long and hard uncovering ancestral lines but has come upon a seemingly impassable barrier:

> [My girlfriend's] grandmother was having considerable difficulty in finding some names on a certain genealogical line. She had done research and, not finding the information, had prayed about the problem. She was in her kitchen one evening, and her husband was in the living room reading the paper. They were alone in the house. Suddenly, they heard the typewriter sounding in the other room. At first, they thought each other was typing, but then they remembered where each other was located in the home. They went in to the room where the typewriter was, with the unfinished pedigree chart still in it. They found that the much sought after names were typed in—in the correct spaces. They firmly believe that it was an act of the Three Nephites.

In other stories a Nephite simply delivers a list of missing names or a newspaper containing crucial information, guides a researcher to a book in the library, or tells one good sister to go to the basement and look in an old trunk located there. In these stories, as in most Nephite accounts, the Nephite delivers his message and then miraculously disappears, thus adding credibility to the message. Such stories persuade struggling genealogists that if they will persist in their work and remain faithful, they too may receive the help they need to reach their goals.

In the temple stories, a Nephite, often appearing as a hitchhiker, warns married people who have not been sealed to each other in the temple to have this ordinance performed, or he encourages others who have already been to the temple to visit there as often as possible because "the time is short." Again he almost always disappears, sometimes leaving no tracks in the snow or along the dusty road where he asks to be let out of the car.

The second major category is missionary work. With over fifty thousand young people serving as full-time missionaries in all parts of the world and with the church's constant emphasis on proselytizing activity, it is again understandable that the Nephites would choose to become involved. On numerous occasions they reportedly have visited a community to prepare it for the message soon to be brought by the missionaries. And from all over the world come accounts of Nephites escorting missionaries through a vicious slum, protecting them from angry crowds, participating with them in street meetings, instructing them in proper proselytizing methods, cheering them when discouraged, and, in time of need, providing them with adequate food, clothing, shelter, and transportation. In recent times, our automobile culture generates many stories. For example:

> This sister missionary said that she and her companion were in a really bad car accident. The car was completely totaled, but neither she nor her companion was seriously hurt. She said that she didn't remember much of what happened at first. She and her companion were kept overnight at the hospital and that night she sort of had a dream or vision or something. She witnessed the entire accident from outside the car. She said she could see that they were being protected during the crash, by what she thought were angels. The angels [thought to be Nephites] had their arms around her and her companion shielding them from the crash itself.
>
> After the car stopped she noticed it was on fire and then noticed two men who came up to the car. Each one helped drag one of the sisters out of the car to a safe distance away and stayed with the sisters till someone else arrived. Then she said they were gone. The sister missionary talked later with the people who found them first and they told her that no one was at the scene of the accident when they arrived.

To struggling young missionaries such stories provide inspiration and motivation for their difficult work, and to their anxious parents back home they give assurance that the Lord and his servants will protect their daughters and sons while they are away.

The third category of stories really subsumes the others. In these narratives, the Nephites come to solve the personal and sometimes desperate needs of individuals—to save them from physical or spiritual danger. Most of the pioneer stories Mormons still relate will, like the following, fall into this category:

> My aunt who lived in Rock Point, Summit County, Utah, was left a widow with a large family. She just wondered how she was ever going to manage, and one day an elderly man came to her home and asked for bread. She said, "Oh, I wonder what I'm going to do! I just have this big family and all." But anyway she gave him a meal and brought him in and fixed him up, and when he left he said, "Sister, you'll be blessed: You'll never see the bottom of your flour bin." And she looked for him when he went out the door, and she couldn't find him anywhere. And she always felt that this visit was from one of the Nephites. She had looked and looked and not any of the other neighbors had ever seen him. And she said as long as she lived she never did see the bottom of her flour bin.

The majority of the stories relating contemporary events also fall into this category. These stories reveal that contemporary Mormon society is not remarkably different from that of the past. The concerns of our pioneer fathers and mothers are still our concerns today—though worked out in modern contexts. Hector Lee argued that as the need for security from the hazards of pioneer living faded, the Nephite stories diminished (1949, 35, 122). This need has not faded; it has merely changed, generating new stories all the while. For example, in pioneer society, where doctors were scarce and medical techniques primitive, the Nephites came often to aid the Saints in times of illness. They frequently administered to the sick through the laying on of hands, or they employed such popular home remedies as tobacco boiled in lard for the caked breast of a nursing mother, grated nutmeg mixed in oil for a child with croup, and an extract from an indigenous herb for a cholera victim.

The Nephite visiting ailing Mormons today will still lay hands on people's heads and bless them, but also frequently relies on the techniques of modern medicine. Today the Nephite pulls a bishop's son from a lake after a canoeing accident and revives him through artificial respiration; he rescues a church official from a fiery automobile accident and treats his wound "in a very professional manner"; and in one instance he actually enters the hospital, operates on a woman the doctors had been unable to treat, and removes a "black-covered growth" from her stomach.

Life on the frontier was dangerous, and the Nephites had their hands full rescuing cattlemen and children from blizzards, guiding wagon trains to water holes, saving them from Indian raids, finding lost oxen, bringing food to isolated and starving homesteaders, pulling wagon drivers from under their overturned conveyances, and harvesting crops for ailing farmers. Today it is the Native Americans who need Nephite protection from the whites; sleek automobiles zip us rapidly over paved roads from one water hole to the next; and government welfare agencies succor the poor and needy. Still, modern life is not without its perils, and the Nephites continue to find ample work. Occasionally they stop to fix a widow's furnace, guide a nurse through a storm to the hospital, help a young man pass an officers' candidate test, or rescue a temple worker locked in the temple after it closed. But for the most part, they are kept busy on the highways. For example:

> A family consisting of parents and three children were on their way to stake conference. They lived on a desert, and it was a hot, dusty ride of two hundred miles to the tabernacle. On the way home the car broke down on a lonely road, which was even more deserted because it was Sunday. The children were hot and hungry, and the poor father could not find the trouble. Just then, two men in white came walking down the road and offered to help. Telling the man to get in his car and start the motor, they lifted the hood. To the family's surprise the car started, and after kissing his wife and hugging his children for joy, he went out to thank the men. They had disappeared.

In other stories the Nephites repair a broken truck axle, tow a stranded automobile to safety, guide motorists lost in blizzards or in the deserts of Death

Valley, keep a long-haul truck driver awake, and pull people from a flaming pileup on the Los Angeles freeway.

As they have done for the past one hundred years, the Nephites still come to comfort mourners, clarify gospel teachings, and encourage devotion to duty, but the spiritual advice they now give speaks to the children of a modern age. For example, a Nephite appears to a woman who has lost her husband and daughter in an airplane crash and tells her that her loved ones have been called on a special mission to the spirit world. In Portland, Oregon, a woman takes a break in the department store where she works and forgets to check out at the time clock; a Nephite meets her at the foot of the stairs and reminds her of her negligence. In Los Angeles, one of the old men appears to the head of the police force vice squad and urges him to give up his wild ways. And in San Diego, a Nephite warns a young parking lot attendant about to be seduced by a woman customer "not to ruin his entire life for a few minutes of pleasure."

In the new stories, then, the scene changes from country to city, but many of the old problems and concerns continue. They are simply changed in form. They are worked out not in pioneer or village cottages with a country road winding pleasantly by, but in urban dwellings, at parking lots, and ice cream stands, with the freeway sounding noisily in the background.

What do the Nephite stories tell us about central issues in the church? Nothing too startling. They show us that the main concerns of the church are also the main concerns of individual church members—living lives that will make them worthy to enter the temple, sealing themselves to their family members, both living and dead, and taking the gospel message to the world. But the stories do more than simply mirror dominant beliefs and principles. They also testify to the validity of church programs and inspire members to follow them. As anthropologist Radcliffe-Brown has pointed out, folklore expresses and cultivates in the minds of individuals those "sentiments" upon which the continuity and existence of a society depend (1922, 376–405). The Nephite stories thus reflect and reinforce church programs and, by endowing them with mystical values, place them beyond criticism or questioning.

They also provide the believer with a sense of security in an unsure world. Just as the early Utah settler living in a hostile physical environment felt safe listening to an account of a Nephite rescuing a rancher from a blizzard, so, too, contemporary Mormons faced with urban congestion, riots, and increasing international tensions are comforted when they hear that Nephites might protect them on crowded highways, guard their children in the mission field, and make sure the right side carries the day in the Middle East.

Perhaps most important, the stories give evidence of a personal, loving and caring God, who sends his servants to succor the weary, protect the helpless, and encourage the wayward to mend their ways.

When physically describing the Nephites, the stories are remarkably inconsistent. The old men have white beards, gray beards, black beards, red beards, neat beards, scraggly beards, no beards at all. And they appear in everything from shabby khaki pants to tuxedos. But despite this variation in dress and appearance, one thing remains constant throughout the Nephite canon: the Nephites come in love and compassion. The following statements from a variety of different stories capture in part the feelings of the narrators toward the Nephite visitor: "[He brought] a very serene, peaceful, and quiet feeling"; "he seemed to bring a good feeling"; "a strange feeling came over the woman as she examined the caller—she noticed a sweet spirit radiate from his eyes"; "he vibrated with kindness and love"; "after he left I had such a peaceful feeling fill my soul and heart"; "[his] personality was overwhelming"; "he seemed to bring peace into the room upon entering"; "in the presence of this man he felt a warmness and friendship that was immediate"; "[he] was extremely kind."

These, kind, compassionate, caring disciples of the Savior come, then, not so much as divine messengers or fearful visitors from the other side, but as brothers and friends, engaged with the people to whom they appear in the same eternal drama and determined to help their brothers and sisters along the way. This gives the Nephite stories a homespun quality and a warmth and immediacy seldom found in other supernatural legend cycles—a warmth and immediacy captured wonderfully in the following story:

> Millie and George were a middle-aged couple who had gone a little to the wayside. When first married, they hadn't thought of ever having a cup of coffee or a shot of whiskey. But now, who's to say they were wrong to just calm their nerves by the coffee or whiskey. In their younger years, they never missed a church meeting or calling. Now, it was harder to get up and wipe the sleep out of their eyes. It was much easier to stay in bed and let Priesthood [meeting] and Sunday school go on without them. When it came time for Sacrament meeting, Millie was too busy fixing dinner and George, he was too tired from lying around all day. This routine went on for quite a few years. One day as Millie and George were riding down a lonely Arizona road, they saw two men who were hitchhiking. Usually, they would never think of picking up hitchhikers, but something told them to pull over and pick up the two men. The men were dressed nicely and looked as if they hadn't walked even a mile. When asked where they were going, they said that they were going anywhere Millie and George were going. Then they began to talk of things which were very extraordinary and unusual. They told Millie and George that they were living in the last days when the Savior of the world was to come again. They told of the great destruction that would come to the wicked if they did not repent. They told them of the wonderful day when Jesus Christ would again come and never leave his brothers and sisters. They talked on about all that was to come for the world and all its inhabitants. Finally, they told Millie and George that if they didn't repent, they were going

> to be two sad people. If they kept on as they were, they would be very unhappy and discontented when they didn't obtain the degree of glory they wanted. It was those little things that were bringing them to destruction. Millie and George just sat there wide-eyed and listening to each word spoken by these two strange men. They couldn't bring themselves to turn around and look at the two men because they knew within what they said was true. Millie finally got up enough courage to turn around to ask the men how they knew so much about her and her husband's personal lives. When she turned around, the two men were gone, and they didn't leave even a hint that they had been sitting in that back seat. This experience shook George and Millie greatly. From then on, they gave up their habits and shortcomings. Millie and George, to this day believe those two men who brought them to the truth were two of the Three Nephites.

What does the future hold for the Nephite legend? Will the old stories continue to be told, and will we still hear about new ones? Or in our supposedly more sophisticated age, will the stories eventually disappear?

To answer these questions, we must ask still others: Will Mormons continue to hold fast to the visions of Joseph Smith? Will they continue to believe that God personally leads the church, rewarding the faithful and punishing sinners? Will church members continue to seek evidence of God's participation in their daily affairs, and will they continue to tell others about this participation? So long as answers to these questions remain affirmative, the Nephite stories will probably remain. Or if they do disappear, they will be replaced by similar stories that meet similar needs in the lives of those who tell and believe them.

What we must remember is that the Nephite accounts are really only a small part of a much larger body of Mormon supernatural lore that shows no signs of diminishing—a lore generated by belief in a personal God who actively intervenes in people's lives. And this lore speaks to the same central issues as those reflected in the Nephite narratives—genealogy work, temple work, missionary work, personal worthiness, and divine help in solving personal problems. In fact, the Nephite stories are so similar in subject matter to the rest of Mormon lore that stories often slip easily from one genre to another. For example, in one of the most popular non-Nephite stories of recent times, a young mother attending a temple to perform vicarious ordinances for the dead suddenly felt that something was wrong at home but was promised by a temple official that if she would complete the session everything would be fine.

> After the session was over she hurried home, and sure enough, there were fire engines and police cars all around her house. As she was running to her house, a neighbor lady stopped her and explained that her daughter had fallen into a ditch and couldn't be

> found. As the lady came to the house, there was her daughter soaking wet and crying. Her mother grabbed her and hugged her. After, the little girl gave her mother a note and explained that the lady who'd pulled her out of the ditch had given it to her. There on the note was the name of the [deceased] lady for whom that woman had gone through the temple that day.

Another story collected just last year has an identical beginning to the one just cited, but the ending takes a different direction:

> They went home, and they really got concerned when they saw a police car and a fire truck outside their house. They ran up to the house and asked the baby sitter what was wrong, and she said their little girl was missing, and they thought she might have fallen into the irrigation ditch because they found her ball in the ditch. So they went searching for her, and about fifteen minutes later she just showed up at the door, and they asked her where she had been, and she said she fell in the ditch, and a man all dressed in white helped her out. I think he was one of the Three Nephites.

That the Nephite tradition was still strong enough to pull this story into the cycle suggests that the stories will be with us for some time to come.

Some may argue that the stories will continue for still another reason—because they are true. If the Book of Mormon is really the word of God, the following Book of Mormon description of the Three Nephites ought to be sufficient explanation for the continuance of the stories: "And they are as the angels of God, and . . . can show themselves unto whatsoever man it seemeth them good. Therefore, great and marvelous works shall be wrought by them, before the great and coming day [of judgment]" (3 Nephi 28: 30–31).

I have no quarrel with this argument. As a folklorist interested in human behavior, I am, to be sure, more concerned with the influence of the stories on the lives of those who believe and tell them than I am with the validity of the stories themselves; and as a literary scholar, intrigued by the struggle for human souls revealed in the Nephite drama, I am more concerned with the artistic tensions developed by the actors in that drama than I am with the historical accuracy of the narratives. But as a Latter-day Saint who believes in the Book of Mormon, I also believe that the Three Nephites may do what the Book of Mormon says they can do. Having read hundreds of Nephite accounts and having compared them with each other, with Mormon folklore in general, and with supernatural legends outside Mormon tradition, I can discount many of the narratives. But I can't discount them all. And I am romantic enough to hope that a story like the following, collected from the young lady who was about to marry the young man in the story, really happened:

> Carol's fiancé, Brent, was called to the Mexico-North Mission. Since Carol had not previously been . . . [through the temple ceremonies], she couldn't go through the temple with Brent to see him . . . [receive his ordinances]. So she stayed outside on the temple grounds of the Mesa, Arizona, Temple. To make her wait a little less tiring and more enjoyable, she took along some embroidery. As she was standing outside the entrance, a short, very old man dressed in white coveralls and carrying a hoe came up to her and said, "You must be very proud of that young man in there," nodding towards the temple. Because she had not seen him standing around when Brent was there, she was very surprised by his remark. He said he was the gardener for the temple grounds and asked if she would like to walk along with him since she had about three hours to wait. She said yes, mostly out of curiosity, she supposed. But as the time went on, he showed her all the flowers on the grounds and explained the lives of some and legends behind others. It seemed his entire life was those flowers. He continued speaking to her, and showed her many things in nature, and she grew to love him in the short time she had known him. He began talking about Brent then. He said she was a lucky girl to have such a man as her future husband. And he went on to explain the importance of marriage. He told her that when Brent came out of the temple, she would see him as she never had before. He then looked at his watch and said, "I suppose your young man will be coming out soon, so we will walk back." As they got back to the waiting room, he thanked her for spending the time with him and asked her to please remember what he had told her that day. Then he left, just as Brent appeared at the desk. Carol looked at him, and she said he had a glow around his entire face. She kissed him and told him to hurry because there was someone she wanted him to meet. They rushed out to catch the gardener, and he wasn't anywhere to be found. Carol looked everywhere they had been and finally she found a very tall man dressed in dirty blue coveralls. She excused herself and asked if he had seen the gardener, and he answered her and said that he was the only temple gardener there had been for the last three years and that he had seen no one there all day.

I see no reason to doubt that the young lady who told this story really had spent the afternoon talking with a stranger. Whether this stranger was simply a kindly old man who had helped a young lady pass the time while she waited for her missionary to go through the temple or whether he was one of the Three Nephites sent to help her understand the significance of the occasion, I leave for each individual to decide.

Stories of the Three Nephites, then, like the stories of Millie and George or of Carol and Brent, are still very much a part of contemporary Mormon society. In our unguarded moments, in a testimony meeting, in a Sunday School class, in intimate conversations with small groups of friends, in the family circle—when critical perceptions are tuned low and the spiritual vibrations are strong—in these moments the Nephite stories circulate among us. And they tell us much of ourselves and of our church. They mirror our attitudes, values, and principal concerns; they reinforce church teachings and persuade us to follow them; they tell us of a personal God concerned with our individual problems; and they provide us with pride in the past, with confidence in the future, and with the means of meeting the crises of modern living with equanimity. So long as the stories continue to meet these ends, they will remain a vital part of Mormon folk tradition, and they will continue to enlarge our understanding of Mormon culture.

NOTE

1. All items of folklore cited in this paper are located in the Brigham Young University Folklore Archive, Provo, Utah.

"Teach Me All That I Must Do"

The Practice of Mormon Religion

I first discovered "'Teach Me All That I Must Do'" not at the 1998 AFS meeting in Portland where it was initially presented, but rather sitting in Bert Wilson's home office.[1] As a folklore graduate student at Brigham Young University, I was writing my thesis on reflexivity and the insider voice in Mormon folklore scholarship. Although Bert was retired and had no obligation to participate in yet another MA thesis, he generously agreed to help me with a chapter on his contribution to the field and shared with me several of his unpublished works, including this article.

After reading "'Teach Me All That I Must Do,'" I immediately associated it with several of Bert's other articles from the late 1990s that evaluate the trajectory of Mormon folklore scholarship. In fact, his article "Folklore, a Mirror for What? Reflections of a Mormon Folklorist" (1995), is almost a prologue to "'Teach Me.'" In that article, he points out a serious weakness in the field of Mormon folklore: "The problem is that I, and others like me, who know what Mormons really do talk about, have played too willingly to the expectations of outsiders and have thus reinforced their own misconceptions" (1995, 19). His point resonates with both my research on and participation in Mormon culture. Despite the fact that well-known Mormon folklore like J. Golden Kimball narratives and Three Nephite legends beg for cross-cultural comparison with trickster heroes and vanishing hitchhikers, they are often not the heart of Mormon vernacular and expressive communication. Thus, in this article Bert focuses on the "seldom . . . collected and less often studied" stories of service that form a core of Mormon experience.

"'Teach Me All That I Must Do'" is also significant in the way it reflects and contributes to the reflexive trend in American folkloristics. Recent years have seen extensive questioning of the goals of folklore research and the ethics of representation. In this article, Bert participates in this academic conversation, and I see in his argument similar self-reflection and concern with the ethical and fair depictions of the life experiences of others. Furthermore, he acknowledges the value of the insider voice, not

---

This paper was read at the annual meetings of the American Folklore Society at Portland, Oregon, on October 31, 1998.

just because in matters of folk expression the insider has the right to be heard, but more importantly because the insider can shed light on what is really happening. It is ironic that Bert would critique his own work as not reflecting enough of an insider perspective since the corpus of his research, which has made him the preeminent Mormon folklore scholar, has been more concerned with the insider's perspective than previous research on Mormon folklore (for example, the work of Austin and Alta Fife or Hector Lee). Thus, even though Bert seeks in "'Teach Me'" to refocus his work, this article is also an extension of his legacy as a scholar of Mormonism: his presentation of an emic, or insider, understanding of Mormon folklore.

As an act of reflexivity this article does more than some reflexive studies by moving past paralyzing self-inspection to present new ways of approaching Mormon folklore. One new direction for which Bert lays a foundation (even if he does not specifically address it) is a greater reliance on the tools of performance analysis in examining "the practice of belief." In the conclusion, he suggests the ethnographic value of looking "not just at a body of abstracted beliefs but at actual behaviors, at the process of believing, at *how* religious people, Latter-day Saints and others, enact their convictions in daily life." Because of arguments like this, ultimately I read "'Teach Me All That I Must Do'" as a call to more fully observe and analyze the performance of Mormon folklore. Even though Bert's article does not attempt such a performance-oriented analysis, it engages the theoretical justification of such studies, and thus, in the end, this should be an article that influences another generation of Mormon folklore scholarship.

—*David A. Allred*

STUDENTS OF RELIGION SOMETIMES DIVORCE THE BELIEFS OF THE GROUPS they study from the practices in which these beliefs are embodied (from participating in sacred ritual to carrying on the routine of daily life), leaving in their place only empty abstractions that yield little understanding of what religious people really take seriously and of what moves them to action in pursuit of their religious ideals.[1] Certainly, this holds true for the study of Mormon beliefs.

In a recent article in the *Journal of American Folklore*, entitled "The Practice of Belief," Marilyn Motz writes: "Examining believing as a practice rather than belief as an entity—using the form of a verb rather than a noun—is a crucial distinction. The usefulness of folklore scholarship lies not in its ability to collect and categorize beliefs but in its ability to explore how people believe" (1998, 349). Some years ago, in a course at Indiana University, Professor David Bidney told class members, "If you want to know what people really believe, look at what they do" (1962). In this paper, I will, as Motz suggests, look at belief as a "process"—believing—and will focus on *how* members of the Church of Jesus Christ of Latter-day Saints, the Mormons, believe by looking, as Bidney suggests, at what they *do*.

This approach may be particularly helpful in the study of Mormon folklore because the Latter-day Saint church, perhaps more than most religious denominations, strongly emphasizes the doing of religion. According to the Book of Mormon, which Latter-day Saints accept as scripture, "it is by grace that we are saved, after all that we can do" (2 Nephi 25: 23). The phrase "after all we can do" is important; it suggests that works are not a consequence of grace but rather precede grace—that we must be doing, not just believing. Thus the semiofficial *Encyclopedia of Mormonism* states: "God has made provision through the atonement of Jesus Christ for the salvation of the human family. Those things that God does for mankind are called 'grace.' Those things that people have to do for themselves are called 'works.' Both are necessary" (Ludlow 1992, 4: 1587). In other words, in terms of necessary and sufficient causes, while both works and grace are necessary, neither without the other is sufficient. Thus Mormons are prone at times to skip over Paul, as they read the New Testament, and quote James's statements that we should be "doers of the word and not hearers only," that "by works a man is justified, and not by faith only," and that "faith without works is dead" (James 1: 22, 2: 24, 2: 20).

The importance of work, of doing, is inculcated in Mormons from their youth on. They grow up hearing proverbial expressions urging them "to work out their salvation" and "to pray as though everything depended on the Lord and to work as though everything depended on them." From their hymnal they sing songs with titles like the following: "Do What is Right," "Carry On," "Choose the Right," "I Have Work Enough To Do," "Keep the Commandments," "Let Us All Press on in the Work of the Lord," and "Put Your Shoulder to the Wheel"—this last hymn urges its singers to "push every worthy work along" (1985 *Hymns of The Church of Jesus Christ of Latter-day Saints*, nos. 237, 255, 239, 224, 303, 243, 252). And they are reminded that Spencer W. Kimball, president of the LDS church from 1973 to 1985, had a placard on his desk that stated simply: "Do It!" Spencer W. Kimball was the nephew of J. Golden Kimball, the crusty Mormon divine noted for sprinkling his sermons with "hells" and "damns." Considering the strong emphasis placed on following the advice of church leaders, it was probably inevitable that a riddle-joke would develop asking, "What do you get when you cross Spencer W. Kimball with J. Golden Kimball?" Answer: "Do it—damn it!"

Converts to the Mormon church are sometimes startled when they discover that they have adopted not just a new theological system but a new social system as well, a social system which, in Mormon parlance, keeps them "anxiously engaged" in church activities and eats up huge hunks of their time. All who serve in the Mormon church, except those at the very top of the hierarchy, are lay workers, volunteers who, while holding down regular jobs outside the church, serve in the church, without pay, in various positions for designated periods of time. The *Encyclopedia of Mormonism* states:

> In practice, the building up of the kingdom of God on earth is accomplished by individuals serving in numerous lay assignments, or callings. They speak in Church meetings and serve as athletic

> directors, teachers, family history specialists, financial secretaries, children's music directors, and women's and men's organizations presidents. . . . Millions of people serve in the Church, and that service represents a significant time commitment. (Thompson 1992, 2: 814)

A Mormon myself, I could add a number of tasks to those listed here. The following parody comes perilously close to the truth: "Mary had a little lamb; / She also had some sheep; / But then she joined the Mormon church; / And died from lack of sleep" (Gault 1972).

What I have described above, intense service willingly given by church members, is seldom reflected in most of the folklore made available to the non-Mormon world through past scholarly studies, including, I must confess, many of my own. There are two reasons for this: first, the focus already mentioned on belief rather than practice; second, a focus in these studies on dramatic tales of the supernatural rather than on less dramatic stories of losing oneself in service, stories that really go to the heart of what it means to be Mormon. Most of the supernatural narratives recount stirring instances in which God or his angels intervene in the lives of church members to save them from spiritual or physical distress—suggesting, almost, that all one need do to get out of a tight situation is pray for help and an angel will pop up from behind some cloud to solve all his or her problems. Abstracted from the culture that produces them, these supernatural narratives, which certainly do exist, can easily give one the impression that Mormonism is an entirely *me*-centered religion whose members are concerned most with what God can do for them. While it is true that Mormons seek God's help in personal matters, their religion itself is primarily an *other*-centered religion whose members are encouraged to sacrifice their own interests and devote themselves to the service of others.

Though this service can take many forms, I will mention just three: missionary service, in which church members take their gospel message to the world; sacred temple service, in which members vicariously perform ordinances such as baptism for deceased ancestors who died without benefit of gospel law; and humanitarian service, in which members reach out to members and nonmembers alike to help them in times of spiritual, physical, or financial distress.

At the moment, some 59,000 Mormon missionaries serve throughout the world at their own expense. To those of you who have had a couple of these missionaries appear at your doors, smiling broadly, eager to convert you, their efforts may seem more a nuisance than a service. From their perspective, however, they are fulfilling the Lord's injunction to take the gospel of salvation, as they understand it, to all the world. They know they will not be welcomed at most doors. Behind those broad smiles, we will often find quivering, frightened young men or women, terrified by the hostility they might encounter. But they knock anyway, convinced that it is their duty. Mormon lore is replete with stories of dedicated missionaries sticking to their tasks in spite of the abuses they must endure. A Mormon missionary was reently attacked and murdered in Russia, an all too common occurrence, and his companion was severely wounded. Interviewed on TV, his family, though mourning his loss, also reaffirmed their commitment to the church's missionary efforts and expressed no regrets at sending their son and brother to serve. That story, I am sure, will circulate broadly, as will and have other stories recounting the great personal and financial sacrifices some families make in order to keep their young men and women, sometimes two or three at a time, in the field. I recall many stories of widowed mothers working fingers to the bone to support a missionary. Such stories have seldom been collected and less often studied.

Just as Mormons are convinced that they must take the gospel to the living, they are equally convinced that they must make its saving ordinances available to their "kindred dead" who died without knowledge of these ordinances. Thus, through intense genealogical research, they seek out the names of their deceased ancestors and then, in their holy temples, vicariously perform these ordinances on their behalf. Achieving these goals requires tremendous effort, almost all of it carried out by volunteers. At the present, there are well over one hundred Mormon temples operating throughout the world. Many of these temples are open from 5:00 a.m. to 10:00 p.m. (a few stay open around the clock). In addition to those who come to the temples to perform vicarious ordinances for the dead, hundreds of others must serve in the temples as officiators in these ordinances. Whereas most missionaries are young people (though in recent years significant numbers of senior couples have also entered the field), most who work in the temples are older—the average age is about seventy. Once again, stories of the dedication and sacrifice of these temple workers abound but have seldom been collected or studied—stories of people leaving their homes to serve in temples in foreign lands, stories of people hampered by crippling disease who still show up at the temples regularly to carry on the work, stories of people who sacrifice their retirement years and lives of ease to advance the cause.

Once one understands the behavioral emphases lying behind the practices described above, then other stories, those dramatic tales of divine intervention, take on an entirely different character. They can be seen not simply as accounts of how God has helped individuals with their personal problems but as behavioral models urging individuals to help others as God has helped them. Two examples will have to suffice:

> Two missionaries were on a Navajo reservation and were driving their car. It was snowing up a storm when their car went into a drainage ditch. They pulled themselves loose and started walking down the road. They were super cold and didn't think they'd make it. They prayed that someone would come. Just then a truck came outta nowhere and [the driver] asked them if they needed a ride. The guy told them that he was on his way to work at the trading

> post. He dropped them off at their place and the next day they went to the trading post to thank him, and the lady said only she and her husband worked there and no one else. (Watt 1993)

> I heard a story about a lady who was very much interested in genealogy, and of course she belonged to the church. She had gathered quite a few names but she couldn't find her grandmother's name, when she was born, or when she died. This lady lived in Norway and she had prayed a lot about getting the information about her grandmother.
>
> One day it was snowing outside and it was in the morning and she was sitting eating her breakfast and somebody knocked at the door. And an elderly, well-dressed man came in and asked if he could have a little something to eat, and at first she thought it was kind of funny because she could always see people go by the kitchen window but she hadn't seen this man go by, but she invited him in and gave him breakfast. She had a funny feeling all the time they were eating and talking at the table, and when he was through eating he thanked her and left. Again she thought it was funny that she couldn't see him go by the window, and she looked outside and there was no trace of footsteps on the snow.
>
> She thought that was kind of funny, but as she gathered the dishes she took his plate, and under his plate was a piece of paper and on that piece of paper was her grandmother's full name, and her birthdate and when she died, and when she even married! (Browne 1968)

It would be easy enough to catalogue Mormon beliefs embedded in these two narratives. Both reflect a belief in the existence of heavenly beings who can appear to and assist people in distress. Both engender in teller and listener a sense of obligation to commit themselves to missionary, genealogical, and temple work. If the Lord's messenger really saved the missionaries from the storm, if the mysterious stranger left under his plate the genealogical information the Norwegian woman had been seeking—if these events really happened, then missionary, genealogical, and temple work must be true principles; and if they are true principles, then we should diligently pursue them; and if we pursue them, then the Lord will help us serve as instruments in saving others. He will help us practice what we profess. These are the stories' most important messages.

The third practice around which stories circulate is humanitarian service. These stories are perhaps the most abundant but least collected and studied of all Mormon narratives. The Book of Mormon states that "when ye are in the service of your fellow beings ye are only in the service of your God" (Mosiah 2: 17), echoing Christ's statement: "Inasmuch as ye have done [it] unto one of the least of these my brethren, ye have done [it] unto me" (Matthew 25: 40). The first verse of a popular Mormon hymn relates directly to these scriptures. It begins with a series of questions followed by a comment followed by still more questions: "Have I done any good in the world today?" asks the hymn. "Have I helped anyone in need? / Have I cheered up the sad, and made someone feel glad? / If not, I have failed indeed. / Has anyone's burden been lighter today / Because I was willing to share? / Have the sick and the weary been helped on their way? / When they needed my help was I there?" The refrain then exhorts those who have failed in their duty to mend their ways: "Then wake up and do something more / Than dream of your mansion above. / Doing good is a pleasure, a joy beyond measure, / A blessing of duty and love" (1985 *Hymns*, no. 223).

Simply doing good, then, is one of the central emphases of the church. The church itself has in recent years expanded its humanitarian efforts, especially in former eastern-block and third-world countries, sending out senior couples not to proselytize but to provide educational, medical, agricultural, and other services. Most stories, however, speak of ordinary members who during the routine of daily life take time out to help others. The following three examples are typical:

> When we moved here our neighbor, Hyrum Babcock, was in the late stages of multiple sclerosis. Our priesthood quorum organized itself to care for him. Each day one of us would read to him for a few hours, and each night one of us would help him bathe. A member had built a motorized sling to lift him from his wheelchair into the tub, which a single person could operate with a little training, and that is what we used so he could have a full body bath each day, which helped immensely in avoiding bedsores. This went on for about five years until he died. (England 1998)

> A Mormon woman in England, hearing constantly on TV of the plight of Bosnians during that war, organized a food convoy, including getting the trucks donated, collecting food, clothing and medicine, and with fellow Mormons driving the convoy to Bosnia and delivering the supplies. She did it again the next year. (England 1998)

> My father [the reference is to my own father] was a section foreman on the Union Pacific Railroad when the great depression began. He was cut back to regular section hand but, fortunately, had enough seniority to keep his job. He voluntarily took a half-time work schedule so that someone else could also work half time and thereby keep his family fed. He sold Watkins products door to door in his free time in an effort to make up the lost wages.

Other stories tell of Relief Society women in a local congregation taking turns sitting with the ill or dying; of a graduate student at the University of Chicago, who spent his Saturdays tutoring children from disadvantaged homes on Chicago's south side; of a soldier during the Korean War who donated his entire mustering out pay to a Korean orphanage; of a scoutmaster who held an incapacitated scout on his shoulders throughout a very long and very hot pioneer days parade; of a financially strapped church member in Finland who rode his bicycle across town early in the morning to clear a frail widow's walkway after each snow storm; of a church member who, upon finding a drunk man lying in his own vomit, picked him up, cleaned him up, took him to a hotel, and arranged his night's lodging.

The acts of service described in these stories are certainly not peculiar to Mormons. They are the kinds of actions one hopes each decent human being might undertake when encountering fellow human beings in need. For Mormons striving to practice their religion, however, they are centrally important, as they attempt to wake up, in the words of the song, and do something more than dream of their mansion above. Though more pedestrian in character than dramatic supernatural tales, these stories take us much closer to the core of Mormon moral and humane values than the supernatural stories ever will. In studying Mormon folklore, we neglect them at our peril.

A popular Mormon children's song, composed in 1957 by Naomi Ward Randall and performed again and again by most Mormon children as they grow toward maturity, ends with the line, "Teach me all that I must do / To live with him someday." In the original version of the song, the line read: "Teach me all that I must know. . . ."; but during his presidency, Spencer W. Kimball, who had the "Do it!" placard on his desk, changed "know" to "do"—teach me all that I must do—recognizing perhaps that as children are enculturated into Mormon social worlds, doing, or practicing religion, may be more important than knowing it (*Children's Songbook* 1989, 2). Few Mormon children will have any kind of sophisticated knowledge of the theological beliefs underpinning their religion, but most of them will have internalized the behaviors expected of them—missionary service, temple service, humanitarian service—as they face the realities of everyday living. Students of religious folklore could take a lesson here. If we will look not just at a body of abstracted beliefs but at actual behaviors, at the process of believing, at how religious people, Latter-day Saints and others, enact their convictions in daily life, we may discover what we have been after all along—a better understanding and appreciation of what these people feel and believe most deeply. So let's do it—damn it!

NOTE

1. A number of the examples used in this paper are drawn from narratives I have heard all my life growing up and living in Mormon society. It is impossible to document these with any exactness. Examples not drawn from my own experiences are documented in the traditional manner.

Personal Narratives

The Family Novel

The first time I ever heard Bert Wilson tell one of his mother's stories about growing up in Riddyville, Idaho, was around a campfire up Logan Canyon at the beginning of an early Fife Folklore Conference. As the flames illuminated his face in the chill June twilight, Bert's voice carried us back to another time and place where young girls rode horses to school every day and the sweet smell of baking bread frequently filled the log cabin she called home. What I remember most about that night was the way all of us were enraptured by the power of his story: It wasn't another legend about the vicissitudes of modern life or a ballad culled from pioneer songbooks—entertaining performances that we'd been enjoying all evening. Instead, Bert shared a part of his family memory with us and in the sharing made personal the deep connections between the land and the people of the Rocky Mountain valleys. Years later, when "The Family Novel" was first published, it became clear to me exactly where the power of that personal campground narrative originated; for in this seminal article, Bert Wilson articulates most convincingly the significance of family stories like the one he related to his friends that evening when his words warmed us more deeply than even the roaring fire.

Reading the article again today, I realize just how profoundly "Personal Narratives: The Family Novel" has influenced the discipline of folklore during the last decade and a half, and more personally, how it has provided the inspiration for the evolution of my own career as a folklorist. In this one article I find again and again not just the underpinnings of an articulate theory of personal narrative, but more importantly a complex matrix of theory and story woven together that beckons each reader to become part of the larger endeavor of "listening to all the voices in our great land."

This paper was delivered as the annual Archer Taylor Memorial Lecture at the meetings of the California Folklore Society in Santa Rosa, California, on April 26, 1990. It was published in *Western Folklore* 50 (1991): 127–49. Reprinted by permission of the Western States Folklore Society.

When Bert presented this piece to the California Folklore Society as the 1990 Archer Taylor Memorial Lecture, the relevance of personal experience narrative to the wider folklore agenda was becoming more and more apparent. Sandra Dolby Stahl's *Literary Folkloristics and the Personal Narrative* (1989) had been published just the year before, drawing attention to the correspondences between the personal narrative and other more "literary" forms. Yet in this article Bert went far beyond Stahl's important work in demonstrating quite dramatically that, while literary scholars were expanding their canon in terms of diversity of gender, race, class, and ethnicity, folklorists—who had frequently led the way for such expansion—had neglected the one group closest to us: ourselves!

In calling for an examination of "the swirl of stories that have surrounded us since we were born," Wilson demanded a reevaluation of the place of the individual in any analysis of personal experience narrative and at the same time insisted on the recontextualization of such stories within the family circle. This emphasis on the context of narrative performance draws heavily on the earlier work of Roger Abrahams, Richard Bauman, Amèrico Paredes, Barbara Kirshenblatt-Gimblett, and Dan Ben-Amos, among others. However, here Wilson pushes towards a theoretical model that is actually performative in its rhetoric stance: the article actually *is* the story it professes to examine. As Bert tells the story of his own coming to terms with the significance of his mother's narratives in his own life and work, the reader/listener is artfully and effectively drawn into that narrative context in a way that demands participation.

Through such a performative model, Bert entices us into a narrative world where at last the significance of active listening reveals several essential understandings. First of all, he suggests the primacy of thematic meaning over linear historical structure. Here Wilson reminds us that personal experience stories are not really "personal history," but rather more like fiction, like novels where events are always told in relation to other stories. Drawing on the work of Sharon Kaufman, Wilson demonstrates the multifaceted ways recurrent values and themes must also be understood in relationship to each other. Such intertextuality demands that all family stories—like Navajo coyote stories—must be "heard" in the context of the entire repertoire. Here too, where individual listeners construct their own lives in listening to each other's stories, there is simply no such thing as "fixed meaning."

As readers participate in the performance in this article, we are increasingly convinced that we *do* all have stories to tell, and that we now know more certainly how to begin to *listen* actively to each story we hear. The truth of this statement is evidenced by the recent work of a number of folklorists engaged in personal narrative research (folklorists like Pat Mullen, Elaine Lawless, Leonard Primiano, and myself, among many others) who have relied heavily on the wisdom and perceptive analysis presented in "Personal Narratives: The Family Novel" to extend our own understanding. And each time I read this masterful piece, I think back once more to that June evening around the campfire where I first met Bert's mother through the eloquence of his words. Through "The Family Novel" I now know where that eloquence came from—and where it is going.

—*Margaret K. Brady*

In my formal education and in my personal study, I have probably spent as much time in the social sciences as in any other discipline. But I still remain what I was as I began folklore study years ago—an unregenerate humanist. It is from a humanistic perspective, therefore, that I shall address the subject of this essay.

In a world challenged by polluted air, disappearing natural resources, a depleted ozone layer, unchecked diseases, crowded highways and airways, burgeoning crime rates, killing drugs, and rapidly shifting geopolitical borders and alliances, a commitment to the study and advancement of the humanities may seem at times an unaffordable luxury. It is in such a world, seeking desperately for solutions to its problems in improved technology and more effective social orders, that President Bush can, as he did in his 1990 State of the Union address, sound a clarion call for excellence in education, can demand that by the year 2000 United States children be "first in the world in math and science," and can pass by in thundering silence a corresponding need for our children to excel in their understanding and appreciation of arts and letters—of the humanities.

A few years ago, the faculty of the university where I was teaching became embroiled in one of those too-typical wranglings over allocation of resources. One faculty member—or so it was reported to me; I was not at the meeting—addressed his colleagues from the English department with the scornful and, in *his* judgment, rhetorical question: "You certainly wouldn't give up a cure for cancer for poetry, would you?" I have always been sorry I was not at that meeting so I could have responded: "For one poem, maybe not; but for poetry—yes."

And I would have said that as one who has watched his own father and several loved relatives die of cancer and who has suffered two primary cancers himself. One quiet night, in the darkened silence of my hospital room, with the terrifying words of the pathology report swirling again and again through my head—"well-differentiated carcinoma"—it was not the hope of some miraculous cancer cure looming on the horizon that got me through to morning but rather defiant phrases like those of the poet Dylan Thomas, hurled angrily and repeatedly at approaching and inevitable death and reminding me all the while of my individual and human worth:

> Do not go gentle into that good night.
> Rage, rage against the dying of the light. ([1952] 1973, 911)

I would not belittle or detract from the serious work of those in the social and physical sciences as they struggle to solve problems that bedevil the world. I would simply remind them, and all of us, that it is the humanities—the products of the imperishable human spirit—which teach us that these struggles are worth carrying on, that we and this world we occupy are worth saving.

My argument is that we folklorists must contribute to this effort by broadening prevailing concepts of the humanities, and of literature in particular (my special field of interest), and by persuading our friends in other disciplines and among the general public to seek evidence of the significance of human life, not just in those canonized masterworks taught in our literature courses but in works of our own invention and in our own capacity to create and appreciate beauty. My plea, therefore, is that we seek courage to face the future by learning to celebrate ourselves.

Most of you are aware of recent attempts to expand the traditional literary canon to include those who have been excluded from it on the bases of race, class, or gender. In our pluralistic society, with its many voices—all different but all American—we have come gradually to understand that if we really cherish the democratic ideals of equal worth of all our citizens, then we must learn to listen to their diverse and endlessly interesting artistic voices—not just to those who happen to be primarily white, male, middle-class Anglo-Saxons.

Folklorists, of course, have long been in the vanguard of those seeking to reach our democratic ideals by focusing on the expressive cultures of all our people; but one important group we have continued to neglect—ourselves. We may have studied the narrative traditions of any number of regional, occupational, ethnic, and religious groups; but many of us have paid inadequate attention to the swirl of stories that has surrounded us since we were born—stories we have ourselves listened to or told about the events of everyday life and about the worlds we have occupied.

Fortunately, we have in recent years begun to remedy this neglect, especially in our work with personal narratives—and, for the purposes of this paper, I take as already established that personal narratives comprise a legitimate folklore genre. As Elliott Oring points out, folklorists, while employing the methodologies of other disciplines, have been more willing "to view their own immediate environments and behaviors as material worthy of serious contemplation, analysis, and interpretation." Such study, he says, can "begin simply as an encounter with objects and behaviors in one's own living room" (1988, 148).

It is to the personal and family narratives told in these living rooms that I would like to direct our attention. To do so I will have to be personal myself, something Oring, in encouraging us to conduct field work in our living rooms, has not necessarily recommended. Indeed, in an essay on the construction of autobiography, he analyzed data he had collected over twenty-one years earlier, arguing that such a time lapse would make possible his treating his data "dispassionately and without the feeling of exposure that might otherwise attend the discussion of more contemporary work" (1987, 241–42). I shall make no such attempt here. I shall discuss my data both passionately and at great risk of exposure. And I shall do so because I do not believe we can understand the emotional force narratives might exert in the lives of others until we have dealt with that force as honestly as possible in our own lives.

Though we folklorists may have been at the game longer than most, we are by no means the only scholars to pay heed to personal narratives. In fact, in recent years everyone has gotten on the bandwagon. Literary scholars have examined oral narratives to discover how literary texts are constituted, sociologists to catalogue customs and lifestyles, organizational behaviorists to record the corporate myths that lend cohesiveness to organizations, historians to take the pulse of a particular era, anthropologists to elucidate larger cultural patterns.

But in all this the individual—the creator and teller of the stories—gets lost. His or her narratives become means to ends rather than ends themselves. Even in the study of personal narratives this can sometimes be so. As Barbara Kirshenblatt-Gimblett notes, as we focus on typical or traditional components of personal narratives in order to justify their study as folklore, we tend to overlook what is most typical about them—that is, that they are personal (1989, 134). However much the narratives may help us understand the larger societies of which they are constituent parts or recurring communally-based narrative patterns, from a humanistic perspective, the stories need no further justification for being than their own existence. It is as personal stories of individual, breathing human beings—not as dots on a chart of social norms—that they speak to us of our humanity.

The most essential of these stories may be those we tell about our family lives and narrate primarily in family contexts. I can't imagine that you will be overly interested in my particular family, but by showing you how such stories have operated there perhaps I can lend you new lenses to look at ways they operate in your families. Before doing that, I must lead into my discussion by telling you a little of my own personal narrative. And to do that, I have to begin with the principal storyteller in my family, my mother, Lucile Green Wilson.

My mother is a product of Welsh and English stock. Her mother's Welsh parents, Jonah Evans and Jane Morse Evans, had been hard working, loyal to their Mormon church, fiery in temperament, and stubborn—especially stubborn. One of their children, my mother's uncle Victor, matched his parents in hard-headedness and, in a rather strange way, characterized the family's persistence to principle:

> They said when Grandpa baptized Uncle Victor, Uncle Victor didn't want to be baptized—Uncle Victor was always kind of a rebel, and he didn't want to be baptized, and Grandpa baptized him anyway. And every time he would come up out of the water Uncle Victor would swear, and he would duck him in again. And it went on for I don't know how many times before Uncle Victor finally quit swearing and got baptized. [pause] I don't think it ever took.

My mother's English grandfather, Robert Green, a widower the whole time my mother knew him, was a different sort. According to family tradition, he had as an infant been given a blessing by Mormon church founder Joseph Smith, but that must not have taken either because he was not much of a churchgoer and liked an occasional drink. One day, in his cups, he drove his favorite team of horses, old Cap and Seal, full speed into the farmstead and almost mowed down my mother—an event that stirred to considerable pitch his daughter-in-law's Welsh temper. But Robert Green was also a soft and gentle man, never speaking harshly to anyone, generous, quick of wit, a lover of books.

From these forebears, then, came my mother, an amalgamation of their characteristics, plus others forged by the harshness and poverty of frontier life—intelligent, sensitive, eager to learn, witty, hard working, proud of her achievements, determined, but shy, and, during her teenage years, embarrassed in the presence of townspeople by her country-girl's dress and manners. Out of her inheritance and out of her experiences came also an ability to capture in concrete detail the events of her life and to make them memorable to others—that is, the capacity to tell stories.

I owe my own love of words to my mother. Although my father had many virtues, verbal dexterity was not one of them. My mother, on the other hand, grew up immersed in words, and she immersed me in them. In the homesteading cabin of her youth, her own mother would gather her children around her each night and read from books borrowed from the library. "I can still remember," my mother said, "how fun it was for all of us just to sit around and listen to Mama read." Describing her experiences in elementary school, Mother said, "I remember that one morning when she [her teacher] picked up that book and said, 'Tom, oh Tom,' and I just got goose pimples. I knew we were going to hear another good story. It was *Tom Sawyer*."

During my own formative years, we were fortunate enough to live in a house with no electricity, surrounded by almost no neighbors, and with few means of entertainment besides ourselves. I can still remember those dark winter nights when my mother dressed me and my sister in our pajamas, then, before tucking us in bed, gathered us into the light of the coal oil lamp, and, like her mother before her, read us magical stories from books.

But my mother also taught me to love words in other ways, by using them well, by bringing to life the world of her past through well-wrought oral narratives. Her family simply lived by the spoken word. Family gatherings at my grandparents' home were, in fact, one long stream of story, with my mother's brothers, railroaders all, regaling each other with accounts of their occupational and heroic exploits—each narrator trying to top the others. My mother did not participate much in these exchanges, though her storytelling ability matched that of her brothers. Hers were more quiet narratives, told in the privacy of our home and bringing to life for me and my sisters the village of her youth, a place called Riddyville, west of McCammon, Idaho, where, following the turn of the century, thirteen families homesteaded neighboring sections of land recently released from the Fort Hall Indian Reservation. Through my mother's stories, the excitement, the passion, the sorrow and heartbreak experienced by those Riddyville pioneers became a treasured part of my life.

When I entered Brigham Young University in 1951, I attempted at first to leave behind the experiences of my youth. I majored in political science and began studying Russian—I think I had dreams of one day parachuting into the Soviet Union as a spy and saving our country from that evil empire. But my love of words artfully employed finally proved too strong—I couldn't resist them. I abandoned my dreams of saving the nation and began instead to study English and American literature, rediscovering in the process much of the magic I had first discovered in the flickering light of a coal oil lamp under the spell of my mother's voice. By the time I had completed an MA, however, I had grown weary of the narrow elitism of the New Critical, or formalist, approaches current at the time—approaches which jerked literature from cultural context and tended to look with condescension at the kinds of stories I had learned from the good people of my rural Idaho and Mormon youth.

So I switched to and earned a PhD in folklore. My research centered first on the folk culture of the land where I had served as a Mormon missionary, Finland, then switched to the Mormon and western culture that had produced me—focusing for the next twenty years not just on the privileged few whose works had made their way into university courses, but on the people next door and on the richness and artistry of the stories they told.

Through all this, however, I was still collecting, analyzing, and celebrating the stories, the creative efforts, of other people, and still using those stories primarily to elucidate larger cultural patterns. I learned a great deal about Mormon society and, I hope, through my studies helped other people bring that society into a little sharper focus. But all the while, in the back of my mind, haunting my reveries, tugging at me in ways I did not understand, demanding my attention, lurked those stories I had learned from my mother, and the country village they had brought to life—Riddyville. Finally, more to exorcise a nagging spirit than anything else, I plunked my mother in front of a tape recorder and said, "All right, tell me again about Riddyville." And she did. For the next ten years, whenever the possibility allowed, we filled tape after tape, grew closer together throughout the process, and experienced together the short but moving life of Riddyville.

The place itself actually got off to a rather inauspicious start. When the Fort Hall land became available for homesteading, farmers lined up at the Marsh Creek Bridge on Merrill Road near McCammon. Someone shot a gun in the air, and the race was off to file claims at the government land office at Blackfoot, Idaho, some forty miles away. Some took the train; others rode horses, with exchange relays set up along the way to speed up the trip. Still, all managed to arrive in Blackfoot about the same time. As the train pulled into town, one hopeful homesteader, Max Cone, eager to file his claim ahead of the others and thus get the best land, jumped from the still moving train and broke his leg. The rest of the crew arrived safely at the land office, only to find it closed. Not until several days later did they finally manage to file their claims, evidently without much contest, and then returned to their new homes. Such was Riddyville's beginning.

Although my grandparents lived on their farm the required time each summer to "prove up" their claim, they did not move the family to Riddyville from their home in Woodruff on the Idaho side of the Utah-Idaho border until 1915, when my mother was eight. At that time, they moved into a newly constructed two-room log cabin, where, for the next twelve years, they lived with their seven children and at times with my grandfather's unmarried brother, Uncle Jim, who also owned a homestead but took turns living with his relatives. Twelve years later, in 1927, my grandfather finally gave up the effort to wrest a living from 160 acres of arid Idaho land, took a job on the railroad, and moved to town. By that time my mother was twenty years old, soon to be married, and Riddyville had become a part of her past, living from then on only in her stories.

When I first began collecting these stories, I sought primarily to recount my mother's history and, to the extent possible, to reconstruct the history of Riddyville. I quickly gave up this attempt as I discovered that while the stories were based on history and occasionally approximated history, they themselves were not history.

This fact was borne home again just the other day. My mother's brother Ralph recently wrote his account of the family's Riddyville years and sent a copy to my mother. The next time I saw him, he said, with a chuckle, "Well, I just got a corrected copy of my history back from your mother." My mother, in turn, explained that she had to correct Ralph's history because it contained so many errors. As I reflected on their comments, I recalled the words of historian Hayden White: "Historiography has remained prey to the creation of mutually exclusive, though equally legitimate, interpretations of the same set of historical events or the same segment of the historical process" (1975, 428).

If my mother and her brother might be called local historiographers, if their equally legitimate stories about the past, derived from equally legitimate perceptions, are based on history, sometimes approximate history, but are not history—that is, are not verifiable accounts of what really happened—then what are they? The answer is: they are fictions—stories created from carefully selected events from their own lives, just as short stories, novels, and epics are created from carefully selected details from the worlds of their authors.

And their appeal is not the appeal of history, but of literature. In a recent article in the *Atlantic Monthly*, Neil Postman wrote:

> A story provides a structure for our perceptions; only through stories do facts assume any meaning whatsoever. This is why children everywhere ask, as soon as they have the command of language to do so, "Where did I come from?" and "What will happen when I die?" They require a story to give meaning to their existence. Without air, our cells die. Without a story our selves die. (1989, 122)

Postman also argued that the stories told by ordinary people about the events of their lives are more profound than novels, plays, and epic poems. I think not. I believe these stories are important precisely because they have the power of literature, because, as I shall try to argue, they actually are, or can be, novels or epics. This explains why I have not been able to get my mother's stories out of my head these many years. Like other works of literature I cherish, they have stayed with me because of their artistic power, because of their ability, as Sir Philip Sydney might say, to hold "children from play and old men from the chimney corner" ([1595] 1956, 285).

Reduced to cold print, the stories may not seem particularly artful. But if you could have been there during the tellings, if you could have seen my mother's gestures and facial expressions, if you could have heard her voice rise in excited exclamation, drop now to a hushed whisper, move to a dry chuckle, break into tears—if you, that is, could have heard these stories in live performance, with a charged and ongoing dynamic relation occurring between teller and listeners, you would have understood their power to excite my fancy, engage my sympathies, and move me with joy or terror.

This fact really should have been obvious to me much earlier. One of the advantages of growing up in a family and hearing someone like my mother tell her stories again and again is that one soon learns to separate recurring, structured narratives from regular discourse. Originally, I attempted to collect my mother's life history from beginning to end, but, as noted, with few satisfactory results. Then I sat down one day and made a list—a long list—of the discrete stories I had heard my mother tell many times—the kinds of stories Sandra Dolby Stahl calls not "one-time narratives" but "stable repeated narratives in the teller's repertoire" (1989, 23), or the kinds of stories Susan Gordon calls "ongoing narratives," narratives told again and again among family members that are both "interruptable and renewable" (Gordon 1986, 370–71). From then on, in our sessions before the tape recorder, I tried to ask questions that would lead my mother into the natural telling of these stories. For example, if I asked about dry fields and struggles over irrigation waters, I knew I would probably learn little about irrigation but that I would in all likelihood get the story about Uncle Jim and Joe Bevan [a pseudonym] fighting over water—a story I'll relate in a moment. Using this method over a ten-year period, I often managed to collect the same story three, four, or five times. And I discovered that different tellings of the same story were remarkably similar in both structure and even in phraseology.

For example, not only my mother's unmarried uncle Jim, but also her grandfather, Robert Green, took turns living with different sons and daughters and thus became close to his grandchildren. My mother, whom Robert Green called Dolly, considered herself one of his favorites. In 1980, she told me:

> When Grandpa would stay with Aunt Vira, her house was kinda up on a hill . . . ; he could go out at the back of their lot and look down where we came with the cows. He was always worrying about me, wondering where I was. He wouldn't rest until he could see those cows coming home. Nona [my mother's cousin] used to get so mad. She'd say, "He wouldn't care if I never got home, and he has

> to go out there [and say], 'I wonder where Dolly is; she ought to be coming by now.'" Said he'd walk out there two or three times.

Three years later Mother embedded the same story in a string of other narratives she was telling:

> Nona used to get mad at him. . . . When Bernice and I used to go get the cows, when Grandpa was up living at Aunt Vira's, you could see way down where—part of the way where we had to go after the cows. And Nona said, he used to go out—he'd say, "I wonder if Dolly's home yet?" He didn't worry about Bernice, I guess. He'd go out there and watch two or three times every night, 'cause we'd fool around, run races on our horses and let the cows mosey on home, and we didn't hurry any, and he'd worry until he'd see us coming, and then he'd settle down. She said, "Ya, he wouldn't worry a bit if it was me, but he always has to see that Dolly gets home all right."

The second narrative is slightly more detailed than the first, explaining why my mother and her cousin Bernice were slow bringing the cows home; otherwise, they are almost exactly the same, though told three years apart. Clearly, then, from the many details she could have talked about, my mother has selected only a few and from them has constructed identifiable recurring narratives. When she has told these stories over the years, she has not been reciting history—she has been presenting herself to the world and capturing through these artistic forms the values and people she holds dear.

How do my mother's stories work as literature? They work, I would argue, the same way a novel works. In fact, I would call my mother's stories, not the family history, but the family novel. Stahl calls stories like those my mother tells "single-episode" narratives (1989, 13). But such a characterization misses the mark. My mother's stories do, to be sure, recount single events, but they do not stand alone; they are always related to other stories and other background events and can be understood only as they are associated with these—something literary critics call intertextuality. It is through this intertextuality that characters in the family oral novel emerge into full-blown, three dimensional individuals, just as well-developed characters emerge gradually from the pages of a written novel—no character is ever fully defined on the first page of a novel. It is also through this intertextuality that events in a number of the stories interlink into coherent meaningful wholes, just as events in a novel unfold and interlink as we push our way through page after page. Really to understand one of these stories, then, one has to have heard them all and has to bring to the telling of a single story the countless associations formed from hearing all the stories.

Unfortunately, you can never fully comprehend my family's novel because you have not lived my life, have not heard the total body of stories I have heard, do not recognize the connections that are obvious to me. But you have heard the novels of your own families, you can make those connections that exist between their various episodes, and you can let the coherent wholes that emerge from the stories play forceful, artistic roles in your lives.

Let me try to demonstrate this intertextuality with an extended example. The dryland homesteads of Riddyville were located on a bench above the valley floor, where ancient Lake Bonneville once made its rush to the sea. The actual farmsteads where the people lived were strung along a winding road below the bench, parallel to Lake Bonneville's dying remnant, Marsh Creek. Water on both the bench and for the gardens below it was always in short supply, especially at my mother's home, where water had to be carried from a neighbor's well, a fact responsible, says my mother, for her long arms. In equally short supply was any money to buy delicacies. With those facts in mind, consider the following brief story:

> One time we had—we carried water all summer to water some pumpkins. You never heard of canned pumpkins, and we all liked pumpkin pies. And we carried water all summer, and those pumpkins were so nice. And on Halloween, Joe Bevan's kids came and tipped our toilet over and put all of our pumpkins down in it.

A typical rural Halloween prank? Maybe. But in another telling of that same story my mother said, "After he [Bevan] got on the rampage, being ornery, that's when their kids . . . tipped our toilet over and put all our pumpkins down the toilet hole." Clearly, when my mother says "after he got on the rampage," she is depending on my already knowing other connected stories.

Of the thirteen families that lived in Riddyville, all but one, the Bevan family, were related either by blood or marriage and stuck together like glue. Joe Bevan was friendly enough at first, until he ran for trustee for the village school. His family voted for him; the other twelve families voted for their family candidate, and Joe's political career came to a quick end. So, too, did his good cheer. "He used to call us the 'Cat Family,'" said my mother; "he hated us"—a fact borne out by the following story:

> There was one patch on top of the dugway that belonged to Joe Bevan, and we used to always go—there was a little road went right through it into our field—and when he got on the rampage, he fenced our gate shut. And Dad went up there one day and couldn't get through, so he cut the wire, and Joe came after him and was going to hit him over the head with a club.

Now let's move for a moment to my mother's unmarried uncle, Jim. A shy, sensitive man, with a perpetually watery eye that made him look less attractive than he actually was, he had been jilted in his youth by his one true love and never again tried to marry. A little slower in wit than his married brothers, with their dry, but quickpaced, frontier humor, Uncle Jim occasionally became the subject of humor himself, though almost always in an affectionate manner. He bought a car but never learned to drive, leaving that task primarily to his nephews. One day two of these trickster nephews took him to Lagoon Amusement Park, in his own vehicle, and somehow coaxed him onto the roller coaster. When the coaster car arrived at the crest of the first hill and Uncle Jim surveyed the trip that lay ahead, he decided not to take it, and stood up to get out. Only the most strenuous efforts of his nephews kept him in his seat. The following story, which might have come right out of James Thurber, casts in relief not only Uncle Jim but many of the Riddyville characters of which he was a part:

> Orville Harris [my mother's cousin] lived just up above us, up the road from us, and he and Hazel [his wife] had gone some place—Detta [another cousin] was staying there, and she wanted Bernice and me to stay all night with her. And—so we talked—she had been working in Pocatello, and she told us about one night when she was on her way home from work and somebody followed her and how scared she was and how she went up on somebody's steps until this man disappeared, or went away. So we were already in a scary mood, and then there was a hole in the window, and there was a black cat'd keep jumping in through that hole, and we'd put him out, and he'd come right back. We were spooky anyway. But we finally went to sleep, or Bernice and I did. And after while Detta woke us up, and she said there was a man in the house. We told her, "Oh, it's just your imagination," after all this stuff we had been talking about. She said, "No, sir," she saw him on his hands and knees in that bedroom door. So about this time we could hear somebody walking outside—we lit the lamp—had lamps, you know—and started to dress because we weren't—she said we couldn't stay there any more. So we each got ahold of our shoe to defend ourselves, and Clyde Ketchum, her brother-in-law, walked up to that window and laughed. And it's funny we didn't all have heart attacks—we were so scared. And he claimed that he couldn't sleep, so he came up to Orville's—he lived, I imagine, a good mile and a half or more away. But he said he came up to Orville's to see if he could get some of his records he wanted to play. But Detta didn't believe him. She figured he came up there because he knew she was alone. Anyway we all dressed and decided to go down to our house to spend the rest of the night. Well, in the meantime, Leland Harris, Detta's brother, and Glade Allen had gone to the show. And they had guns, a gun or something with them—they'd been to McCammon to the show. And on the way home, when they got about even to our house, our dog [Sport] went out after 'em barking, and one

> of them shot, just to scare the dog. And the dog disappeared. Albert [my mother's brother] and Uncle Jim were sleeping outside. In the summer time, we always put the cot that they slept on outside, and they slept out there. So Albert kept worrying about old Sport, thought maybe those kids really had shot him. And so he finally got Uncle Jim to get up and—of course, there were never cars or anything in Riddyville in the night—he got Uncle Jim to get up and go with him, and they went up the road looking for old Sport just about the time that we were coming down to come to our place to stay all night. And they heard us coming, and they ran—poor old Uncle Jim with his bare feet, just a storming at Albert for doing this. We were already scared, and then we saw these two white things a running down the road. They had their underwear on—of course, we didn't know it was them. But we decided we'd rather face whoever it was than go back up to Orville's house. So we went on home, and when we got there Albert was just in hysterics laughing cause he'd—and Uncle Jim was so mad at him for getting him in such a predicament, and his feet hurting, running on those rocks. Then we all got to laughing about it afterwards.

But Uncle Jim was not just a humorous character—he was a generous and kindly man, much loved by all his family, often using his own money to come to the aid of his more financially strapped brother, my grandfather, Bert Green. When my mother's sister Jessie died, a little girl to whom Uncle Jim had grown very close—she would climb into his lap and call him Gee—Uncle Jim dug into his own pocket to help pay for her casket, at the same time vowing that "he was never going to get that attached to 'another youngun,' 'cause it was too hard."

We must really know all this and more before we can finally bring Uncle Jim and Joe Bevan together in the following story and make it understandable:

> The water we had came down Dry Holler—we always called 'em hollers—and it went past Joe Bevan's house. And it was Uncle Jim's turn to have it, but Joe Bevan just turned it off his—it was a dry year, I guess—and he turned Uncle Jim's water off and put it on his crop there, whatever he had, and Uncle Jim went up and turned it back, and Joe Bevan came out and hit him in the face. And poor old Uncle Jim—he had a tender skin anyway—and when he came home, why, it was just, the skin was just knocked off of his cheek where he had hit him. And I usually didn't hate anybody, but that day I hated Joe Bevan, cause I couldn't stand it to have anybody hurt Uncle Jim.

We've come some distance from the pumpkins in the toilet and a little closer, I hope, to understanding the intertextuality that can tie seemingly disparate narratives together, providing texture and unity to the oral novels that circulate in our families.

As we collect our family stories, we must, as Elliott Oring suggests of autobiographical stories in general, put them into some sort of structural frame; otherwise, we have little hope of understanding them. Oring himself recommends an historical structure, "a chronological conceptualization of related events and experiences." Although history, as Oring acknowledges, is only one of many "paradigms of coherence" available to us (1987, 258), it is the one, I suspect, collectors most often impose on their material—thus, the well-accepted term, "life history."

But structuring my mother's narratives historically, however convenient for the collector, would cause one to miss what is most important to her. She has absolutely no sense of chronology. "I can't remember," she says, "when all these [different] things happened." And she can't remember not because she lacks the capacity to do so—she has a quick and agile mind—but because she simply has no interest in chronological sequence.

What is true of my mother is probably true of most family storytellers—their narratives will focus primarily on recurrent values and themes. For example, in studying narratives of the famous Texas storyteller Ed Bell, Richard Bauman argued that eliciting a lifecourse history from Bell would not be very productive. He chose instead to examine Bell's "active performance repertoire"—stories that Bell, like my mother, told again and again—to show how Bell's narratives were "systemically" related—that is, how they clustered around and illustrated particular themes important to Bell (1987, 197–219).

Commenting on this tendency of narrators like my mother or Ed Bell to focus on themes, Sharon Kaufman writes:

> Though they are not deliberately fashioned, the themes people create [in their stories] are the means by which they interpret and evaluate their life experiences and attempt to integrate these experiences to form a self-concept.
>
> In the description of their lives, people create themes—cognitive areas of meaning with symbolic force—which explain, unify, and give substance to their perceptions of who they are and how they see themselves participating in social life. . . . [Through the themes drawn from their life experience], individuals know themselves and explain who they are to others.
>
> Old people [adds Kaufman—and I would say most people] do not define themselves directly through a chronology of life experiences. Rather, they define themselves through the expression of selected life experiences . . . ; people crystallize certain experiences into themes. These themes, as reformulated experience, can be considered building blocks of identity (1986, 25–26).

My attempt in studying my mother's stories—and the approach I recommend—has been to discover how the individual narratives through which she explains herself to others are systemically related—that is, linked together into an artistic whole—by clustering around certain themes and individuals important to her. The unity in her family novel lies not in a linear plot leading from event to event toward any logical conclusion, but rather, as in some modern novels, in the clustering of motifs around given themes, with my mother always at the center. This process is also similar to what one finds in epic traditions where unity is derived from the accretion of narratives around cultural heroes and heroines and around dominant cultural values.

I could spend the next several days elucidating themes in my mother's stories and showing how they relate to her and to her world. But space will permit only a few examples. One of the major themes in her stories is the grinding poverty that characterized her Riddyville youth. Year after year she watched her father watch the skies for clouds that seemed never to bring rain in time to save the crops from ruin and listened to him come in from the fields and say, "Well, it looks like the south forty's beginning to burn." When he would get up in the middle of the night, dress, and pace the roads of Riddyville, worrying about the survival of his family, she would lie awake herself worrying about both him and the family. Once he borrowed money to buy a herd of Holstein cows to try and get ahead. My mother explains the results:

> They just couldn't make the payments—we had em for quite a long while; it was so nice to have a nice herd of milk cows. Then the bank finally foreclosed. And that day they came over—we didn't know how we were even going to live, cause that's all the money we had was cows. Anyway, I don't know who came from the bank, but they went down the road with our cows, and we all stood on the porch. That was a sad old day; we just stood there and watched them take our living away, all of us crying. . . . We all felt the end of the world was coming. We had no money, no way to live except cream checks. We survived somehow.

When my mother reached high school age and began riding her horse each day to attend school in McCammon, about four miles away, she felt the effects of her family's poverty even more keenly, as she now had to compare herself with the better-to-do, and supposedly more sophisticated, girls from town. She said:

> I made one dress in the fall, sent for some old ugly material and made a dress. . . . And I had to wear that all winter. I had to wear it to school; I had to wear it to church; I had to wear it anyplace I went. . . . A school teacher [who] lived across from us loaned me

> her dress one night to go to the New Year's Eve dance over to Robin. And, oh, I felt like—I wouldn't have been so stupid and backward if I'd a had some clothes and coulda looked like other people. That night I just felt like a different human being to have that pretty dress on. It was a kelly green—it had a wide belt. I danced a lot and I just felt like I was somebody else. You don't know how that makes you feel to have to look like a dope all your life. They didn't have any—my folks didn't have any money.

Such accounts make my mother's story of finally getting a pretty dress even more poignant.

> It was one of the first times for a long while that I had new clothes. I had a new dress. I'd made this dress [at the end of my senior year] in school, and it was really pretty, and Mama had managed somehow to get me some new shoes and a new hat. And I was so happy to have a whole new outfit. And we were gonna go to [church] conference in Arimo, and we had to go in the buggy. And I had to run out to the corral to do something before we left, and I didn't want to get my new shoes dirty, so I put on my old horrible ones that I used to milk cows in, had manure and milk and everything else all over 'em. And I went out, and when I came back, I forgot to put my decent shoes on. We got almost up to Arimo, and I discovered what shoes I'd had on. So then I—it was too late to go back, so the rest of them went to church, and I drove the team down under the hill and sat there all day all by myself waiting for two sessions of conference to end. It was horrible. I was so proud of my new clothes. I thought for once—I never had new clothes. I hadn't had any for ages, and I was so happy to have a whole complete outfit all at once. Then I ruined it. I don't ever remember wearing it any other time—of course, I did, but I can't remember it. All I remember about that dress was that terrible day.

In spite of the poverty, my mother loved Riddyville—loved the horses she rode, the games she played with friends, the visiting among neighbors, the smell of baking in the house when she came home from school—her mother baked eight loaves of bread every other day; she loved the generosity of people, the kindness of the men, the faith of the village women who gathered en masse at her house, formed a circle around her mother's sick bed, and knelt in prayer. But always there was the ambivalence. "Everybody was just like family," she said; "everybody helped each other, and everybody loved each other, and we were just—it was just a nice place to grow up, when you didn't mind not having any money."

But a compensating theme, just as strong as that of poverty, also pervades the narratives—that of never giving up no matter what the odds. I could illustrate this theme with a dozen stories—from Mother's learning how to deal with cows by learning how to swear at them to her bringing runaway horses under control, but I will use just one. Weakened by an earlier case of mumps and by too much hard work for a young girl, my mother first lost thirty-seven pounds and then came down with rheumatic fever while she was in high school. The breakdown occurred something like this:

> This one winter day I rode my horse to school, and it was thirty below zero. I was just so cold, and then when I got just about where you turn to go into McCammon, I felt like it was getting warm. I thought, "Gee, that weather's changed; it's warm now." But by the time I got into town where I had to tie the horse up, I knew that it wasn't warm, that I might be trying to freeze. . . . Anyway, I could hardly tie the reins, and I got up to school; and on the way up there, if I'd had much further to go, I think I'd laid down. That snow looked so soft, and I was so tired. But I got there.

She got there, but that was about all. She moved through the rest of the day in something of a trance. The doctor who examined her the next day said she wouldn't live six months, that the valves in her heart were gone. Her response to that death sentence rings more strongly in her own words:

> I stayed in bed for about six weeks . . . , and then I started to get up about eleven and stay up two or three hours, and I kept doing a little more. And one day in February [she had taken ill at Christmas], it was nice and warm—kinda thawing—warm sun was shining on the porch. Mama went to town, and I said, "Go ask that doctor if I can go outside." When she came back, she said he about had a fit. He said, "Why if I went outside, I'd have pneumonia, and that'd be the end of me." But I said, "Well, I've been out all day—all afternoon." I'd bundled up and sat out there. And I kept doing it. And that spring I rode my horse and went back to school.

Not only did she go back to school. Of the thirty students who started with her, fourteen finished—and she graduated second in the class.

From the events of her past, then, my mother has selected details and created a body of stories that place her in the center of and in control of her universe—stories that may not always be historically accurate but that have over time and through repeated tellings become what T. S. Eliot might call "objective correlatives"—artistic representations for what she holds most dear and would most eagerly communicate to others ([1919] 1975, 48). Though I have been able to give you only a brief glimpse of her stories—I intend eventually to bring them all together—I hope I have demonstrated that through their intertextuality and their systemic unity, they form a powerful whole capable of moving us as good literature always moves us. I hope also that I have inspired some of you to seek in your family narratives the novels that may help shape your lives.

As you do so, don't be overly concerned with meaning. What do family stories mean to those who tell them? As you seek to answer that question, I recommend the words of Paul Ricoeur: "Like a text, human action is an open work, the meaning of which is 'in suspense.' It is because it 'opens up' new references and receives fresh relevance from them that human deeds are also waiting for fresh interpretations to decide their meaning" (1973, 103). In other words, stories like my mother's do not have fixed, determinate meanings, even to the narrator—and having once created the stories, the narrator in future recitations becomes both teller and audience. They serve rather as the means by which the storyteller structures her life and presents it to the world. Through such stories, as Sharon Kaufman points out,

> the self draws meaning from the past, interpreting and recreating it as a resource for being in the present . . . ; from this perspective, individual identity is revealed by the patterns of symbolic meaning that characterize the individual's interpretation of experience . . . ; people formulate and reformulate personal and cultural symbols of their past to create a meaningful, coherent sense of self, and in the process they create a viable present. In this way the ageless self emerges: its definition is ongoing, continuous, and creative. (1987, 14)

What do my mother's stories mean not just to her but also to me, and what might similar stories from your families mean to you? Even if these narratives did contain fixed meanings, we could never get at them precisely because that symbolic and imperfect system we call language would stand always in the way. But that shouldn't dishearten us because as we listen to the stories, we also are creating a meaningful, coherent sense of self, constructing our own lives in the process. If literary criticism has taught us anything in recent years, it has taught us that meaning lies as much in what we take to a text as in the text itself. What Robert Scholes says of reading can apply equally well to listening to stories:

> If a book or a story or any other text is like a little life, and if our reading actually uses up precious time in that other story we think of as our lives, then we should make the most of our reading just as we should make the most of our lives. Reading reminds us that every text ends with a blank page and that what we get from every text is precisely balanced by what we give. Our skill, our learning, and our commitment to the text will determine, for each of us, the kind of experience that text provides. Learning to read . . . is not just a matter of acquiring information from texts, it is a matter of learning to read and write the texts of our lives. (1989, 19)

Scholes's statement explains why it might be best to call my mother's narratives both a *family* novel and a *personal* novel. It is family because it belongs to us all—each of us in the family having heard the same stories about the same family members in similar family settings, and each of us having access to many of the associations that make the stories understandable. It is personal because it belongs to each of us differently—each of us having filled in the blank page with which the novel ends in an individual way, according to individual need, and each of us having moved from the stories themselves to compose the individual texts of our lives.

For this reason I prefer to speak not of what the novel means to me, in any ultimate sense of meaning, but rather of what it does for me. It can give me a glimpse, as Sandra Dolby Stahl points out, of "a pearl of great price, another person's soul" (1989, xi). That in itself is enough, but it does still more. On a lazy summer afternoon, with the oblique rays of an Idaho sun flickering through the curtains and highlighting the deep wrinkles in my mother's face, we have sat before the tape recorder—laughing together, arguing, sometimes crying—as my mother has told her stories still another time and as a young girl from Riddyville has ridden once more through both our imaginations.

As I have listened to my tapes of these sessions, I have heard in the background the steady, constant ticking of my mother's old grandfather's clock. Her grandfather, Robert Green, had bought the clock for himself and later given it to my grandparents on their marriage; my mother inherited it from them; and I hope one day to inherit it from her. I have heard the ticking of that clock all my life, just as I have heard my mother's stories all my life. As I listened to it on the tape, it seemed not just to tick away time but to dissolve time, making me one with all those people in Riddyville and placing me in the center of narratives like the one below, a narrative about the first owner of the clock, Robert Green, who had fussed over my mother, worried about her, spoiled her—and whom she probably loved above all other people. One time, says my mother,

> I went when he was up to Aunt Vira's when he was real sick, and I went up to see him, and I was going to comfort him, and he wound up comforting me. I just looked at him and started to cry, 'cause I couldn't stand it if anything happened to Grandpa. He said, "Now, don't cry, Dolly; I'll be all right."

Because she couldn't stand it if anything happened to him, Robert Green's accidentally poisoning his beloved team of horses, old Cap and Seal, proved to be one of the most tragic days in my mother's young life. Here is the story:

> Grandpa thought nobody had horses like his and nobody's watch told time [like his]. Even the railroad [time], if his was a little different, it was the railroad that was wrong, not his watch. He always said he had the correct time. . . . Anyway, we used to have poisoned

> oats and put them out around the fields to kill the squirrels in the summer, because they would eat the crops. And Grandpa always bought his horses oats. He always had oats to feed old Cap and Seal. And this one time, he got in the wrong—he was staying with Uncle Dan then, or the horses were—and he got in the wrong sack of oats and fed them the poisoned oats. And—anyway they got real sick, and I wasn't up there; I wasn't in on this first part—the whole town was there doing everything they could possibly think of to save those horses. And old Cap was Grandpa's favorite. Cap was just a plain bay, and old Seal had a little bit of brown mixed in with him—and he loved them both, but Cap was his favorite. And old Seal died first. And then—they were all still trying to save old Cap—and Grandpa came down to our place—he couldn't stand it anymore to be around them—and he came down to our place and stayed all night. And the next morning Uncle Jim came down and Grandpa went out to the gate to meet him, and he says, "Well, what about it, Jimmy?" And Uncle Jim says, "Well, the old boy's gone." Then, of course, all of us started to cry—Mama and everybody—and we missed Grandpa; we didn't know where he was. And Mama kind of had an idea. So she went out to the old outside toilet, and he was sitting in there crying. . . . And then Uncle Jim—he dragged [old Cap and Seal] down in the hills there, and laid them just straight, so they would be side by side.

A couple of years ago I drove my mother to what once had been Riddyville. She showed me where their home had been, across from the two-room schoolhouse, where Aunt Vira had lived, where Uncle Dan had lived, where she had spent the afternoon in a tree, chased there by a raging bull, where she had jumped her horse across a rock-filled ravine none of her companions dared jump. Nothing remained, except one old house that would soon join the others in ruin. I left my mother in the car briefly and walked over to the house, startling out a deer taking shade under a decaying roof from the afternoon sun. As I walked back to the car through sagebrush and weeds grown higher than my head, across fields rutted by erosion, I could almost feel all the life that had once been there—children playing "Fox and Geese," teenagers racing their horses down the road, men sharing labor during threshing, women scrubbing plank floors until they were white, young homesteading couples tilling their fields and dreaming of independence.

Now only the stories remain. But they do remain. And that family novel developed from those stories, created first by my mother as she shaped her life and then re-created by me as I have shaped mine, persists in my mind as powerful and as artistically moving as the works of literature that line my library shelf.

As I lay in my hospital bed years ago wondering what that well-differentiated carcinoma would finally do to me, it was not just Dylan Thomas's "Do not go gentle into that good night" that brought me through the dark; it was also my mother's line: "And that spring I rode my horse and went back to school." More than that—it was all that vigor, all that passion, all that humor, all that joy and tragedy, all that *life* that had been Riddyville, living in my memory not as historical narrative but as the artistic rendering of significant human experience—that is, as literature, literature that testified to me once again of the indomitable nature of the human spirit and of its capacity to create and enjoy beauty.

William Faulkner tells us that it is the poet's duty to write about these things "which have been the glory" of our lives ([1952] 1966, 1249). Too long we have looked for the expressions of this glory only in the canonized works of the received literary tradition. It is time now to realize our democratic ideals by listening finally to all the voices in our great land. Especially is it time to seek in our own family stories the Riddyvilles that have created, expressed, and given direction to our own lives. It is time at last to celebrate ourselves; we all have stories to tell.

A Daughter's Biography of William A. Wilson

In 1951 my father, William Albert (Bert) Wilson, enrolled at Brigham Young University (BYU) and began an academic life that would consume his energies for the next forty-five years. He interrupted his studies once, in 1953, to serve a two-and-a-half-year mission in Finland for the Church of Jesus Christ of Latter-day Saints (the Mormons); but even that adventure proved to be important preparation for future academic endeavors. Dad studied, taught, and fell in love not only with my mother, Hannele Blomqvist Wilson, but with the Finnish people, who would become the focus of his doctoral dissertation, *Folklore and Nationalism in Modern Finland.* The vitality and quality of Dad's academic endeavors are evidenced best by the publication of his dissertation, as well as over eighty scholarly articles on folklore. In addition, Dad has directed folklore archives at BYU and Utah State University (USU), has served at BYU as English department chair and director of the Charles Redd Center for Western Studies, has edited *Western Folklore,* has been elected a fellow of the American Folklore Society, and has received many prestigious awards for both scholarship and teaching.

In light of these facts, readers should know that Dad never took a college prep class in high school. In fact, he rarely even took home his books. Before and after school he worked manual labor for local farmers, for town businesses, and for his father, a railroad section foreman and owner of an eighty-acre irrigated farm in Downey, Idaho. Further, the hours Dad spent *in* school seem to have been devoted as much to mischief making as to learning. One of Dad's few memorable grade school writing experiences occurred during his fourth grade year. His teacher, Miss Salvesen, punished misbehaving students by requiring them to copy a page of their history book for each of their ill deeds. Dad and his lifelong friend Eugene England memorized the shortest page in the book, wrote it out many times, and kept the copies on hand as a hedge against future punishments. Similarly, Dad's *last* memorable writing experience in public school occurred during his senior year, when his history teacher/principal caught him and his friend Freddy Pickren sword fighting with yardsticks in the hall during class time and consequently assigned them both to write an essay on the United Nations.

The explanations for Dad's misbehavior are many, but lack of interest in school is not really one of them. Even in his youth Dad found that rigorous academic work made him feel more fully alive and more fully human. In fact, having recently read a considerable amount of material about the United Nations, he was delighted by the principal's writing assignment and worked diligently to produce an essay that he delivered (with a dramatic bow) to his amazed principal that same afternoon. ("Poor Freddy," says Dad, had to work many days to complete the essay.) Had more of such work been required of Dad at Downey High School, he probably would have gotten into less mischief. Unfortunately, he would have to leave his community behind in order to find enough intellectual challenges to keep him out of trouble.

In other ways, though, Dad never really left Downey. Rather, he became its ardent spokesman, devoting his professional life to recording and preserving the "lore" of close-knit communities like his Downey friends. During his college years when Dad switched his emphasis from English literature to folklore, I believe that it was the communal nature of folk art that appealed to him the most and that the reasons were intensely personal. He was moved not only by artistic appreciation of "lore" but by deep bonds of affection which he felt for the "folk" from his youth. And the older Dad became, the more his scholarship was driven by a passionate desire to illuminate, validate, and honor the culture that produced him. It is important, then, to understand Dad's youth in Downey, not because he left it so far behind, but because he *refused* to leave it completely behind; though Dad would live an adult lifestyle far different from that of his boyhood, his academic work was not the antithesis of his past but rather a natural extension of it.

Downey is currently only a ghost of its former self. The population within city limits has decreased from 750 in 1950 to 613 today, and most of the many family farms that once surrounded the town have returned to sage brush. By the time my grandmother died in August of 1996, only the bank, the post office, and one grocery store opened their doors for business on a Main Street full of otherwise vacant, boarded up buildings. Some newcomers have moved in to replace an aging, dying population, but many of the new residents commute some forty miles to work in Pocatello, Idaho, or in other communities and are not intimately acquainted with their neighbors.

In contrast, when Dad was a boy the town boasted (in addition to the bank and post office) a pharmacy, several major car dealers and garages, a number of "farm implement companies," three grocery stores, three hardware stores, three pool halls, a lumber yard, four cafes, and a theater, with an attached confectionary, which opened every night of the week. When I began interviewing Dad in 1996 (just one month after Grandma's death), his stories about his youth were in large measure a tribute to this golden age. Downey "was a real town," he explains, and in the absence of televisions, computers, and freeways, people depended on the town for both their entertainment and their livelihood.

Students were not bussed, as they are now, says Dad, to "a potato field in Arimo [a nearby community]" to attend a consolidated school with students drawn from towns throughout the valley. Rather, children who lived in town walked to Downey Grade School (containing grades one through eight) and Downey High School. Of the twenty-three members of Dad's senior class of 1951, fourteen also appear in his second-grade picture. As had many of their parents a generation earlier, these children attended church together, played together, suffered through adolescence together, and understood each other as adults in ways most of us today will never understand our neighbors.

Adult community members also were both self-sufficient and interdependent in ways that most people of my generation can hardly imagine. For example, Grandpa raised cows, chickens, and pigs and grew a large garden. For their winter food supply, Grandma and Grandpa stored potatoes and carrots raised in the garden or purchased from local farmers, and Grandma canned produce from the garden such as corn, beets, peas, and beans and a lot of fruit (peaches, apricots, pears, and berries) which they brought home in a trailer from family excursions to nearby farms in Utah. My grandparents in turn sold much of the milk from their cows to local residents. To make ends meet, they thus depended on the goods and services, as well as on the business, of their neighbors.

Additionally, community members often worked *together* to produce the goods they needed. During harvest season especially, local farmers teamed up to help each other and employed "extra" young laborers from town. Besides cleaning toilets in the motel across the street, washing dishes in Jack's Café, grinding meat into hamburger in the grocery store, and helping his dad with work on their own farm, Dad worked seasonal jobs with his friends (picking potatoes; thinning and topping beets; tying grain sacks; plowing gardens; cutting, raking, and stacking hay) for other farmers. When he got older, Dad also worked alongside family members and neighbors for the Union Pacific Railroad, and sometimes they all worked under the direction of Dad's father, William (Bill) Wilson, who was a section foreman.

Grandpa experienced a unique set of challenges in being "boss" to people who sat by him in church and even ate Christmas dinner at his table. In response, he led with both firmness and kindness, as well as by example. His men knew he was capable of firing even good friends who did not take their jobs seriously, but they also heard his reassuring praise as he labored beside them. The rewards of Grandpa's efforts were the love and respect of family and community. Though he had only sporadically experienced six years of formal education, Grandpa was, in Dad's view, widely esteemed as a man of intelligence, gentility, and integrity.

As the son of Bill Wilson, Dad felt his place among a close-knit community of laboring-class workers and participated fully in the traditions and celebrations that resulted from their associations. Dad's stories passionately recount the predictable rhythm of Downey community life and the gathering places that facilitated it. He describes the grain elevators and flour mills where young boys gathered to play hide-and-seek and shoot rubber bands at each other with homemade guns; the ball games and dances that everyone in town, not just the teenagers, attended; the movie theater, the soda fountain, and the swimming pool where teenagers mingled after school and on weekend dates; the pool hall, where young men especially hung out against their Mormon parents' wishes; the daily schedule that all good housewives followed (my grandmother and her neighbor, Mrs. Austin, competed every Monday morning to get their laundry on the line first); the Bannock County Fair, in which community members displayed prized animals, foods, and handwork; the sewing club my grandmother attended for forty years; the easy and comfortable family gatherings with relatives who all lived a short drive or train ride away; and the marvelous storytelling sessions that occurred over and over again at all of these family and community functions.

This cohesive community clearly provided Dad with a sense of place and belonging, which served as an anchor for him for the rest of his life. Once when he and his sister Gloria were playing, coatless, in a snowbank, the town doctor drove by, stopped the car, and marched into the house to scold my grandmother for not dressing her children appropriately. Years later, on the night before Dad left for his mission, the entire town gathered for a dance in his honor. How could one *not* feel nostalgic about such a place?

Dad was also, however, restless as a boy in Downey, and it would be misleading to suggest otherwise. He was, after all, the son not only of Bill Wilson but also of Lucile Green Wilson. Dad idolized his father, but in talent and temperament he clearly favored my grandmother. Specifically, he shared her keen mind; her musical ear; her quick wit; her inability to relax or sit still; her belief that if things could go wrong they usually would; her ability to find humor and value in the human condition, in spite of its essentially tragic nature; and her need to capture and communicate that value and humor through language—especially through the medium of story. As Dad explains in his essay about her, she and her extended family filled his youth with good conversation, much laughter, and moving, artistic narratives about their lives—narratives which, Dad argues, show the "indomitable human spirit" as artistically and movingly as any canonized literature he has read.

As a storyteller, Grandma represented a culture whose narrative traditions were preserved orally, rather than in written form. However, Grandma also was unique in her culture in that she took her schooling seriously and graduated from high school second in her class, in spite of serious health problems which at one time caused her to miss a year of elementary school. As a mother, she cared about her children's education and, by reading nightly to Dad, instilled in him a love of books that would carry him through many long hours of solitude in his father's fields (between irrigation water changes) or in railroad cars (between work shifts).

Through his love affair with literature, Dad acquired some sense of the largeness of the world and an interest in the people beyond Downey who occupied that world. His love of story would also lead to acting and writing experiences during which he discovered some natural ability. For example, during his eighth grade year, he rode a horse on stage while vigorously singing "My home's in Montana." According to Dad, his robust performance delighted everyone except his mother, who was distracted by worries that the horse would mess on the stage. As he grew older he dreamed, like every other boy in Downey, of being a sports star and felt that nothing else really "counted" in Downey, but he still made time to perform in several school and church plays and to edit his high school newspaper—until the principal "fired" him for writing an editorial against school consolidation.

Unlike most people in his family and community, Dad also decided, at his mother's encouragement, to continue his education beyond high school. He enrolled at BYU with plans to major in political science and, though not a stellar student his first two years (he certainly had not learned to study in Downey), enjoyed most of the classes he managed to attend. He especially credits a freshman composition teacher, Nan Grass, for "turning [him] into a college student" (even though he never showed her his full capabilities) and a history teacher for assigning him essay questions like "Discuss all the major developments in slavery from the arrival of the first slaves in 1619 to the Emancipation Proclamation in 1863."

If going to college helped expand Dad's worldview, serving a mission in Finland (also at his mother's encouragement) did so even more. Dad was moved not only by lush forests and lakes that covered the land but also by the stoic people whose reserved nature and dry humor appealed to him. He found their history fascinating and admirable, and he enjoyed learning their language. He was impressed by thoughtful Sunday School discussions among well-educated, literate, committed Mormon church members, and he was especially charmed by a Hannele Blomqvist from Lahti, Finland, who had joined the church a year earlier and was now serving a mission in her own country. After Mom and Dad had both completed their missions and resumed acquaintances at BYU, they married in the Salt Lake Mormon temple.

After his mission and marriage, Dad seems to have found more motivation and direction in his schooling. Having developed good study habits in Finland and satisfied the longing of his heart for love, he settled into a life of a serious student, abandoned his earlier plan to become a spy, yielded to "the allure of story," and completed a bachelor's degree in English, followed by one year as a high school English teacher in Bountiful, Utah, and then a master's degree (again at BYU) in English literature.

At first, Dad explains, he thought he had to leave behind the stories of his youth and study more sophisticated literature. However, he eventually became "weary of the narrow elitism" of then-popular formalist literary criticism which "jerked literature from cultural context" and "tended to look with condescension" at the kinds of stories that had captivated him in his youth. Though deeply moved by much canonized literature, he objected to the notions that only educated people could craft good stories and that only educated people could determine what constituted good art.

Searching for a more inclusive discipline, he enrolled at Indiana University in a PhD program in folklore and focused his research on the political use of the *Kalevala* (an epic work based on ancient Finnish folksongs) in awakening a spirit of nationalism. With this focus he was able to combine his interests in politics and literature with his love of "all things Finnish," and he was able to expand his study of literature to include the tales of common, working class peoples.

I believe that in studying the lore of common peoples, Dad made a highly symbolic (though probably not fully conscious) choice to stay loyal to his roots, no matter how much his new lifestyle would differ from that of his boyhood. But because his new lifestyle was indeed different, not to mention demanding, Dad would wander far beyond Downey (both literally and figuratively) for many years. "The damned dissertation," as it was known in our house, was a nine-year project that took us back and forth between Bloomington, Indiana (where Dad earned his PhD), Helsinki, Finland (where Dad studied on a Fulbright scholarship), and Provo, Utah (where Dad eventually returned to BYU as a faculty member before actually completing said damned dissertation). And what I learned from both my parents during those years was not the importance of having roots but rather the excitement of cultural diversity.

This family focus on other cultures continued even after the PhD ordeal was over and we settled into more permanent residence in Provo and later in Logan, Utah. Mom, who knew well the pain of homesickness, often rounded up Dad's international students and brought them to our house for holiday dinners. She also fraternized with a large group of Finnish women who, like her, had emigrated to Utah and married young American men. As a social worker, Mom introduced us to people from different socioeconomic groups (for example, Native Americans, patients at the hospital for the mentally ill, and migrant workers), with whom we would not otherwise have come in contact. And as a folklorist in a world of very few folklorists, Dad communicated often with colleagues all over the world. He went to conferences with them and took interest in the cultures they were studying. Sometimes these folklorists discussed their studies at our dinner table.

In short, the father I knew was not exactly the same boy my grandparents had raised. The youth who had milked cows before dawn became a college professor who haunted empty libraries and wandered the halls of his university department in his stockinged feet until three and four o'clock in the morning. The young farmer who had once been "terrified" by the prospect of sitting by an African American woman on a bus in California now enthusiastically studied cultures far different from the one that had produced him. From a very early age, I understood that both my parents had a genuine desire really to understand their brothers and sisters of all cultures, and I recognized Dad's interest in folklore as a means of gaining that understanding.

On the other hand, Dad's folklore studies also gradually led him to a greater appreciation of and interest in his own culture. When Dad first began his PhD program, he had never really considered that folklore existed in his own culture. Folklore, he thought, belonged to other people; he had come to IU to study the folklore of the Finns. He therefore found very unusual a suggestion by his IU mentor, Richard Dorson, that he ought to collect some Mormon folklore. However, his views began to change in 1964 after he collected from his Bloomington ward (parish) members forty-five stories about the three Nephite prophets who, according to Mormon belief, have wandered the earth since the time of Christ.

By the time he returned to BYU as a faculty member, Dad had begun writing about western and especially Mormon folklore, and after finishing his dissertation, he began to pursue this interest full time. His studies over the course of many years have helped him to explain Mormon culture to non-Mormons as well as to define his own place within that culture, and in recent years he has especially found satisfaction in collecting his own family folklore. These accomplishments have motivated him to emphasize to his students that folklore is not just a collection of antiquated stories from the past; rather, folklore is constantly created by every kind of community imaginable in the *present.* Office mates at work, sports team members, neighborhood children at play, women's bridge clubs, and small cohesive towns like Downey—all of these "communities" develop traditions, rituals, and stories, in an attempt to create order, meaning, and beauty from their everyday experience, and all of their artistic expressions have meaning and aesthetic form unique and fully understandable only to the members of those communities or "folk groups."

This definition of folklore was (and still often is) unfamiliar to nonfolklorists both within and without academia. Dad and his fellow folklorists thus have faced the monumental yet heady task of exploring with their students the implications of this definition and convincing those who make administrative decisions that folklore scholarship is a field worth supporting and funding.

Dad's approach to this task has been to encourage his students to start their folklore studies, not by studying a different culture, as he did, but by focusing on their own cultures and then by expanding out to a comparative study of other cultures—to a broader understanding of the ways culture works and to an understanding that all cultures are rooted in a shared humanity. He has found that his students initially understand the significance of their own cultures' folklore in ways that they never could understand that of other cultures and consequently are able to make meaningful contributions to academic discussions across many disciplines, including sociology, psychology, anthropology, political science, and even international relations. These students often have expressed gratitude for an opportunity to study subjects which really matter to them on deep, personal levels. In applying scholarly analysis to their own cultures, they have acquired a deeper understanding of themselves, and sometimes this understanding has helped them come to terms with the more painful, disturbing elements of their heritage. Always it has helped prepare them for the equally important task of sensitively and fairly interpreting the folklore of *other* cultures.

In our current age of multicultural education, Dad's approach might not seem so revolutionary, but in the 1960s, when Dad began teaching folklore at BYU, the folklorists were way ahead of their time. In an age of formalist literary criticism, it was especially difficult for some humanities professors to consider that the communal stories, jokes, traditions, and creations of everyday people could have nearly as much artistic merit as the formalized art taught in university classrooms.

As the only folklorist at both BYU and USU for many years, Dad was keenly aware of these attitudes and, consequently, of the precarious position of most university folklore programs. He understood that he had to spread his message beyond the classroom in order to keep folklore scholarship alive. Consequently, he spoke often in college English classes, in university lecture series, and even in Mormon "firesides"; and he continues today, even in retirement, to address church and university classes—especially about the importance of family folklore. Above all, Dad has shared his message by befriending students and colleagues and taking an interest in their stories. I remember often being designated by my mother to pick him up from his office while she waited with a younger brother in the car. Mom usually brought reading material with her for this occasion because it was always a long, drawn-out affair. Besides having to return to his office three or four times for things he had forgotten, Dad also had to stop and visit everyone whose door was open between his office and the stairs. Almost always I heard stories during these occasions, and though I was too young at the time to consciously realize it, I think now that the stories were especially well told by English professors who knew Dad was paying attention to every aspect of their storytelling performance. Dad hasn't yet converted all his friends and colleagues, but as they have shared their stories, especially with such an interested listener, many of them have begun to recognize how the stories have shaped their own lives and moved them as profoundly as any novel or poem.

It would be grossly simplistic and unfair of me, however, to suggest that Dad's networking habits have all been politically or professionally motivated. Mainly, they are just indicative of the person he was reared to be. Dad simply enjoys hanging out with a close-knit group of friends and habitually works to develop a sense of community and trust among them. As a child I saw evidence of these friendships when students came to our home for dinner or cohorts came for a visit or a card game. (I'll forever cherish the memory of Eloise Bell's bellowing laughter pervading my dreams and pushing them in pleasant directions.) Sometimes these associates even came to help with home maintenance projects. I believe half the English department helped paint our house after Dad's malignant thyroid was removed in 1969. Twenty-five years later, when my husband and I were building our own home, Dad, with English department colleagues Doug Thayer and Eugene England, showed up at our doorstep one day to help us meet the bank's completion deadline. While I felt deeply grateful to these men, I realized that their actions had little to do with me and everything to do with lifelong patterns of interaction with each other. And, though I can't speak for Doug Thayer, I know that both Dad and Eugene credited some of those patterns of interaction to customary behavior which they both had learned as young boys in Downey.

As a folklorist, Dad has integrated the best of two worlds he loves. He has helped document, preserve, and even perpetuate the values and lifestyle he enjoyed in the western, Mormon, agrarian culture that produced him while still satisfying his desire for an academic lifestyle and for companions who share his intellectual interests. In other words, Dad has gradually developed a network—a community or folk group, if you will—of devout, Mormon intellectuals like himself.

But Dad also has done more than this. In bringing Downey with him to the university, he has made the academy a much more relevant, accessible place for many students and has thus helped other folklorists to create a new, worldwide community of scholars not so far removed from the various "folk communities" that have produced *them*—a community of scholars not hiding out in an ivory tower but actively bridging cultural divides by interpreting different communities for each other.

All of the essays in this book show evidence of this bridge building. No matter what Dad writes, I believe he always envisions an audience full of family and friends, as well as academic colleagues. Never wanting to alienate any reader, Dad always starts by defining folklore, and he illustrates academic terms and concepts with stories which people outside his discipline can understand. Especially I think he writes (even now, after her death) for his mother, who read everything he wrote and was immensely proud of him. In the essay devoted entirely to her stories, he closes with a statement which I believe he would want you, the readers, to understand more than any other.

> Too long we have looked for the expression of . . . glory only in the canonized works of the received literary tradition. It is time now to realize our democratic ideals by listening finally to all the voices in our great land. Especially it is time to seek in our own family stories the . . . [communities] that have created, expressed, and given direction to our lives. It is time at last to celebrate ourselves; we all have stories to tell.

—Denise Wilson Jamsa

William A. Wilson's Published Works

BOOKS

Folklore and Nationalism in Modern Finland. Bloomington and London: Indiana University Press, 1976.

Kalevala ja kansallisuusaate [The *Kalevala* and the National Idea]. Helsinki: Työväen Sivistysliitto, 1985—A translation, with a new introduction, of *Folklore and Nationalism in Modern Finland*.

WORKS EDITED

Book Review Section. *Western Folklore*, 1972–1978.

Mormon Folklore. Special issue of *Utah Historical Quarterly* 44, no. 4 (Fall 1976).

Western Folklore, 1979–1983.

Stories, Songs, and Opinions of the Idaho Country. Special issue of *Rendezvous* 17, nos. 1 and 2 (1982). (Served as contributing editor.)

ARTICLES

Mormon Legends of the Three Nephites Collected at Indiana University. *Indiana Folklore* 2 (1969): 3–35.

On Our Down-Again Up-Again Society. *Newsletter of the Folklore Society of Utah* 7 (June 1970): 3–5.

Editorial: The Demise of the Coalville Tabernacle. *Newsletter of the Folklore Society of Utah* 8 (April 1971): 1.

Independence or Dependence: The Fate of Our Folklore Society. *Newsletter of the Folklore Society of Utah* 8 (April 1971): 4–7.

On Silver Bullets and Mad-Stones. *The Possible Sack* 2 (September 1971): 7–12.

Folklore and History: Fact amid the Legends. *Utah Historical Quarterly* 41 (1973): 40–58.

Herder, Folklore, and Romantic Nationalism. *Journal of Popular Culture* 6 (1973): 819–35.

And They Spake with a New Tongue (On Missionary Slang). In *Conference on the Language of the Mormons*, ed. Harold S. Madsen and John L. Sorenson, 46–48. Provo: Brigham Young University Language Research Center, 1974. (With John B. Harris.)

The *Kalevala* and Finnish Politics. *Journal of the Folklore Institute* 12 (1975): 131–55.
My Road into Folklore. *Folklore Forum*. Bibliographic and Special Series, no. 14 (1975), 61–62.
"The Vanishing Hitchhiker" among the Mormons. *Indiana Folklore* 8 (1975): 79–97.
A Bibliography of Studies in Mormon Folklore. *Utah Historical Quarterly* 44 (1976): 317–29.
The Evolutionary Premise in Folklore Theory and the "Finnish Method." *Western Folklore* 35 (1976): 241–49.
The Paradox of Mormon Folklore. In *Essays in the American West, 1974–1975*, ed. Thomas G. Alexander, 127–47. Charles Redd Monographs in Western History, no. 6. Provo: Brigham Young University Press, 1976.
The Study of Mormon Folklore. *Utah Historical Quarterly* 44 (1976): 317–28.
Utah Folklore and the Utah Librarian. *Utah Libraries* 20 (Spring 1977): 25–36.
Editorial Statement. *Western Folklore* 38 (1979): 1–2.
Folklore in *Giant Joshua*. In *Proceedings of the Symposium of the Association for Mormon Letters, 1978–79*, ed. Steven P. Sondrup, 57–63. Provo, Utah, 1979.
Folklore of Utah's Little Scandinavia. *Utah Historical Quarterly* 47 (1979): 148–66.
The Curse of Cain and Other Stories: Blacks in Mormon Folklore. *Sunstone* 5, no. 6 (November–December 1980): 9–13. (With Richard C. Poulsen)
On Being Human: The Folklore of Mormon Missionaries. Utah State University Faculty Honor Lecture Series. Logan: Utah State University Press, 1981.
Richard M. Dorson's Theory for American Folklore: A Finnish Analogue. *Western Folklore* 41 (1982): 36–43.
From the Editor. *Western Folklore* 41 (1983): 247–48.
Mormon Folklore. In *Handbook of American Folklore*, ed. Richard M. Dorson, 155–61. Bloomington: Indiana University Press, 1983.
Trickster Tales and the Location of Cultural Boundaries: A Mormon Example. *Journal of Folklore Research* 20 (1983): 55–66.
USU Fife Folklore Archive. *Folklore Society of Utah Newsletter* 17, no. 2 (1983).
Contributor to *Popular Beliefs and Superstitions from Utah*, coll. Anthon S. Cannon, ed. Wayland D. Hand and Jeannine E. Talley. Salt Lake City: University of Utah Press, 1984.
Idols and Myths in Music: A Comment. *Musiikin Suunta* 7, no. 3 (1985): 9–13.
Kalevala riemuvuosi Petroskoissa 1935 [The Kalevala Jubilee in Petroskoi, 1935] and Kansanrunouspropagandaa itsenäisessä Suomessa [Folklore Propaganda in Independent Finland]. *Aikamerkki* (January 1985), 8–12.
The Seriousness of Mormon Humor. *Sunstone* 10, no. 1 (1985): 6–13.
The Outlaw Hero in U.S. Legend and Song. Special issue of *Musiikin Suunta* 7, no. 1 (1985): 80–88.
"We Did Everything Together": Farming Customs of the Mountainwest. *Northwest Folklore* 4, no. 1 (1985): 23–30.
And Not To Yield. *Fellowship*, 8–12. Addresses Delivered at Annual University Conference. Provo, Utah: Brigham Young University Press, 1986.
Austin and Alta Fife: Pioneer Folklorists. *Utah Folklife Newsletter* 20, no. 2 (Fall 1986): 2–4.
Documenting Folklore. In *Folk Groups and Folk Genres: An Introduction*, ed. Elliott Oring, 225–54. Logan: Utah State University Press, 1986.
In Memoriam: Austin E. Fife, 1909–86. *Utah Historical Quarterly* 54 (1986): 288–90.
The Need Beyond Necessity. *BYU Today* 41, no. 5 (October 1987): 32–37, 47–52.
Partial Repentance of a Critic: The *Kalevala*, Politics, and the United States. In *Folklife Annual 1986*, ed. Alan Jabbour and James Hardin, 81–91. Washington, D.C.: American Folklife Center at the Library of Congress, 1987.

Dealing with Organizational Stress: Lessons from the Folklore of Mormon Missionaries. In *Inside Organizations: Understanding the Human Dimensions*, ed. Michael Owen Jones, Michael Dane Moore, Richard Christopher Snyder, 271–79. Newbury Park, California: Sage Publications, 1988.

The Deeper Necessity: Folklore and the Humanities. *Journal of American Folklore* 101 (1988): 156–67.

Freeways, Parking Lots, and Ice Cream Stands: The Three Nephites in Contemporary Mormon Culture. *Dialogue: A Journal of Mormon Thought* 21, no. 3 (Fall 1988): 13–26.

Preface to *Heaven on Horseback*. By Austin and Alta Fife, v–ix. Logan: Utah State University Press, 1989.

Richard M. Dorson as Romantic-Nationalist. *Journal of Folklore Research* 26 (1989): 36–42.

The Study of Mormon Folklore: An Uncertain Mirror for Truth. *Dialogue: A Journal of Mormon Thought* 22, no. 4 (Winter 1989): 95–110.

In Praise of Ourselves: Stories to Tell. *Brigham Young University Studies* 30 (1990): 5–24.

Mormon Folklore and History: Implications for Canadian Research. In *The Mormon Presence in Canada*, ed. Brigham Y. Card, et al, 150–66. Edmonton and Logan: University of Alberta Press and Utah State University Press, 1990.

Juanita Brooks and Family Narratives. Juanita Brooks Lecture Series. St. George, Utah: Dixie College, 1991.

On Teaching the *Kalevala* to Advanced Students. In *Studies in Finnish Language and Culture*, ed. Melvin J. Luthy, 35–40. Proceedings of the Fourth Conference on Finnish Studies in North America. Helsinki: Ministry of Education, 1991.

Personal Narratives: The Family Novel. *Western Folklore* 50 (1991): 127–49.

The Spinner of Tales. *Sunstone* 15, no. 3 (September 1991): 50–52.

Folklore. In *Encyclopedia of Mormonism*. 5 vols. New York: Macmillan, 1992, 2: 518–20.

Kalevala, ideologia ja moderni elämä [The *Kalevala*, Ideology, and Modern Life]. *Elias*, no. 3 (1992): 10–14. [*Elias* is the official publication of the Finnish Literature Society.]

Three Nephites. In *Encyclopedia of Mormonism*. 5 vols. New York: Macmillan, 1992, 4: 1477–78.

Mormon Folklore: Cut from the Marrow of Everyday Experience. *Brigham Young University Studies* 33 (1993): 521–40.

Suomalaiset Uudessa Maailmassa—folkloristinen näkökulma [Finns in a New World: A Folkloristic Perspective]. *Kalevalaseuran Vuosikirja* [Kalevala Society Annual] 72 (1993): 182–95.

Austin and Alta Fife. In *Utah History Encyclopedia*, ed. Allan Kent Powell, 187. Salt Lake City: University of Utah Press, 1994.

It All Depends on What You Mean by Family. *Southern Folklore* 51 (1994): 73–76.

Kalevala, ideologia ja moderni elämä [The *Kalevala*, Ideology, and Modern Life]. *Kalevalaseuran Vuosikirja* [Kalevala Society Annual] 73 (1994): 249–54.

The Power of the Word. *The Association for Mormon Letters Annual*, (1994): 8–14.

Powers of Heaven and Hell: Mormon Missionary Narratives as Instruments of Socialization and Social Control. In *Contemporary Mormonism: Social Science Perspectives*, ed. Marie Cornwall, Tim B. Heaton, and Lawrence A. Young, 207–17. Urbana and Chicago: University of Illinois Press, 1994.

Folklore, A Mirror for What? Reflections of a Mormon Folklorist. *Western Folklore* 54 (1995): 13–21.

Mormon Folklore—Faith or Folly? *Brigham Young Magazine* 49, no. 2 (May 1995): 46–54.

Mormon Narratives: The Lore of Faith. *Western Folklore* 54 (1995): 303–26.

Arts and the Family. *Ovations* (Fall 1996): 2.

Building Bridges: Folklore in the Academy. *Journal of Folklore Research* 33 (1996): 7–20.

The Lore of Polygamy: Twentieth-Century Perceptions of Nineteenth-Century Plural Marriage. *Weber Studies* 13 (Winter 1996): 152–61.

Mormon Folklore. In *American Folklore: An Encyclopedia*, ed. Jan H. Brunvand, 493–96. New York and London: Garland, 1996.

Sibelius, the *Kalevala*, and Karelianism. In *The Sibelius Companion*, ed. Glenda Goss, 43–60. Westport, Connecticut: Greenwood, 1996.

Folk Ideas of Mormon Pioneers. *Dialogue: A Journal of Mormon Thought* 31, no. 3 (January 1998): 81–99. (With Jessie Embry.)

Kalevala. In *Encyclopedia of Folklore and Literature*, ed. Mary Ellen Brown and Bruce A. Rosenberg, 347–51. Santa Barbara, Denver, and Oxford: ABC-CLIO, 1998.

Krohn, Karl Leopold. In *Encyclopedia of Folklore and Literature*, ed. Mary Ellen Brown and Bruce A. Rosenberg, 360–64. Santa Barbara, Denver, and Oxford: ABC-CLIO, 1998.

Lönnrot, Elias. In *Encyclopedia of Folklore and Literature*, ed. Mary Ellen Brown and Bruce A. Rosenberg, 392–94. Santa Barbara, Denver, and Oxford: ABC-CLIO, 1998.

Mormon Folklore: Grammar for a Discourse Community. In *Annual for the Association for Mormon Letters* 1998, ed. Lavina Fielding Anderson, 54–57. Salt Lake City: Association for Mormon Letters, 1998.

Nationalism. In *Encyclopedia of Folklore and Literature*, ed. Mary Ellen Brown and Bruce A. Rosenberg, 441–44. Santa Barbara, Denver, and Oxford: ABC-CLIO, 1998.

Settlement Folk Ideas: Stories for the Mormon's Move West. In *Annual for the Association for Mormon Letters* 1998, ed. Lavina Fielding Anderson, 57–68. Salt Lake City: Association for Mormon Letters, 1998. (With Jessie Embry.)

Eighteen Years Later: A Retrospect on "On Being Human," *Sunstone* 22, nos. 3–4 (June 1999): 57–60.

The Folk Speak: Everyday Life in Pioneer Oral Narratives. In *Nearly Everything Imaginable: The Everyday Life of Utah's Mormon Pioneers*, ed. Ronald W. Walker and Doris R. Dant, 485–503. Provo: Brigham Young University Press, 1999.

Misquotes and Misfires: William Wilson Responds to Christopher Caldwell and George Will. *American Folklore Society News* 28, no. 1 (February 1999): 24–25.

The Concept of the West and Other Hindrances to the Study of Mormon Folklore. In *Worldviews and the American West: The Life of the Place Itself*, ed. Polly Stewart, Steven Siporin, and Charles Sullivan, 167–90. Logan: Utah State University Press, 2000.

The Role of Religion in Cultural Policy in Utah. In *Cultural Policy in the West: Symposium Proceedings*, 103–10. Aspen, Colorado: Aspen Institute, Western State Arts Federation, 2000.

A Sense of Self or a Sense of Place: Personal Narratives and the Construction of Individual and Regional Identity. *Southern Folklore* 57 (2000): 3–11.

Folklore of Dixie: Past and Present. *Juanita Brooks Lecture Series*. St. George, Utah: Dixie College, 2005.

REVIEWS

Review of *Finnish Folklore Research 1818–1918*, by Jouko Hautala, in *Journal of American Folklore* 86 (1973): 67–69.

Review of *Bill Bailey Came Home*, by William A. Bailey, ed. Austin and Alta Fife, in *Utah Libraries* 17 (Fall 1974): 38–39.

Review of *Utah Folk Art: A Catalog of Material Culture*, ed. Hal Cannon, in *Utah Endowment for the Humanities News and Information* (January 1981).

Reviews of *The Finnish Revolution, 1917–1918*, by Anthony F. Upton, and *Finland in the Twentieth Century*, by D. G. Kirby, in *Scandinavian Review* 69, no. 3 (September 1981): 84–85.

Film review of *Kathleen Ware: Quiltmaker*, by Sharon Sherman, in *Journal of American Folklore* 95 (1982): 378–80.

Review of *The Vanishing Hitchhiker: American Urban Legends and Their Meanings*, by Jan H. Brunvand, in *Utah Endowment for the Humanities News and Information* (February 1982).

Review of *Studies in Finnic Folklore*, by Felix J. Oinas, in *Journal of Baltic Studies* 17 (1986): 372–73.

Review Essay of *Early Mormonism and The Magic World View*, by Michael D. Quinn, in *Brigham Young University Studies* 27 (1987): 96–104.

Review of *Early Mormonism and the Magic World View*, by Michael D. Quinn, in *Western Historical Quarterly* 20 (1989): 342–43.

Review of *Nordic Folklore: Recent Studies*, ed. Reimund Kvideland and Henning K. Sehmsdorf, in *Scandinavian Studies* 65 (1993): 244–48.

Review of *George Q. Cannon: A Biography*, by Davis Bitton, in *BYU Studies* 39, no. 3 (2000): 190–93.

TRANSLATIONS

Honko, Lauri. Memorates and the Study of Folk Beliefs. *Journal of the Folklore Institute* 1 (1964): 5–19.

Haavio, Martti. The Oldest Source of Finnish Mythology: Birchbark Letter No. 292. *Journal of the Folklore Institute* 1 (1964): 45–66.

Works Cited

Abbreviation: BYUFA = Brigham Young University Folklore Archive

Abrahams, Roger D. 1966. Some Varieties of American Heroes. *Journal of the Folklore Institute* 5: 341–62.

———. 1968. Introductory Remarks to a Rhetorical Theory of Folklore. *Journal of American Folklore* 81: 143–58.

———. 1972. Folklore and Literature as Performance. *Journal of the Folklore Institute* 9: 75–94.

———. 1976. The Complex Relations of Simple Forms. In *Folklore Genres*, ed. Dan Ben-Amos, 193–214. Austin: University of Texas Press.

———. 1977. Toward an Enactment-Centered Theory of Folklore. In *Frontiers of Folklore*, ed. William R. Bascom, 79–120. Boulder, Colorado: Westview Press.

———. 1993. Phantoms of Romantic Nationalism in Folkloristics. *Journal of American Folklore* 106: 3–37.

Ames, Kenneth L. 1977. *Beyond Necessity: Art in the Folk Tradition.* Winterthur, Delaware: Winterthur Museum.

Anderson, Nels. [1942] 1966. *Desert Saints: The Mormon Frontier in Utah.* Chicago: University of Chicago Press.

Anderson, P. K., collector. 1967a. BYUFA. Call Number L3.5.2.2.4.1.

———, collector. 1967b. BYUFA. Call Number L3.2.1.5.1.23.1.

Arrington, Leonard J. 1958. *Great Basin Kingdom: An Economic History of the Latter-day Saints, 1830–1900.* Cambridge: Harvard University Press.

———. 1974. The Many Uses of Humor. Paper read in Last Lecture series at Brigham Young University, Provo, Utah. 17 January.

Arwidsson, Adolf Ivar. 1909. *Tutkimuksia ja kirjoitelmia.* Translated by Severi Nuormaa and Edv. Rein, in *Suomalaisuuden syntysanoja*, 2, Suomalaisen Kirjallisuuden Seuran Toimituksia, no. 105. Helsinki: Suomalaisen Kirjallisuuden Seura.

At Laskiainen at Palo, Everyone Is a Finn. 1983. Tom Vennum Jr., Elli Köngäs Maranda, and Marsha Penti, Project Directors. Produced by the Smithsonian Institution, Office of Folklife Programs.

Baer, Florence E. 1982. "Give me . . . your huddled masses": Anti Vietnamese Refugee Lore and the "Image of Limited Good." *Western Folklore* 61: 275–91.

Ball, James A., collector. 1992. BYUFA. Call Number L3.2.1.5.1.30.1.

Barton, Sydney, collector. 1974. Four Functions of Medical Folklore. BYUFA. Field Project No. 154.

Bascom, William R. 1954. Four Functions of Folklore. *Journal of American Folklore* 67: 333–49.
Bauman, Richard. Verbal Art as Performance. 1975. *American Anthropologist* 77: 290–311.
———. 1987. Ed Bell, Texas Storyteller: The Framing and Reframing of Experience. *Journal of Folklore Research* 24: 197–221.
Bauman, Richard, and Charles L. Briggs. 2003. *Voices of Modernity*. New York: Cambridge University Press.
Ben-Amos, Dan. 1971. Toward a Definition of Folklore in Context. *Journal of American Folklore* 84: 3–15.
———. 1977. The Context of Folklore: Implications and Prospects. In *Frontiers of Folklore*, ed. William R. Bascom, 36–53. Boulder, Colorado: Westview Press.
Benfey, T. 1869. *Geschichte der Sprachwissenschaft und orientalischen Philologie in Deutschland*. Munich: J. G. Gotta.
Bidney, David. 1962. Classroom lecture in Indiana University course, The Theory of Myth. Recorded by author.
Blackham, Doris, and Susan Christensen, collectors. 1971a. BYUFA. Call Number L3.2.1.5.22.1.
———, collectors. 1971b. BYUFA. Call Number L3.2.1.5.1.27.1.
———, collectors. 1971c. BYUFA. Call Number L3.2.1.5.1.24.1.
———, collectors. 1971d. BYUFA. Call Number L3.2.1.3.12.1.
———, collectors. 1971e. BYUFA. Call Number L3.2.1.5.2.2.1.
Blegen, Theodore. 1947. *Grass Roots History*. Minneapolis: University of Minnesota Press.
Blumenreich, Beth, and Bari Lynn Polanski. 1974. Re-evaluating the Concept of Group: ICEN as an Alternative. In *Conceptual Problems in Contemporary Folklore Study*, ed. Gerald Cashion, 12–17. Folklore Forum Bibliographic and Special Series, No. 12, Indiana University.
Boas, Franz. [1927] 1955. *Primitive Art*. New York: Dover.
Bowman, Reynold E., collector. 1972. Invasion of 1970: The Mormon Conspiratorial Mind. BYUFA. Field Project No. 169.
Brady, Margaret K., ed. 1984. Ethnic Folklore in Utah. Special issue of *Utah Historical Quarterly* 52/1.
Browne, James D., collector. 1968. BYUFA. Call Number N256.
———, collector. 1969. BYUFA. Call Number N246.
Browning, Diane. 1986. Bangerter Says Tight Budget Will Mean Sacrifices. *Herald Journal*, 14 February.
Brunvand, Jan Harold. 1981. *The Vanishing Hitchhiker: American Urban Legends and their Meanings*. New York: W. W. Norton.
Bryant, Patricia, collector. 1972a. BYUFA. Call Number 181.2.
———, collector. 1972b. BYUFA. Call Number 181.14.
Bryner, Don, collector. 1970. BYUFA. Call Number L3.2.2.1.8.1.
Butler, Jon. 1990. *Awash in a Sea of Faith: Christianizing the American People*. Cambridge: Harvard University Press.
Caldwell, Christopher. 1998. Art for Politics' Sake. *Commentary* (February): 55–57.
Campbell, Barbara, collector. 1970a. Polygamy Stories: Harmony and Disharmony. BYUFA. Field Project No. 191.
———, collector. 1970b. BYUFA. Call Number 191.4.
Card, Laura Dene, collector. 1971. BYUFA. Call Number L3.5.2.3.3.1.
Carson, Ema, collector. 1973a. BYUFA. Field Project No. 194.7.
———, collector. 1973b. BYUFA. Field Project No. 194.4.
Carter, Thomas, ed. 1988. The Tangible Past. Special issue of *Utah Historical Quarterly* 56/4.

Castrén, Liisa. 1951. *Adolf Ivar Arwidsson isänmaallisena herättäjänä.* Historiallisia Tutkimuksia, no. 35. Helsinki: Historiallinen Seura.

Cheney, Thomas E., ed. 1968. *Mormon Songs from the Rocky Mountains: A Compilation of Mormon Folksong.* Publications of the American Folklore Society, Memoir Series, vol. 53. Austin: University of Texas Press.

———. 1974. *The Golden Legacy: A Folk History of J. Golden Kimball.* Salt Lake City: Peregrine Smith.

Children's Songbook. 1989. Salt Lake City: The Church of Jesus Christ of Latter-day Saints.

Child, Francis James, ed. [1884–1898] 1965. *The English and Scottish Popular Ballads.* 5 vols. New York: Dover.

Chinn, Jennie. 1986. The Nature and Scope of a State Folklorist's Responsibilities: An Overview. Paper Read at Folklore and Mythology Studies: Retrospect and Prospect. University of California at Los Angeles, 30 May.

Clark, Robert T. Jr. 1947. Herder, Cesarotti and Vico. *Studies in Philology* 44: 657–59.

———. 1955. *Herder: His Life and Thought.* Berkeley: University of California Press.

Clements, William M. 1974. The American Folk Church: A Characterization of American Folk Religion Based on Field Research among White Protestants in a Community in the South Central United States. PhD diss., Indiana University.

———. 1978. The American Folk Church in Northern Arkansas. *Journal of the Folklore Institute* 15: 161–80.

———. 1983. The Folk Church: Institution, Event, Performance. In *Handbook of American Folklore,* ed. Richard M. Dorson, Inta Gale Carpenter, Elizabeth Peterson, and Angela Maniak, 136–44. Chicago: University of Chicago Press.

Cornwall, Marie, Tim B. Heaton, and Lawrence A. Young, eds. 1994. *Contemporary Mormonism: Social Science Perspectives.* Urbana and Chicago: University of Illinois Press.

Cracroft, Richard. 1980. "Freshet in the Dearth": Samuel W. Taylor's *Heaven Knows Why* and Mormon Humor. *Sunstone* (May–June): 31–37.

Danielson, Larry. 1979. Ethnic Folklore. Lecture delivered at the Fife Folklore Conference, Utah State University.

Degh, Linda and Andrew Vazsonyi. 1973. *The Dialectics of the Legend.* Folklore Preprint Series 1, no. 6. Bloomington: Indiana University Folklore Publications Group.

Dorson, Richard M. [1952] 1972. *Bloodstoppers and Bearwalkers: Folk Traditions of the Upper Peninsula.* Cambridge: Harvard University Press.

———. 1957. A Theory for American Folklore. *Journal of American Folklore* 72 (July–September): 197–215.

———. 1959. *American Folklore.* Chicago: University of Chicago Press.

———. 1962. *Folk Legends of Japan.* Rutland, Vermont: Charles E. Tuttle.

———. 1964. *Buying the Wind: Regional Folklore in the United States.* Chicago: University of Chicago Press.

———. 1969. A Theory for American Folklore Reviewed. *Journal of American Folklore* 82 (July–September): 226–44.

Dundes, Alan. 1969. The Devolutionary Premise in Folklore Theory. *Journal of the Folklore Institute* 6: 5–19.

———. 1971. Folk Ideas as Units of Worldview. *Journal of American Folklore* 84 (January–March): 91–103.

———. 1977. Who Are the Folk? In *Frontiers of Folklore,* ed. William R. Bascom, 17–35. Boulder, Colorado: Westview Press.

Easten, Charlotte, collector. n.d. BYUFA. Call Number L3.2.1.5.1.8.1.

Ekman, Karl. 1936. *Jean Sibelius: His Life and Personality.* Trans. Edward Birse. London: Alan Wilmer.

Eliade, Mircea. 1959. *The Sacred and the Profane: The Nature of Religion.* Trans. Williard R. Trask. New York: Harvest.

Eliot, T. S. [1919] 1975. *Hamlet.* In *Selected Prose of T. S. Eliot*, ed. Frank Kermode. New York: Harcourt Brace Jovanich.

England, Eugene. 1996. Introduction: One View of the Garden. In *Tending the Garden: Essays on Mormon Literature,* ed. Eugene England and Lavina Fielding Anderson, xiii–xxxv. Salt Lake City: Signature Books.

———. 1998. Letter to William A. Wilson.

Ergang, Robert R. [1931] 1966. *Herder and the Foundations of German Nationalism.* New York: Octagon Books.

Ervasti, A. V. 1880. *Muistelmia matkalta Venäjän Karjalassa kesällä 1879.* Oulu.

Falnes, Oscar J. 1933. *National Romanticism in Norway.* New York: Columbia University Press.

Faulkner, William. [1952] 1966. The Writer's Duty. In *Literature of the United States*, ed. Walter Blair et al., 2: 1248–49. Glenview, Illinois: Scott, Foresman and Company.

Fife, Austin E. 1940. The Legend of the Three Nephites among the Mormons. *Journal of American Folklore* 53: 1–49.

———. 1942. Popular Legends of the Mormons. *California Folklore Quarterly* 1: 105–25.

———. 1948. Folk Beliefs and Mormon Cultural Autonomy. *Journal of American Folklore* 61 (194–98): 19–30.

Fife, Austin E., and Alta S. Fife. 1956. *Saints of Sage and Saddle: Folklore among the Mormons.* Bloomington: Indiana University Press.

Finnish American Lives. [1982] 1984. Produced and Directed by Michael Loukinen. Marquette, Michigan: U.P. North Films, Northern Michigan University.

Finno, Jacobus Petri. [1583] 1988. *Yxi wähä suomenkielinen wirsikirja.* Helsinki: Suomalaisen Kirjallisuuden Seura.

Flint, Aili. 1985. The *Kalevala* as a Bridge between Finland and the United States. Paper read at the Library of Congress, Washington, D.C., 24 January.

Florinus, Henrik. [1702] 1987. *Wanhain suomalaisten tawaliset ja suloiset sananlascut.* Jyväskylä: Gummerus Oy.

Folk Arts 85/86. 1985. Washington, D.C.: National Endowment for the Arts.

Frost, Robert. 1969. *The Poetry of Robert Frost.* Ed. Edward Connery Lathem. New York: Henry Holt.

Gardner, David Pierpont. 1986. The Humanities and the Reform Movement: What Can Be Done? *National Forum* 66 (2): 9–11.

Gault, Constance, collector. 1972. BYUFA Call Number 11.1.19.2.

Geary, Edward A. 1977. Mormondom's Lost Generation: The Novelists of the 1940s. *BYU Studies* 18 (Fall): 89–98.

Geary, Janet, collector. 1968. BYUFA. Call Number N341.

George, De Anne, collector. 1982. BYUFA. Call Number L3.2.1.3.14.1.

Georges, Robert A. 1969. Towards an Understanding of Storytelling Events. *Journal of American Folklore* 82: 313–28.

———. 1978. Conceptions of Fate in Stories Told by Greeks. In *Folklore in the Modern World*, ed. Richard M. Dorson, 301–19. The Hague and Paris: Mouton.

———. 1979. Feedback and Response in Storytelling. *Western Folklore* 38: 104–10.

———. 1980. Toward a Resolution of the Text / Context Controversy. *Western Folklore* 39: 34–40.

Georges, Robert A., and Michael Owen Jones. 1995. *Folkloristics: An Introduction.* Bloomington: Indiana University Press.

Gillies, Alexander. 1937. Herder's Essay on Shakespeare: 'Das Herz der Untersuchung.' *Modern Language Review* 32: 262–80.

———. 1945. *Herder*. Oxford: B. Blackwell.
Gomme, George Laurence. 1908. *Folklore as an Historical Science*. London: Methuen.
Gordon, Susan Judith. 1986. *Characterizing "the Other": Costa Ricans' Ambivalent Attitudes Expressed Traditionally about Each Other and Their Nicaraguan Neighbors*. PhD diss. University of California at Los Angeles.
Gottlund, Carl Axel. 1817. *Svensk Literaturtidning*, no. 25, 21 June.
Granger, Byrd. 1977. *A Motif Index for Lost Mines and Treasures Applied to Redaction of Arizona Legends and to Lost Mine and Treasure Legends Exterior to Arizona*. Tucson: University of Arizona Press.
Greenway, John, ed. 1969. *Folklore of the Great West: Selections from Eighty-three Years of the* Journal of American Folklore. Palo Alto: American West Publishing.
Greenway, John. 1964. Introductory Note to Memories of a Mormon Girlhood, by Juanita Brooks. *Journal of American Folklore* 77: 195–219.
Grimm, Jacob. 1882–88. *Teutonic Mythology*. 4 vols. Trans. James Stephen Stallybrass. London: George Bell and Sons.
Haavio, Martti. 1949. *Kalevalakultti*. In *Kalevala: kansallinen aarre*, ed. F. A. Heporauta and Martti Haavio, 240–75. Porvoo and Helsinki: Werner Söderström.
———. [1943] 1985. *Viimeiset runonlaulajat*, 3rd edition. Porvoo, Helsinki, and Juva: Werner Söderström Osakeyhtiö.
Hand, Wayland D. 1938. The Three Nephites in Popular Tradition. *Southern Folklore Quarterly* 2: 123–29.
———. 1983. Magic and Supernatural in Utah Folklore. *Dialogue: A Journal of Mormon Thought* (Winter): 51–64.
Hansen, Peggy, collector. 1971. BYUFA. Field Project No. 253.
Haring, Lee. 1994. Response to Felicia R. McMahon. Folklore E-Mail Discussion List. 28 November.
Hart, John L. 1997. Ten Million Members Worldwide. *LDS Church News*, 1 November, 3, 5.
Hautala, Jouko, ed. [1948] 1974. *Vanhat merkkipäivät*. Hämeenlinna: Suomalaisen Kirjallisuuden Seura.
———. 1954. *Suomalainen kansanrunoudentutkimus*, Suomalaisen Kirjallisuuden Seuran Toimituksia, no. 244. Helsinki: Suomalainen Kirjallisuuden Seura.
Hayes, Carlton J. H. 1926. *Essays on Nationalism*. New York: Macmillan.
———. 1960. *Nationalism: A Religion*. New York: Macmillan.
Heikinheimo, Ilmari. 1933. *Kaarle Aksel Gottlund: Elämä ja toiminta*. Porvoo and Helsinki: Werner Söderström Osakeyhtiö.
Herder, Johann Gottfried Von. [1877–1913] 1967–1968. *Sämtliche Werke*, 33 vols. Ed. Bernhard Suphan. Hildesheim, Germany: Georg Olms.
Herlevi, Waino. 1986. Interviewed by author. Orem, Utah, 19 August. Interview in possession of author.
Hirn, Yrjö. 1939. Kalevala-romantiikka ja Akseli Gallen-Kallela: Sekä muutamia mietteitä karelianismista Suomen sivistyselämässä. In *Matkamiehiä ja tietäjiä*, trans. Maijaliisa Auterinen, 203. Helsinki: Otava.
Hobsbawm, Eric, and Terence Ranger. 1983. *The Invention of Tradition*. Cambridge: Cambridge University Press.
Hornborg, Eirik. 1963. *Suomen historia*. Trans. Kai Kaila. Porvoo and Helsinki: Werner Söderström.
Honko, Lauri. 1982. UNESCO Work on the Safeguarding of Folklore. *NIF Newsletter* 10, nos. 1–2. Turku, Finland.
———. 1988. Australia in the Frontline of the Safeguarding Process. *NIF Newsletter* 16, nos. 3–4. Turku, Finland.

Hymns of the Church of Jesus Christ of Latter-day Saints. 1985. Salt Lake City: Deseret Book.

Inha, Into K. 1911. *Kalevalan laulumailta: Elias Lönnrotin poluilla Vienan Karjalassa*. Helsinki: Kansanvalistusseura.

Ives, Edward D. 1985. In *Folklife Annual 1985*, ed. Alan Jabbour and James Hardin, 74–85. Washington, D.C.: Library of Congress.

Järnefelt, Eero. 1921. Muistelmia Larin Paraskesta. *Kalevalaseuran Vuosikirja* 1: 94–95.

Jones, Michael Owen. 1981. Prologue, Section Introductions, Epilogue. In *Foodways and Eating Habits: Directions for Research*. Special issue of *Western Folklore* 40: vi–xii, 1–3, 41–44, 91–93, 134–37.

———. 1987a. *Exploring Folk Art: Twenty Years of Thought on Craft, Work, and Aesthetics*. American Material Culture and Folklife Series. Ann Arbor: UMI Research Press.

———, ed. 1987b. Folk Poetry, Finnish Identity, and Lönnrot's *Kalevala*. In *The World of the Kalevala*, 1–25. Los Angeles: UCLA Folklore and Mythology Publications.

Jones, Michael Owen, Michael Dane More, and Richard Christopher Snyder, eds. 1988. *Inside Organizations: Understanding the Human Dimensions*. Newbury Park, Calif.: Sage.

Jones, Steven Swann. 1984. *Folklore and Literature in the United States: An Annotated Bibliography of Studies of Folklore in American Literature*. New York and London: Garland.

Jutikkala, Eino. 1961. *A History of Finland*. Trans. Paul Sjöblom. New York: Frederick A. Praegen.

Kallio, Kyösti. 1936. Eduskunnan tervehdys. *Kalevalaseuran Vuosikirja* 16: 60.

Kansalliseepoksista. 1910. *Karjala*, no. 48.

Kaufman, Sharon R. 1986. *The Ageless Self: Sources of Meaning in Late Life*. Madison: University of Wisconsin Press.

Kimball, Spencer W. 1977. The Gospel Vision of the Arts. *Ensign* 7 (July): 5.

King, Marion, collector. 1945. BYUFA. Call Number N1092.

Kirshenblatt-Gimblett, Barbara. 1983. Studying Immigrant and Ethnic Folklore. In *Handbook of American Folklore*, ed. Richard M. Dorson, 39–47. Bloomington: Indiana University Press.

———. 1989. Authoring Lives. *Journal of Folklore Research* 26: 123–49.

Knuuttila, Seppo. 1989. What the People of Sivakka Tell about Themselves: A Research Experiment in Folk History. In *Studies in Oral Narrative*, ed. Anna-Leena Siikala. Helsinki: Finnish Literature Society.

Kohn, Hans. 1946. *Prophets and Peoples*. New York: Macmillan.

———. 1960. *The Mind of Germany*. New York: Scribner.

———. 1961. Nationalism. *Encyclopaedia Britannica* 16: 149–50.

———. 1967. *The Idea of Nationalism*. New York: Macmillan.

Kolodny, Annette. 1992. Notes toward a New Literary History of the American Frontiers. *American Literature 64/1*: 15.

Krohn, Helmi. [1931] 1943. Jean Sibelius lapsena. In *Lukemisto Suomen lapsille*, vol 4, ed. M. Airila, Mandi Hannula, Eero Salola. Helsinki: Valistus.

Kuusi, Matti. 1953. *Vanhan kansan sananlaskuviisaus*. Porvoo and Helsinki: Werner Söderström Osakeyhtiö.

Lampila, Hannu-Ilari. 1985. Program Notes to Compact Disc Recording of the *Kullervo* Symphony. Hayes Middlesex, England: EMI Records.

Larsen, Genevieve, collector. 1974. BYUFA. Call Number L3.2.1.4.4.2.

Larson, Gary O. 1997. *American Canvas: An Arts Legacy for Our Communities*. Washington, D.C.: National Endowment for the Arts.

Larson, Gustive O. 1947. *Prelude to the Kingdom: Mormon Desert Conquest, a Chapter in American Cooperative Experience.* Francestown, New Hampshire: M. Jones.

Lassila, Pertti. 1985. *History of Finnish Literature.* In *Finnish Features,* 2. June. Helsinki: Ministry of Foreign Affairs.

Lawless, Elaine J. 1984. "I Know If I Don't Bear My Testimony I'll Lose It": Why Mormon Women Bother to Speak at All. *Kentucky Folklore Record* 30: 79–96.

———. 1988a. *God's Peculiar People: Women's Voices and Folk Tradition in a Pentecostal Church.* Lexington: University Press of Kentucky.

———. 1988b. *Handmaidens of the Lord: Pentecostal Women Preachers and Traditional Religion.* Philadelphia: University of Pennsylvania Press.

———. 1993. *Holy Women, Wholly Women: Sharing Ministries of Wholeness through Life Stories and Reciprocal Ethnography.* Philadelphia: University of Pennsylvania Press.

———. 1996. *Women Preaching Revolution: Calling for Connection in a Disconnected Time.* Philadelphia: University of Pennsylvania Press.

Lee, Hector H. 1949. *The Three Nephites: The Substance and Significance of the Legend in Folklore.* University of New Mexico Publications in Language and Literature, no. 2. Albuquerque: University of New Mexico Press.

———. 1964. *J. Golden Kimball Stories.* FTA-25 Folk-Legacy Records.

———. 1988. Introduction to *Exploring Western Americana,* by Austin E. Fife, ed. Alta Fife, xv–xviii. Ann Arbor: UMI Research Press.

Leino, Eino. 1917. Kansallisviikko: Kalevala johtotähtenä. *Sunnuntai,* February 25: 1–2.

Leone, Mark P. 1973. Archeology as the Science of Technology: Mormon Town Plans and Fences. In *Research and Theory in Current Archeology,* ed. Charles L. Redman, 125–50. New York: John Wiley and Sons.

Leppänen, A. 1935. Kansanrunous ja Suomen porvariston imperialistiset pyrkimykset. *Punainen Karjala,* 22 February. *Kalevala* Newspaper Clipping File, Manuscript Archive, Finnish Literature Society, Helsinki.

Lindström-Best, Varpu. 1988. *Defiant Sisters: A Social History of Finnish Immigrant Women in Canada.* Toronto: Multicultural History Society of Ontario.

Linsén, Johan Gabriel. 1961. Address to the Finnish Literature Society–16 March 1836. In *Pysy Suomessa pyhänä: Suomalaisen Kirjallisuuden Seuran esimiesten puheita vuosina 1834–1946,* ed. Eino Nivanka, 11. Suomalaisen Kirjallisuuden Seuran Toimituksia, no. 268. Helsinki: Suomalaisen Kirjallisuuden Seura.

Lockwood, Yvonne Hiipakka. 1990. A Special Issue: Finnish American Folklife. *Finnish Americana: A Journal of Finnish American Culture* 8: 4–5.

Lönnrot, Elias. [1835] 1993. *Kalevala taikka vanhoja Karjalan runoja Suomen kansan muinosista ajoista.* In *Elias Lönnrot:Valitut teokset,* 5: 175–315. Suomalaisen Kirjallisuuden Seuran Toimituksia, no. 580. Helsinki: Suomalaisen Kirjallisuuden Seura.

———. [1840] 1982. *Kanteletar.* Vaasa, Finland: Suomalaisen Kirjallisuuden Seura.

———. [1849] 1984. *Kalevala.* Suomalaisen Kirjallisuuden Seuran Toimituksia 14. Mikkeli, Finland.

———. 1990. Letter to Carl Niklas Keckman, 6 February 1835. In *Elias Lönnrot Valitut Teokset,* ed. Raija Majamaa, 1: 91. Suomalaisen Kirjallisuuden Seuran Toimituksia, no. 510. Helsinki: Suomalaisen Kirjallisuuden Seura.

Ludlow, Daniel H., ed. 1992. Work. In *Encyclopedia of Mormonism,* 4: 1587. New York: Macmillan.

Lundell, Linda, collector. 1974. BYUFA. Call Number L3.2.1.5.1.26.1.

Lundwall, N. B. 1952. *The Fate of the Persecutors of the Prophet Joseph Smith.* Salt Lake City: Bookcraft.

Madsen, Harold S., and John L. Sorenson, eds. 1974. *Conference on the Language of the Mormons.* Provo: BYU Language Research Center.

Martin, Timo, and Douglas Sivén. 1984. *Akseli Gallen-Kallela: Elämäkerrallinen rapsodia.* Helsinki: Watti-Kustannus.

Mather, Cotton. [1702] 1853. *Magnalia Christi Americana: Or, the Ecclesiastical History of New England.* 2 vols. Hartford, Conn.: S. Andrus & Son.

McCauley, Enid, collector. 1971a. BYUFA. Call Number L3.2.2.1.6.1.

———, collector. 1971b. BYUFA. Call Number L3.6.2.2.1.

McCauley, Michael, collector. 1968. BYUFA. Call Number L3.5.2.2.3.1.

McDaniel, Maren, collector. 1972. BYUFA. Call Number L3.6.2.1.1.

McDonald, Janet, collector. 1984. BYUFA. Call Number L3.2.1.5.1.6.2.

Montesquieu, Charles de Secondat, baron de. [1748] 1900. *The Spirit of Laws [De l'Esprit des lois].* Rev. ed. trans. Thomas Nugent. 2 vols. New York: The Colonial Press.

Motz, Marilyn. 1998. The Practice of Belief. *Journal of American Folklore* 111 (Summer): 339–55.

Nevins, Allan. 1962 [1938]. *The Gateway to History.* Garden City, New York: Anchor Books.

Niemi, A. R. 1898. *Kalevalan kokoonpano*, Suomalaisen Kirjallisuuden Seuran Toimituksia, no. 90. Helsinki.

Nurmio, Yrjö. 1947. *Taistelu suomen kielen asemasta 1880-luvun puolivälissä.* Helsinki.

Oaks, Dallin H., and Marvin S. Hill. 1975. *Carthage Conspiracy: The Trial of the Accused Assassins of Joseph Smith.* Urbana: University of Illinois Press.

Oinas, Felix J. 1964. Lecture in course on Russian Folklore, Indiana University, Bloomington, Indiana.

Oring, Elliott. 1975. The Devolutionary Premise: A Definitional Delusion? *Western Folklore* 34: 36–44.

———. 1981. *Israeli Humor: The Content and Structure of the Chizbat of the Palmah.* Albany, New York: State University of New York Press.

———. 1986. On the Concepts of Folklore. In *Folk Groups and Folklore Genres: An Introduction*, ed. Elliott Oring, 1–22. Logan: Utah State University Press.

———. 1987. Generating Lives: The Construction of an Autobiography. *Journal of Folklore Research* 24: 241–62.

———. 1988. Rechnitzer Rejects: A Humor of Modern Orthodoxy. In *Between Two Worlds: Ethnographic Essays on American Jewry*, ed. Jack Kugelass, 148–61. Ithaca, New York: Cornell University Press.

Paasikivi, J. K. 1959. *Toimintani Moskovassa ja Suomessa 1939–41.* Porvoo, Helsinki, Juva: Werner Söderström Osakeyhtiö.

Packer, Boyd K. 1977. The Arts and the Spirit of the Lord. In *1976 Devotional Speeches of the Year.* Provo, Utah: Brigham Young University Press.

Penti, Marsha. 1990. Juhlat: Good Times for Finns. *Finnish Americana: A Journal of Finnish American Culture* 8: 12–19.

Peterson, Levi. 1982. The Christianization of Coburn Heights. In *Canyons of Grace*, 79–101. Urbana: University of Illinois Press.

Postman, Neil. 1989. Learning by Story. *The Atlantic* 264, no. 6: 122.

Poulsen, Richard C. 1988. Violence and the Sacred: Mormon Jokes about Blacks. In *Misbegotten Muses: History and Anti-History*, 24–36. New York: Peter Lang.

Quinn, D. Michael. 1987. *Early Mormonism and the Magic World View.* Salt Lake City: Signature Books.

Radcliffe-Brown, A. R. 1922. The Interpretation of Andamanese Customs and Beliefs: Myths and Legends. In *The Andaman Islanders*, 376–405. Cambridge: Oxford University Press.

Redfield, Robert. 1930. *Tepoztlan, a Mexican Village: A Study of Folk Life.* Chicago: University of Chicago Press.

———. 1941. *The Folk Culture of Yucatan.* Chicago: University of Chicago Press.
———. 1947. *The Folk Society.* Indianapolis: Bobbs-Merrill.
———. 1955. *The Little Community: Viewpoints for the Study of a Human Whole.* Chicago: University of Chicago Press.
Rees, Gordon, collector. n.d. BYUFA. Call Number L3.2.1.3.13.1.
Reichel, Edward. 1999. Spectacular Abravanal Hall. *Deseret News,* 16 September, Focus section.
Reitala, Aimo. 1987. Romantiikasta Modernismiin. In *Sortokaudet ja Itsenäistyminen,* vol. 6 of *Suomen historia,* ed. Jukka Tarkka, 11–45. Espoo: Weilin-Göös.
Ricks, Joel. 1924. Pioneer Narratives Collection. Utah State University Special Collections Library, Logan, Utah, File MS 389.
Ricoeur, Paul. 1973. The Model of the Text: Meaningful Action Considered as Text. *New Literary History* 5: 91–117.
Roberts, Kathleen J., collector. 1974. BYUFA. Call Number L3.2.1.5.1.17.1.
Runeberg, Johan Ludvig. 1835. Nionde runan i Kalevala. *Helsingfors Morgonblad,* November 23.
Ryan, Charles William, collector. 1970. BYUFA. Legend Collection L6.6.2.8.1.
Saarimaa, E. A. 1921. *Kansanrunouden asema suomenkielisten oppikoulujen äidinkielen opetuksessa.* Virittäjä 25: 1–6.
Sabin, Randall, collector. 1961. BYUFA. Call Number L3.2.1.3.1.1.
Santino, Jack. 1982. Catholic Folklore and Folk Catholicism. *New York Folklore* 8: 93–106.
Scholes, Robert. 1989. *Protocols of Reading.* New Haven and London: Yale University Press.
Setälä, E. N. 1923. Kalevala ja Karjala. *Kalevalaseuran Vuosikirja* 3: 11–12.
Sewell, Ernestine P. 1989. *Eats: A Folk History of Texas Foods.* Fort Worth: Texas Christian University Press.
Sidney, Sir Philip. [1595] 1956. An Apology for Poetry. In *Renaissance England: Poetry and Prose from the Reformation to the Restoration,* ed. Roy Lamson and Hallett Smith, 271–309. New York: W. W. Norton.
Sihvo, Hannes. 1973. *Karjalan kuva.* Suomalaisen Kirjallisuuden Seuran Toimituksia, no. 314. Helsinki: Suomalaisen Kirjallisuuden Seura.
Silmäys Kalevalaamme. 1910. *Turun Kuva-Lehti,* February 23 and March 2.
Siporin, Steve. 1992. *American Folk Masters: The National Heritage Fellows.* New York: Harry N. Abrams.
Smith, Henry Nash. 1950. *The Virgin Land: The American West as Symbol and Myth.* New York: Vintage.
Smith, Holly Sue, collector. 1982. BYUFA. Call Number L3.5.2.0.14.1.
Smith, Joseph Fielding. 1938. *Life of Joseph F. Smith: Sixth President of the Church of Jesus Christ of Latter-day Saints.* Salt Lake City: Deseret News Press.
Stahl, Sandra Dolby. 1989. *Literary Folkloristics and the Personal Narrative.* Bloomington and Indianapolis: Indiana University Press.
———. 1983. Studying Folklore and American Literature. In *Handbook of American Folklore,* ed. Richard M. Dorson, 422–33. Bloomington: Indiana University Press.
Steed, Leesa, collector. 1984. BYUFA. Call Number L3.5.2.0.15.1.
Stegner, Wallace. 1942. *Mormon Country.* New York: Bonanza Books.
Stewart, Polly, Steve Siporin, C. W. Sullivan III, and Suzi Jones, eds. 2000. *Worldviews and the American West: The Life of the Place Itself.* Salt Lake City: Utah State University Press.
Strong, Mary, collector. 1965a. BYUFA. Call Number L3.5.2.2.2.1.
———, collector. 1965b. BYUFA. Call Number L3.6.2.3.1.

Tarkiainen, Viljo. 1922. *Piirteitä suomalaisesta kirjallisuudesta*. Porvoo: Werner Söderström.

Tawaststjerna, Eric. 1976, 1986. *Jean Sibelius*. Trans. Robert Layton. 3 vols. London: Faber & Faber.

Taylor, Samuel. 1994. *Heaven Knows Why*. Salt Lake City: Aspen.

Thatcher, Elaine. 2003. Interview with William A. Wilson. In possession of Elaine Thatcher.

Thomas, Dylan. [1952] 1973. Do Not Go Gentle into That Good Night. In *The Norton Anthology of Modern Poetry*, ed. Richard Ellmann and Robert O' Clair, 911. New York: W. W. Norton.

Thompson, Paul. 1992. Lay Priesthood and Leadership. In *Encyclopedia of Mormonism*, 2: 814–16. New York: Macmillan.

Timonen, Senni, ed. 1982. *Näin lauloi Larin Paraske*. Helsinki: Suomalaisen Kirjallisuuden Seura.

Titon, Jeff Todd. 1988. *Powerhouse for God: Speech, Chant, and Song in an Appalachian Baptist Church*. Austin: University of Texas Press.

Toelken, Barre. 1976. The "Pretty Languages" of Yellowman: Genre, Mode, and Texture. In *Folklore Genres*, ed. Dan Ben-Amos, 145–70. Austin: University of Texas Press.

———. 1979. *The Dynamics of Folklore*. Boston: Houghton Mifflin.

———. 1991. Traditional Water Narratives in Utah. *Western Folklore* 50: 191–200.

Tometich, Shirley, collector. 1967. BYUFA. Call Number L3.5.2.2.8.1.

Torma, Carolyn. 1990. Ethnicity and Historical Preservation. *Finnish Americana: A Journal of Finnish American Culture* 8: 24–31.

Trachtenberg, Joshua. 1942. The Folk Element in Judaism. *Journal of Religion* 22: 173.

Tradition Bearers. 1987. Produced and directed by Michael Loukinen. Marquette, Michigan: U.P. North Films, Northern Michigan University.

Turner, Frederick Jackson. 1920. *The Frontier in American History*. New York: Henry Holt.

Turner, Victor W. 1969. *The Ritual Process: Structure and Anti-Structure*. Chicago: Aldine Press.

Tymms, Ralph. 1955. *German Romantic Literature*. London: Methuen.

Tyson, Ruel W., Jr., James L. Peacock, and Daniel W. Patterson, eds. 1988. *Diversities of Gifts: Field Studies in Southern Religion*. Urbana: University of Illinois Press.

United States Congress. 1976. American Folklife Preservation Act. Public Law 94–201. Washington, D.C.

Utter, David. 1892. Mormon Superstitions. *The Folk-Lorist* 1: 76.

Väisänen, A. O. 1921. Jean Sibelius vaikutelmistaan. *Kalevalaseuran Vuosikirja* 1: 77.

Valkonen, Markku. 1989. *Kultakausi*. Porvoo and Helsinki: Werner Söderström.

Vernon, Gregory, collector. 1968. Missionary Stories. BYUFA. Field Project No. 427.

Vico, Giambattista. [1744] 1961. *The New Science*. Trans. Thomas Bergin and Max Harold Fisch. Garden City, New York: Doubleday.

Vilkuna, Kustaa. [1950] 1968. *Wuotuinen ajantieto: Vanhoista merkkipäivistä sekä talous- ja sääkalenterista enteineen*, 2nd ed. Helsinki: Otava.

Vogt, Evon Z., and Ray Hyman. 1959. *Water Witching U.S.A.* Chicago: University of Chicago Press.

W:nen, J. 1901. Kalevala-tutkimuksen tulokset. *Uusi Suometar*, 6 November.

Walker, Ronald W. 1984. The Persisting Idea of American Treasure Hunting. *BYU Studies* 24 (Fall): 452–59.

Walker, Steven C., collector. 1964. BYUFA. Call Number L3.6.2.4.1.

Wargelin, Marianne K. 1990. Ethnic Identity for Sale: The Finnish American Gift Shop. *Finnish Americana: A Journal of Finnish American Culture* 8: 32–37.

Watt, Kevin. 1993. BYUFA, Wilson Missionary Collection #4025.
Webb, Walter Prescott. 1931. *The Great Plains.* Boston: Ginn.
White, Hayden. 1975. *Metahistory: The Historical Imagination in Nineteenth-Century Europe.* Baltimore and London: Johns Hopkins University Press.
Wiklund, K. B. 1902. Är Kalevala ett folkepos? Ett slutord. *Finsk Tidskrift* 53: 470–73.
Will, George F. 1998. Arts, Humanities Endowments Take Populist Road to Survival. *Deseret News* (5 April): AA6.
Wilson, William A. 1963. A Review of *Saints of Sage and Saddle.* Seminar Paper. Indiana University.
———. 1969. Mormon Legends of the Three Nephites Collected at Indiana University. *Indiana Folklore* 2, no. 1: 3–35.
———. 1971. Independence or Dependence: The Fate of Our Folklore Society. *Newsletter of the Folklore Society of Utah* 8 (April): 4–7.
———. 1973a. Folklore and History: Fact amid the Legends. *Utah Historical Quarterly* 41 (Winter): 40–58.
———. 1973b. Herder, Folklore, and Romantic Nationalism. *Journal of Popular Culture* 6: 819–35.
———. 1975. The Vanishing Hitchhiker among the Mormons. *Indiana Folklore* 8, nos. 1–2: 79–97.
———. 1976a. *Folklore and Nationalism in Modern Finland.* Bloomington and London: Indiana University Press.
———. 1976b. The Evolutionary Premise in Folklore Theory and the "Finnish Method." *Western Folklore* 35: 241–49.
———. 1976c. The Paradox of Mormon Folklore. *Brigham Young University Studies* 17: 40–58.
———, ed. 1976d. Mormon Folklore. Special issue of *Utah Historical Quarterly* 44/4.
———. 1979 Folklore of Utah's Little Scandinavia. *Utah Historical Quarterly* 47: 148–66.
———. 1981. On Being Human: The Folklore of Mormon Missionaries. *Utah State University Faculty Honor Lecture Series.* Logan: Utah State University Press.
———. 1982. Richard M. Dorson's Theory for American Folklore: A Finnish Analogue. *Western Folklore* 41: 36–42.
———. 1983a. Mormon Folklore. In *Handbook of American Folklore,* ed. Richard M. Dorson, 155–61. Bloomington: Indiana University Press.
———. 1983b. Trickster Tales and the Location of Cultural Boundaries: A Mormon Example. *The Journal of Folklore Research* 20: 55–66.
———. 1985. The Seriousness of Mormon Humor. *Sunstone* 10, no. 1: 6–13.
———. 1987a. Partial Repentance of a Critic: The *Kalevala,* Politics, and the United States. In *Folklife Annual 1986,* ed. Alan Jabbour and James Hardin, 81–91. Washington, D.C.: Library of Congress.
———. 1987b. Review Essay of *Early Mormonism and the Magic World View,* by Michael D. Quinn. *BYU Studies* 27: 96–104.
———. 1989. Freeways, Parking Lots, and Ice Cream Stands: The Three Nephites in Contemporary Mormon Culture. *Dialogue: A Journal of Mormon Thought* 21 (Fall): 13–26.
———. 1990. Mormon Folklore and History: Implications for Canadian Research. In *The Mormon Presence in Canada,* ed. Brigham Y. Card, et al., 150–66. Edmonton and Logan: University of Alberta Press and Utah State University Press.
———. 1995. Folklore, A Mirror for What? Reflections of a Mormon Folklorist. *Western Folklore* 54: 13–21.

———. 1996. Arts and the Family. *Ovations* (Fall), 2.

———. 2000. A Sense of Place or a Sense of Self: Personal Narratives and the Construction of Personal and Regional Identity. *Southern Folklore* 57: 3–11

Wixom, Marion, collector. 1975. BYUFA. Call Number 453.5.

Woodhouse, Jillian A., collector. 1975. BYUFA. Call Number L3.2.1.3.5.1.

Wordsworth, William. [1807] 1948. Composed upon Westminster Bridge. In *Anthology of Romanticism,* ed. Ernest Bernbaum, 223. New York: Roland Press.

Wright, Kathryn. 1975. Manuscript. BYUFA.

Wuorinen, John H. 1931. *Nationalism in Modern Finland.* New York: Columbia University Press.

Yoder, Don. 1974. Toward a Definition of Folk Religion. *Western Folklore* 33: 2–15.

Contributors of Introductions to Essays

David A. Allred is assistant professor of English at Snow College in Ephraim, Utah, where he teaches folklore, American literature, and composition. His dissertation focused on performance theory and the intersection of folklore and literature. He has published articles on nineteenth-century American literature, Mormon history, and Mormon folklore.

Richard Bauman is distinguished professor of folklore and ethnomusicology, communication and culture, and anthropology, and chair of the Department of Folklore and Ethnomusicology at Indiana University, Bloomington. He has served as president of the Society for Linguistic Anthropology and the Semiotic Society of America, and as editor of the *Journal of American Folklore*. Among his publications are *Verbal Art as Performance* (1977), *Story, Performance, and Event* (1986), *Voices of Modernity* (with Charles L. Briggs, 2003), and *A World of Others' Words* (2004).

Margaret K. (Meg) Brady is professor of English and ethnic studies at the University of Utah, where she has taught courses in folk narrative, women's folklore, and American Indian Studies for over twenty-five years. She is also the founding director of YourStory: Record and Remember. Her most recent book, *Mormon Healer and Folk Poet: Mary Susannah Fowler's Life of "Unselfish Usefulness"* (2000), won the American Folklore Society's Elli Kongas-Maranda Prize.

Simon J. Bronner is distinguished university professor of American Studies and folklore at the Pennsylvania State University, Harrisburg, where he also serves as director of the Center for Pennsylvania Culture Studies. He has published more than fifteen books on folklore and cultural history; his most recent titles are *Folk Nation: Folklore in the Creation of American Tradition* (2002), *Lafcadio Hearn's America* (2002), and *Following Tradition: Folklore in the Discourse of American Culture* (1998). He is also editor of the Material Worlds Series for the University Press of Kentucky and the Pennsylvania German History and Culture Series for Penn State Press.

Thomas A. DuBois has written extensively on Finnish folklore and the *Kalevala*, as well as other Nordic topics. He is professor of Finnish at the University of Wisconsin-Madison, where he also serves as a faculty member in the interdisciplinary program in Folklore Studies. His books include (with Leea Virtanen) *Finnish Folklore* (2000); *Nordic Religions in the Viking Age* (1999); and *Finnish Folk Poetry and the Kalevala* (1995).

HENRY GLASSIE is college professor of folklore at Indiana University. He loves the music and architecture of the southern United States, the landscape and stories of Ireland, the ceramics and textiles of Turkey and Japan, the life in the streets in India and Bangladesh. Books he has written on topics like these have won many awards, and three of them—*Passing the Time in Ballymenone* (1982), *The Spirit of Folk Art* (1989), and *Turkish Traditional Art Today* (1993)—have been named among the notable books of the year by the *New York Times.*

DAVID J. HUFFORD is university professor and chair of humanities, professor of family and community medicine, and professor of neural and behavioral sciences at Penn State College of Medicine. He is also adjunct professor of religious studies at the University of Pennsylvania. He has taught, studied, and published on folk belief, spirituality, and health for over thirty years. In 1992 he received the Manuel de la Cruz Award from the Mexican Academy of Traditional Medicine for his research in folk medicine. Hufford's research focuses on the role of experience in the development of traditional healing approaches and in spiritual belief.

MICHAEL OWEN JONES, who has known Bert Wilson since graduate school, has taught folklore at UCLA since 1968. Past president of the American Folklore Society, he has authored 150 articles, monographs, and books on folk art, food symbolism, organizational folklore, folk medicine, fieldwork, and methods and theories in folkloristics.

PHILLIP MCARTHUR is associate professor of international cultural studies at Brigham Young University Hawaii, where he teaches courses on theory, folklore, performance studies, and Oceania. His research and publication is centered on oral narrative, cultural performance, cosmology, social power, nationalism, and globalization in the Marshall Islands.

ELLIOTT ORING is professor of anthropology at California State University, Los Angeles. He has published numerous books and articles on folklore, humor, and cultural symbolism. He is a member of the Society of Fellows of the American Folklore Society and a folklore fellow of the Finnish Academy of Science and Letters. His most recent book was *Engaging Humor* (2003).

GEORGE H. SCHOEMAKER is currently folk arts specialist for the Utah Arts Council Folk Arts Program, a division of the Utah Department of Community and Culture. He teaches courses in humanities, world mythology, and American popular culture at the University of Phoenix, Utah campus. At the Utah Arts Council he administers the Folk Arts Apprenticeship Grant, public programming of artists, and partnering with rural, tribal, and other arts organizations to develop programs and opportunities for economic growth through the arts.

Steven Siporin, associate professor of English and history at Utah State University, teaches a wide variety of folklore courses and writes on Italian Jewish culture, foodways, western folk art, and oral narrative. His book, *American Folk Masters: The National Heritage Fellows* (1992), celebrates a gifted group of American folk artists.

David Stanley teaches folklore and literature at Westminster College in Salt Lake City. He has published books, articles, and recordings on gospel music, storytelling, ethnic music, and the folklore and humor of folklorists. He edited *Folklore in Utah: A History and Guide to Resources* (2004). He also coedited a collection of essays, *Cowboy Poets & Cowboy Poetry* (2000), and produced a recording, *Cowboy Poetry Classics*, for Smithsonian Folkways. He previously worked as a folklorist for the Utah Arts Council.

Beverly Stoeltje teaches anthropology and folklore at Indiana University, where she is associate professor of anthropology, with a joint appointment in the Department of Folklore and Ethnomusicology. She has published on women of the West, cowgirls, rodeo, festival and ritual, Asante Queen Mothers in Ghana, narrative in Ghana, legal anthropology, and women, language, and law in Africa.

Elaine Thatcher is associate director of the Mountain West Center for Regional Studies at Utah State University, and is a folklorist who has worked closely with many ethnic, occupational, and geographic communities of the West. Past projects include work on sense of place and land-use ethics. Her publications include *Cowboy Poets & Cowboy Poetry*, coeditor (2000) and an essay on public sector folklore in *Folklore in Utah* (2004).

Jacqueline S. Thursby, associate professor of English at Brigham Young University, teaches English education, folklore, mythology, multicultural pedagogy, and women's culture. She has published books and articles on Basque American women, Latter-day Saints, food lore, funeral and cemetery studies, and folklore pedagogy.

Kristi A. Young is curator of the Wilson Folklore Archives in the L. Tom Perry Special Collections at Brigham Young University. She has published book reviews in *Journal of American Folklore* and *BYU Studies* and is the author of several courtship-related entries in the forthcoming *Encyclopedia of American Folklife*. She is the codirector of the American Folklife Center and Brigham Young University Folklife Field School for 2004 and 2005 and also serves as the director of the Utah Heritage Project.

Index